Supported Employment

Supported Employment
Strategies for Integration of Workers with Disabilities

Paul Wehman, Professor
Department of Physical Medicine and Rehabilitation,
Medical College of Virginia

Director, Rehabilitation Research and Training Center
on Supported Employment for the Severely Disabled,
Virginia Commonwealth University

Paul Sale, Assistant Professor
Division of Teacher Education and Special Education,
Virginia Commonwealth University

Wendy S. Parent, Research Associate
Rehabilitation Research and Training Center on Supported
Employment for the Severely Disabled, Virginia Common-
wealth University

Andover Medical Publishers
Boston London Oxford Singapore Sydney Toronto Wellington

Andover Medical Publishers is an imprint of Butterworth–Heinemann.

Library of Congress Cataloging-in-Publication Data
Supported employment : strategies for integration of workers with disabilities / [edited by]
    Paul Wehman, Paul Sale, Wendy S. Parent.
        p. cm.
    Includes bibliographical references and index.
    ISBN 0–9626521–7–2 (hardcover : alk. paper)
    1. Vocational rehabilitation—United States.   2. Handicapped-Employment—
United States.   I. Wehman, Paul.   II. Sale, Paul.   III. Parent, Wendy S.
    [DNLM: 1. Handicapped. 2. Rehabilitation. Vocational. HD 7255.5
    S9585]
    HD7256.U5S878   1992
    331.5'9'0973—dc20
    DNLM/DLC
    for Library of Congress   92–10960
                               CIP

British Library Cataloguing in Publication Data
A catalogue record for this book is available from the British Library.

Butterworth–Heinemann
80 Montvale Avenue
Stoneham, MA 02180

10 9 8 7 6 5 4 3 2 1

Printed in the United States of America

Contributors

Christine Groah, M.Ed., /Clinical Coordinator

Marshall Manor

John J. Kregel, Ed.D., Associate Professor

Division of Teacher Education and Special Education, Virginia Commonwealth University and

Associate Director, Rehabilitation Research and Training Center on Supported Employment for the Severely Disabled, Virginia Commonwealth University

Pam Sherron, M.Ed., Director of Employment Services

Rehabilitation Research and Training Center on Supported Employment, Virginia Commonwealth University

Michael West, M.Ed., Research Associate

Rehabilitation Research and Training Center on Supported Employment for the Severely Disabled, Virginia Commonwealth University

Pamela S. Wolfe, Ed.D., Assistant Professor

Pennsylvania State University, Department of Special Education

Dedication

This book is dedicated to the people who bring the most joy to our lives: Brody, Cara, Blake, Amanda, Stephanie, Betsy, and Steve.

Contents

Preface

The 1980s were a time of vocational rehabilitation innovation for persons with severe disabilities. Research and demonstration efforts early in the decade cultivated new rehabilitation approaches. An approach focusing on job placement and on the job training for individuals for whom employment was an elusive and often unmet reality evolved from these early efforts. This place-train approach, now called supported employment, was developed to ensure that persons with severe disabilities have access to fair wages for valued work, integration with non-disabled peers, and on-going support. During the mid and later 1980s significant federal, state, local and consumer initiatives propelled the implementation of supported employment into virtually every rehabilitation system in the country. By 1990 over 72,000 Americans had received supported employment services given by over 2,600 programs (Wehman, 1991).

The purpose of this book is to assist supported employment providers, employment specialists, rehabilitation counselors, and educators in the implementation of quality supported employment for persons with a range of abilities and severe disabilities. The exponential expansion of supported employment has created a dearth of personnel trained in the unique (though hybrid) methodologies of supported employment. We believe that this book will provide a solid foundation upon which employment specialists and others can create solutions to employment problems experienced by persons with severe disabilities.

The book has been conceptualized into three major sections: *Supported Employment Foundations, Supported Employment Implementation Strategies, and Special Issues in Supported Employment.* As primary authors we have tried to gain the advantages of a non-edited text, while drawing on expertise from several of our colleagues. Unless otherwise noted below, chapters without bylines were contributed by one of the major authors. The *Foundations* section begins with a chapter by Paul Wehman and John Kregel that provides a historical and current prospective of how supported employment has grown and touched the lives of thousands of consumers. Chapter 2, by Mike West and Wendy Parent, is a powerful description of how the notions of real choice and substantive empowerment of consumers are the driving forces behind supported employment. The next two chapters describe the similarities and relative strengths of the individual placement approach, Chapter 3, and the group models, Chapter 4, written by Pam Wolfe.

The *Supported Employment Implementation Strategies* section melds together approaches from special education and rehabilitation and applies those approaches to the sometime unique supported employment venue. The section begins by reemphasizing the critical importance of consumer and family choice in supported employment and provides techniques for insuring adequate consumer and family input. Chapter 6, written by Pam Sherron, Christine Groah, and Wendy Parent, details how to systematically assess consumer abilities and disabilities, how to identify valued jobs in a variety of settings, and finally, how to make that all important match between consumer and job. Chapter 7 provides an overview of issues and potential resolutions related to training on the job site for consumers with a range of disabilities. Chapter 8, by Michael West, provides methodologies to insure that supported employees keep their jobs after the employment specialists leaves the job site. Chapter 9 concludes this section by equipping readers with pragmatic suggestions of how to deal positively with non-task related behavioral obstacles often found on job sites.

The last section, *Special Issues in Supported Employment*, addresses critical concerns shared by many individuals in the supported employment field. Chapter 10 discusses the concern of maintaining the highest possible quality within individual local programs. Chapter 11 provides insight into one of the litmus tests of quality supported employment, vocational integration. Finally, Chapter 12 details the important task of staffing supported employment programs and provides illustrative material on hiring supported employment personnel.

The continued growth and quality improvement of supported employment will depend, to a large extent, on those current and prospective "front line" staff who daily make significant differences in the lives of persons with disabilities. This text is written with those staff in mind. We wish them continued success.

Reference

Wehman, P. (1991). Supported employment national implementation outcome data for 1986–1990. Presentation made at the Supported Employment State Director's Meeting, September 11, 1991, Washington, DC.

Acknowledgements

The preparation of this book required significant contributions by many individuals other than the primary and chapter authors. We wish first to thank the hundreds of consumers with whom we have collectively worked and who assisted us in our learning about supported employment. Second, we are indebted to our colleagues at the Rehabilitation Research and Training Center on Supported Employment who have shared their wealth of experience with us. Additionally, we would like to express gratitude for the never ending manuscript preparation which was handled expertly by Tricia Baker, Jeanie Dalton, and Emily Fisher. Finally, each of us is thankful for the unending support that we receive from significant others in our lives.

Part I

Supported Employment Foundations

1

Supported Employment: Growth and Impact

Paul Wehman, Ph.D.

John Kregel, Ed. D

There is little doubt that when the period of 1980 to 1990 is looked back upon, supported employment will be considered one of the major new programs in the fields of rehabilitation, developmental disabilities and special education. For thousands of unemployed people with severe disabilities, this avenue of rehabilitation has opened a new door to expanded vocational opportunities. With unemployment rates as high as 80% to 90% for persons with mental retardation (Wehman, Kregel, and Seyfarth 1985), supported employment has been the only vehicle toward competitive employment.

Supported employment has consistently been demonstrated as a program approach that works. The goal is paid work in the normal workplace with whatever levels of support are necessary to enhance work outcome. There was a time in 1980 that it was considered highly unlikely to think that a person with measured intelligence or IQ of 35 could work in competitive employment. Within the past decade that perception has changed significantly. It is the purpose of this book to discuss how persons who are seriously challenged with severe disabilities can work with support. This book is directed to those students and professionals who are looking for a comprehensive approach to learning about supported employment program development and implementation

The Rehabilitation Act Amendments of 1986 authorized funds for supported employment in all 50 states through the Title 6 C program. These funds are given to states in a formula based on the state population. In addition to these dollars, there are Title III discretionary funds for model demonstration grant programs. These resources along with many other state funds from mental health, mental retardation and developmental disabilities, and the Joint Training Partnership Act have been increasingly funnelled into supported employment.

CHARACTERISTICS OF SUPPORTED EMPLOYMENT

What, then, is supported employment? What features are indigenous to every supported employment program? At a minimum, pay for real work, integrated work settings, at least 20 hours per week, and usually some degree of ongoing support are essential. Today, increasing numbers of students with severe disabilities are graduating from school and looking for paid employment. From research, we know these students can perform jobs that involve difficult tasks.

Encouraged by both current research and experience gained from access to education, parents, advocates, and people with disabilities have raised their expectations for the future. Yet many community programs still only offer to get students "ready" for work, while too few actually provide the assistance students need to get and keep a job.

Supported employment is a strategy for changing the mismatch between employment expectations for people with severe disabilities and the limited options available in most communities. Federal initiatives, through the Developmental Disabilities Act of 1987 and the Office of Special Education and Rehabilitative Services (OSERS), have paved the way for the development of programs offering supported employment.

Supported employment is defined as paid employment for persons with developmental disabilities for whom competitive employment at or above the minimum wage is unlikely and who, because of their disabilities, need ongoing support to perform their work. Support is provided through activities such as training, supervision, and transportation. Supported employment is conducted in a variety of settings, particularly, work sites in which persons without disabilities are employed.

Supported employment is a combination of employment and ongoing services. *It is a type of employment, not a method of employment preparation nor a type of service activity.* It is a powerful and flexible way to ensure normal employment benefits, provide ongoing and appropriate support, create opportunities, and achieve full participation, integration, and flexibility.

Federal initiative has created a climate of opportunity to develop new employment options for people with severe disabilities. However, the future lies in the hands of employers, service providers, parents, and people with disabilities to realize these opportunities.

Features of Supported Employment

Six important features of supported employment programs help to explain how they differ from a traditional service approach.

1. **Employment.** The purpose of these programs is employment with all the regular outcomes of having a job. Wages, working conditions, and job security are key considerations.

2. **Ongoing support.** The focus is on providing the ongoing support required to get and keep a job rather than on getting a person ready for a job sometime in the future.
3. **Jobs not services.** Emphasis is on creating opportunities to work rather than just providing services to develop skills.
4. **Full participation.** People who are severely disabled are not excluded. The assumption is that all persons, regardless of the degree of their disability, have the capacity to undertake supported employment if appropriate ongoing support services can be provided.
5. **Social integration.** Contact and relationships with people without disabilities who are not paid caregivers are emphasized. Social integration can with co-workers, supervisors, and others occur at work, near work, during lunchtimes or breaks; or during nonwork hours as a result of wages earned.
6. **Variety and flexibility.** Supported employment does not lock programs into one or two work options. It is flexible because of the wide range of jobs in the community and the many ways of providing support to individuals in those jobs.

Integrated Work

A hallmark in human services during the 1980s was the educational integration of children and youths with disabilities into schools and classrooms with nonhandicapped peers. The underlying philosophy behind this move away from segregation has been the opportunity to have access to normal activities in environments in which there is no stigma attached. While there has been a steady level of progress in the nation's schools toward educational integration, the latter half of the last decade also witnessed an extension of this philosophy into the workplace.

For a number of years during the 1970s and into the 1980s, researchers became more and more proficient at helping people with severe disabilities attain vocational skills. However, for the most part, this work did not occur in normal work settings typically associated with competitive employment. Techniques for systematic instruction, behavior management and rehabilitation engineering were not provided directly at job sites. Furthermore, these advances did not necessarily lead to improved employment outcomes.

With the advent of supported employment programs, integration in the workplace and paid work became the "gold standard" of adult services. Pay levels, work conditions, and amount of hours worked quickly became relatively easy to evaluate in terms of attractiveness. Integration, that is, opportunity to interact with and work with nonhandicapped co-workers, has not been such an easy aspect to assess. The nature of the work tasks, the work schedule, and difficulty in observation of crowded work environments has made vocational integration challenging for job developers and supported employment specialists.

Determining the quality of integration available in the workplace is an important process in supported employment. Since many jobs for supported employees are entry-level and do not often differentiate in terms of pay, the opportunity for friendships, and new co-worker relationships can become deciding factors in which job to select. Looking at company indicators, benefit equality, employee treatments, and the work area in general can provide insight into the quality of vocational integration that will be available.

Later in this book (see Chapter 11), we will examine, in much greater depth, vocational integration and the various aspects of its measurement.

Supported Employment Implications for Rehabilitation Counselors

The emergence of supported employment as an option for job placement of clients with severe disabilities has provided rehabilitation counselors with an important alternative when helping clients gain employment. The rehabilitation counselor is the person who frequently initiates supported employment services in local communities and is the professional who usually arranges for these or other necessary vocational services. Many people with severe disabilities have been considered unemployable because their disability was evaluated as being too severe. As noted earlier, the use of staff support, such as a job coach at the point of placement (i.e., the business setting), is a significantly different way of approaching the problem of challenging rehabilitation cases.

However, with this alternative approach to services has come the responsibility for rehabilitation counselors to learn more about the strengths and weaknesses of supported employment. In the past, most rehabilitation counselors did not have the choice to utilize employment specialist services in their communities for difficult-to-place clients. The idea of supported employment was, at best, experimental. However, it is noteworthy that in recent years many of the supported employment models and concepts have been embraced by most states in the country. Consider for example some of the following information:

- A 50 state analysis recently conducted (Wehman and Kregel and 1990) showed that the numbers have increased from 9,876 supported employment clients in 1986 to over 32,000 in 1988. (This report is represented in much greater detail in the latter half of this chapter).
- In the same study, it was found that over 50% of supported employment clients were in the individual placement model of competitive employment.
- In states such as Virginia, Michigan, Colorado, Pennsylvania, Nevada, North Dakota, Illinois, and many others, significant and dramatic growth of supported employment placements is occurring; for example (See Figure 1.1), in Virginia over 10 quarters of placements have increased

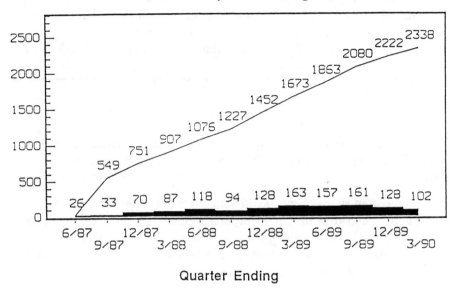

Quarterly and Cumulative Totals of
Placements Reported in Virginia

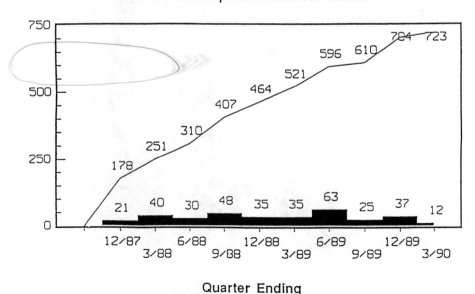

Quarterly and Cumulative Totals of
Placements Reported in North Dakota

Figure 1.1

cumulatively from approximately 500 to over 2300. During a similar time frame, North Dakota has gone from 0 to 723.

- In California (see Figure 1.2), the number of vocational rehabilitations has increased dramatically between 1986 and 1989.
- In Pennsylvania, the 1989 winter edition of the *Supported Employment Newsletter* reports that 596 placements have been made, with over 1.3 million dollars earned by clients, $274,000 in taxes paid, $546,000 in SSI/SSDI costs served, and another $1.1 million saved in day program costs.

These figures are provided only as a small amount of evidence to capture the growth of supported employment. What seems to have made this approach so attractive is:

1. Supported employment provides an alternative to an unsuccessful closure and gives the counselor an additional option(s) to draw upon.
2. Supported employment is *outcome* oriented, that is, counselors can purchase services which lead directly to paid employment, not activities that are only preparatory in nature.

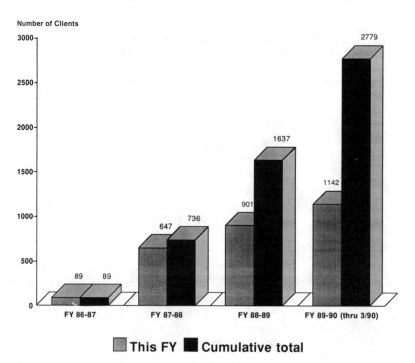

Figure 1.2   VR Rehabilitations since program onset in California.

In the most comprehensive study to date in this area, Shafer (1990) queried over 700 rehabilitation counselors nationally to assess their level, of knowledge in supported employment. While it is not surprising, counselors in system change states had a higher knowledge level at the point the survey was completed; it is also interesting that most counselors, regardless of the state, were in favor of trying supported employment. The systems change strategy is discussed below.

NATIONAL STRATEGY TO IMPROVE SUPPORTED EMPLOYMENT OUTCOMES

In 1985, the United States Department of Education, Office of Special Education and Rehabilitative Services embarked on a national strategy to change the adult service system for persons with severe disabilities. The strategy was based upon the competitive allocation of large ($500,000) awards to states to stimulate change annually from day programs to integrated employment programs. A total of 27 states (portrayed in Figure 1.3) received Title III funds over the five year period of 1986–1991 with the expressed purpose of implementing supported employment programs for persons with severe disabilities (Wehman, Kregel, and Shafer 1989).

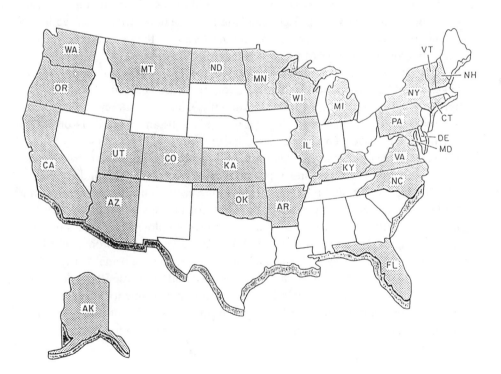

Figure 1.3   State recipients of Title III systems change grants (1985–1900).

This strategy was viewed by many as a bold initiative to modify or alter the way vocational and other adult services were delivered to people with severe disabilities who were typically housed in sheltered workshops or adult activity centers. There was, and still is, considerable controversy on how aggressive or quickly these changes should be made; what additional dollars or resources are needed; how to best communicate these changes to families; and perhaps above all, how to recruit and train staff to meet these new challenges. It is probably safe to say that this strategy has been a highly effective means of fostering change. The preliminary data shown in the Wehman, Kregel, and Shafer monograph seem to support this strategy. As this chapter is written, the Rehabilitation Services Administration is planning to provide funds for another 17 states to embark upon further state systems change during the time period of 1991–1994.

Overview of Supported Employment Progress in the United States

The federal government has directed recent policy and funding initiatives toward enhancing the development of supported employment service opportunities in not just 25, but all 50 states. Vocational rehabilitation agencies in all 50 states and the District of Columbia are now actively involved in the development and provision of supported employment services. The federal/state cooperative initiative has resulted in the provision of supported employment services for a substantial and continuously growing number of persons with severe disabilities.

The study report that follows was developed by Virginia Commonwealth University and clearly indicates the success of the focused federal effort to develop supported employment opportunities nationally. The study surveyed all 50 states to see the progress made between 1986 to 1988. Substantial numbers of historically noncompetitively employed individuals with severe disabilities have entered the competitive labor force through the vocational rehabilitation system. Extended services to maintain persons in supported employment are being funded by agencies other than vocational rehabilitation for persons with mental retardation, and also in a steadily expanding number of states, for persons with mental health or physical disabilities. The capacity of the supported employment services provider system has grown rapidly, and, annually, increasing amounts of nonfederal funds are being utilized. State systems of supported employment are being clearly defined in policies and procedures in both Title III-funded and non-Title III-funded states. The 1986–1988 period represents a developmental time frame for the federal supported employment initiative with many indicators of significant progress in integrating persons with severe disabilities into the competitive labor force.

Emerging Policies and Procedures

Availability and sources of funds for the provision
of initial placement and ongoing support services.
States were asked to indicate whether ongoing support funds were available for seven specific groups of individuals with disabilities.

These disability groups were:

- Mental Retardation
- Mental Illness
- Brain Injury
- Cerebral Palsy
- Other Physical Disability
- Hearing Impairment
- Visual Impairment

State responses for *initial placement* funds were classified by general availability/nonavailability for each disability group. State responses for ongoing support funds were classified as being available statewide, or available in some localities, or not available by disability. States classified as having ongoing support funds available statewide were those which had state or local agency budgets with a significant source of funds for supported employment ongoing support services that were equally available to individuals in all areas of the state (see Figure 1.4).

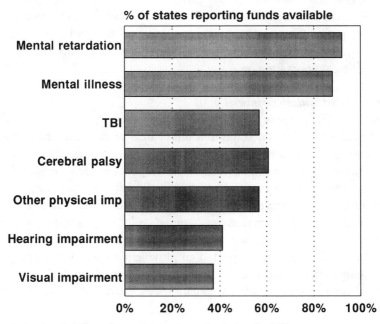

Figure 1.4   Availability of ongoing support funds by disability.

A total of 47 (92.2%) of the states reported being able to provide initial placement and ongoing support services statewide for individuals with mental retardation. In 45 states (88.2%), persons with long-term mental illness were able to access supported employment services. For persons from various physical disability groups, ongoing support services were available in a smaller percentage of states: for persons with traumatic brain injury (56.9%); cerebral palsy (60.8%); other physical disabilities (56.8%); hearing impairments (41.2%) and visual impairments (37.3%).

The states reported numerous sources of *ongoing support* funding as a result of cooperative planning between state and local agencies and organizations. Cited sources of ongoing support funds included state general revenue funds; local community agency funds; Job Training Partnership Act (JTPA) funds; Medicaid waiver funds for waiver-eligible consumers; special state appropriations for specific groups of individuals (e.g., transition-aged individuals with autism); and private funds (e.g., United Way or other charitable contributions).

States were also requested to provide information regarding the content of *cooperative funding* agreements, specifically concerning the point in time that limited funding from the rehabilitation agency is terminated and ongoing support funding is provided by another agency. Approximately 51% of the states have specific guidelines in effect that determine the duration of time-limited funding as a function of the amount of services provided in relation to the hours of employment during a specified period of time. For example, time-limited funding would cease and ongoing support service funding begin when an individual in supported employment demonstrated stability of task performance as measured by job site, and related intervention services at or below 20–25 percent of the hours worked for a specified time period. Some states have less specific criteria and rely on the local rehabilitation counselor or local interagency teams to make the decision on movement to ongoing support funding.

Policies associated with the conversion of facility-based services to supported employment.

The specific responses given by states to a survey item on changing the workshops and other segregated day programs to supported employment are presented in Figure 1.5. Of the states responding, 27.6% identified policies that *encouraged* the reallocation of existing day program slots or the elimination of existing sheltered employment/day activity programs. Only 5.3% of the states indicated that reallocation of existing day program slots was a *mandated* state policy. In comparison, 30.3% of the states indicated policies that maintain current levels of alternative day program availability and use supported employment as one of the alternatives available, along with traditional programs, for future expansion. Similarly, 15.8% indicated policies that would limit new expansion exclusively to supported employ-

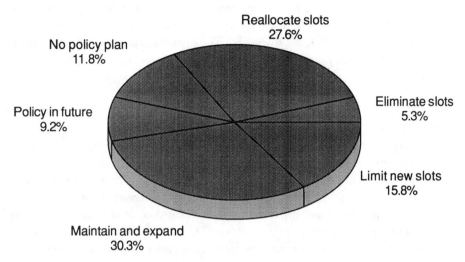

Figure 1.5   State policies regarding existing day programs and future growth of supported employment.

ment. Approximately 11.8% responded that they had no plans to issue policies regarding conversion, while 9.2% indicated that they intended to do so in the future.

The most prominent examples of significant changes taking place in state systems are the 15.8% of the states that have formal plans to limit the future expansion of day service programs to supported employment. At the beginning of Fiscal Year 1986, many of these states had few, if any, supported employment programs in operation and very limited formal policy definition regarding the role of supported employment services as an alternative to traditional day programming for persons with developmental and other severe disabilities.

Policies to insure the participation by persons with severe
handicaps and to establish local supported employment programs
The survey requested information regarding the strategies and procedures being used to encourage the participation of individuals with the most severe handicaps in supported employment programs, including persons with severe or profound mental retardation. Demonstration or start-up grant programs operated by the state vocational rehabilitation agency served as the primary strategy for encouraging the participation of persons with the most severe disabilities. A small number of states utilized their demonstration and start-up grant program to serve individuals from specific disability categories, including persons with severe or profound mental retardation, severe mental illness, autism, multiple handicaps, or traumatic brain injuries. The alternative strategy used by a number of states was to rely upon

grant applicant agencies to fulfill a commitment, as specified in the *Request for proposals,* to serve individuals with the most severe disabilities, without setting disability specific criteria or providing oversight. The demonstration and start-up grant strategy was the primary strategy utilized to establish local supported employment programs.

Growth in Supported Employment Participation
Number of participants in supported employment.

Table 1 presents 1986–88 data on the number of supported employment participants as reported by all 50 states and the District of Columbia. These data represent the total number of supported employment participants that could be identified by the major state agencies providing funding for supported employment. In some states, these data were provided by state vocational rehabilitation agencies only, by state mental health/mental retardation (MH/MR) agencies, or some combination thereof. In every state, however, representatives from all identified agencies were contacted and requested to submit data.

The total number of individuals served in supported employment is presented in Figure 1.6. Based upon data submitted by a total of 20 states, a total of 9,876 individuals were served in supported employment in Fiscal Year 1986. The remaining states either indicated that they had not yet begun to provide supported em-

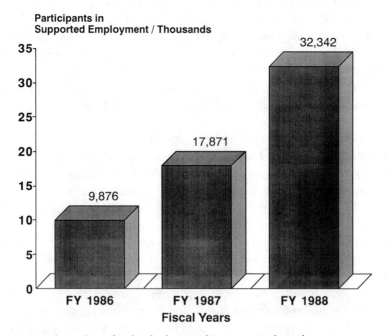

Figure 1.6   Total number of individuals served in supported employment.

Table 1.1 Growth in supported employment participants fiscal years 1986–1988

States	FY 86 Supported Employment Participants Total	FY87 Supported Employment Participants Total	FY88 Supported Employment Participants Total
AK	45	96	142
AL	NA	50	105
AR	0	15	17
AZ	0	0	NA
CA	812	1,803	3,276
CO	323	909	1,073
CT	763	1,467	2,658
DC	0	6	40
DE	22	106	170
FL	0	232	721
GA	NA	491	1,072
HI	16	31	63
IA	0	0	433
ID	0	0	153
IL	0	394	700
IN	0	97	374
KS	0	64	130
KY	51	197	286
LA	0	20	25
MA	0	0	2,064
MD	627	976	1,035
ME	NA	0	138
MI	0	327	600
MN	3,047	4,425	4,587
MO	59	98	237
MS	0	0	378
MT	70	98	156
NC	0	0	311
ND	0	178	305
NE	0	0	NA
NH	100	300	705
NJ	150	323	555
NM	0	0	0
NV	0	0	12
NY	612	1,000	2,350
OH	0	0	81
OK	0	20	78

Table 1.1   Growth in supported employment participants fiscal years 1986–1988 *(cont.)*

States	FY 86 Supported Employment Participants Total	FY87 Supported Employment Participants Total	FY88 Supported Employment Participants Total
OR	147	147	642
PA	0	89	245
RI	0	0	543
SC	0	0	176
SD	0	0	49
TN	0	0	117
TX	0	138	696
UT	0	62	150
VA	184	420	715
VT	226	281	502
WA	913	1,087	1,265
WI	1,691	1,797	1,985
WV	0	86	160
WY	18	41	67
Total	9,876	17,871	32,342
Number of States Providing Data	20	36	48

ployment services or that they did not have such data available. By Fiscal Year 1987, the total number of participants had increased to a total of 17,871, representing an 81% increase over the total number served in FY 1986. The FY 1987 figure was based upon data provided by a total of 36 states. For FY 1988, a total of 48 states provided data and reported a cumulative total of 32,342 individuals served in supported employment. The FY 1988 total represented an 81% increase over the FY 1987 number of participants and a 226% increase over the FY 1986 number of participants.[1]

Primary Disability of Supported Employment Participants

Information regarding the primary disability of supported employment participants was provided by a total of 45 states for FY 88, the most recent year that these data

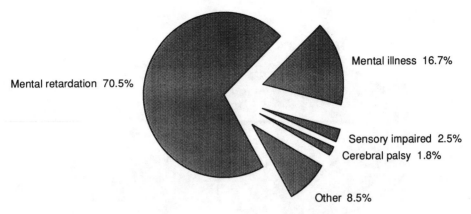

Figure 1.7 Primary disability of participants, N = 25,383; 45 states reporting. (Preliminary data-subject to verification January 30, 1990)

were available. The 45 states provided primary disability information on a total of 25,383 individuals. This figure represents approximately 78% of the total number of FY 88 participants. As the data in Figure 1.5 indicates, individuals identified as mentally retarded comprised slightly more than 70% of those individuals for whom such information was available. Individuals with long-term mental illness represented 16.7% of all participants. The remaining 12.8% of the participants consisted of individuals identified as experiencing sensory impairments (2.5%), cerebral palsy (1.8%), or other disabilities (8.5%), such as traumatic brain injury, autism, and other unspecified disabilities.

A total of 37 states were able to provide FY 88 data on the functioning level of supported employment participants for whom mental retardation was identified as their primary disability. The data in Figure 1.8 indicates that individuals considered mildly mentally retarded (IQ = 55–69) represented 46.3% of all individuals identified as mentally retarded and served in supported employment. Individuals considered moderately mentally retarded represented 37.5% of the sample, while individuals considered severely mentally retarded (IQ = 25–39) comprised 11.6% of the participants with mental retardation and approximately 8% of all participants.

Data regarding the type of mental illness diagnosed for those individuals with a primary diagnosis of mental illness were also solicited from the states in the second wave of the survey. Three categories were provided in the questionnaire, using the same categories employed by the RSA 911 case reporting system. Eleven states from the second stage survey sample responded to this item and provided data representative of 351 individuals. Based upon the data provided by these eleven states, individuals experiencing psychosis represented 52.1% of the sample,

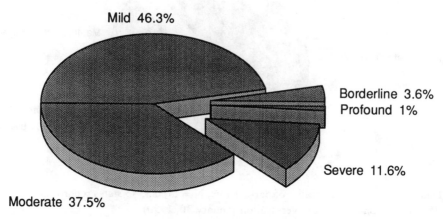

Figure 1.8   Supported employment participants identified as mentally retarded, N = 13,219; 37 states reporting.

while those individuals experiencing neurosis constituted 27.9% of the sample. Finally, persons experiencing personality disorders represented 19.9% of all supported employment participants for whom mental illness was a primary diagnosis.

IMPACT UPON THE REHABILITATION SERVICE SYSTEM

The impact that supported employment has had upon the vocational rehabilitation system can be assessed from a variety of perspectives. In this section, data are presented that summarize the number of new clients determined eligible for vocational rehabilitation services and for whom supported employment was identified in their Individual Written Rehabilitation Program (IWRP); the number of supported employment clients who were successfully (status 26) and unsuccessfully (status 28) rehabilitated by the state agency; and finally, the number of individuals served in traditional, nonsupported employment, day services.

New Clients to the State VR Agencies

The number of states capable of providing data on new VR supported employment clients has increased progressively between FY 1986 and 1988. For 1986, 10 states reported that a total of 912 new, eligible clients had entered their vocational rehabilitation agency as a result of supported employment.

By FY 1987, this figure, as reported by 21 states, had increased to 3,899 clients. In FY 1988, a total of 39 states provided data indicating that a total of 8,552 clients had become eligible for vocational rehabilitation services as a direct result of supported employment. Eleven states provided data for all three fiscal years and reported a net FY 1986–1988 increase of 165% in new VR clients as a result of supported employment.

Successful and Unsuccessful Rehabilitants

The ability of state agencies to retrieve information on successful and unsuccessful supported employment closures has been limited. Until recently, many states did not specifically identify supported employment clients within the case reporting system. As the required supported employment data elements for RSA 911 become consistently implemented by all state agencies, this information will undoubtedly become more readily available. For FY 1986, only 5 states were capable of reporting data on status 26 and 28 supported employment closures. These states' data identify a total of 138 successful supported employment closures and 20 unsuccessful closures. By 1987, the number of states providing these data had risen to 16. These 16 states reported a total of 582 status 26 successful closures, as compared to 134 status 28 unsuccessful closures. Finally, for FY 1988, a total of 2,372 status 26 closures were reported by 31 states, while 451 status 28 closures were reported for the same fiscal year.

Impact Upon Traditional Day Service Programs

In order to assess the impact that supported employment has had upon traditional day programs and facility-based service programs, states were requested to provide figures on the number of individuals served in all facility-based, day activity, work activity, extended sheltered employment, and psycho-social rehabilitation programs. These program options represent the most common service delivery systems from which potential supported employment clients will be referred. In many states, this service taxonomy was not recognized, or, the states were capable of providing aggregated figures only. As such, data are only presented regarding aggregated, total clients in traditional day programs.

A total of 27 states were able to provide data on the number of clients served in these alternative day programs and supported employment for each of the fiscal years under analysis. These data reveal that the number of persons served in traditional day programs has increased by 16,500 individuals between 1986 and 1988, representing a growth rate of 8.9%. In comparison, these same states, all of whom reported supported employment participants for the same three years, indicated that the number of clients served in supported employment had grown by 17,380, representing a net growth in supported employment of 181% during the three-year fiscal period. The number of individuals served in supported employ-

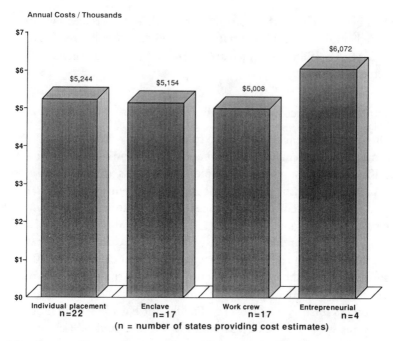

Figure 1.9   Comparative yearly costs of providing supported employment.

ment, when expressed as a percentage of all alternative day and supported employment participants, grew from 4.9% in FY 1986 to 11.74% in FY 1988.

Cost Estimates for Supported Employment and Traditional Day Service Programs

States were requested to submit information on the average annual costs in FY 88 for serving individuals in the four predominant models of supported employment and the four previously identified models of alternative day services. The number of states providing these data varied extensively for each of the identified models. Additionally, the range of reported costs varied dramatically. Figure 1.9 presents the annual average cost estimates reported by states for serving individuals in each of the identified supported employment models. As these data indicate, the average cost for these services appears fairly consistent, ranging from a low of $5,008 for serving individuals in mobile work crews, to a high of $6,072 for serving persons in entrepreneurial businesses. This latter figure, however, should be viewed with extreme caution as only 4 states provided data on this model.

While the reported average annual costs across supported employment models were fairly consistent, states reported a wide range of costs within each model. Individual placement model costs ranged from a low of $1,545 to a high of

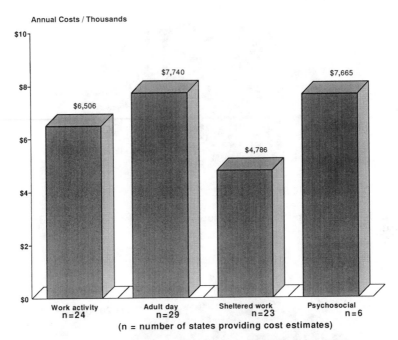

Figure 1.10   Comparative yearly costs of providing traditional day services.

$10,000, with a standard deviation of $1,875. Likewise, enclave costs estimates ranged from a low of $1,705 to a high of $8,007, with a standard deviation of $1,813. In comparison, mobile work crew cost estimates ranged from a low of $1,650 to a high of $10,000, with a standard deviation of $2,050.

Cost estimates were also solicited for providing alternative day service programs. As displayed in Figure 1.10, sheltered employment was identified as having the lowest annual cost at $4,786, while adult day activity programs had the highest cost estimate at $7,740. Sheltered employment cost estimates ranged from $475 to $10,080, with a standard deviation of $2,648. In comparison, adult day activity program cost estimates ranged from $3,272 to $25,000, with a standard deviation of $4,438. Work activity center cost estimates averaged $6,506 and ranged from $2,920 to $11,500, with a standard deviation of $2,426. Finally, psycho-social rehabilitation cost estimates ranged from a low of $838 to a high of $13,750, with an average cost estimate of $7,665 and a standard deviation of $4,329.

KEY OUTCOMES FOR SUPPORTED EMPLOYEES

States were requested to provide information on a variety of key outcomes experienced by the individuals participating in supported employment. In this section,

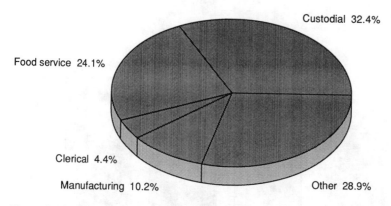

Figure 1.11   Types of positions held by supported employees, N = 9,327; 35 states reporting.

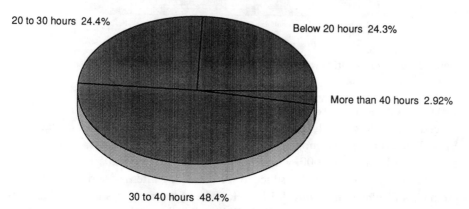

Figure 1.12   Average weekly hours of employment based upon data from 27 states representing 21,319 supported employees.

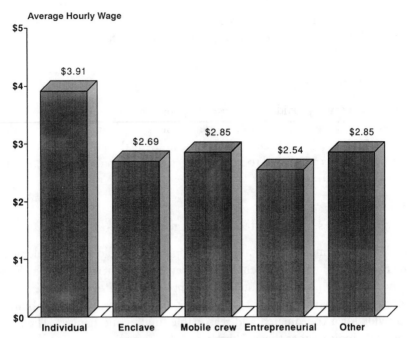

Figure 1.13   Comparative hourly wage rates by model based upon data provided by 27 states.

data are presented regarding the types of job in which consumers are employed, the amount of hours worked each week, and finally, their average hourly and yearly wages.

Types of Jobs Held by Supported Employees

Thirty-five states submitted data regarding the types of jobs in which supported employees were working in FY 1988. These data, representing 9,327 participants, are presented in Figure 11. Custodial and food service positions represent the two largest job categories, encompassing 32.4% and 24.1% of the sample, respectively. It is noteworthy that an additional 28.9% of the sample of participants were employed in other positions not represented by the four categories that were identified by the questionnaire.

Weekly Hours of Employment

Figure 1.12 presents data on 21,319 supported employees that were submitted by 27 states regarding the average weekly hours of employment for these participants. These data indicate that approximately 76% of the participants for whom these data were available were employed in excess of 20 hours per week. Over half (51.3%) of this sample were employed in excess of 30 hours per week.

Average Hourly Wages

Twenty-seven states provided data regarding the average hourly salary of supported employees working in the various models of supported employment. As depicted in Figure 1.13, participants employed in the individual placement model averaged $3.91 per hour, as compared to hourly wages, which ranged from $2.54 to $2.85 for the other identified models of employment.

Emerging Policies in Supported Employment

Among the more critical aspects of supported employment implementation is the extent to which state agencies have developed policies and procedures that (1) encourage the provision of supported employment by service delivery agencies; (2) promote the participation of individuals with the most severe disabilities; and (3) provide for a coordinated and reasonable funding mechanism. The above re-ported data indicate that the establishment of such policies has begun to occur in some states; however, it is clear that much work must still be done in this regard.

Provider Incentives.

As reported earlier, the approach states have taken in converting traditional, seg-regated vocational alternatives to supported employment may best be character-ized as indirect and encouraging. It is clear that the majority of state agencies are not yet mandating the elimination nor actual conversion of day program/sheltered employment program slots to supported employment. Typically, it appears that state agencies are viewing supported employment as a growth option, allowing pro-viders to convert or "rollover" existing program slots as they desire.

While not evident from these data, interviews and informal contacts with state agency representatives revealed a lack of true incentives for local providers to begin implementation of supported employment. For example, the unit rate at which supported employment is funded in many states does not provide adequate fiscal compensation for the agency. In California, for example, a flat unit rate of $20 per hour was implemented for the funding of individual placement services. Similarly, the state of New York has mandated a maximum hourly rate of $14 per hour.

These unit rates are significantly higher than those typically provided for Work Adjustment Training, Vocational Evaluation, or other traditional facility-based services, which may often be purchased by state agencies at rates ranging from $15–35 per day. Typically, facility-based providers are able to make use of contract generated revenue from their sheltered employment enterprises to compensate for the insufficient funding of these services. For providers operating without a sheltered employment component, or those attempting to downsize or convert their sheltered employment, this option is not available nor desirable. Clearly, if supported employment implementation is to occur at any significant level, appropriate funding levels and procedures must be in place that entice and encourage facilities to shift their service orientation.

Another issue that we identify as a serious disincentive to supported employment implementation is the availability of extended services funding. The survey data indicate uneven availability of ongoing funding based upon disability. Additionally, based upon our discussions with state agency representatives and other individuals within the states, it is clear that extended services funding is insufficient and uncoordinated in many states. Quite often, providers are left to their own devices, with little, if any, support or technical assistance to identify and secure ongoing funding sources as required in the IWRP. The result has been inadequate support provision as agencies attempt to maximize their spending by maintaining excessively high caseloads for their employment specialists, and/or minimizing the amount of extended services provided to individual consumers.

Clearly, interagency coordination and funding that is mandated at the state agency level and aggressively pursued and implemented at the local level is needed to assure providers that reliable, stable funding for extended services is available. In North Dakota, for example, the administration and funding of ongoing support services has been transferred from the Division of Human Resources to the Department of Vocational Rehabilitation, thereby offering providers a single source entity from which to obtain funding for supported employment. Many other states have clearly articulated and implemented local interagency funding mechanisms.

Consumer Assessment and Identification.

The ability to determine the appropriateness of potential clients for supported employment or predict their ongoing support needs represents a significant need for state agencies and providers alike. Rehabilitation counselors are in need of guidelines to assist them in identifying appropriate supported employment clients, determining the ongoing support needs of clients, and recognizing the supported employment potential of individuals with the most severe handicaps.

At this time, few state agencies have done much to operationalize the eligibility requirements for entry into supported employment programs. The result has been extreme variability in the type of individuals served in supported employment programs across various states. The lack of more specific information regarding client appropriateness/eligibility may also result in a tendency to be less than aggressive in arranging and providing supported employment services for individuals with the most severe handicaps (e.g, multihandicapped, dually diagnosed, dual sensory impairments, profound mental retardation, etc.).

Quality Assurance and Program Evaluation

State agencies almost universally report an urgent need to devise program evaluation and quality assurance mechanisms for use in effectively monitoring local community supported employment implementation and guaranteeing that quality outcomes are achieved by supported employment participants. Many states are attempting to move from simple regulatory compliance to sophisticated program evaluation mechanisms designed to improve the quality of supported employment services provided by local programs. However, few states have established and implemented formal, statewide, evaluation/technical assistance systems and few resources are available to assist them in this effort. Many states lack the basic program outcome data available through management information systems and other sources that allow state agencies to identify problems and track progress over time. This lack of information is becoming particularly critical as supported employment moves beyond the isolated demonstration into statewide implementation.

Survey respondents indicated that the standards on which the quality of supported employment programs should be judged have changed rapidly over time. While initially the focus was simply on hourly wages and hours worked per week, recent conceptualizations of success, in many states, have centered on additional variables, such as fringe benefits, career advancement, increased wages over time, and social integration. Many other quality assurance issues, which until recently had received very little attention from policymakers and program managers, are clearly major concerns of the survey respondents. For example, to what extent are consumers exercising maximum freedom of choice in determining whether or not they participate in supported employment and making other major career decisions? Or, although supported employment is clearly improving the physical integration of participants, are consumers also socially integrated into work settings, or are many individuals becoming socially isolated in the community? These "second generation" quality assurance issues, along with others, are becoming the focal point of many states' technical assistance and staff development activities.

Systems Change

The ultimate size and extent of our nation's supported employment program is yet to be determined. It is safe to hypothesize that rapid growth in the program will continue over the next several years. However, supported employment participants still represent only a very small percentage of all individuals participating in most states' rehabilitation and day programs for individuals with severe disabilities.

While the large influx of federal rehabilitation monies and state expansion funds has spurred the development of supported employment, the program cannot continue to grow at its present rate without a significant reallocation of existing resources.

Without continued, effective systems change efforts the progress made during the past several years will slow or fade. Policies and regulations must continue to be refined until supported employment is viewed as an integral component of each state's rehabilitation program and the roles of all participating agencies are clear. Consensus building efforts must occur that will forge state and local agreement on the extent to which supported employment alternatives will replace existing day program options. Partnerships with business and industry must continue to be cultivated. Finally, sufficient resources must be identified, through new and creative approaches, to adequately finance the national supported employment effort into the 1990s.

Promising Trends

In spite of the policy issues just discussed, there are some very positive and promising indications that supported employment is taking hold in many states. Perhaps one of the more significant indications of this initiative has been the tremendous growth that has been witnessed in the total number of supported employment participants. As reported in Table 1.1, 48 states submitted data indicating that a total of 32,342 individuals participated in supported employment in FY 1988.

While this figure is indeed impressive, it pales in comparison to estimates of the total day activity/sheltered employment census of individuals with mental retardation or developmental disabilities. Buckley and Bellamy (1985), for example, estimated that, in 1983, 185,536 individuals were served in day and vocational programs supported by state mental retardation/developmental disability agencies. Clearly, supported employment participation continues to represent the exception, rather than the rule, in vocational service options for persons with disabilities.

There is little doubt, however, that the national trend is toward supported employment. Our own data, based upon information submitted from 27 states capable of providing three year data on supported employment and alternative day program enrollments, suggest that the growth in facility-based service options has begun to slow as supported employment has become available. Projected growth rates in facility-based program slots among these 27 states was estimated at 8.9%, while growth rates for supported employment within the same states was projected at 181% during a three year period. These findings corroborate our observations regarding the established conversion policies of state agencies; there remains a high demand for day vocational services, and as such, supported employment is being implemented as one option among many to respond to this ever increasing demand. Based upon recent data regarding future special-education graduates, the demand for day services and supported employment can be expected to remain strong (Ward and Halloran 1989).

Clearly, there remains significant work to be done in order to more fully incorporate this innovative service into the existing array of options available to persons with severe disabilities. However, there should be little question regarding the effectiveness of recent federal initiatives and policies; supported employment is emerging as a major, significant factor in the vocational rehabilitation of Americans with severe disabilities.

2

Consumer Choice and Empowerment in Supported Employment

Michael D. West

Wendy S. Parent

Most individuals treasure and guard the control that they exert over their own lives—where they work, where they live, their style of dress, their preferences for food, the company they keep, and other major and everyday decisions. To a great extent, the choices and preferences we express and the decisions we make define ourselves. They reveal our values, our priorities, our goals, our needs, our contentment with the present, and our hopes for the future. Learning to make decisions and choices is as much a part of the developmental, process as learning to take care of one's bodily needs, to communicate, and to coexist with the rest of society.

Yet, for many individuals with severe disabilities, the opportunities to learn and practice decision making and self-direction are limited or circumvented. More and more, it is becoming evident that the reasons these individuals experience such powerlessness and lack of self-direction have less to do with their limitations and impairments and more to do with the attitudes and practices of caregivers, service providers and funding agencies, and social institutions. For example, individuals may not be given the opportunity to learn how to make appropriate choices or to practice decision making; they may not be given adequate information or experience to make good decisions or choices; options may be artificially preselected and restricted; or, in many cases, the "choices" offered to and then selected by individuals or their families may not be choices at all, but the avoidance of undesirable alternatives or threats (i.e., agreeing to live with incompatible roommates in a group residence to avoid movement to a more restrictive setting). It is only in recent years that the empowerment of individuals with disabilities and their families has received any substantial attention in the rehabilitation literature and in direct service technology (Bannerman, Sheldon, Sherman, and Harchik 1990; Guess, Benson, and Siegel-Causey 1985; Lovett 1991; Shevin and Klein 1984).

This chapter will examine consumer empowerment issues in human services and supported employment in particular. First, we will describe, in general terms, how consumers can be given more control over supported employment services and, by extension, their work experiences. Then, we will examine consumer empowerment from the perspective of the various disability groups typically served in supported employment programs, giving relevant case examples to show the effects of choice and, in one case, the absence of choice on individuals' satisfaction with employment and general well-being.

CONSUMER EMPOWERMENT AND CHOICE MAKING

Historically, recipients of human services have not been given much of a voice in what services are offered, how services are administered, or what the outcomes of services should be. The prevailing attitude on both sides of the provider-recipient fence seems to have been that "beggars can't be choosers." However, in recent years, we have witnessed a growing belief that consumers should gain some power over human services and, in the process, gain or regain power over their own lives. *Empowerment* can be broadly defined as the transfer of power and control over the values, decisions, choices, and directions of human services from external entities (i.e., government agencies, service providers, social forces, etc.) to the consumers of services. The likely effects of the transfer of choice making to consumers would be increased independence, greater motivation to participate and succeed, and a greater degree of dignity for the consumer.

Choice is defined as "the act of an individual's selection of a preferred alternative from among several familiar options" (Shevin and Klein 1984). This implies that choice making involves two parts identifying one's preferences and then expressing those choices. Individuals with severe disabilities may have difficulty with one or both of these skills due to a lack of training on how to make choices, inexperience with choice making, little knowledge about possible alternatives, limitations with communication, or frustration over not having choices respected in the past. Persons who have communication difficulties may express preferences through overt actions, whose meanings are not easily interpretable. Individuals with disabilities frequently respond positively to a question or answer in a manner they feel the questioner would prefer, because often they do not understand what is being asked, are not aware of the given alternatives, or do not want to jeopardize the chance to receive employment services. Unfortunately, these "choices" often translate into service delivery with little regard for whether the response reflects what the individual actually wants. It is likely that individuals with severe disabilities will require additional assistance, support, or time in order to make and express their preferred choices.

CHOICE AND EMPOWERMENT
IN SUPPORTED EMPLOYMENT SERVICES

In the past individuals with severe disabilities were not given a choice regarding vocational services. An individual either met the eligibility criteria for rehabilitation services (Bitter 1979) or was referred for extended evaluation, training, or work adjustment to "get ready" to go to work. With supported employment, individuals are not excluded or prepared; rather the delivery of services is built around his or her *current* skills, abilities, interests, and preferences. The foundation of this model is the provision of individualized supports that will assist a person who has a severe disability participate in the roles and settings that he or she prefers and chooses. Flexible, individualized supports allow an individual to rely on personal skills and resources to achieve his or her chosen lifestyle (Smull and Bellamy 1991). Supported employment extends the right of choice to those persons who typically have had few opportunities to choose how they want to live their life, where they want to work, and the services they would like to receive. Williams (1991) expresses this right as follows:

> Every person, regardless of the severity of his or her disabilities, has the right and ability to communicate with others, express everyday preferences, and exercise at least some control over his or her daily life. Each individual, therefore, should be given the choice, training, technology, respect, and encouragement to do so (Williams 1991, 543).

The opportunity to choose where one wants to work and the chance to change one's mind when that choice is no longer desirable has been shown to have a significant effect on the degree of job satisfaction that an individual experiences. Studies investigating job satisfaction of nonhandicapped workers have reported that the meaning of the concept is very individualized and factors such as the amount of pay, the personal relationships on the job, the amount of autonomy, the challenge of the work, the prestige of the position, or the steadiness of employment all vary in importance, depending on the individual. (Moseley 1988). The factors associated with job satisfaction are no different for workers with a disability and will vary in importance for each person, depending upon his or her job values and personal preferences. Summarizing her experiences as a vocational counselor involved with supported employment, McDonnell (1991) reported "client involvement in actively choosing a work field and taking an active role in developing a job in that area creates a commitment by the consumer which tends to enhance job satisfaction" (p. 3). Unfortunately, the opportunity to choose a job and to make decisions about the delivery of supported employment services is frequently determined more by an individual's disability label rather than the importance autonomy and control has on personal satisfaction and job retention. Within supported employment services, there are ample opportunities to empower all

Table 2.1   Empowering Consumers in Supported Employment

- Provide opportunities to choose from a variety of interesting, motivating, and socially and personally valued career areas. It is in these areas that job development or job tryout activities should be concentrated.
- Provide opportunities for expressing preferences and making choices between specific jobs based on such factors as pay, work hours, work expectations, compatibility with the supervisor or co-workers, and the degree to which the consumer feels comfortable interacting with co-workers or customers.
- In areas where there are multiple providers of employment services, provide the opportunity to express a preference for a particular provider, based on personal experiences or track records.
- Provide opportunities to express a preference for particular job coaches, again based on prior experience or track record.
- Provide opportunities for expressing preferences in training methods, adaptive devices, or compensatory strategies, based on ease of use, comfort or discomfort, stigmatizing effects, or any other factor.
- Allow consumers choice in either keeping a position, changing job responsibilities, or resigning and seeking a more compatible position.

consumers. Table 2.1 provides a listing of these opportunities, and some of them will be described here.

Choosing a Career Area

For some individuals, who have had community-based vocational training, career counseling, or a previous work history, valued job preferences may have already been identified. However, for others, whose life experiences have been very limited or who have received little support or encouragement, job choices may be based more on wanting to work or professional opinion rather than the desired option. Several strategies can be used by the employment specialist to assist the individual with making an informed career choice. These include (1) computer software and microfiche career exploration packages, such as Virginia View; (2) videotapes displaying the work environment and job responsibilities of a variety of jobs; (3) repeated personal conversations between the employment specialist and consumer to share job information, to get to know the individual's likes and methods of expression, and to build trust so that honest feelings are shared; and (4) participation in community-based situational assessment experiences (see Chapter 6 for more information on situational assessments).

Melinda was targeted for a supported employment placement during her last year of school at a segregated special education center. She was enrolled in a class for students with severe and multiple handicaps where she was working on IEP goals of number recognition, letter recognition, counting coins to $.50, making a bed, making a sandwich, and collating papers. Melinda's vocational program included working in the school's sheltered workshop three days a week for four hours a day. Melinda has disability labels of severe mental retardation, cerebral palsy, vision impairment, and medication controlled seizures.

The employment specialist found out from Melinda that she would like a job where she could be around other people, but was unsure of what kind of work she would like. A situational assessment was scheduled for Melinda at a local hospital where she could try out several jobs, each for a four hour period. The first day, Melinda worked in the supply room, where she was responsible for pushing the supply cart, guiding the dust mop, and emptying the trash cans. She had overall difficulty with gross motor movements and strength when lifting and pushing. Melinda's fine motor skills were much better, and she was able to orient independently in the large supply room after one demonstration by the trainer. After about thirty minutes of working, Melinda began to whine and sit down repeatedly. She came back to work when the trainer ignored her whining and reinforced her for working, but she continued to sit down whenever the trainer was not providing reinforcement.

The second day, Melinda worked in the kitchen of the hospital, where she was responsible for clearing patient trays, loading dishes and trays into the dishwasher, and replacing the tray carts. She required a verbal prompt to start working and several subsequent prompts to continue working. Melinda cried and argued with the trainer when she was told to return to work. She was able to perform the job tasks after a short training period but required some assistance with moving the cart, due to limitations with gross motor movements. When clearing trays, Melinda did not appear to have difficulty discriminating between the items that needed to be sorted, but she did close her eyes and look away from her work frequently.

Melinda worked in the laundry room, where she folded and stacked pajamas and towels. She worked for three hours before stating she was tired and would like a break. Her folding rate was average, but her overall pace was slow, as she had difficulty making the small folds in the pajamas and stacking them in piles. She frequently initiated interactions with other employees and stopped working several times to approach another co-worker to ask her if she could help. It appeared as though Melinda really enjoyed the type of work she was doing and the environment she was in, as evident by her work performance and social interactions. Melinda said the job she most enjoyed was folding clothes, and she asked the trainer if she could come back and work in the laundry room again the next day.

Choosing a Specific Job

Identified career preferences provide broad parameters, which can guide the employment specialist's job development activities. However, the specific characteristics of each potential job opening and work environment (i.e., salaries, benefits, degree of integration and interaction, etc.) are going to vary and affect the desirability of the specific job to the consumer. For example, an individual may prefer the higher wages of one job over the nine to five hours of another. Similarly, an individual may choose the social atmosphere of one job over the geographical location of another. Indications of which job characteristics are valued by an individual can be identified during the consumer assessment process when completing the following activities: (1) interviewing the consumer and family members, (2) observing the consumer in different environments, (3) reviewing records and evaluations documenting previous experiences, (4) repeatedly visiting and communicating with the consumer and/or family in familiar surroundings, (5) conducting community-based situational assessment work experiences, and (6) arranging on-site visits at different businesses in the community.

> As a teenager, George had been diagnosed as having schizophrenia. For the past twenty years, he experienced repeated hospitalizations in psychiatric institutions and for many years sat at home with his parents. At the age of 36, George was referred to the state vocational rehabilitation agency where he was determined eligible for services and considered to be a good candidate for supported employment. An employment specialist met with George and conducted a consumer assessment to gather information about George's work characteristics and job preferences so that he could be assisted with identifying a good job match. George told the employment specialist he really wanted a job and reported that he had worked in the back of a kitchen at several of the hospitals and enjoyed it tremendously.
>
> The employment specialist targeted job development activities at local restaurants to find a kitchen job that would match George's interests and support needs. Several jobs were found including a dishwashing and a pot scrubbing position. The employment specialist discussed the jobs with George at great length and took him on an interview at both restaurants so that he could observe the job setting and duties firsthand. George did not have previous work experience in a community setting and had difficulty deciding which job might be best for him. He stated that he didn't care as long as he could work, and he asked the employment specialist to select between the jobs. The employment specialist remembered a friend who owned a similar restaurant and arranged for George to have a chance to try out each job, to see which one he liked best.

George arrived at the restaurant, and the employment specialist showed him how to scrub the pots. He picked up the first pot and after a few seconds of washing it, began to scream loudly and threw the pot across the room. George continued to scream and to throw pots on the floor. The employment specialist had never seen George exhibit these behaviors before and suggested they move over to the dishwashing job. The employment specialist showed George how to load and unload the dishwasher and George immediately jumped right in. George continued to work for four hours until a co-worker approached him about taking a lunch break. It was evident that George preferred the dishwashing job; this was confirmed by his statement that he wanted to be a dishwasher.

Choice of Agency and Job Coach

In areas where there are multiple providers of employment services, funding and referral agencies can give consumers and their families the opportunity to express a preference for a particular supported employment provider. This preference may be based on prior experiences, good and bad track records with job placements and retention, proximity, or level of comfort with agencies or staff within agencies.

Usually, a supported employment program manager will assign a job coach or employment specialist to assist a consumer according to availability and case loads. Typically, an individual will not know the employment specialists well enough to select one over another at the time of referral. As the consumer and employment specialist work together more closely during job development, consumer assessment, and particularly during job site training, provisions should be made to accommodate an individual's request for a different job coach. Just as nonhandicapped people do not like everyone, the consumer may find that he or she cannot work with or doesn't like the job coach assigned or the two of them have conflicting values or ideas regarding employment. It is important to listen to what the individual with a disability is saying and to pay attention to a change in behavior at the job site, which may signal a problem with the current training arrangements. Perhaps a satisfactory solution can be identified that could alleviate the problem without changing job coaches. If another job coach is not available to accommodate the consumer's request, then he or she should be given an estimated time frame of how long the wait may be so that a choice between realistic alternatives can be made.

Leroy is a 20-year-old student enrolled in a self-contained school for individuals with severe and profound handicaps. He has been assessed as having severe mental retardation and fragile x syndrome. Leroy's speech is limited to a few words, such as yes or no, and some repetitive phrases. He frequently exhibits multiple stereotypic and self-injurious behaviors. Leroy's teacher and his mother both feel he should work, and Leroy always answers positively when asked if he would like a job. He was targeted by a supported employment program for placement.

Robin, the employment specialist, met with Leroy, his mother, and his teacher on several occasions to identify job development leads. He also took Leroy out into the community for lunch and other activities so that they could get to know each other before beginning a job placement. A dishwashing position was located in a cafeteria near Leroy's home and determined by everyone to be a good job match. Leroy and Robin both arrived at the restaurant everyday wearing the same uniform and followed the same daily schedule. During the slow periods, Robin used systematic instruction to teach Leroy how to clean the trays, load and unload the dishwasher, and put the dishes away. During the lunch rush, Robin would do the work while Leroy cleared the trays; a task he was able to do with minimal verbal prompting.

After working together five days a week for four weeks, Robin explained to Leroy that he would not be there for a few weeks because another person he had worked with needed some assistance. Robin began preparing Leroy several days in advance of the switch and stayed on the job site a few days with Leroy and Susan, the new employment specialist. Leroy nodded positively when Robin asked if he liked Susan and would like to work with her. Everything went well the first day that Leroy and Susan worked together. The next morning Leroy's mother reported that he had come home the night before and thrown things around the house, refused to eat, and kept banging objects against the wall in his bedroom, keeping everyone up most of the night. The following day at work Leroy kept saying "where's Robin," "Robin go home," and "don't want to work." Leroy frequently sat down at the job and refused to clear the trays or allow Susan to assist him with learning how to perform the rest of his job tasks.

Leroy and Susan worked together for five days, and each day his behavior became more disruptive both at work and at home. The employer told Susan he thought he would have to terminate Leroy if his performance did not improve. Susan contacted her supervisor who recommended that she, Robin, and Susan meet to come up with a solution for the problem. It was decided that Robin and Susan would switch positions, and Robin would return to work with Leroy. Beginning the first day back together, Leroy performed the job the same as he had before Robin left and did not exhibit any of the behaviors at work or at home that were reported during Robin's absence.

Choice of Methods

Consumers of services can also be involved in selecting training methods, adaptive devices, or compensatory strategies. They may have ideas about which would be more effective for them, which would be more comfortable to use, or which would have a less stigmatizing effect on them. They may also have preferences concerning the level of intervention that is being provided at the job site. They may feel the employment specialist is checking up too often, embarrassing them in front of co-workers. They may feel that picture prompts are too juvenile for them or call attention to the consumer's inability to read or follow instructions. When conspicuous methods cannot be avoided, the employment specialist should make every attempt to fade them as rapidly as possible.

Jack is a man in his late twenties who sustained a severe head injury as a teenager. He exhibits impairments in his speech, memory, reasoning, and motor coordination. He is also known to have episodic loss of inhibition and self-control, at which time he will fly into a rage toward anyone for any reason. His work history, prior to supported employment, consisted of several jobs that he quickly lost when he could not remember his duties or became angry when corrected. His employment specialist helped him locate and land a job as a stock clerk in an electrical and plumbing supply warehouse. Jack's duties consisted of retrieving items listed on customers' invoices and keeping the warehouse clean and organized.

The employment specialist designed aids to enable Jack to remember his duties and make decisions for carrying them out. Several posters with large lettering describing Jack's duties were placed on the walls. They were designed and positioned so that Jack could read them from several distant locations on the warehouse floor. Under some of the job duties, such as where items were located, when to empty trash barrels, etc., were also listed corresponding decision rules that Jack was to employ in carrying out the particular duty.

Jack occasionally referred to the posters, but he usually ignored them, with many subsequent errors. When prompted by the employment specialist to refer to the posters, Jack became angry with her and threatened to destroy them. It took a while for the employment specialist to understand that Jack's noncompliance stemmed from the aids themselves. They served as continual reminders to Jack and his co-workers that he was "different" and could not think or remember as clearly as the other workers. They made him feel that he was stupid or perceived as stupid.

The employment specialist took down the posters and worked with Jack to redesign the memory aid so that Jack was comfortable with it. Jack's duties and decision rules were typed on a sheet of paper, which was then clipped onto a clipboard. Jack could clip the invoices over the list so that it could be seen only by himself. The newly-styled aid was not as durable and had to be replaced frequently. Jack sometimes forgot to take the clipboard with him or left it in places around the warehouse, so the new aid was somewhat less convenient. But it was immensely more effective because Jack used it.

Choice of Keeping or Resigning a Job.

Perhaps this area of choice is the most problematic for supported employment agencies to accept and implement. Because of financial and personnel commitments, relationships with employers or state vocational rehabilitation counselors, and other economic and political considerations, providers will frequently attempt to maintain placements as long as possible, regardless of the level of satisfaction or vocational aspirations of the supported employee. Consumers may even be intimidated with threats of extended unemployment should they follow through with a desire to terminate their employment.

By statutory definition, supported employment clients either have never worked competitively or have not had success working competitively. They are individuals who are typically excluded from work experience programs that allow clients to explore career interests. They have significant deficits in cognition, social skills, or emotional stability, or they require extensive adaptations to jobs and workplaces, all of which will tax the patience and resources of most employers and co-workers. By and large, they are placed in entry-level positions that have high turnover and low satisfaction rates, even for nondisabled workers. Should it come as a surprise that a large number of supported employees leave their jobs voluntarily or involuntarily after a short period of time (see Lagomarcino 1990)?

In terms of consumer empowerment issues, supported employment provider agencies have two major tasks before them. First, to acknowledge that long-range vocational success for their clients begins with consumer-directed placement (Martin and Mithaug 1990). Too often, agencies target positions into which the greatest number of potential clients can "fit", rather than attempting to match the abilities and interests of individuals with motivating, challenging jobs. Second, supported employment provider and funding agencies need to develop more positive attitudes regarding job separations. Job separations should not be viewed as failures on anyone's part, but as stages of growth in the consumer's development of both work preferences and work capacity. That is, the consumer has learned more about the types of work situations that he or she prefers and/or dislikes and has established a competitive employment baseline (i.e., one week, one month, six months, etc.) on which to improve during the next attempt.

COMMON EMPOWERMENT ISSUES

Consumers with Mental Retardation

Persons with significant mental retardation are highly unlikely to develop sufficient abilities to achieve complete self-direction, independence, and autonomy. However, the complete absence of choice is undignified and frequently leads to "learned helplessness" and total dependence on others (Guess et al. 1985). Therefore, a central theme of any treatment or educational program should be that persons with mental retardation are allowed to show preferences, make choices and decisions, and exercise some control over their own day-to-day activities and long-term goals. Individuals with significant mental retardation can be trained to discover and express their preferences and to make choices and decisions. Learning to make good decisions requires experience with the process of decision-making, with alternatives, and with the consequences of decisions. In areas where independent choice making is not feasible or safe, choice making can be adapted or supported, and individuals can partially participate in decision-making processes (Sharpton and West 1992).

Even if they don't always agree with the result, supported employment service providers should respect the employment decisions made by people with significant mental retardation. They should keep in mind that making choices is a means of establishing one's own identity and individuality. They should also keep in mind that it is part of the human condition to make bad decisions on occasion and to learn from mistakes.

Judy is 23 years old and has been assessed as having mental retardation in the severe range, according to standardized test scores. She also has cerebral palsy, which is evident in decreased motor functioning and a slow unsteady gait. Judy has poor fine motor skills and low muscle tone, which makes her appear very weak. She has good social skills but speaks in unclear sentences. Judy frequently verbalized phrases, such as "yabadabado" and "look at me," which are described by her teacher as inappropriate, nonsensical, and excessive. She attended a self-contained school for individuals with moderate to profound mental retardation. Judy's vocational program involved community-based training on stocking food at a local grocery store. She had no paid employment experiences and had not participated in any type of program since leaving school.

Judy was targeted to receive supported employment services during her transition meeting, which was conducted during her last year of school. The rehabilitation counselor completed the necessary paper work and referred her to a supported employment provider for services. Judy was placed in a job as a bathroom attendant in the food court area of a local shopping center. She worked 20 hours a week and earned $4.15 an hour. Throughout her shift, Judy was responsible for monitoring, cleaning, and supplying the restrooms. She had frequent opportunities to socialize with the public and other co-workers during the work day. Both she and her mother were very excited about Judy's job and felt she was well-suited for the position.

Judy learned the skills necessary to complete her job duties through one-on-one training with the employment specialist for a period of four months. Modifications were made to the supply room so that Judy's cleaning products were clearly marked in a designated location. In addition, a co-worker who worked the same shift, was identified to assist Judy with tying her apron and using the time clock each day. A behavior intervention program was implemented to reduce, but not eliminate, the number of vocalizations Judy shouted out while working. The supervisor evaluations indicated her work to be satisfactory and reported that Judy was well-liked by the other employees.

Judy's employment specialist systematically faded her presence from the job site over a three month period and gradually introduced the follow-along service provider to Judy and the job site. The follow-along provider regularly visited Judy twice a month to assess her work performance. He would talk to Judy, who said she liked her job, and the supervisor, who reported that he was seeing significant changes in her work performance. The supervisor evaluations reported Judy's work to be below average both in quality and productivity. Several weeks after leaving the job site, the employment specialist stopped by to have lunch with Judy and was surprised to see her sitting in the bathroom talking to herself and the customers, despite an obvious mess. Judy's follow-along service provider assured her that Judy was receiving services and the situation was under control. Three weeks later the employment specialist stopped by the job site again to visit Judy and was informed by the supervisor that Judy had been terminated. Six months later Judy's mother called the employment specialist desperately trying to find out when Judy would return to work. The rehabilitation counselor was hesitant to re-open Judy's case, since he was informed by the follow-along service provider that Judy had lost her job due to a poor work attitude and an inability to work competitively.

Judy's case illustrates the importance of the right of choice and the problems imposed when professional opinion replaces that right. It is clearly evident that Judy performed her job to the employer's standards when she received the level and intensity of support services that she needed to work successfully. Although the follow-along provider visited Judy twice a month, the minimum required by law, the intent of the ongoing service modality was not fulfilled. Judy did not receive proactive assessment, ongoing training and support, or intensive intervention as needed to assist her with maintaining her employment status. Instead, Judy was expected to "fit" the follow-along provider's service delivery schedule and when that was insufficient, she lost her job. Unfortunately, the responsibility for job loss was inappropriately placed on Judy, a label likely to affect the choices and opportunities available to her for years to come.

Consumers with Mental Illness

Anthony and Blanch (1987) were among the first to describe supported and transitional employment services for individuals with psychiatric disabilities. They noted that consumer choice had not received much emphasis in the supported employment literature because the target populations have consisted primarily of persons with significant mental retardation and other disabilities. These individuals tend to be "matched" to jobs rather than to select jobs. Persons with mental illness, on the other hand, represent a wider range of intellectual abilities, skills, interests, and desires for advancement, and they must have the opportunity to select jobs that meet their criteria.

While we strongly argue that all consumers, regardless of disability level, have wide ranges of skill levels, interests, etc., and that choice is equally important for each potential consumer, Anthony and Blanch (1987) make a valid point about the necessity for consumer-centered placement activities to achieve successful and satisfying placements. This point was underscored in findings by Fabian (1989), who reported that consumers of a psychosocial rehabilitation program who were placed into jobs did not report a higher level of life satisfaction than those who were not working. Fabian noted that these clients tended to be placed in whatever jobs were immediately available, regardless of the consumer's individual abilities and interests, and therefore, the jobs in and of themselves were insufficient to improve the quality of life of the consumer group.

Jason completed a special education program located in a separate classroom of a regular high school. He had been diagnosed with the labels of manic depressive disorder, mild mental retardation, behavior disorder, and sexual deviancy (never confirmed). Jason's school did not have any formal transition program and no referral for adult services was made before he exited the school system.

Jason was raised by his mother who expected him to work and contribute to the household expenses after he finished school. She assisted him with getting hired, at minimum wage, as a utility worker at a fast-food restaurant close to their home. Jason soon learned how to do his job, however, due to the cyclical nature of his disability, his performance and attendance was very inconsistent. Shortly after he lost his job, Jason and his mother found a similar position in another fast-food restaurant. This job soon ended for the same reasons. A long string of short-lived, fast-food restaurant, janitorial/utility positions continued to follow with similar outcomes.

When Jason was 26 years old, his mother remarried and he and his new stepfather did not get along with one another. His mother felt Jason should move and assisted him with finding a room in a boarding house close by. She handled his monthly bills and provided support with grocery shopping, medical care, housekeeping, and job searches. Jason started working at another part-time dishwashing job and became bored with all of his free time. He soon visited his high school's coach, who had always been helpful and showed an interest in Jason's well-being. Mr. Williams gave Jason a volunteer position handing out towels and equipment to the members of the sports teams. This allowed him to attend the games, something he really enjoyed. He also made a few phone calls and referred Jason to the Mental Health/Mental Retardation agency for case management services.

Jason was found eligible for services and his case manager quickly referred him to a variety of agencies and programs that she thought would benefit him, such as Social Security, Medicaid, and supported employment services. He was considered to be inappropriate for services from the local supported employment program since they only served individuals who had mental retardation in the moderate to severe range. (The supported employment program was a demonstration project funded prior to the passage of the Rehabilitation Act Amendments of 1986, which established supported employment as a viable service within the federal/state rehabilitation program.) The supported employment program director and the case manager had worked together on many occasions in the past and personally communicated with each other regarding Jason's situation. They both recognized Jason's need for services and the unfortunate circumstances of his falling between the cracks. In addition, Jason was calling both providers on a regular basis reporting his current status, checking on employment options, and looking for someone who would just listen to him.

The program director contacted a rehabilitation counselor at the State vocational rehabilitation agency with whom she had developed a good working relationship. She explained Jason's situation and tried to find out if he could receive any support from the agency, even though he was working part-time and needed ongoing as opposed to time-limited support services. The rehabilitation counselor determined that Jason was eligible for services and found him a full-time job, with benefits, as a utility person for a restaurant with a very supportive supervisor and staff. He also arranged for other services, such as independent living skills training, money management, and financial assistance, such as purchasing uniforms and submitting impairment-related work expense deductions. Jason was also assisted with moving into a supported living arrangement so that he could be less dependent upon his mother and still have access to assistance as needed.

The case manager, rehabilitation counselor, and program director continued to provide support and identify needed resources for Jason long after his case was closed as successfully employed. Jason would call each person when he felt the need to talk with someone, solve a problem, or get more information. He would fluctuate between weeks of not contacting anyone and, during his low periods, calling several times a day. After two years, Jason lost his job and his rehabilitation counselor reopened his case and supported a second placement in a "mom and pop" type restaurant. Jason continued to receive personal assistance from all three providers, however,and over time his need to call and "check in" became greatly reduced to about one call every four to six months. When supported employment services became a part of the vocational rehabilitation agency, Jason's rehabilitation counselor referred him to a supported employment provider, who assisted Jason with obtaining a job at the YMCA and provided the support he needed to maintain his employment situation.

Jason's case represents the problems associated with a lack of choice simply because the options are not known or because an individual's disability label restricts the alternatives from which to choose. Fortunately, Jason was highly motivated to work and did not give up trying to find the assistance that he wanted, despite repeated letdowns. He also had his own support network, first with his mother, then high school coach, and later the three professionals who helped him target the services and resources that he needed and was entitled to receive. Jason's story has a happy ending, although the road to get there was long, bumpy, and never easy. Eight years was an inordinate amount of time to have to search, ask, and wait for the individualized supports that allowed Jason to live and work in the community settings of his choice.

Consumers with Traumatic Brain Injury

Individuals who have sustained severe traumatic brain injury (TBI) typically exhibit cognitive deficits in memory, reasoning, and executive functioning. They may also have physical impairments (mobility, strength, coordination, visual or hearing impairments, etc.) or emotional/behavioral disorders (inappropriate social skills, disinhibition, verbal or physical outbursts, unusual behaviors, etc.). Very few survivors of severe TBI return to work following rehabilitation efforts, and even fewer return to work at their preinjury levels of skill and pay (Ben-Yishay, Silver, Piasetsky, and Rattok 1987; Brooks, McKinlay, Symington, Beattie, and Campsie 1987). In recent years, supported employment has been proposed as a service alternative for assisting individuals with severe TBI return to competitive work (Wehman et al. 1990).

A common problem associated with cognitive impairment from severe TBI is that many of these individuals have unrealistic impressions of their own problems, abilities, and chances for returning to the preinjury occupation or lifestyle

(Tyerman and Humphrey 1984). While many of these individuals are aware of the dissonance between their preinjury and postinjury status, their expectations for recovery and return to work are often unrealistic (Tyerman and Humphrey 1984; Nockleby and Deaton 1987). Deaton (1986) and Tyerman and Humphrey (1984) suggest that denial of limitations may serve as a coping mechanism, reducing the distress that brain-injured persons would otherwise feel about their conditions.

Acceptance of the "new self" and its accompanying abilities and limitations is a critical antecedent of postinjury vocational adjustment. Employment specialists and counselors must sometimes balance the self-perceptions and interests of the head-injured client against the real demands of the work world and help the client to develop reasonable, obtainable career goals. Mutual participation in identifying and making vocational choices during the placement phase is the first step towards long-term job retention (Kreutzer and Morton 1988).

David was involved in a car accident at age 21, resulting in a severe head injury and accompanying physical handicaps and cognitive deficits. He has right side hemiplegia with no use of his right upper extremity and left hand ataxia with an absence of fine movement and slow gross movement. His ambulation is difficult, with poor balance and a pronounced limp in his gait. He tires easily, has poor short-term memory, and has difficulty processing information.

Following his injury, David received vocational rehabilitation which included vocational evaluation and therapeutic services, such as physical and occupational therapy and independent living skills training. He expressed an interest in computer programming to his rehabilitation counselor, who then enrolled him in an introductory data processing course at a local college. He experienced difficulty completing his course assignments satisfactorily and on time, so his course work was discontinued. His vocational evaluation regarding competitive employment was not encouraging. David, however, continued to be interested in data processing and computer operations and worked for a short time as a volunteer at a local hospital. Through a neighbor, he was also able to work part-time as a data entry operator, when work was available.

Four and one-half years after his injury, David was referred for supported employment services. After assessing his skills and interests and screening the local job market, the employment specialist helped David acquire a job as an order entry operator at a major pizza delivery business. His duties consisted of taking incoming calls from customers ordering pizzas and routing the order to the appropriate distribution center via a computer terminal. He earned $4.15 per hour, 22 hours per week.

There were minimal problems with David acquiring the necessary skills to perform the job. To neutralize his short-term memory deficit, a memo station was mounted above and to one side of his work station. This provided a list of important steps which David could refer to when taking orders. The memo station also described steps for orders that required changes in David's routine (i.e., large orders receiving a 10% discount). His primary work problems centered on his inability to keep up with incoming calls because of his physical and cognitive limitations. Factors that contributed to his poor work speed were an inability to press the shift key with other keys simultaneously, periods of increased extraneous movement caused by his ataxia, and generally poor fine motor skills. He also became frustrated when correction procedures were implemented by the employment specialist.

The employment specialist arranged for an occupational therapist to visit the work site and the three parties discussed changes and adaptations that would help David increase his speed. One adaptation was a wooden lapboard built to fit David's chair. This expanded his work space and stabilized his ataxia. Three lap boards were designed and constructed before one was accepted as optimal for David's working position. A city map was laminated, with tabs added to the edges of the pages to make page turning easier. Finally, with the assistance of a rehabilitation engineer, a shift key adaptation was added to the computer keyboard to allow upper-case lettering with one hand. During the time that adaptations were being planned and fabricated, the employment specialist completed part of the work for David to keep his productivity within acceptable limits.

David held this position for over 18 months and earned $7,112, receiving very favorable evaluations from his supervisor and a raise in pay. Eventually, however, for a number of reasons, his enthusiasm for the job began to wane, and problems with attendance and punctuality developed. Through conversations with David, his family, and his supervisor, the employment specialist determined that David was bored with the job. Attendance and punctuality problems were David's way of expressing the need for a change.

A part-time maintenance and custodial position was located at a private fitness club. David receives $4.50 per hour for 20 hours per week, with paid sick and annual leave and free use of the facilities. This last benefit is very motivating for David because exercise is very important to him. He has worked for 18 months at this position, which includes a brief layoff because of slow business during the winter.

David's case represents not only the value of choice in getting and keeping a job, but also the attitude of the program toward voluntary job separation. During job development, David's interests took precedence over the results of formal vocational evaluation, with obvious payoffs. David was motivated to learn and to stay with a difficult but preferred job and develop an 18-month work history. Then, despite the significant expenditure of time and money for supported employment services, adaptations, and assistance from specialists, and in spite of David's many positive experiences in the position, his employment specialist helped him search for another job when it became clear that David needed a change.

Consumers with Severe Physical Impairments

Individuals with physical disabilities have motor impairments related to a variety of diagnoses including cerebral palsy, muscular dystrophy, multiple sclerosis, rheumatoid arthritis, traumatic brain injury, and spinal cord injury (Wood 1988). In addition, many individuals have secondary disabilities of perceptual or cognitive deficits and concomitant handicaps, such as sensory impairments or medical conditions (Matich-Folds 1991; Wood 1988). Individuals with physical disabilities may have multiple needs and frequently require assistance in mobility, communication, learning, self-care, or decision-making.

Employment issues for individuals with physical disabilities can be quite different from those of persons with severe cognitive impairments. The term "job-site enabling" is frequently used, which focuses less on job-site training and more on modifications, adaptations, and compensatory strategies to assist an individual with functioning more independently (Wood 1988). Other services from an occupational therapist, physical therapist, or speech therapist may be needed to assist with positioning, mobility, adaptive equipment, and communication needs (Matich-Folds 1991). Due to the lack of a single agency being assigned responsibility for the coordination of services for individuals with physical disabilities, employment specialists may find themselves identifying and accessing services from other agencies or service providers, normally the role of a case services coordinator. Similarly, not having an agency responsible for the delivery of services has created additional limitations with funding, administering, and staffing ongoing, follow-along services essential for supported employment. Transportation problems can further restrict employment options since specialized services or lift-equipped buses are often necessary.

Decisions regarding employment choices are also affected by the same issues confronted during service delivery. Communication, motor, and sensory impairments can make it difficult for an individual to express his or her preferences and be accurately understood by another person. The use of augmented communication systems and adaptive equipment can enhance one's ability to express choices and participate in the ongoing decision-making process. Emphasizing the physical environment (e.g., calm, comfortable, free of stress) and providing ample time (e.g., not rushing, waiting during pauses) are critical for valid choice making. Slow or uncontrolled motor movements and unclear speech should not be interpreted as an inability to choose, but rather as a signal to the employment specialist to utilize adaptations, modifications, or other techniques to make communication easier for the individual. Often, just spending time together, listening to how an individual speaks and observing his or her mannerisms of expression can eliminate the need to utilize additional supplemental aides.

Owen dropped out of high school to enter the work force. At the age of 19, he began to suffer frequent falls and injuries. While hospitalized for a mild work-related injury suffered in a fall, he was diagnosed as having multiple sclerosis. After discharge from the hospital, Owen returned to his parents' home. For the next seven years, he experienced a gradual deterioration of his physical functioning. Eventually, he lost the use of both legs and one arm and hand, and much of the strength and range of motion of his other arm and hand. He also lost control of his bladder and was fitted with a Foley catheter and collection bag. He was and is still able to control his bowel movements, but he must be transferred to the toilet.

Owen's parents were soon overwhelmed by the demands of caring for him, and sought a residential placement. However, because of his physical care needs, he was ineligible for any MR/DD-funded residential programs in the area, and both he and his parents desired that he remain close to them. The only option available to them was a nursing facility, and Owen, at the age of 34, was admitted. As of this writing, he has been a resident of nursing homes for 11 years.

Although Owen knows he does not fit in at the nursing facility and would rather live with people his own age (no one else is under 65) he is resigned to living there. He realizes that his options are limited and rationalizes that the facility is "just a place to sleep and eat for the time being." and not really his home.

For the past two years, Owen has been attending a sheltered workshop, where he receives work adjustment training, paid for by his vocational rehabilitation counselor. Along with other clients, all of whom are mentally retarded, he spends about 5 hours a day stuffing envelopes and earns from $1 to $5 a week. He finds the work dull and meaningless. He knows there are machines that can do their day's work in a matter of minutes, and that some of the work has been given to the workshop as charity. But he prefers the drudgery and indignity of the workshop to "sitting around watching people die." Owen would like to try a real job, but he knows that he could not compete with nonhandicapped workers. Because of his severe limitations and his catheter and collection bag, he feels that he would have a hard time finding work he could perform in a receptive business. He has never heard of the concept of supported employment from either his workshop staff or his rehabilitation counselor.

Unfortunately, as is too often the case with people with severe disabilities, Owen's story does not yet have a happy resolution. His life has become a succession of monotonous, meaningless days, without highs or lows, without a hint of progress towards an end, and without hope that it will someday be better. Somehow he manages to keep a sense of humor about his status, but more often his words ring of fatalism and powerlessness.

Owen's sad case shows the effects that an absence of options and choices can have on people's lives. Owen simply has no options, not where he lives, not where he works, nor how he spends his time. The service delivery system has artificially restricted his options. He is ineligible for those that currently exist because of his physical care needs, and none will be developed to meet those needs. When options are so severely limited, people usually wind up in situations that are the most inappropriate for them, as Owen has done.

CONCLUSION

Human service providers sometimes talk about people who "fall between the cracks" in the service delivery system, as if people whose preferences and needs don't "fit" the available options are a distinct minority. But the simple truth is that human services are generally designed for the masses, to meet perceived needs of groups of people with similar problems, and not for the individuals themselves. Thus, there is an expectation that clients will have a homogeneous set of needs, abilities, desires, and limitations, and options are therefore limited to those meeting a "lowest common denominator" criteria. In essence, service options tend to be designed for stereotypes, not human beings. Thus, everyone, in some way or another, becomes a crack-dweller.

Employment services are no exception. For contracted work, as in many sheltered workshops, enclaves, and work crews, agencies typically seek out jobs that can be performed by the greatest number of clients, or by the most limited of clients. Therefore, the opportunities for offering the maximum degree of satisfaction and challenge to individuals are artificially limited. Agencies can impose artificial limits on consumers in individual placements as well. They can do this by targeting jobs simply because the positions are frequently available, because they are relatively easy placements, and because a lot of clients can meet the minimum requirements, instead of considering whether or not those jobs are desired by their clientele or motivating to them. Some consumers may indeed find a satisfying job using a "first available job" mentality. However, for most supported employees, this strategy is self-defeating, for no amount of job support or remuneration will keep consumers in jobs that they do not find intrinsically motivating and rewarding.

3

Supported Employment: A Critical Analysis of Individual Placement Approaches

As emphasized in Chapter 1, the unique attributes of supported employment that set it apart from more traditional vocational rehabilitation service delivery models are its thrust on fair wages, integration, and ongoing support for persons with severe disabilities. Over the ten years that these critical values have been embraced by many rehabilitation professionals, there has been a remarkable display of creativity to make these seemingly simple attributes a reality within programs that work with consumers who have disabilities. The notion behind all supported employment is that workers should be placed in valued, integrated jobs and then trained to perform that job to employer expectations. At a macroscopic level, this creativity has engendered a variety of supported employment implementation approaches.

Moon and Griffin (1988) describe four broad implementation approaches (often referred to as "models"): individual placement, enclave, mobile crew, and entrepreneurial or small business model. The individual placement approach pairs one rehabilitation professional (often titled an "employment specialist" or "job coach") with only one consumer at a job site. Unlike the individual model, the enclave, mobile crew, and entrepreneurial approaches implement supported employment with between two and eight consumers within the same general work space at the same time. The latter three approaches are commonly referred to as "group" approaches and will be described extensively in Chapter 4.

The purpose of this chapter is to acquaint the reader with the common ways in which the individual approach has been utilized and to discuss the outcomes of this approach in terms of wages, integration, ongoing support, and benefit costs. Applications across disability groups and trends and issues associated uniquely with this model will also be examined. It is important to realize that the individual approach is currently the prevalent approach to supported employment. Over half of all consumers served in supported employment are served by the individual approach.

DESCRIPTION

The individual approach to supported employment, sometimes referred to as the supported work model of competitive employment, is founded on the general premise that one employment specialist will support only one consumer at a job site. The employment specialist's time on-site initially matches the consumer's work hours, but gradually tapers off until only periodic contact with the consumer, on or off of the job site, occurs. These two fundamental characteristics contrast with the basic attributes of group models, which advocate training of more than one person at a job site and the ongoing presence of a trainer/supervisor during most of the work day and throughout the life of the job.

The technologies used to provide the support to consumers in the individual approach are *job development, consumer assessment, job placement, job-site training*, and *ongoing assessment and follow-along* (Moon, Goodall, Barcus, and Brooke 1986). Figure 3.1 illustrates how these technologies relate to each other. For a full description of each of the technologies discussed below, see Section II: Supported Employment Implementation Strategies.

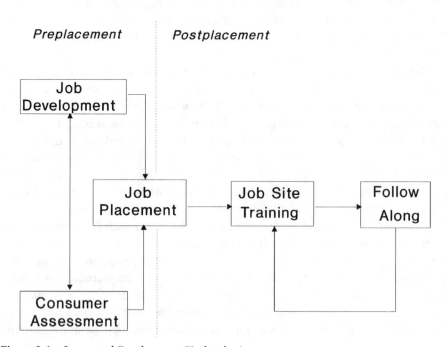

Figure 3.1   Supported Employment Technologies

Job Development

The process of identifying vacancies within the local labor market is referred to as job development. The initial step in *job development* is screening the community job market. The purpose of this screening process is to acquaint the employment specialist with the local labor market and general requirements for the various employment sectors found in the labor market. After this initial screening is complete, the employment specialist makes contact with employers who may have positions suited for the consumers with whom the employment specialist works. As appropriate job vacancies are located and employers demonstrate a willingness to work with supported employment, specific job requirements and duties are identified. The result of the job development process is a pool of potential jobs that can be filled by the consumers in the employment specialist's caseload.

Consumer Assessment

The purpose of *consumer assessment* is to identify consumer attributes and interests that will potentially facilitate or inhibit employment. Consumer assessment generally occurs concurrently with job development. The processes used to conduct consumer assessment include interviewing the consumer and significant others, observing the consumer in a variety of settings, gleaning salient information from formal educational, psychological, vocational and medical evaluations, and sometimes conducting a situational assessment, during which the consumer can be observed performing tasks in a work-like situation for short periods of time. Consumer assessment results in a robust appraisal of consumer characteristics that will ultimately be used to determine which available job vacancy will be filled by the consumer. Unlike many assessment processes, consumer assessment in supported employment does not typically yield standardized or normative data. Likewise, the information obtained through consumer assessment is not used to "qualify" someone for supported employment.

Job Placement

Job placement refers to the process of matching a particular consumer with a particular job vacancy and securing of employment in that vacancy. At this point in the supported employment process many resources have been allocated to carefully scrutinizing a variety of jobs and painstakingly assessing the consumers to be served. Based upon the specific job and consumer attributes a "match" between job and consumer is made. Once a pairing of job and consumer has occurred, the employer is approached and job interviews occur. The result of job placement is the acquisition of a job for a consumer.

Job-Site Training

Individuals with disabilities, like all people, come to new jobs needing training in certain areas. *The job-site training* phase of supported employment assures that consumer training needs are addressed systematically and efficiently. Most often this training is facilitated by the employment specialist who obtains assistance from the employer, direct supervisor if different than the employer, and co-workers. Specific techniques such as applied behavior analysis, counseling, and cognitive strategies may be utilized to facilitate job-skill acquisition. The choice of strategies depends entirely upon the consumer attributes and the job setting and are therefore necessarily individualized. Strategies typically used with various disability groups will be discussed later in this chapter. The outcome of effective job-site training is a consumer who possesses all of the job duty-specific and social skills needed to maintain the job.

Ongoing Assessment and Follow-along

A characteristic that distinguishes supported employment from other vocational rehabilitation services is its never-ending nature. During the *follow-along* phase of supported employment, the employment specialist makes recurrent contact with the employer and consumer to ensure that both are satisfied with the job placement. Should problems arise (as they often do), the employment specialist initiates the necessary corrective actions to remediate the problems. Corrective action may involve job restructuring, additional job-site training, and/or referral to other services.

IMPLEMENTATION CONFIGURATIONS

The processes portrayed in Figure 3.1 and described above are fundamental to all individual (and most group) approaches to supported employment. However, there is more than one configuration through which the individual placement model has been implemented. Included under the general heading of "individual placement approach" are three configurations: basic, multiple, and cluster placements. Figure 3.2 illustrates the different configurations graphically. Each is described below and in the accompanying case studies.

Basic

The basic configuration is the way most early individual placements were made and is the "truest" of all the individual placement approaches. In this configuration, only one supported employee works within a job site. As with all of the individual approaches, after a job match is made and placement occurs, the employment specialist proceeds through a period of initial training (during which the employment

Individual Approach Configurations

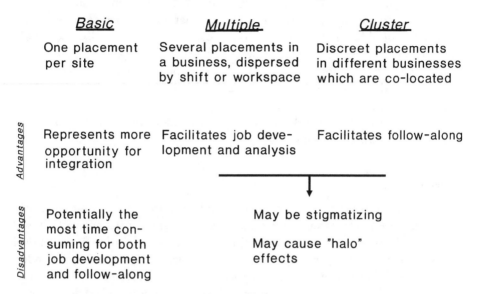

Basic	*Multiple*	*Cluster*
One placement per site	Several placements in a business, dispersed by shift or workspace	Discreet placements in different businesses which are co-located

Advantages

Represents more opportunity for integration	Facilitates job development and analysis	Facilitates follow-along

Disadvantages

Potentially the most time consuming for both job development and follow-along	May be stigmatizing May cause "halo" effects

Figure 3.2   Individual Approach Configurations.

specialist facilitates the acquisition of all work-related skills), stabilization (during which the employment specialist facilitates maintenance and behavioral generalization of acquired skills across materials and supervisors), and fading (during which the employment specialist systematically and gradually withdraws from the job site). The initial consumer placed at the job site is the only consumer that works at that site.

Multiple

This configuration can be conceptualized as a *consecutive* series of more than one basic placement within the same business. Typically, the first consumer is placed at a job site as described above. After fading is complete, another consumer is placed at the same job site during either a different shift or in a location that is physically distinct from the initial placement. There are several advantages to this configuration. First, during the first placement, rapport between the employment specialist and employer is often strengthened, making job development for a second position easier. Second, job-analysis procedures can be implemented during the fading phase of the first placement, thus efficiently utilizing the employment specialist's time at the job site. And finally, during the follow-along phase, fewer resources will be needed because of the proximity of the consumers to one another.

There are also disadvantages to this configuration. The first disadvantage, and perhaps the one that contraindicates use of the multiple configuration in many cases, relates to the often negative stigmatization that occurs when disproportionate numbers of disabled persons work in one location (e.g., sheltered workshops or segregated educational settings). Suspect are those multiple placement configurations in which the proportion of workers with disabilities to workers without disabilities exceeds the proportion of individuals with disabilities in the general population. Second, problems that arise on the job site with one worker may influence the perceptions of the co-workers and supervisors about the second worker. This may lead to a multiple job loss.

Cluster

In this configuration, multiple supported employees are placed in different businesses that are in the same geographic proximity. This works particularly well when the placements are within a shopping mall or other location in which businesses are congregated. This configuration makes use of the follow-along and, to some extent, job development advantages of the multiple placement, but generally alleviates the disadvantages. The criteria of natural proportion should, however, be considered in this placement configuration.

OUTCOMES OF THE INDIVIDUAL APPROACH

Supported employment is said to be an "outcome-oriented" vocational option. The outcomes (benefits that accrue for consumers in supported employment and the rehabilitation service system) as a result of the individual approach can be categorized into four interrelated areas: wages, integration, ongoing support, and economic-benefit costs. The magnitude of each of the outcomes is best described in terms of their relation to group supported employment approaches and traditional vocational rehabilitation programs.

A discussion of each of the outcomes for the individual placement approach is found below. The reader should keep in mind, however, that the persons served in each supported employment model and the traditional vocational rehabilitation programs are not necessarily homogeneous. For example, Kregel, Wehman, and Banks (1990) found that persons with severe/profound mental retardation were more likely to be served by the enclave model. Persons with ambulation impairments were more likely to be served in the entrepreneurial model; yet there were no significant differences in visual or hearing impairments, fine-motor impairments, nor communication impairments. Thus, although it is appropriate to compare the approaches to supported employment, it should be done cautiously until effective statistical standardization of consumer characteristics can be implemented.

Wages

An important value of supported employment is that individuals, regardless of disability, earn fair wages for real work. One may assume, though errantly, that access to at least minimum wage is available to all Americans. Many persons with disabilities, and in particular, persons with severe disabilities, have not been afforded this opportunity through more traditional vocational rehabilitation services, such as work-activity and sheltered employment. For example, wages earned within day activity centers range from zero (some states disallow paid work) to $2.00 *per day* (Bellamy, Rhodes, Mank, and Albin 1988). Kiernan and colleagues reported that the average sheltered employment wages for persons with developmental disabilities was $1.47 per hour for full-time workers and $1124 per hour for part-time workers. More than 50% of the workers earned less than $1109 per hour (Kiernan, McGaughey, and Schalock 1986). Persons in sheltered workshops typically earn one-third of the prevailing minimum wage (Kiernan, Schalock, and Knutson 1989).

Recent wage data from 27 states on all models of supported employment demonstrates that individuals served by supported employment enjoy much better pay than sheltered employees. Supported employees in the individual placement model earn an average of $3.91 per hour (Rehabilitation Research and Training Center 1990). These wages also compare quite favorably with the average wages earned by individuals in enclaves ($2.69), mobile crew ($2.85), and entrepreneurial ($2.54) approaches to supported employment.

The wage data favors the individual approach, in a large part, because individuals served in sheltered workshops and group supported employment options are frequently paid under a *subminimum wage certificate* issued by the United States Department of Labor. Under this special certificate, workers with disabilities can be paid wages *commensurate* with their productivity. While on the face this seems fair, critical access to appropriate training and support is often unavailable, and therefore, individuals paid these commensurate wages may not have an opportunity to reach their maximum productivity. Consumers with disabilities who are placed using the individual approach most often work for employers who do not possess a subminimum wage certificate and are therefore bound to pay at least minimum wage to all of their workers. It can be argued that no individual should be paid less than the prevailing minimum wage. To do so with persons who have disabilities is establishing a "class" distinction based on disability and can be argued as discriminatory. Unfortunately, this argument is not supported by statute or practice at this time.

Integration

Historically, persons with severe disabilities have been both physically and socially *segregated* in vocational, educational and residential settings from persons without disabilities. Ready examples include sheltered workshops, special public schools that serve only persons with disabilities, intermediate care facilities for the mentally retarded (ICF-MR), and the Special Olympics. In each of these cases, access to social and cultural aspects of life have been limited due to the service delivery systems created by federal, state, local, and private entities.

The social and cultural attributes of a job setting are considered important as each of us decides whether or not to accept or retain a given position. The concept of *vocational integration* professes that workers with disabilities have as much access to these important social and cultural job characteristics as do workers without disabilities. Mank and Buckley (1989) describe vocational integration as "adherence to regular and ordinary patterns of minute-to-minute and day-to-day working life" (p. 320). They go on to describe four levels of integration including physical integration, social integration, relationships, and social networks.

Data empirically documenting the total vocational integration of persons in the individual approach are scarce. In a recent study, the physical and social integration of 1,608 supported employees was measured on a five point Likert Scale by Kregel et al. (1990). Individuals in the individual placement model had a higher mean-level of integration than any of the group models. There was a statistically significantly lower level of integration for supported employees in work crews and enclaves.

Intuitively, the individual approach offers more *physical* integration because the supported employees are colocated with nondisabled individuals. This contrasts with the usual implementation of the group models in which supported employees are colocated next to other persons with disabilities. As described in Chapter 4, employee placement is a critical consideration with group models, in general, and enclaves, in particular.

The degree to which social integration (e.g., elective personal interactions) is occurring within job sites using the individual approach is unclear. In the most pertinent study to date, Parent and her colleagues (1990) found a similar frequency of interactions between mentally retarded and nondisabled workers. However, the nondisabled employees interacted more during break time and participated in more work-related interactions than did their disabled counterparts. Again, by structure, it would appear that more opportunity for social integration exists for persons served in the individual approach than in either traditional sheltered work facilities or either of the other group approaches to supported employment.

The development of relationships and social network building of supported employees have also not been adequately researched to date. A new tool that will measure all aspects of integration will soon be available. *The Vocational Integration Index* (Parent, Kregel, Wehman and Metzler, in press) will measure company, work area, employee, and benefits indicators that lead to enhanced vocational integration.A discussion of *The Vocational Integration Index*, vocational integration in general, and specific techniques that enhance vocational integration can be found in Chapter 11.

Ongoing Support

Prior to supported employment, persons placed in competitive job sites often did not (and still do not) enjoy ongoing support. Supported employees, by statute, must receive ongoing support. At least two monthly on-site visits are required to meet the federal definition of supported employment.

As stated earlier in this chapter and in detail in Chapter 4, a basic assumption of all group models is the nearly continuous presence of a supervisor allocated specifically to the group of supported employees. Persons served in the individual placement model "lose" the continual presence of their job coach during the fading and follow-along phases. Thus, supported employees in the individual approach receive the least amount of ongoing support from service providers when compared to consumers in group models.

In an effectively operating individual approach program, frequent information gathering and retraining-as-needed is always provided. The fewer actual on-site hours afforded by the individual model is not a negative aspect of the approach. In fact, continual ongoing support, as provided in the group models, tends to stigmatize the workers and increase the likelihood of prompt and artificial reinforcement dependency. Indeed, the use of *natural supports* (utilizing existing job-site personnel and material resources) may be enhanced with the individual placement approach out of necessity of job-coach fading.

Benefit-Costs

A program evaluation that examines economic outcomes is typically called *benefit-cost* analysis. Writing about the individual approach to supported employment, Hill states, "It is indeed rare for consumers and taxpayers alike to prosper financially through the implementation of a social program" (Hill 1988, 40). The positive benefits relative to costs of the individual approach to supported employment have been empirically demonstrated (for persons with mental retardation). For example, using Virginia consumers served by a University project as a database, Hill found that each consumer gained (after loss of government benefits) an average of $3,894 per year. Taxpayers saved over $4,063 annually through the implementation of the individual approach.

Similar in-depth benefit-cost data are not available for the other approaches of supported employment. However, FY 1988 cost data (no benefit data) comparing the four approaches to one another have been aggregated (RRTC, 1990). The data indicate near equivalence of the four models, with the average annual cost of the individual approach being $5,244, enclaves $5,154, work crews $5,008, and, based on an extremely small sample, entrepreneurial $6,072. The data reported were not standardized for the severity level of disabilities of consumers served.

No supported employment approach is inherently better than another. By its very nature, the provision of supported employment services is individualized, and a particular approach should only be utilized after careful consideration by service providers, rehabilitation professionals, the consumer, and significant others in the consumer's life. The quality of life of the consumer and his or her preferences and functional abilities should form the basis of all decisions. It is also very important to recognize that, in most cases, the individual approach should be the first choice of approaches because of generally better wages, a higher probability of integration with nondisabled individuals, and its relative cost effectiveness.

TRENDS AND ISSUES ASSOCIATED WITH THE INDIVIDUAL PLACEMENT APPROACH

Supported employment services, in general, and the utilization of the individual placement approach, specifically, have increased dramatically during the 1980s. Blossoming from a few demonstration projects to a major, national vocational rehabilitation initiative, the implementation of the individual approach is now occurring in every state of the Union. With this growth, several trends seem to be emerging, and several issues have yet to be resolved. A most notable trend has been the use of the individual approach with persons who have disabilities other than mental retardation. Critical issues that have evolved include, among others, continued funding for supported employment, the utilization of employers to implement supported employment, and, perhaps most importantly, how services to *severely* disabled individuals will be delivered. Each trend and issue is discussed below.

Application Across Populations

Supported employment was first used primarily for persons with mental retardation. Recently, efforts have been made to expand supported employment overall and in particular to the individual placement approach and to consumers who have disabilities other than mental retardation. For example, this approach has been used with persons with sensory impairments, criminal offenders, and individuals with traumatic brain injuries, psychiatric disorders, and physical disabilities. A brief description of the current status of supported employment with three of the most prevalent populations follows.

Traumatically Brain-Injured
Individuals in this group have received a head injury usually resulting in post traumatic amnesia and/or unconsciousness. This group differs quite dramatically in

terms of demographics and functional characteristics. For example, most traumatically brain-injured consumers held a job prior to their injury. Cognitive deficits, especially problems with memory, and a high incidence of alcohol/substance abuse are frequently associated with this population.

Supported employment does work for this population. Wehman and associates (1989) found in a study of 20 consumers that the mean wages for traumatically brain-injured supported employees before injury, after injury but before supported employment, and with supported employment were $5.11, $3.45, and $4.52 respectively. Thus, although supported employees in this group did not return to preinjury wages, there was a significant change after supported employment.

There is a growing literature base that indicates that the individual approach is effective with consumers who have sustained brain injuries (see Wehman et al. 1989). The direct service technologies needed to effectuate job acquisition and retention for this group have yet to be fully articulated and empirically demonstrated. The reader is referred to Wehman and Kreutzer (1990) for a more detailed discussion of the individual approach to supported employment with this population.

Long-term Mental Illness

Persons with chronic and persistent mental illness are also beneficiaries of the individual approach to supported employment. Long served by transitional employment programs, these individuals do not typically need the intensive on-site job training traditionally provided by the individual approach. Therefore, the emphasis with this population is more on appropriate job selection that matches the personality and job-ability strengths of the consumer with the job. A second and equally important aspect is the significant amount of ongoing support needed to assist the consumer with coping with the job-site environment.

The Center for Psychiatric Rehabilitation (1988) has developed an innovative "Choose-Get-Keep" approach that utilizes many of the basic tenets of supported employment to provide ongoing vocational services to persons with long-term mental illness. In this approach, consumers are first provided assistance in clarifying vocational goals, interests, and abilities. Next, job selection processes are facilitated to enhance the probability of a good job-consumer match. Finally, routine follow-along is provided to assist the consumer in meeting the ongoing challenges of their work and disability.

Because the application of supported employment to this population is not yet out of the demonstration phase, measurement on its employment effectiveness has not been adequately achieved. There is also considerable uncertainty about which approach will ultimately prove the most effective and cost-efficient (Noble and Collignon 1988).

Physically Disabled

The direct service technologies utilized for persons who have physical disabilities closely resemble those used for persons with mental retardation (Wood 1988). The major variant is that the use of structural job-site modifications and adaptations is often increased. Prostheses are also more likely to be used with this population. Because of modifications/adaptations and prostheses, the services of a rehabilitation engineer are frequently utilized to enhance the employment outcomes of persons with physical disabilities.

Yet to be evaluated with this population is the level of ongoing support needed and the cost effectiveness of supported employment. Again, as with programs designed to serve traumatically brain-injured persons and persons with long-term mental illness, systematic documentation of costs and benefits needs to be done.

Funding

Supported employment services received by a consumer are initially funded via vocational rehabilitation monies. To date, the funding has been accomplished using two streams: case service dollars (allocated through Title I of the Rehabilitation Act and utilized for case services of all types, not just supported employment) and specific monies for supported employment (allocated through Title VIC of the Rehabilitation Act). An additional, major funding source for supported employment demonstration has been through Title III of the Rehabilitation Act. Persons needing supported employment to achieve meaningful, paid work should always have theoretical access to Title I monies but, from a pragmatic point of view, will have to compete among less severely disabled persons for those case service dollars. It has not yet been demonstrated that Title I monies will sustain supported employment services. The continued allotment of funds through Title VIC and supported employment funds in Title III is not assured. At this writing, it is unclear how stable the funding through these two Titles will remain.

At a predetermined point (usually after the initial intervention is completed), funding switches to another source, frequently, mental health/mental retardation agencies. Similar to Title I rehabilitation funding, these ongoing funds are competed for by a variety of service providers and programs, only some of which are providing follow-along services to persons served with the individual approach. How much funding will be obtained by supported employment service providers is a never-ending question. In times of fiscal scarcity, it should not be assumed that funding increases or decreases will be equitably applied across the supported employment and other treatment programs. Complicating the ongoing funding issue even more, some funding agencies have specific mandates that allow them to spend money for supported employment on specific populations. Therefore, the continued utilization of supported employment across an increasingly diverse group of persons with disabilities is tied directly to these ongoing funds.

Employer Utilization

Traditionally, the individual approach to supported employment has utilized employers in only one way: as a supplier of jobs. As a result, the role of the employment specialist has been to ensure that there was an adequate supply of jobs to meet the demands of his or her caseload. This task was accomplished primarily through one-on-one job development. As supported employment enters its second full decade, both the role of the employer in relation to the implementation of supported employment with a specific consumer and the methodologies of securing an adequate number of jobs in a cost-efficient manner are being reexamined.

Employers as Providers

Typically, employers train and support their nondisabled employees. Traditionally, employers have not expended the resources to extend training and support opportunities to persons with significant disabilities. As a result of the supported employment initiative, companies are now seeing that persons with disabilities can be assets rather than liabilities.

This change in perspective has caused some to believe that it is more normalizing to have employers provide the follow-along and even initial training to the persons with disabilities. Still in its formative stages, this concept could ultimately move supported employment service provision from the public to the private sector. For example, in the future organizations may either employ their own job coach to implement the direct-service technologies of supported employment, or they may contract individually with other entities that specialize in supported employment services.

Corporate Involvement

Approaching corporate chief executive officers to obtain multiple positions (dispersed throughout the organization) is another emerging trend. For example, as a corporative initiative, Pizza Hut, Inc. has recently implemented an initiative to bring supported employees into its franchises. This "top-down" approach may increase both the efficiency with which an adequate number of jobs can be made available and the investment, both programmatic and fiscal, of the employers.

Population Served

At its inception, supported employment was designed for persons with severe disabilities. The data presented in Chapter 1 raise clear questions as to whether or not this intent has been met. With all of the populations served by the individual approach, defining "severe" is an elusive task. For example, if one uses only IQ to determine the severity level of a person with mental retardation (a risky but frequently used application of IQ), supported employment, at this time, is absolutely not meeting the original intent. Findings related to the functional characteristics of individuals in supported employment indicate that persons with severe or profound disabilities represent a small minority of the population served (Kregel and Wehman 1989).

The reasons for such representations are not clear-cut. The absence of significant numbers of persons with severe disabilities may be the result of inadequate training of vocational rehabilitation counselors and/or service providers. The service system itself may not yet have been modified adequately to encourage service provision to the most challenging individuals. This current minority status may or may not be able to be changed in the future. Only time will tell.

SUMMARY

The individual placement approach is the most prevalent approach to providing supported employment services. It is arguably the most normalizing. It certainly results in the highest average wages. The benefit-costs of the approach have been demonstrated with some certainty with persons with mental retardation and to a lesser degree with other individuals. Funding, employer involvement, the application of supported employment to a wider variety of persons, and the severity level of persons served are all important and unresolved content areas to be watched in the 1990s.

Is the individual placement approach appropriate for all consumers in supported employment? Certainly not. Should the individual placement approach be the approach of first choice for all consumers in supported employment? Certainly.

4

Supported Employment: A Review of Group Models

Pamela S. Wolfe

Recent legislation has extended the traditional vocational options for individuals with disabilities. The Developmental Disabilities Act of 1984 (P.L. 98-527) emphasized the need for paid work in a variety of settings for individuals with disabilities for whom competitive employment at or above minimum wage would be unlikely and who would need ongoing support to perform. Further, the Rehabilitation Act Amendment of 1986 (P.L. 99-506) encouraged conversion of center-based programs to industrial-based employment (Hill, Wehman, Kregel, Banks, and Metzler 1987). Supported employment has emerged as a means with which individuals with disabilities can successfully obtain and sustain work in integrated settings.

From its legislative inception, supported employment has been intended for those individuals with severe disabilities who could not participate in work without support. The combination of the unique strengths and challenges individuals with disabilities bring to an employment setting, together with the service needs of the community has resulted in the evolution of a variety of vocational placements. Supported employment placements can include both individual and group placements. Individual placements typically enlist a job coach to accompany an individual with disabilities on a job where he or she is provided with the necessary support until competency is reached and supervision is gradually "faded." Group models, however, place more than one individual at a site, and ongoing supervision is provided throughout placement. The provision of continued support has meant group models are often recommended for individuals with more severe disabilities, who may require more supervision. Group models may differ on several dimensions, including the type of work performed, where the work occurs, the availability of opportunities for integration, and how consumers are paid and benefits accrued. What follows is a review of group models, including enclave, mobile work crew, and small business models. A description of each model is provided, as well as a review of literature on employment outcomes. The primary studies reviewed are listed in Table 4.1.

Table 4.1   Primary Studies Reviewed for Group Model Analysis

Source	*Characteristics of the Sample*
Kregel, Wehman and Banks (1990) (a)	1550 individuals from statewide supported employment programs operated by vocational rehabilitation agencies in Virginia, North Dakota and Nevada, secondary school-based programs in California, and United Cerebral Palsy affiliates in New Jersey, Alabama and Illinois. Categorized models as individual (1215), enclave (145), work crew (132) and small business (58).
West, Kregel and Banks (1990) (b)	1150 individuals tracked by RRTC serving 96 provider agencies in eight states. Categorized models as individual (1215), enclave (145), work crew (132), and small business (158).
Wehman (1990) (c)	Survey of 50 states and District of Columbia resulting in sample size of 51. Within each state, Vocational Rehabilitation agencies were contacted. Additional information was collected by contacting appropriate representatives from mental retardation/developmental disabilities, mental health and other agencies associated with supported employment. Survey was conducted between 1988 and 1990. Categorized models as individual placement (13,085), enclave (3845), work crew (3205), entrepreneurial (1844), TEP (1250), and other (1880).
Utah Supported Employment Program (1990)(d)	Annual report of USEP project in implementing supported employment in Utah, supported by a five year grant initiated in 1985 from the Rehabilitation Services Administration. Categorizes models as individual placement (65%), enclave (20%), work crew (13%), and transitional employment for persons with mental illness (2%).
California State Department of Rehabilitation (1990) (e)	Individuals employed through provision of services by the Habilitation Services in the Department of Rehabilitation. Total number of clients employed currently exceeds 5,000. Data of clients in VR plan status FY 1989-90. Categorizes models as individual placement (1334), enclave (583), and work crew (434).
Rusch, Johnson and Hughes (1990) (f)	264 supported employment employees served by community rehabilitation facilities implementing supported employment projects in the state of Illinois. Selected for study if mental retardation was reported as the primary disability and complete data were available on co-worker involvement. Data obtained from July, 1987. Categorized models as individual placement (118), clustered (123), and mobile work crew (23).

Table 4.1 Primary Studies Reviewed for Group Model Analysis *(continued)*

Source	Characteristics of the Sample
UCU, RRTC North Dakota (1990) (g)	From RRTC tracking system. North Dakota supported employment providers from January 1, 1990 to March 31, 1990. Categorized models as work activity (O), entrepreneurial (51), mobile work crew (60), enclave (51), supported job (91), supported competitive (468), time limited (2), and other (O).
RRTC Virginia (1990) (h)	From RRTC tracking system of 2338 individuals in Virginia. Categorized models as work activity (O), entrepreneurial (16), mobile (150), enclave (273), supported job (28), supported competitive (1769), time limited (101), and other (O).
Western Michigan University (1990) (i)	Data from 42 agencies in Michigan through March 31, 1990. 877 individuals were involved in supported employment. Categorized models as individual placement (520), enclave (284), mobile work crew (65), and transitional (7).
Illinois Supported Employment Project (1990) (j)	772 individuals served in supported employment programs through the Illinois Supported Employment Project at the Transition Institute during FY 1990. Categorized models as individual (458), clustered (259), and mobile (44).

SUPPORTED EMPLOYMENT: WHAT ARE THE CHOICES?

Enclave

The enclave model places a group of individuals with disabilities in competitive industry while providing full supervision and support in the setting. Enclaves are usually comprised of three to eight individuals (in order to comply with the Federal Register definition of supported employment). The enclave is often presented as a vocational option for individuals with more severe disabilities and behavior problems (Moon and Griffin 1988; Mank, Rhodes, and Bellamy 1986; Rhodes and Valenta 1985[a]) because the work is often repetitious and relatively stable over time (Mank et al. 1986). Individuals with severe disabilities are placed in companies in industry, often called "host companies." In exemplar programs, workers receive pay that is commensurate with nondisabled workers producing the same amount and are given comparable fringe benefits (Mank et al. 1986). Supervision can be provided by either the host company or a nonprofit organization. Quality characteristics of an industry-based model are outlined in Table 4.2.

Table 4.2 Desirable Characteristics of Enclave Models

1. Enclave employees who require intensive ongoing support.
2. Physical space in close proximity to nondisabled co-workers.
3. Work that is typical of work performed by co-workers.
4. Employees are employed by the host company.
5. Pay and benefits based on productivity and are commensurate with the wages/benefits received by nondisabled co-workers.
6. Transportation is provided by public or company transportation.
7. Enclave represents approximately 1% or less of total work force or numbers less than eight in compliance with Federal Register (1984).
8. Work routines, such as hours worked, days worked, and breaktimes, are the same as nondisabled co-workers.
9. Supervisor is familiar with company procedures and brings supervision skills to the company.
10. Support organization maintains low visibility, but intervenes when necessary. Provides training to other company employees on behavior management and other skills to increase productivity and integration of enclave employees.

Adapted from Rhodes and Valenta (1985[b]). Enclaves in industry. In P. McCarthy, J. M. Everson, M. S. Moon, and J. M. Barcus (Eds.), *School-to-work transition for youth with severe disabilities* [Monograph, pp. 129-149]. Richmond: Virginia Commonwealth University, Project Transition into Employment, Rehabilitation Research and Training Center.

The type and amount of integration afforded in an enclave is largely dependent on company characteristics (Moon and Griffin 1988). Opportunities for integration can be "engineered" by the use of public transportation, break and lunch periods that are synchronized with nondisabled co-workers, and use of company recreational activities (Mank et al. 1986).

Implementation issues often occurring with the enclave model of supported employment include locating a suitable host company and initial start-up costs. Mank et al. (1986) have suggested that three to nine months of planning may be needed to initiate and organize an enclave's introduction into an established industry. Companies selected should be large and well-established in order to ensure economic stability and opportunities for integration (Rhodes and Valenta 1985 [b]). Initial monies for start-up costs must also be available for staff, training, and supplies. Further, supervisors must be able to guarantee a set amount of productivity and quality (Mank et al. 1986). Workers can be paid either directly by the host company, or indirectly, in which the host company pays the sponsoring organization who then pays employees. Most enclaves are using an indirect payment route (Moon and Griffin 1988). The introduction of an enclave into a host company can be enhanced by incentives, such as guaranteed productivity, effective training and supervision, detailed production information, affirmative action assistance, tax credits, possible reduction in employee turnover, and improved public relations (Mank et al. 1986).

Rhodes and Valenta have described an enclave model operating in a biomedical electronics device manufacturing company in Washington. In a company of approximately 900 individuals, six individuals with severe disabilities work on the production line. Supervision is provided by a lead supervisor (initially paid by a nonprofit organization) and a "model" worker (provided by the host company to increase productivity). An individual is hired directly by the company when his or her productivity over a three month period averages 65% of the productivity of nondisabled workers. Rhodes and Valenta found that after one year of operation, all employees were producing at or above 50% of employees without disabilities, with average monthly earnings of $323.

More recent data reveal that enclave models typically serve less than a quarter of participants in supported employment. Of the studies reviewed, the percentage of consumers served in the enclave model ranged from a high of 34% in Illinois (1990) to a low of 7.1% in North Dakota (1990). A national analysis by Wehman found that 15.3% of individuals in supported employment were served in an enclave model (Wehman 1990).

In the state of Michigan (1990) it was found that the greatest number of participants in the enclave model (41%) were classified as mildly-handicapped, with IQs ranging from 55 to 70, followed by individuals with moderate mental retardation (29%). The smallest group served were individuals classified as borderline mentally retarded (.08%) or above (.04%). Individuals with profound/severe mental retardation represented 15% of individuals in the enclave model. Similarly, Kregel, Wehman, and Banks (1989) found the largest group served in the enclave model to be individuals with mild disabilities (approximately 40%), followed by individuals with moderate mental retardation (26%), severe/profound mental retardation (22%), borderline (7%), and physical and sensory impairments (5%). Illinois (1990) reported similar results with 48% of their sample classified as mildly retarded, 25% as moderately retarded, and 9% as severe/profoundly retarded.

Typical occupations for enclave workers have included janitor, housekeeper/assistant, clerk/clerical, material handler/porter, packer, and food service worker (Illinois 1990). Wages for consumers in enclave models ranged from an average of $231.19. per month (Utah 1990) to $435.34 (Western Michigan 1990), with average hourly rates of $2.69 (Wehman 1990) to $3.52 (Illinois 1990). Average hours worked per week ranged from 17.11 (Michigan 1990) to 28.7 (Kregel et al. 1989).

Thirty-two percent of individuals participating in the enclave model received no fringe benefits (West, Kregel, and Banks 1990). The most common fringe benefits offered to enclave employees were vacation/annual leave (55%), sick (37.5%) and medical/health benefits (36.4%). Enclave workers received dental benefits and medical/health benefits more frequently than other group model workers (West et al. 1990).

Rhodes and Valenta (1985[a]) provided estimates of start-up costs of approximately $4,682 for staff salary, staff training, administrative support, and supplies. Further, Rhodes and Valenta estimated an income/benefit cost ratio (found by dividing the total earnings of the program employees by the total public costs) to be 1126 or$1.26 earned for every dollar invested. More recent program costs for established enclave programs reveal that enclave models are comparable in costs to other group models. Utah (1990) reported yearly costs of $5150, while Wehman (1990), in an analysis of the 50 states, found an average yearly cost of $5154, with model costs ranging from $1705 to $8007 per year to operate. Noble and Conley (1987) also cite an average monthly reduction of $81.22 in SSI/SSDI as a benefit of the Physio-Control enclave model.

In an analysis of opportunities for integration, Kregel Wehman, and Banks (1989) found enclaves providing less opportunity for physical and social integration than small business models. Michigan (1990) computed the average percent of individuals in the immediate work group who have disabilities, illustrative of the level of integration with nondisabled peers, and found that 82.86% of the individuals surrounding enclave workers were disabled. Such a high percentage contrasts with a low of 41.69% found in individual placement models. Rusch, Johnson, and Hughes (1990) examined the level of integration experienced by consumers in individual, clustered, and mobile crew placements. Similar to enclave models, clustered placements were defined as a "situation where two or more supported employees work for a single employer, typically performing similar job duties" (p. 35). Results were coded as "associating," "befriending," "advocating," "data collection," and "evaluation." (See Table 4.3 for a definition of the categories). Rusch et al. found significant differences between the frequency of occurrence and nonoccurrence for each type of co-worker involvement. Rusch et al. found indi-

Table 4.3   Definitions of Co-worker Involvement Defined by Rusch et al. (1990)

Advocating—Co-worker advocates by optimalizing, backing, and supporting the target employee's status. Optimizing refers to encouraging a supervisor to assign high-status and relevant tasks to the target employee; backing refers to supporting target employee's rights, which includes speaking up or offering explanations during differences of opinion; supporting refers to the provision of emotional support through friendship.
Associating—Co-worker interacts socially with the target employee at work.
Befriending—Co-worker interacts socially outside work.
Collecting data—Co-worker collects data by observing and recording social and/or work performance.
Evaluating—Co-worker appraises target employee's work performance and provides written or oral feedback.
Training—Co-worker provides on-the-job training.

Adapted from Rusch, Hughes, McNair, and Wilson (1989) cited in Rusch, Johnson, and Hughes (1990).

Table 4.4   Characteristics of the Enclave Model

Percent served in model	Range 7.1% (g) to 34% (j)
Population served	Range profound mental retardation to borderline mental retardation
Percent of individuals with severe/profound disabilities served	Range 9% (j) to 22% (a)
Average hours worked per week	Range 17.11 (i) to 28.7 (a)
Average monthly wage	Range $231.19 (d) to $435.34 (i)
Percent receiving one or more fringe benefit	67.4% (b)
Intervention hours (coached to worked, 10-12 months on job)	18.31% (i)
Average cost to operate model	$5154 (c)
Percent rehabilitated	11% (e)

viduals in the cluster sample to experience associating most frequently (85%) and data collection least frequently (9%). Individuals in the cluster sample experienced all types of co-worker involvement more frequently than mobile work crews, but less frequently, or the same, as individual placement. Only 24% of individuals in the clustered model experienced befriending.

Mobile Work Crew

A mobile work crew provides group vocational opportunities for a small group of individuals with disabilities (typically three to eight). Supervised by one or two individuals, the mobile work crew providing services travels from site to site in the community. The mobile work crew model is often recommended for individuals with severe disabilities and behavioral problems, although Mank et al. (1986) have suggested that crew participation may be inappropriate for individuals with severe physical or behavioral disabilities due to the extensive staffing they may require and the frequent variation in tasks. Advantages of this particular model have included its flexibility in meeting the varied needs of different communities, its opportunities for integration, and high public visibility (Moon and Griffin 1989; Mank et al. 1986). Table 4.5 outlines some preimplementation considerations for a mobile work crew.

An example of a mobile work crew is described by Mank et al. (1986). Typical contracts included grounds-keeping and janitorial work, with wages ranging from $130 to $185 per month. More recent data reveal that from 6% (Illinois

Table 4.5   Implementation Considerations for a Mobile Work Crew

1. *Market*—Labor needs must be ascertained through a market analysis prior to implementation.
2. *Equipment and supplies*—Equipment needs must be analyzed and decisions regarding whether to rent, lease, or purchase equipment considered. Cost, expected return on investments, complexity of the operation regarding training for use and maintenance of the equipment, and ease of transportation of equipment must be assessed.
3. *Transportation*—Vehicles used for transportation must be secured and accommodate workers and staff, as well as equipment, safely and conveniently.
4. *Insurance*—Additional insurance coverage, including bonding, may be necessary to cover damage to customers' property and theft.
5. *Staff*—Staff must be hired and trained. Staff skills must encompass vocational training, job development, equipment usage, computation of payroll, data collection, and transportation of workers. Staff may also include a nonhandicapped worker to increase productivity and handle excess work.

Adapted from Bourbeau, (1989). Mobile work crews. An approach to achieve long-term supported employment. In P. Wehman & J. Kregel (Eds.), *Supported Employment for persons with Disabilities Focus on excellence* (pp. 83–94). NY: Human Sciences Press.

1990; Virginia 1990) to 18% (California 1990) of consumers in supported employment participated in mobile work crews. Wehman (1990) reported a national average of 12.8%. Typical contracts have centered primarily on janitorial work (Illinois, 1990). In fact, the only other occupations for enclave workers listed by researchers at Illinois, were food service and maintenance/utility worker, each representing only one supported employment consumer (Illinois 1990).

Individuals with mild mental retardation were the largest group being served in the mobile work crew model. Kregel, Wehman, and Banks (1989) reported that approximately 48% of their sample in a mobile work crew was comprised of individuals classified as mildly mentally retarded and only 7% of individuals were classified as severe/profound mentally retarded. Data from Western Michigan (1990) revealed that individuals with IQs of 55 to 69 comprised 48% of their sample, while 27% were classified as severe/profoundly mentally retarded (IQ of 0 to 39). Illinois (1990) reported 52% of their mobile work crews to be classified as mildly mentally retarded, with no individuals classified as severe/profoundly retarded participating. Average hours worked per week ranged from 12.23 (Michigan, 1990) to 27.6 (Kregel et al. 1989). A national analysis by Wehman revealed an average hourly wage of $2.85, with Illinois reporting a slightly higher hourly wage of $3.03. Average monthly wages ranged from a low of $199.68 (Illinois 1990) to a high of $381.24 (Michigan 1990). Twenty-eight percent of consumers in mobile work crews received no fringe benefits, however, 59.7% of consumers received sick leave, and 62.9% received vacation/annual leave with greater frequency than other group model participants (West, Kregel, and Banks 1990).

Mank et al. (1986) report start-up costs for mobile work crews of approximately $5,000 to $8,000, primarily for the initial acquisition of equipment. Utah (1990) found the yearly cost of running mobile work crews to be $5150, comparing closely with Wehman's national analysis of $5008, with programs ranging from $1650 to $10,000.

Kregel, Wehman, and Banks (1989) found that of all the models assessed (enclave, small business and individual placement) mobile work crews offered the fewest opportunities for integration. Michigan (1990) found 78.36% of the individuals surrounding workers in a mobile work crew to be other individuals with disabilities, indicating a fairly low level of integration with nondisabled peers. Rusch, Johnson, and Hughes (1990) found that mobile work crew participants experienced the lowest percentage of involvement with nondisabled co-workers in all categories of involvement. Only one individual out of 23 in a mobile crew experienced befriending. Rusch et al. caution that mobile work crews may be an inappropriate placement due to limited opportunities for nondisabled co-worker support. Table 4.6 lists some characteristics of the mobile work crew model.

Benchwork or Small Business

Small businesses, alternatively known as benchwork or entrepreneurial models, can offer manufacturing services or subcontract work (Moon and Griffin 1988). Small businesses typically operate as small, single-purpose, nonprofit businesses in which individuals with disabilities can receive training and supervision for contract work

Table 4.6 Characteristics of a Mobile Work Crew

Percent served in model	Range 6% (j, h) to 18% (e)
Population served	Range severe/profound mental retardation to borderline mental retardation
Percent of individuals with severe/profound disabilities served	Range 0% (j) to 27% (i)
Average hours per week worked	Range 12.23 (i) to 27.6 (a)
Average monthly wages	Range $199.68 (j) to $381.24 (i)
Percent receiving one or more fringe benefits	71.2% (b)
Intervention hours (coached to worked, 10-12 months on job)	25.13% (i)
Average cost to operate model	$5008 (c)
Percent rehabilitated	10% (e)

(Mank et al. 1986). The benchwork model has been suggested for individuals with the most severe disabilities, who may need constant supervision (Boles, Bellamy, Horner, and Mank 1984; Mank et al. 1986; Moon and Griffin 1988), because smaller staff to client ratios are utilized (e.g., 1:5 reported by Mank et al. 1986)

The small business model is similar in many ways to a typical workshop. Contract work is usually performed in the businesses' own work space, and the businesses are responsible for securing subcontract work. The model differs from a traditional workshop model in that most benchwork models are smaller (8 or fewer individuals), many serve individuals with the most severe disabilities who may not be admitted to workshop programs, and long- and short-term parts-contracts reduce overhead costs (O'Bryan 1985). O'Bryan (1989) has outlined some model components listed in Table 4.7.

Small business models are usually staffed by a manager, product manager, and personnel, all with direct-line responsibilities (O'Bryan 1989). Consumers are paid wages at a by-the-piece rate, but wages are often dependent on the success of the business (O'Bryan 1989). Because the small business operates within its own work space, opportunities for integration may be limited, and supervisors must often actively arrange for community interactions (O'Bryan 1989).

An example of the small business or benchwork model is the Special Training Program (STP) developed by the University of Oregon between 1973 and 1982 (O'Bryan 1989). Utilizing small electronics assembly businesses, the STP model was replicated in 17 communities, (Mank et al. 1986). O'Bryan (1989) reports that small business or benchwork models are dwindling; STP programs have decreased from 17 to 12 since 1973.

The benchwork model was the least frequently utilized of all the group models, with the percentage of consumers served ranging from 7% (Virginia 1990) to 7.3% (Wehman 1990). The largest group represented in the small business model

Table 4.7   Components of Small Business Models

Commercial Operations—Development of policies and procedures for marketing and sales, job design, production operations, and production control. To help assure success, small businesses must invest in technical expertise and equipment, offer competitive pricing, and provide quality assurance.

Habilitation and Training—Development of goals and objectives for consumers with emphasis on choice, skill acquisition, behavioral training, and opportunities for community integration outside the work place.

Management and Finance—Organizational structure, staffing, and direction and control of the business outlined and deliniated.

Adapted from O'Bryan (1989). The small-business supported employment option for persons with severe handicaps. In P. Wehman, and J. Kregel (Eds.), *Supported Employment for persons with disabilities. Focus on excellence* (pp. 69-82). NY: Human Sciences Press.

consisted of individuals classified as mildly mentally retarded (49%), followed by borderline mentally retarded (18%), severe/profound mentally retarded (13%), long-term mental illness (7%), physical and sensory impaired (7%), and moderately mentally handicapped (6%). (Kregel, Wehman, and Banks 1989).

Average hourly wages were also the lowest reported for all the models, with rates ranging from $1.00 per hour (North Dakota 1990) to $2.42 per hour (Wehman 1990). Kregel et al. (1989) found the average hours worked per month to be 25.4. Monthly wage averages ranged from $125 (O'Bryan 1989) to $149 (Kregel et al. 1989). Ninety-four percent of individuals participating in small business models did not receive any fringe benefits, by far the largest percentage of any individuals across all group models (West, Kregel, and Banks 1990). No employees included in the sample were given dental benefits, employee discounts, or free/reduced meals. However, lack of such benefits is reasonable given the type and location of work. Almost 7% received sick leave, medical/health benefits, and vacation/annual leave. (West et al. 1990). Clearly, the small business model provided very few fringe benefits for its participants.

In a benefit-cost analysis of the STP model, Noble and Conley (1987) found that the cost of the model exceeded client earnings. Noble and Conley also report that, in 1985, the STP model had an average monthly cost of $355, while benefits in the form of client earnings, averaged only $42 per month. While Noble and Conley note that earnings ranged from 0 to $754, low average monthly hours (28.7) contributed to costs exceeding benefits. Mank et al. 1986) report start-up costs for the benchwork model of approximately $15,000 to $25,000. Wehman (1990) found the small business model to cost an average of $6072, the highest of the group models compared.

Kregel, Wehman, and Banks (1989) surprisingly found the small business model to provide more opportunities for integration than either enclave or mobile work crews. Table 4.8 lists some components of the small business model.

SYNTHESIS OF GROUP MODEL DATA

Table 4.9 represents a synthesis of some of the features examined in supported employment group models. Of the group models analyzed, enclaves served the most consumers in group supported employment, and small businesses served the fewest. Wehman et al. (1989) noted that the number of both enclave and small business models increased between 1986 and 1988. Only the mobile work crew experienced a decrease in number dropping from 14.4% in 1986 to 5.9% in 1988.

Despite the fact that supported employment has been designed to serve individuals with severe disabilities who would not be able to sustain work without support, many individuals participating in group models are individuals classified as mildly handicapped. The percentage of individuals classified as severely/profoundly mentally handicapped ranged from 13% to 17% and remained close across models

Table 4.8   Characteristics of the Small Business Model

Percent served in model	Range 7% (h) to 7.3% (c)
Population served	Range severe/profound mental retardation to mild mental retardation
Percent of individuals with severe/profound disabilities served	13% (a)
Average hours per week worked	6.35 (a)
Average monthly wage	Range $125 (O'Bryan 1989) to $149 (a)
Percent receiving one or more fringe benefits	5.6% (b)
Intervention hours (coached to worked, 10-12 months on job)	N/A
Average cost to operate model	$6072 (c)
Percent rehabilitated	N/A

Table 4.9   Characteristics Across Group Models

	Enclave	Mobile Crew	Small Business
Percent Served	20.5%*	12%*	7.15%*
Percent individuals with severe/profound disabilities served	15.5*	13.5*	13
Average hours worked per week	22.9*	19.9*	6.35
Average monthly wages	$333.27*	$290.46*	$137*
Percent receiving one or more fringe benefits	67.4%	71.2%	5.6%
Percent receiving Medical/Health benefits	36.4%	18.6%	6.9%
Intervention hours (coached to worked 10-12 months)	18.31%	25.13%	N/A
Average cost to operate	$5154	$5008	$6072
Percent rehabilitated	11%	10%	N/A
Integration ranking among models (low to high)	medium	low	high

*Figures represent average of percentages and therefore only provide a rough estimate.

(e.g., enclave, 17%; mobile work crew 13%; and small business 13%) indicating that individuals with severe disabilities are not served more frequently in one model over another.

Most individuals, regardless of model, worked less than full-time. The average hours per week were comparable across models, however, discrepancies were evident in different programs (e.g., Michigan 1990 reported much lower average hours per week than those found by Kregel et al. 1989).

Along with low hours, it is clear that many individuals participating in group models are poorly remunerated. Consumers in the small business model were paid the lowest monthly wages. Many of the programs, regardless of group-model type, paid subminimum wages. For example, small business consumers in Virginia received hourly wages ranging from a minimum of $0.50 to a maximum of $3.60 (Virginia 1990). When low hours are coupled with low hourly wages, it is clear why many individuals with disabilities do not earn a "living wage." Interestingly, an examination of the monthly earnings of supported employment consumers as compared to earnings attained prior to placement in supported settings found all employees, regardless of group model, to experience an increase in wages (Kregel et al. 1989). Kregel et al. also found an increase in earnings after placement in supported employment of 349% for consumers in enclave models, 164% in mobile work crews, and 224% in small businesses.

The percentage of individuals receiving fringe benefits varied fairly widely among the models, with consumers in mobile work crews receiving benefits fairly frequently (71.2%) and small business consumers very infrequently (5.4%) (West et al. 1990). Although West et al. identified the type of position held and size of the company as possible conflicting variables, the authors note that almost all group model participants included in their study were employees of placement agencies rather than the host company. West et al. concluded that full-time versus part-time employment status affected the availability of fringe benefits more than participation in a particular group model. Medical insurance coverage, an important benefit for individuals with disabilities, (Conley, Noble and Elder 1986; Kiernan and Brinkman 1988; West et al. 1990), was often not available for group model participants; only 6.9% of consumers in small business models received medical benefits. As supported employment models become more established, the type and availability of fringe benefits may figure heavily into the assessment of the best placement for consumers with disabilities.

Small business models appear to be the most expensive group model option. The models show great diversity in the range of costs within each model, with enclaves ranging from $1705 to $8007, and mobile work crews ranging from $1650 to $10,000. An analysis of the training provided to consumers in group models revealed that mobile work crew members received the most job coach training (percentage of coached hours to worked hours after ten to twelve months on the job). Johnson and Rusch (1990) found the hours of direct training provided to supported employment consumers in enclave (or clustered) and mobile work crew placements did not change over time. Johnson and Rusch suggest that lack of fading may be due to reasons other than actual training needs, such as the expectations of the employment specialist that training will be provided on a continuous basis and who, in turn, may market such placements to employers with the promise that staff intervention will be constant.

Integration, an important outcome of employment placement, is often difficult to quantify. Michigan, (1990) in an attempt to quantify integration, assessed the number of individuals in mobile work crews and enclaves, who were classified as disabled, and found a fairly high percentage of individuals surrounding those workers in both mobile work crews and enclaves to be disabled (small businesses were not included in their analysis). An analysis of the different group models did reveal differences in opportunities for, and types of, interactions. Kregel et al. (1989) reported significant differences in opportunities for integration among the models. Enclaves and work crews provided less opportunity for physical and social integration than small businesses, and mobile work crews provided the fewest opportunities of all models. Similarly, Rusch et al. (1990) found mobile work crew's consumers to experience a low percentage of involvement across all categories of involvement (See Table 4.3 for a review of categories of involvement). As Rusch et al. suggest, the type of contract work secured may impact on opportunities for integration. Contracts requiring work after normal office hours or away from other workers may seriously affect the viability of mobile work crews to offer satisfactory opportunities for integration.

Analysis of the type of co-worker involvement revealed individuals in clustered placements (likened to enclaves) experienced a fairly high amount of "associating" and "evaluation". All model participants experienced very little "befriending" or "data collection" involvement. The low percentage of individuals experiencing befriending suggests that interactions are restricted to the work place. Rusch et al. note that data collection might not aid in the development of friendships, hence the low percentage of data collection occurring might be viewed as a positive outcome.

Supported employment closures, or consumers identified as "rehabilitated" (status 26), were available only from California (1990) and only for enclave and mobile work crew models. Individuals served in both models were rehabilitated at a comparable rate (11% and 10, respectively). Due in large part by the ability of the agencies to retrieve and report the necessary information, analysis across all models, including individual placement, showed an increase in successful closures. (Wehman 1990).

SELECTING A MODEL

A look at outcome data in supported employment highlights the need to examine many diverse elements. Table 4.10 summarizes critical performance evaluation in-

Table 4.10   Critical Performance Evaluation Indicators

1. Participant characteristics
   age
   gender
   disability level
   SSI/SSDI recipient
2. Setting prior to supported employment placement
3. Supported employment environment
4. Employment data
   wages per hour
   average hours per week
   weeks worked since placement
   taxes paid
5. Occupational category during supported employment
6. Level of integration
7. Hours of job support
   training
   assistance
   supervision
   transportation
   case management
8. Job movement patterns
   change status with each move to reflect present employment environments.

Adapted from Schalock (1988). Critical performance evaluation indicators in supported employment. In P. Wehman and M. S. Moon (Eds.), *Vocational rehabilitation and supported employment* (pp. 163–174). Baltimore: Paul Brookes Publishing Co.

dicators cited in Schalock (1988); which synthesizes outcome indicators in supported employment from a number of authors (Kiernan, McGaughey and Schalock 1986; Mank et al. 1986; Wehman, Hill, Hill, Brooke, Pendleton, and Britt 1985).

Outcome data illustrate that many components represent success in a vocational placement. Further, important outcomes, such as job satisfaction and increased feelings of self-esteem, cannot be overlooked.

As in any evaluation of outcome, the assessment of success will depend, to a large extent, on the perception of the individual making the evaluation. Multiple perspectives will also be evident in assessment of group models. Schalock (1988) notes that many individuals are involved in the evaluation of supported employment models, including the consumer, his or her family, nonprofit organization employees, program personnel, and federal and state policy-makers (Schalock 1988). Table 11 outlines some of the elements individuals may want to consider when selecting a group model. Each element should be viewed with consideration to the perspective of the individual making the selection. However, clear acknowledgement and understanding of consumer needs and wants should figure heavily into any placement decision.

Table 4.11   Elements to Consider in Model Selection

1. What work arrangement is the consumer best suited for?
2. What work arrangement is the consumer most comfortable with and most enthusiastic toward?
3. What work arrangement is the family most comfortable with and most enthusiastic toward?
4. Which model(s) are currently available and established?
5. Which model(s) can be effectively established in a given community?
6. How much will each model cost?
7. Which model affords the consumer opportunities to be independent and increase his or her quality of life?
8. Which model affords the greatest opportunity for physical and social integration?
9. Which model offers the best benefits?
10. Which model offers opportunities for advancement and job satisfaction?

1. What work arrangements is the consumer vocationally best suited for?

Compatibility between an individual and a job requires a match between an individual's skills and strengths and the requirements of a job. An assessment of a consumer's strengths and weaknesses should be undertaken to see how these fit into the jobs available in the community or presently available in each model. For instance, an individual with physical disabilities may have difficulty participating in a mobile work crew in which mobility in the community is necessary. Equally, an individual with the ability to remain flexible in many jobs may find a mobile work crew a challenge. Staff to client ratios should also be assessed. Individuals who require a great deal of supervision may have difficulty in a mobile work crew or in an enclave, depending on the type of work secured.

An analysis of a consumer's strengths and weaknesses can be done via a situational analysis. A situational analysis, as the name implies, analyzes an individual in an actual job setting. An environmental assessment or situational assessment consists of identifying potential environments in which a consumer may function and observing him or her in the actual setting performing the work or actions required in that setting (Moon et al. 1990). Information can also be gleaned from interviews with the consumer, his or her family, program managers of program models, and past employers. All the information gathered can be synthesized into the best fit between the consumer and the jobs available or typical of each model.

2. What work arrangement is the consumer most comfortable with and most enthusiastic toward?

Even if a suitable match can be made between a consumer and a job, the consumer must feel comfortable with the settings and tasks. Obviously, if a consumer feels less than enthusiastic toward a job or setting, the situation may be doomed for failure. Individuals who feel uncomfortable in the presence of a great number of people may dislike an enclave that requires contract work in a large factory. Similarly, loud noises or closed spaces may be a problem for consumers and must be acknowledged. Assessment can be undertaken via a situational analysis and interviews.

3. What work arrangement is the family most comfortable with and most enthusiastic toward?

The need for family involvement in the service provision for individuals with disabilities has long been acknowledged. Family members intimately know the consumer and can usually provide valuable information to aid in decision making. If placement decisions are made without interest in and respect for the parents' and family members' priorities and wishes, targeted plans may fail. Such information is best secured through interviewing family members and acknowledging their feelings toward supported employment placements.

4. Which model(s) are currently available and established?

While it should not serve to deter individuals from seeking to establish needed services, a look at the availability of existing programs and models may be helpful. Typically, established models have the advantage of providing information on retention, wages, benefits and jobs available. Information concerning already established models can be obtained through local rehabilitation counselors, nonprofit organizations for individuals with development disabilities, and state funding agencies for individuals with developmental disabilities.

5. Which model(s) can be effectively established in a given community?

Because a proper match between a consumer and jobs available in existing models may not exist, it may be necessary to establish new options within a given community. To help ascertain what jobs, and hence models can successfully operate in a community, a market analysis is useful. Steps undertaken in a market analysis are outlined in Table 4.12.

It may also be helpful to interview major employers in the community and contact the local Chamber of Commerce to better understand the job market availability in the community. An examination of supported employment programs in surrounding communities may also prove beneficial.

6. How much will each model cost?

While we would like to believe otherwise, cost often figures heavily in the choice of a model. The cost of a program is a complex combination of many different factors. Benefit-cost analyses can examine many different variables. Hill, Wehman, Kregel, Banks, and Metzler (1987) analyzed the following in their assessment of benefit-cost analysis: months worked , staff intervention time, reduction in SSI, estimated alternative program costs savings, estimated total taxes paid, total public

Table 4.12   Questions Related to Analysis of the Local Labor Market

1. Who are the major employers in your community?
    a. Number of employees
    b. Type of work performed
    c. Entry level requirements
    d. Community reputation
2. What types of employment are most commonly found in your community?
3. Which companies or types of employment have the largest turnover rates in your community?
4. Which companies or types of employment are anticipating growth (new job opening) in the next year?
    a. Market trend
    b. Potential date for job vacancies
5. What companies are known to have hired persons with disabilities?
    a. Type of employment
    b. Name of employer
    c. Types of disabilities
6. Does your community have seasonal employment?

Moon, M.S., Inge, K. J., Wehman, P., Brooke, V., and Barcus, J. M. (1990). *Helping persons with severe mental retardation get and keep employment. Supported employment issues and strategies.* Baltimore: Paul Brookes Publishing Co.

savings, Targeted Jobs Tax Credit (TJTC), total project expenditures, consequences to taxpayers, and total wages earned. From the consumer's standpoint, important variables might include wages and fringe benefits. Each model brings with it different and unique costs in program establishment. For example, a mobile work crew might need a van for transportation and insurance for work in the community or transportation of consumers. Contract work for small businesses that entails shipping of assembled parts must figure the cost of distance and weight in transporting items. Equipment needs will depend greatly on the contracts secured or the type of work required. Information on the benefit-cost ratio of various models can best be secured through agencies employing group models and from current literature on models in operation.

7. Which model affords consumers opportunities to be independent and increase feelings of self-esteem?

Opportunities for individuals with disabilities to function independently is limited either by the situation or the technology available to restructure the situation. Independence is fostered through choice in work, living arrangements, and recreational activities. Within a work setting, vocational independence can be enhanced through the manner in which consumers arrive and depart from work. For example, consumers afforded opportunities to arrive at work independently, usually through the use of public transportation, may feel more in control of their lives. How workers are paid may also serve to affect feelings of control. Consumers participating in an enclave, who are paid directly by the host company, may experience greater independence than consumers paid by a service organization. Assessment of how "normalized" work conditions are may help provide a picture of the amount of independence available to consumers. Such assessments can be made through the use of situational assessments and interviews with service agencies and host companies.

8. Which model affords the greatest opportunities for physical and social integration?

Opportunities for integration are an important component of supported employment. An individual's success on the job and his or her satisfaction with their work will depend, to a large extent, on opportunities for integration. Integration entails far more than simple physical proximity, although once in closer physical proximity, the greater the probability of encountering opportunities for social integration. Models may vary in the amount and type of integration that can occur between consumers and individuals without disabilities. Assessment of the physical space of the companies in which contracts or work is procured may lend insight into integration opportunities as well as access to the surrounding community. For example, an enclave might offer a consumer the opportunity to work along side many other individuals without disabilities, particularly if the enclave workers are scattered throughout the work site. Participation in a mobile work crew may also mean consumers, as they travel from site to site, are exposed to opportunities for interactions with many different individuals. The small business model may also provide integration opportunities through lunch breaks at a nearby restaurant. Further, each model may provide different levels of "structured" opportunities for integration. For example, the benchwork model may provide extensive training in the acquisition of social skills and may provide opportunities to gain social skills with others. Opportunities for interactions may also be a function of the number of other individuals in the vicinity. Enclave workers in large factories may have an advantage over small business workers, who are not exposed to as many other individuals.

Opportunities for integration may also be affected by the patterns of socialization of co-workers in the sites available in various models. Assessment of how often and when co-workers socialize and whether the company has formalized venues for interactions (company softball teams, picnic, etc.) may be helpful. Finally, the age of other workers may also impact on opportunities for interactions. If workers in one model differ significantly in age from the consumer, this may further serve to limit opportunities for integration by decreasing chances for the development of friendships in and out of work.

9. Which model offers the best package of benefits for the consumer?

Models may vary in their ability to provide wages, adequate hours, and fringe benefits for consumers. Individuals may need to assess company policies for workers and benefits. Further, benefits may be different if work is available only part-time. Some models may not be able to provide full-time work and may limit the number of hours available for consumers to work. A mobile work crew member who works with a grounds-keeping crew may find seasonal work restricting the number of hours available to work in winter months. Similarly, a small business consumer may find that short-term contracts disrupt stable work patterns.

Individuals must also be aware of the production rate necessary to attain before "full-time" status or fringe benefits are available. Information concerning wages, fringe benefits, and hours available to work can be obtained by contacting host companies or service organizations.

10. Which model offers opportunities for advancement and job satisfaction?

Qualify-of-life issues recently have begun to emerge in the human services field. No longer is simply job placement the ultimate outcome for individuals with disabilities, but rather placement in jobs that are personally satisfying and offer opportunities for advancement. Individuals must be aware of the production requirements of companies in which the models are based as well as those with whom contracts are secured. If a nonprofit organization is the mainstay of the model chosen, one should ascertain the frequency of movement of consumers from more to less restrictive environments.

Table 4.13 provides a chart useful for group model selection. The chart may be filled out by different individuals, each with a unique perspective on group placement options, and responses may be compared and contrasted (as in a consumer's rating and a policy-maker's rating). Comparison of different perspectives may facilitate prioritization of options and elements within each employment outcome.

Table 4.13   Group Model Selection Chart

Directions: Rate each variable within each group model option as 1 (most favorable alternative) to 3 (least favorable alternative).

Elements	Enclave	Work Crew	Small Business
Vocational fit	———	———	———
Emotional fit	———	———	———
Family attitude	———	———	———
Established models	———	———	———
Community fit	———	———	———
Benefit/cost	———	———	———
Independence	———	———	———
Integration	———	———	———
Benefits to consumer	———	———	———
Job satisfaction	———	———	———

Part II

Supported Employment Implementation Strategies

5

Family Influence in Identifying a Job

Family involvement in the supported employment process has been identified as a critical factor related to the successful employment of an individual with a disability. Research has indicated that a lack of family support has a negative effect on employment outcomes and job retention (Rehabilitation Research and Training Center Newsletter 1986; Schutz 1986). A survey of national experts on supported employment reported family beliefs and concerns to be a major barrier to supported employment implementation preceded only by economic disincentives and employer attitudes (Bateman, 1990). In addition, the positive role of parents in employment has been demonstrated in a study of 462 special education graduates in Vermont in which 80% were reported to be working in jobs found through the self-family-friend network (Hasazi, Gordon, and Roe 1985). The strength of families in influencing the service delivery system has been witnessed repeatedly, as evident by the deinstitutionalization movement and the establishment of free and appropriate education for all children. More recently, parents and family members have focused these efforts on developing, expanding, and improving community employment and residential programs (Gartner, Lipsky, and Turnbull 1991).

Parent and family participation offers many advantages to professionals assigned the responsibility of placing an individual with a disability into employment. First, families are the experts on their son, daughter, or family member with a disability and can provide valuable information about his or her vocational interests, skills, and abilities to assist with making a good job match (Moore 1988). Second, parents and family members can share information about the family to assist with the identification of work that is consistent with the philosophy, values, and beliefs held by the family. Third, families are a valuable and constant source of support throughout the employment tenure of a worker with a disability, quite unlike the ever-changing co-workers, supervisors, and professionals associated with the job placement. Fourth, families who are given the opportunity to choose and participate are likely to feel invested in the employment situation and to be more willing to provide assistance when needed.

Parents and family members who are actively involved with supported employment services also experience multiple benefits. Family members can receive information from professionals that explains employment options, community resources, and supported employment service characteristics, which can help answer questions and alleviate concerns. In addition, choice and control in planning and decision making is a significant source of stress reduction for parents and family members (Carney 1987; Turnbull, Summers, Backus, Bronicki, Goodfriend, and Roeder-Gordon, nd). Expressing preferences and choices gives parents and family members the opportunity to build on the family's strengths and to determine the direction of their own lives (Turnbull and Turnbull 1990). Finally, family participation increases the likelihood of personal satisfaction and the achievement of individual and family goals and aspirations.

The purpose of this chapter is to identify the role of parents and family members in supported employment and the ways in which professionals can best work with families to facilitate their support. First, the perspective of the family will be presented through a discussion of family dynamics and expectations. Second, communication techniques that stimulate and foster collaborative family-professional relationships will be identified. Third, the role of the family in the job identification and placement decision process will be discussed. Finally, strategies for increasing family support and involvement in supported employment will be suggested.

UNDERSTANDING FAMILY PERSPECTIVES

Family Dynamics

The family operates as a system, so the actions of one family member influences the actions of all other members (Turnbull and Turnbull 1990). Similarly, a change in one member's behavior typically causes change in the behavior of other members as well The family life-cycle concept suggests that families pass through a series of predictable stages, each with its own set of developmental tasks (Carney 1987). These stages include (1) couple, (2) birth of first child, (3) school-age children, (4) adolescent children, (5) children leaving home, and (6) retirement/old-age (Carney and Kraft 1987). Transition from one stage to the next produces change and creates stress and a need for adjustment within the family (Turnbull, Summers, and Brotherson 1986).

The transition for a family with a disabled member is likely to be less clear, as additional challenges are presented with each new stage, while the responsibilities from previous stages continue to demand attention. For example, most nonhandicapped children obtain employment and independent living arrangements after graduating from high school, which tends to result in a decrease in family dependency. In contrast, fragmented and unavailable services frequently result in an individual with a disability having more time to sit at home after exiting the school system and actually increases their dependency on family support.

Any change to the family unit or a family member can create stress regardless of whether that change is positive or negative. Stress tends to be reduced when individual roles are well-defined and transition from one stage to another is fairly well-expected (Turnbull and Turnbull 1986). Although some change and stress can be expected with any child, for those parents who have a child with a disability, changes in the individual's life often are more traumatic (Moore 1988). It is likely that parents do not have the information and experience that could assist them with making a smooth progression through each stage for several reasons. Often, parents do not receive the financial, professional, or service support that would allow them to easily and successfully make the transition from one stage to another. In addition, parents may have hopes and desires for their son or daughter, but lack the resources to be able to best help him or her accomplish these goals. Finally, families may find it difficult to obtain desired information as they frequently must juggle the maze of existing disability programs and fight for the development of new services.

A family with a disabled member is more similar to other families than it is different (Gartner, Lipsky, and Turnbull 1991). Despite the similarities, all families are unique with specific needs that change over time. Factors influencing how disability affects a family include (1) the characteristics of the disability, (2) the characteristics of the family, (3) the personal characteristics of each family member, and (4) the special needs of the family and other family members (Turnbull and Turnbull 1990). Therefore, families will typically react to and cope differently with the demands associated with disability and life-cycle changes depending upon their unique qualities and available supports.

Throughout history, parents have been assigned many roles in association with their son or daughter with a disability; for example, parents as the source of their child's problem; parents as disability organization members; service developers; recipients of professional decisions; learners and teachers; political advocates; and educational decision makers (Turnbull and Turnbull 1990). It can be assumed that family members, such as a spouse or sibling, who are closely and actively involved with the individual with a disability are considered to share similar roles. Families have also been assigned the additional label and stigma that is often given to their son, daughter, or family member with a disability, such as being referred to as an "autistic" or a "head-injured" family (Gartner, Lipsky, and Turnbull 1991). More recently, parents have been viewed as family members with unique strengths and individualized needs that must be addressed for successful family life (Turnbull and Turnbull 1990). Professionals need to assist families with identifying their personal needs, desires, and expectations, as well as aim to provide the support that will help them accomplish the goals that they and their family member with a disability would like to achieve.

Family Expectations

Each family enters into the employment service arena with its own preconceived notion of what the individual with a disability can and should do. It is likely that these ideas are influenced by each family's culture, characteristics, history, and previous experiences with disability services. Most would agree that families only want what is best for their son or daughter and something that he or she would like to do. Many parents and family members are well aware of the employment potential of the individual with a disability and will not compromise their desires by settling for a sheltered workshop or day program placement. In Oregon, a study of 165 parents who had a son or daughter with mental retardation enrolled in a high school program reported that when making vocational placement decisions, they were most interested in job training and security,(McDonnell, Wilcox, Boles, and Bellamy 1985). The respondents emphasized a need for training activities that focused on developing more interesting jobs rather than just security, indicating a preference away from sheltered nonvocational programs.

In contrast, a large number of families have developed very low expectations as a result of receiving discouraging, inaccurate, or no information about the employment options that are available for their family member who is disabled. In fact, for many families whose son, daughter, or relative is severely disabled or was born before the passage of the Education for All Handicapped Children Act of 1975, employment may have never been presented as an alternative. For others, sitting at home, long waiting-lists, or adult day programming may have been suggested as the only post school options available. Hill, Seyfarth, Banks, Wehman, and Orelove (1987) surveyed 660 parents and guardians whose sons or daughters were receiving mental retardation services from agencies in Virginia and found that only 12% indicated a preference for competitive employment. Furthermore, parents of a son or daughter with severe and profound mental retardation selected an activity center as the optimal placement, while those parents whose son or daughter had a label of mild and moderate mental retardation reported a preference for a sheltered workshop placement.

It is important for professionals to remember that the preferences families express may not necessarily reflect their preferred choice for vocational services, but rather their expected or learned response. All too often, families have heard, "your son, daughter, spouse, or relative will never work" or "the sheltered workshop would be the most appropriate placement for your disabled family member". Is it any wonder then that families may appear skeptical the first time an employment specialist visits them and says, "I'm here to place your son, daughter, or spouse into a job"? Regardless of whether the family wanted or expected employment for the individual with a disability, if they have not been prepared that this might be a possible alternative, it is likely that at first they will proceed cautiously.

Low expectations should not necessarily be interpreted negatively as strict, unyielding opinions, but rather as evolving personal goals based upon the quality of information at hand. Professionals need to provide families with the resources that will empower them to make informed choices about the employment outcomes for their family member with a disability. It is important that service providers explain the different alternatives to families and help them exercise choice to obtain their preferred option (Wehman 1990). The necessary, first step is communicating with parents or family members to identify just what it is they would really like to see their son, daughter, spouse, or relative accomplish.

COMMUNICATING WITH FAMILIES

Relationship Building

It is evident that a positive working relationship between families and professionals is a critical component of vocational services, however, many parents report interactions with professionals to be more of a source of stress than help (Turnbull, Summers, Backus, Bronicki, Goodfriend, and Roeder-Gordon, nd). Professionals who are identified as being most helpful are those who understand family systems, family life-cycles, and family stress and coping styles (Singer and Irvin 1991). In addition, effective professionals apply that knowledge to their regular interactions with families in an attempt to establish equal, respectful, and mutually satisfying relationships. Some of the professional qualities reported to be important for effective helping include being enthusiastic, open-minded, competent, efficient, and practical (Huang and Heifetz 1991). The foundation for a rewarding partnership is the recognition that each family is unique and contributes valuable skills that complement rather than hinder the role of the professional. (Gartner, Lipsky, and Turnbull 1991).

The opportunity for developing a family-professional partnership begins at the time of the very first contact, which either party may initiate. Service providers should take special precaution to spend the majority of the time getting to know the family and sharing information about him or herself and the program being represented. It is unfair to assume that family members should disclose extensive personal information about themselves during the first encounter, particularly if interactions during the meeting are formal and one-sided. Parents and family members may be reluctant to initially assume an active role due to being tired of sharing information "just one more time" or with "just one more professional," especially if past experiences have repeatedly failed to result in satisfactory outcomes.

It is not unusual for families to have been and to continue to be inundated with a variety of professionals, each with their own priorities and opinions as to what would be best for the family. Service providers should be sensitive to the variety of professionals that families must deal with and provide assistance with clarifying how the different agencies are related. In fact, hesitancy may be a signal that the family does not understand the services being offered or feels that they are already receiving similar services. For example, a parent may decline an offer for supported employment services since his son is already "employed" in the sheltered workshop through an arrangement made by the other agency representative.

Although the family may be interested in employment, it may not be their one and only priority, as they must also contend with daily schedules and a multitude of other family demands. Too often, families are labeled as being uncooperative or unsupportive when, in actuality, they are fearful, cautious, or perhaps just not operating on the same timetable as the service provider. Furthermore, an entirely unrelated explanation may account for a family's display of "disinterested" behaviors. For example, logistical problems, such as lack of transportation, inconvenient scheduling, or no child-care provisions may be the real explanation for a family's reluctance to schedule an appointment or for repeated cancellations of previously scheduled meetings. A parent's recommendations to professionals for reducing barriers and increasing rapport include showing support, offering praise, appearing genuinely interested, being positive and optimistic, and creating a trusting and supportive atmosphere (Rehabilitation Research and Training Center Newsletter 1990).

Effective Communication

Research on parent-professional communication in the field of education suggests that parents prefer informal and frequent communication (Turnbull and Turnbull 1990). Personal experience has proven this strategy to be effective when communicating with families regarding supported employment. It is likely that families prefer to have numerous opportunities to ask questions as they arise as well as to be given ample time between contacts to consult other resources and make well-thought-out decisions. Opportunities for communication can occur in a variety of ways, including telephone calls, home visits, and written correspondence.

In addition to professional initiated communication, it is important to encourage family members to contact the employment specialist whenever they think of a question or new information they would like to share. The family's importance and value in the placement decision process is portrayed when members are granted equal control in directing the lines of communication rather than being at the mercy of the professionals who are providing services. An important decision for the employment specialist is whether to give the family a home number to call when they are interested in talking after work hours. The advantage of this is that family members may have difficulty talking freely during the day or are not allowed to receive personal calls during work, which places limitations on their involvement beyond their control. In addition, having a home number to call personalizes the experience and is likely to reassure the family of the employment specialist's commitment to them and the individual with a disability.

The purpose of family-employment specialist communication is to provide both parties with the opportunity to give and receive information. A relationship conducive to open and honest communication must be established if the employment specialist and the family members are to accomplish this goal. The mannerism, communication style, and personality of the employment specialist plays a critical role in just how successful this relationship will be. Several considerations are important to remember when communicating with families. These include (1) being sensitive to the family dynamics and culture; (2) understanding your own perceptions, attitudes, and values (Turnbull and Turnbull 1990); (3) developing good interpersonal communication and listening skills; (4) modeling how to effectively communicate, such as sharing information and asking questions; (5) demonstrating flexibility by adapting to individual family styles, agendas, and preferences; and (6) recognizing and responding to personality differences and conflicts. Specific guidelines on how to effectively communicate with family members are described in Table 5.1.

As previously mentioned, meetings with the family are also a time for the employment specialist to share information about the supported employment program and community-based employment in general. It is important to use a variety of sources when providing information to ensure that a method is utilized that is easily understood by the family. For example, articles and newsletters may be very informative, but if the family cannot read or does not have the time to read a large volume of material, the effort will be meaningless. Techniques for sharing information include verbal communication, published articles and newsletters, conferences or workshops, linkage with other parents and family members, videotapes or slide shows, and contact with local, state, and national resources.

Family Concerns

Frequently, family members will not ask questions or discuss issues with the employment specialist, giving the impression that they understand everything and all of their concerns have been addressed. While this may be the case, it is this author's experience that a lack of communication is more often an indication that the family does not know what questions to ask or is not yet aware of their concerns. This has primarily been due to the newness of the concept being presented, inadequate time to process the information, or uncertainty as to how supported employment will affect them or the personality of the family members. Therefore, it is important to provide the family with all relevant information regardless of whether or not they make specific requests. Table 5.2 provides a listing of program and ser-

Table 5.1   Guidelines for Communicating with Family Members

1. Arrange a meeting time that is convenient for the family. This may mean visiting during the evening or on weekends.
2. Take time for introductions and getting to know each other at the beginning of the meeting.
3. Explain what supported employment is, the services offered by the program, and the ongoing role of the employment specialist.
4. Ask the family about the goals and aspirations that they hold for their family member with a disability.
5. Address any questions or concerns that the family may have. If an answer is unknown, don't guess, but tell the family you are unsure and will get back to them with an answer at a later date.
6. Provide additional information that is important for the family to know, but may have gone unasked.
7. Discuss the types of jobs that the family feels would be most appropriate or desirable for the family member with a disability and brain storm possible job leads.
8. Encourage and practice open and honest communication.
9. Actively listen and observe to get a better understanding of the family dynamics, values, and routines.
10. Determine the family's availability and willingness to provide assistance and support for the individual with a disability.
11. Schedule a second follow-up meeting to review the information presented, answer questions, and discuss job placement ideas in-depth.
12. Give the family written materials or videotapes that further explain and clarify supported employment.
13. Provide the names and numbers of other families whose members have participated in supported employment and would be willing to talk with the family.
14. Give the family a telephone number and address to contact and explain your hours of availability.
15. Assess your attitude and perceptions of the family and address any stereotypes, prejudices, or negative feelings that may exist.

vice. Information that should be shared with families to assist them in making informed choices and assessing service quality. These topics can be used by employment specialists as guidelines for the type of information that should be offered to families as well as to supplement the questions asked directly about the program.

Family members generally have many questions about supported employment that they may or may not feel comfortable asking the employment specialist. For example, transportation, social security, co-worker acceptance, and service stability

Table 5.2 Supported Employment Program and Service Information to be Made Available for Family Members

Program	*Services*
Mission statement/philosophy	Placement services provided
Types of services/supports available	Job training services provided
Program history/development	Follow-along services provided
Service eligibility criteria	Related employment services provided
Procedures for handling referrals	Type of employment model
Number of employment specialists	Waiting lists
Number of persons who have received services	Number of persons placed per year
Program outcomes	Average weekly earnings
Provisions for replacements	Average work hours per week
Resources for family members	Long-term support arrangements
Service recipients/references	Role of employment specialist Retention rates

are questions frequently posed by families. It is important to address these concerns during conversations with the family even though they may not ask the questions directly. Too often, an employment specialist will identify a job that requires an immediate placement decision only to have parents hesitate because they are not sure if Micky should gamble with his SSI check or if Joan will be safe riding the bus or working with the public. Table 5.3 provides a listing of many of the questions and concerns frequently posed by family members. In addition, the employment specialist is provided with responses and resources that can be useful when addressing family concerns. To reduce problems that may arise and jeopardize job placement, it is to the employment specialist's advantage to make this information available, as early as possible, to all family members who are or will be involved with the employment of the individual with a disability.

IDENTIFYING A JOB

There are typically many more job openings in a community then there are supported employment workers or available staff to provide training. The challenge is more often in identifying the job that is best suited for a particular individual

Table 5.3   Employment Specialist Responses and Resources for Addressing
Family Concerns

Concern	Information to be Presented by Employment Specialists	Resources for Parents
Ability to perform the job	Job matching of individual abilities to job requirements	Job analysis information
	Training by employment specialist of work and work-related skills	Employment specialist progress reports and informal communication
	Ongoing assessment and training or support, as needed, for as long as the individual is employed	Supervisor evaluations and feedback
Safety of the job and work environment	Job analysis of work requirements and environment	Job analysis information
	Careful job matching	Ongoing progress reports
	Training provided until individual performs job to company standards	Employment specialist training data
	Job modifications, adaptations, and support provided, as needed	Visit to the job site during individual's lunch or break
Transportation to and from work	Assessment of all possible transportation options and selection of most appropriate mode	Documentation of transportation arrangements (e.g., schedule, routes, bus number, regulations, telephone number).
	Completion of transportation arrangements	Employment specialist training data
	Training by employment specialist until individual can use transportation independently	Employment specialist feedback
	Ongoing assessment and training as needed	

Table 5.3 Employment Specialist Responses and Resources for Addressing Family Concerns *(continued)*

Concern	Information to be Presented by Employment Specialists	Resources for Parents
Loss of Social Security and disability benefits	Wage and benefit needs considered during job match	Local Social Security Administration office
	General explanation of effect of work on individual's benefits	Social Security benefit worksheets for estimating amount of check after employment
	Description of work incentives (e.g., Plans for Achieving Self-Support (PASS), Impairment related work expenses).	Rehabilitation Counselor or Case Manager information
	Assistance with visiting Social Security office	
Co-worker acceptance and social relationships	Matching of individual social interests to job's social environment	Employment specialist feedback
	Employment specialist modeling of appropriate social interactions with co-workers	Reports of satisfaction/ dissatisfaction and number of friendships by individual
	Employment specialist training of social and interpersonal skills	
	Gradual fading of employment specialists time on the job site	
	Assistance with participation in social opportunities and activities	

Table 5.3   Employment Specialist Responses and Resources for Addressing Family Concerns *(continued)*

Concern	Information to be Presented by Employment Specialists	Resources for Parents
Availability of supports	Utilization of formal and informal supports at the job site	Employment specialist contact number
	Linkage with community supports and resources as needed	Employment policies and contact information
	Employment specialist intervention until individual is stable on the job	Long-term provider agency information and contact number
	Arrangements made with long-term support provider	Community resources information
Family roles and responsibilities	Encouragement of family involvement in decision making	Supported employment information
	Assessment of the type and frequency of support that the family is willing to provide	Family support groups (e.g., Parent-to-Parent, Next Step, Head Injury Support Group)
	Frequent and ongoing communication with family members	Networking with members of other families
	Individualized service delivery	Employment specialist communication
Job stability	Ongoing assessment of work performance	Program employment outcomes (e.g., retention rates, waiting lists)
	Intervention provided as needed to maintain job standards and individual satisfaction	Progress reports and performance evaluations
	Provisions for replacement should job separation occur	Individual feedback and self-reports
		Supported employment provider resources and contact information

with a disability rather than in locating businesses that have a job opening. It is not unusual for placement decisions to be based upon convenience (e.g., location, schedule), administrative pressures (e.g., placement numbers, funding), or professional opinion (e.g., perceived compatibility, individual abilities) rather than individual or family choice. Although these methods may result in the desired outcome of employment, the long-term success of such one-sided placements is likely to be sacrificed. The most effective strategy for ensuring that an individual and a job are a good match is to include the individual with a disability and his or her family throughout the entire job identification process. A more thorough discussion of individual choice and empowerment in supported employment is provided in Chapter 6.

Employment Preferences

Family members may have their own ideas about what the individual with a disability can do or what they would prefer that he or she do. For example, Gary's father may want him to work at the factory close to their house, Lucy's mother may have always thought her daughter would work in a day care center, or Michael's wife may want him to work at a prestigious job that offers travel and benefits. No matter how much the employment specialist agrees or disagrees with the family's choice of jobs, it is important to openly discuss their ideas. Perhaps Gary's father has chosen the factory because he works there and feels he can protect his son who is severely physically-disabled from being ridiculed and teased. Maybe Lucy's mother selected day care because the vocational teacher suggested that this would be an appropriate job for an individual with moderate mental retardation. Similarly, Michael's wife may have selected this job in an attempt to restore their life to the way it was before her husband sustained a traumatic brain injury. Family members may not be as committed to a specific job as they are to a desired goal that they feel their selection will help them to accomplish. Listening to the family's job preferences can help identify these underlying motives that may be equally addressed in other employment settings.

Whether or not a family has a particular job in mind, it is important to find out what characteristics of a job would be important to them. In addition to asking about the particular interests and abilities of the individual, the following questions can provide an indication of the job characteristics that the family would prefer and most likely support. What location is most preferred? What type of work do they feel their family member with a disability would be most interested in? What type of job environment would make them feel most comfortable? What hours would be most suitable to the family schedule? What kind of wages and benefits are important? What type of assistance would the family be willing to provide? What other issues does the family feel are a priority? For example, a mother may state that she would like a job where her daughter with cerebral palsy will have a two-week vacation so that she can accompany the family to Europe next summer. Even though this demand may limit job opportunities, it is better to identify these types of concerns early rather than place the individual into a job with no vacation, only to have her quit five months later when the family takes their vacation.

Professionals are more likely to identify the family's true preferences if several meeting times are scheduled and all key family members are involved. For example, if all meetings are scheduled during the day with the mother, pertinent information from the father, which may negatively or positively affect the placement, may never be obtained. Much of the information that can really assist the employment specialist with identifying a good match will be gathered through informal conversation on a variety of occasions.

One reason for repeated visits is to enhance trust and confidence so that the family is more willing to share its personal feelings and experiences. Second, family members may have never thought in terms of competitive employment and will need more time to remember important information and to formulate their desires. It is surprising that many family members are given two hours, during one meeting, to voice their preferences for competitive employment even if they have never heard of it before, yet most have had years to contemplate sheltered workshop or day activity program options. Third, families may be experiencing a bad day or the scheduled meeting may not be convenient, so they quickly respond to the service provider's questions without considering the possible long-term ramifications of their answers. Finally, families may underestimate their contribution to the employment process and withhold information thinking it is irrelevant or unimportant. Communicating repeatedly with family members provides both parties with the opportunity to ask questions and share information, which allows service providers and the family to build upon what the other has said.

Placement Decisions

In addition to information sharing, the family also plays an integral role in brainstorming possible employment options that would be best suited for the individual with a disability. For example, Mary may love animals, so perhaps a job in a veterinary hospital or animal shelter may be a good match. Similarly, John's father passes by a large office complex on his way to work and would be willing to provide transportation every day if a job could be identified there. Or, Louis is good at playing some sports, so a job as a locker attendant at the YMCA or as a ticket-taker at the coliseum may be most interesting to him. Spending time discussing job possibilities with the family can provide further opportunities for obtaining information as one idea triggers another potential employment site or important placement consideration. For example, Mary's teacher recommended she get a job as a "sunshine girl" in a hospital, to which her mother added the suggestion that perhaps a nursing home would be more intimate. The employment specialist, remembering laundry skills that Mary demonstrated in her school vocational program, recommended that a laundry job at the local nursing home be targeted as a possible job site for her.

Furthermore, brain-storming sessions create a situation for synthesizing and translating relevant information into practical job development leads. For example, the family would like Susan to work days at a supportive place, close to home, where she could utilize her good social skills and love for people, prompting the employment specialist to remember a little, neighborhood "mom and pop" restaurant that was looking for a dining room attendant. Finally, potential problems, such as transportation and support needs, and family resources, such as job leads and assistance, can be assessed with the input of the key people involved in the placement process.

Family involvement in identifying a job does not cease once job development activities are begun. Frequent communication between the service provider and family is essential as the job leads are contacted and new potential businesses are identified. For example, the department store where Jim's family really wanted him to work did not have any job openings, but the employment specialist found a similar type of janitorial position at a nearby bowling alley and needed to know if the family would be in agreement with this job. It is important for employment specialists to share the information gathered during job development so that families can modify their employment aspirations based upon realistic job demands. For example, Stacy's parents thought she would be best suited to work at a day care center, however, after contacting several locations, the employment specialist found that the job required a license that Stacy would not be able to obtain. The family is sure to be more invested if they receive the same information as the employment specialist and can have the opportunity to use it to brain-storm other possibilities than if they were just told later on that their job choice was not a good idea.

Once a potential job opening is identified, the individual with a disability, employment specialist, and family members should sit down and discuss its compatibility and attractiveness. For example, does Sam like this kind of work? Does the family feel that Debbie would enjoy working there? Is the family comfortable with Amy taking public transportation to work everyday? Is Roger's wife satisfied with the wages and fringe benefits that this job offers? Does Laura agree to work weekends, as the company requires? Some aspects of the job may not be exactly what the family had in mind, and this is the time to figure out if they would be willing to make compromises or if job modifications could be made to accommodate their expectations.

It is better to address any problems before deciding to place an individual into a job, however, it is also important to realize that family concerns are not necessarily an indication of dissatisfaction and can frequently be alleviated with honest and reassuring communication. When employment specialists make job placement decisions, they often feel families should just accept the position and label questioning families as overprotective or interfering. However, most people considering a position would ask the employer numerous questions about the job to assist with their decision to accept or decline employment. Since family members do not have contact with the employer, it is natural for them to direct their questions toward the employment specialist and to expect a voice in the decision process. After all, even after the employment specialist is no longer involved, the family members are the ones who will have to live with the job placement decision and experience the consequences that may occur.

INCREASING FAMILY SUPPORT

Make Multiple Home Visits

> Molly was referred by her special education teacher for supported employment services. The employment specialist initiated assessment activities by scheduling an appointment with Molly's mother. When the employment specialist arrived, Molly's mother was not at home. Several other visits were also missed, and numerous telephone calls were frequently not returned. The teacher told the employment specialist that Molly's mother was not supportive or interested in her daughter's schooling and never showed up for parent-teacher meetings. The employment specialist decided to try one more time and just dropped in on the mother at home one evening. Molly's mother was very receptive and expressed a great deal of support for Molly going to work. In fact, several ideas for job leads were generated, and the mother told the employment specialist to drop by any time to make additional arrangements for Molly to start work.
>
> Molly's mother had been labeled as uncooperative and not supportive of her daughter's future. Repeated home visits proved just the opposite and revealed the underlying factors motivating the mother's behavior. Molly's mother was a single parent raising five children, including one who was severely mentally retarded and one who had severe cerebral palsy. She was often too busy or tired to meet with professionals and had too many other priorities to remember meeting times or return phone calls. In addition, Molly's mother stated that she wanted her daughter to work but was repeatedly told by Molly's teachers that employment was not a realistic goal, and she was often expected to implement time-consuming school programs at home.

As indicated by the above case study, first impressions are not always what they seem. It is important to make frequent contacts with the family to get a true indication of their needs and desires. Past experiences with professionals as well as the present family situation can influence the behavior and expectations of family members. Repeated visits can give families a chance to receive information and assistance and to express their feelings at times that are most suitable for them.

Have Frequent Telephone Contact

The employment specialist was in the process of completing consumer assessment and job development activities for Billy. She had met with Billy's mother and father on two occasions and found them to be interested, but cautious in pursuing supported employment. The employment specialist shared information about concerns typically expressed by parents and gave them her home and office numbers to call if they had any questions. The employment specialist had two telephone messages at work the next day from Billy's father. She returned his calls and answered his questions about safety and supervision at the job site. That night Billy's mother called and asked how Billy would be received by other co-workers, and if he would be exposed to teasing. Billy's mother or father continued to call the employment specialist with questions at least once every day or evening.

The employment specialist decided the parents had been given sufficient information and began avoiding their calls. In fact, out of fear that the parents were overprotective and would jeopardize any employment situation, she and her supervisor were considering not placing Billy into a job. In a casual conversation with Billy's case manager, the employment specialist found out that Billy had been sexually abused at camp several years ago, and the parents had not allowed him to be alone with other people or professionals since then. The case manager was surprised to hear they were even considering employment and was sure a trusting relationship with the employment specialist was critical before the family would allow Billy to go to work.

Family members have a long history of experiences and opinions that they bring into the supported employment process. Frequent communication with the employment specialist gives the family multiple opportunities to share information or ask questions as they come to mind. Families also have a chance to get to know the employment specialist and establish trust and confidence, laying the foundation for an open, honest relationship.

Communicate in a Way the Family Understands

During his school transition meeting, supported employment was identified as being the appropriate vocational goal for Reggie. The rehabilitation counselor was assigned the responsibility of completing the necessary paperwork to receive employment services. He wrote a letter to Reggie's mother asking her to come to his office to sign papers and discuss service arrangements. No response was received, so the rehabilitation counselor sent another letter. Since Reggie's family had no telephone, several additional letters were sent, all with no response. The rehabilitation counselor expressed concern about the family's support in the follow-up transition meeting and suggested that supported employment was not an appropriate placement option for Reggie. Reggie continued to tell meeting participants that he and his mother were interested in his opportunity for employment.

The employment specialist who attended Reggie's meeting decided to visit Reggie's mother at her home. When he arrived, the mother seemed to be extremely excited about discussing employment for Reggie. She said Reggie had told her that he was going to work, and she was anxiously waiting for someone to come talk with her. The employment specialist asked about the letters, and the mother replied that she had received some mail but didn't know what it was. Further discussion revealed that Reggie's mother did not know how to read and did not have anyone around that could help by reading the letters to her. The employment specialist discussed everything with the mother and contacted the rehabilitation counselor, explaining the need to take the papers over in person to be signed.

Families have different lifestyles and cultures that can affect the way they relate to and respond to communication with professionals. It is a mistake to assume that all families are the same or that all professionals and family members will share the same background and values. Every effort should be made to determine the level of communication understood or desired by the family and to provide information in a way that accommodates those needs. Equally important is providing a variety of sources of information so that families can learn what is important and become empowered to make choices.

Share Information and Resources

Alice's family had always felt she would be employed one day and were very excited when a staff person from the sheltered workshop told them she was a candidate for their new supported employment program. This sounded like the opportunity for community participation and security for Alice's future that they were concerned about as they got older. The employment specialist met with Alice's family in the evening several times and explained supported employment. She was surprised when the mother and father didn't have any questions for her and couldn't think of any concerns that the employment specialist could help with. Several job development ideas were generated and one "perfect" position was identified.

The employment specialist contacted Alice's parents and said she had found a job just like the one they had asked for, and the position was available immediately. When the employment specialist visited the family at home that night to make the final arrangements, she could not believe the parents' reluctance. They said they didn't know if Alice could perform the job alone and expressed concern over what would happen to her on the public bus. The parents also expressed skepticism about employment because Alice depended so much on her Supplemental Security Income (SSI) check and couldn't afford to lose it. The employment specialist realized she had moved too fast and had not adequately prepared the family for employment by not responding to their unspoken fears.

Whether or not supported employment is a new concept, it is likely family members will need to hear about this type of service delivery on several occasions in order to understand what it means and what impact it will have on them. It should not automatically be assumed that a lack of questions or doubts by family members indicates unquestioning support. Often, concerns do not surface until family members develop a knowledge base with which to formulate questions or until placement into employment becomes a reality. Experience in providing supported employment services will increase an employment specialist's skills at "reading" family members and proactively addressing their concerns.

Arrange Linkage with Other Families and Available Supports

Cindy was very happy to be back to work again after years of hospitalizations and unemployment. The employment specialist was thrilled that, after only two weeks of trainer intervention, Cindy learned her job so quickly. Cindy seemed to really enjoy her work and the employer thought she was doing a wonderful job. The employment specialist was extremely surprised to receive a phone call from Cindy's employer only a few months after Cindy had been on the job, telling her that Cindy was going to be fired for not showing up at work. The employment specialist visited Cindy at home and was told that Cindy no longer wanted to work.

Cindy, her husband, and the employment specialist talked at length about her job and their day-to-day activities. During the conversation, the husband mentioned that he didn't like driving Cindy to work every day and missed having his dinner fixed every night. Cindy revealed her feelings of loneliness and her fear that her illness would surface and jeopardize her job. Neither seemed to realize that Cindy's return to work would be so disruptive to their lives. In addition, both had been so involved with Cindy's illness for such a long period of time that they had lost touch with their friends and relatives and never heard from them any more.

During the placement process and ongoing support services while employed, other families who have received supported employment services can be a useful source of information for family members and a valuable resource for support. Often, a member of another family who has similar experiences will have much more credibility with the family receiving services than the employment specialist, and if at all possible, arrangements for networking should be made. Identification of family issues and problems and linkage with community supports can assist families with adjusting to the demands that may result due to the change in employment status for the family member with a disability.

SUMMARY

When a family is interested and supportive of employment for their family member with a disability, the employment specialist's job is made much easier. The family can offer valuable information to assist with identifying a good job match and with developing interventions to make the placement successful. In addition, the family can help by providing instruction or reinforcement to support job-site training efforts and by monitoring or assisting with issues related to the individual's ongoing employment. Family support is not a luxury, but rather, a critical element of the entire supported employment process.

For a number of reasons, a family may not share the employment specialist's enthusiasm for employment or may be reluctant to offer any assistance. A review of the dynamics of the family, the type of information provided, the manner in which it was presented, and the communication skills of the employment specialist can provide insight into the factors that may be influencing the family's behavior. For example, does the family understand what supported employment is? Is the family experiencing personal problems, making concentration on employment difficult at this time? Or, does the employment specialist's attitude send a message that the family's input is not important?

A critical role of the employment specialist is communicating with family members and encouraging their active involvement in the decision process. This begins with the initial visit and continues during job identification, job placement, job-site training, and ongoing follow-along. Showing respect, demonstrating good interpersonal skills, accommodating the family's schedule, personalizing the relationship, sharing relevant information, being aware of one's own attitudes, and listening to what the family has to say are important strategies for increasing family support. Failure to make every attempt to gain family support and involvement in the job identification process can seriously jeopardize the future success of the individual's employment situation.

6

Consumer Assessment, Job Development, and Job Placement

Wendy S. Parent

Pam Sherron

Christine Groah

The relationship between quality of work life, job satisfaction, and overall quality of life for individuals who are not disabled has been clearly documented in the literature (Henne and Locke 1985; Moseley 1988; Rice, McFarlin, Hunt, and Near 1985; Rosenthal 1989). The concept of quality of work life first began in the 1960s with General Motors and the United Auto Workers, to describe worker satisfaction and to increase employee involvement in matters related to the condition of their working lives (Goode 1990). As increasing numbers of individuals with severe disabilities began entering the work force, the importance of quality of work life for personal satisfaction and employment success gained recognition as a critical element of service delivery. A National Conference on Quality of Life for Persons with Disabilities, conducted in 1988, reported the following principles regarding quality of work life for individuals with disabilities (Kiernan and Knutson 1990,110). First, quality of work life is the same for people with and without disabilities. Second, quality of work life is a matter of consumer rather than professional definition. Third, quality of work life is a social phenomenon and primarily a product of interactions with others.

Quality of work life is related to the interaction between the characteristics of the work place and the needs and preferences of the individual. Kiernan and Knutson (1990) propose the following definition of quality of work life:

> Quality of work life is an individual's interpretation of his/her role in the workplace and the interaction of that role with the expectations of others.

The quality of one's work life is individually determined, designed, and evaluated. A quality work life means something different to each and every individual and is likely to vary according to the individual's age, career stage, and/or position in the industry (p. 102).

An individual considers a variety of factors when judging whether a job is good or bad, and the importance of each of these factors will vary depending upon the value placed upon each characteristic (Rosenthal 1989). These factors include job duties, working conditions, job satisfaction, period of work, job status, and job security. It is assumed that over time these expectations and attitudes are going to change for the individual and the job. This may be particularly significant for individuals in supported employment, who typically have had a limited or disrupted work history and possibly no prior work experience from which to formulate expectations or to judge quality and satisfaction.

The emphasis on worker involvement in decision making and problem solving for quality of work life indicates that individuals with disabilities need to be involved in deciding where they want to work and the type of job they would like to have if they are going to experience satisfaction with their work (Kiernan and Knutson 1990). Autonomy and control in the development and selection of jobs has been reported to be a critical factor for employment success (Moseley 1988). It is assumed that most individuals like certain aspects of a job more than others and, when selecting a job, will trade off one attribute for another, such as wages versus nonmonetary benefits (Rosenthal 1989). Job satisfaction is considered to result "from the perception that one's job fulfills or allows the fulfillment of one's job values" (Henne and Locke 1985, 222). A careful match between the characteristics of the individual and the environmental attributes of a job is essential for personal satisfaction and employment success (Schalock and Jensen 1986). It is critical for individuals with disabilities to be empowered to make job placement choices if they are going to experience personal satisfaction with their work.

The purpose of this chapter is to describe the job placement process for individuals with disabilities who are receiving supported employment services. First, the process of assessing an individual's skills, interests, and support needs will be discussed. Second, job development strategies for identifying community employment opportunities will be presented. Third, strategies to assist employment specialists with making a good consumer-job match will be described. Finally, activities to be completed for job placement and the first day of work will be reviewed.

CONSUMER ASSESSMENT

During the consumer assessment process, the abilities, preferences, and needs of a consumer are identified so that the characteristics of the individual can be matched to the skill requirements, social dynamics, and available supports of a job. The purpose of consumer assessment is to find out as much information about an individual as possible so that the employment specialist can assist him or her with choosing a job that will be the most satisfying. Information is obtained concerning the individual's vocational interests, adaptive behaviors, parent/family attitudes, transportation possibilities, work skills, social interests, and other relevant factors. It is important to remember that consumer assessment is not conducted to exclude individuals from supported employment opportunities. Rather, useful information is identified that will help the employment specialist best match an individual to a specific job.

Consumer assessment utilizes a functional or ecological assessment approach that focuses on the individual, the job, and the ecology of the workplace (Menchetti and Udvari-Solner 1990). An individual's functional work skills and support needs are interpreted in the context of real job demands rather than a preestablished score or criteria, as is typically done with standardized evaluations, such as a Valpar Work Sample Series or Wechsler Intelligence Test. For example, an individual who scores low on the Valpar may be considered unemployable and receive a recommendation for vocational training to improve work performance. A major problem with this interpretation is that the skills that the standardized test is measuring are not necessarily those that are required to perform a particular job. An individual who cannot sort shapes, discriminate sizes, or coordinate assembly tasks on the Valpar may be very good at a dishwashing, janitorial, micrographics, or landscaping job, whose skill requirements are quite different.

Consumer assessment activities must be conducted at the same time as job development so that placement decisions can be based upon the requirements of local community businesses (Wehman, Wood, Everson, Goodwyn, and Conley 1988). The characteristics of an individual are documented and interpreted in objective terms that can be matched to real-job characteristics. For example, a description that an individual works "too slowly to be competitively employed" is difficult to interpret when making job matching decisions due to the variability in production standards across jobs. Consider the difference in the speed requirements of a dishwashing job in a busy restaurant with a library book-shelving position that emphasizes quality over quantity. Additionally, the production rates of different settings of the same type of job will vary, such as that for a fast-food restaurant versus an elegant, French restaurant.

Completing Assessment Activities

During consumer assessment, an employment specialist is responsible for a variety of activities aimed at gaining a general indication of the individual's work characteristics as well as addressing the individual's and family's concerns. Differing amounts of information from multiple sources are likely to be obtained for each individual. A description of the type of information that may be gathered and possible resources for obtaining it are provided in Table 6.1. The key is to utilize all of the relevant sources that are available to avoid overlooking an important fac-

Table 6.1

Types of Information	Possible Resources
Medical • medical conditions • medications • sensory/perceptual abilities *NOTE - If the consumer is on medication, it is imperative for the employment specialist to know the effects of the medication and possible signs of noncompliance.	• medical records • interview with physician or physiatrist (medical doctor that specializes in rehabilitation) • hospital reports • consumer/family interview
Psychological • mental health • depression • cognitive abilities *NOTE-If the consumer has a diagnosis, it will be important to know the symptoms of the illness and how it may be displayed.	• psychological evaluations • psychiatric hospital reports • mental health services records • consumer/family interview
Substance Abuse • substances used • frequency of use	• vocational rehabilitation records • interviews with family • interviews with consumer
Education and Training • grade completed • post-secondary/college experience • vocational training	• education/rehabilitation records • consumer/family interview • interview with teachers
Employment • work history (includes paid and volunteer, pre- and post-onset of disability)	• Social Security Administration • education/rehabilitation records • interviews with past employers • consumer/family interview
Support Systems • parent/family attitudes • case management • friends/relative support	• vocational rehabilitation records • parent/family interview • home visit • case management needs assessment

Table 6.1 *(continued)*

Types of Information	*Possible Resources*
Abilities • work skills • personal skills • mobility • community functioning	• observation in multiple environments • consumer interview • situational assessment • vocational evaluations/training records • neuropsychological evaluations
Interests • career choices • work preferences • social preferences • hobbies, desired activities	• consumer interview • parent/family interview • vocational rehabilitation records • education/vocational training records • previous employment records; i.e., reasons for separation • visit employment sites, job-site fairs • newspaper (have consumer circle or cut out job advertisements in paper)
Psychosocial Issues • social skills • communication skills • unusual behaviors	• observation • visit consumer in diverse settings and observe how he/she behaves • parents/family interview
Effects on Current Lifestyle • financial/medical benefits • housing situation	• Social Security Records • housing officials • case management assessment
Expectations • wages, benefits, hours, location • type of work and setting	• consumer interview • parent/family interview
Transportation • available options • distance willing to travel • willingness of family or neighbors to transport *NOTE - Naturally, this will be the key in defining the area for job development activities.	• consumer interview • parent/family interview • Department of Transportation; i.e., organized car-pooling • scope neighborhood for bus routes • public and private providers; i.e., bus, taxi, specialized transportation

tor that would affect job placement. When conducting consumer assessment activities the employment specialist's responsibilities include (1) conducting interviews, (2) observing in multiple environments, (3) interpreting formal records, (4) completing situational assessments, and (5) communicating with family members. The degree and intensity to which these activities are performed may vary with different individuals depending upon their past experiences, present situation, and severity of disability.

Conducting Interviews

It is important to interview the individual with a disability to find out his or her preferences and expectations. What better way to find out what an individual likes or dislikes than to ask him or her yourself? In addition, the employment specialist and individual can begin to develop a rapport during in-person and telephone interactions, which can lay the foundation for the more intense relationship that follows.

Interviewing an individual with a severe disability may present challenges that make it difficult to determine if the information gathered truly reflects the individual's feelings. Perhaps the individual does not understand the question or may answer yes to everything or may try to respond in a way that he or she feels the employment specialist expects. The use of multiple types of question formats can increase the likelihood that valid responses are obtained. These include open-ended questions (e.g., What kind of work do you like to do?), multiple choice questions (e.g., What hours do you prefer to work? In the morning, afternoon, or night?) either-or questions (e.g., Would you like to work close by other people or in an area where you are alone?), and yes-no questions (e.g., Do you like emptying the trash at home?). In addition, question formats should be alternated (i.e., use different types of questions throughout the interview), reversed (i.e., ask the question again in a way that presents the opposite scenario), and repeated more than one time (i.e., ask the question again at a different time during the interview). Additional techniques for conducting effective interviews with individuals who have a disability are located in Table 6.2.

The interview is also a good time to identify other persons in the individual's life who could share useful information and to obtain consent to contact them. Talking with the many people who know the individual, either personally or professionally, can provide valuable insight into the individual's typical behaviors and characteristics. For example, family members can tell you what the individual does around the house, the rehabilitation counselor can discuss referral and evaluation information, and the day program staff can relay current training or instructional activities. Depending upon the individual's present and past experiences, additional persons may be appropriate to contact. These can include teachers, employers, siblings, friends, medical personnel, or other service providers.

It is not uncommon for the person interviewed to withhold information out of fear that disclosure will cause the individual to be denied services. For example,

Table 6.2 Techniques for Interviewing Individuals with Disabilities

---

- Select a location where the individual feels comfortable and relaxed.
- Explain the purpose for meeting with the individual in a manner that he or she understands.
- Take time to get acquainted with each other before beginning the actual interview.
- Use a variety of question formats throughout the interview.
- Actively listen to what the individual is telling you.
- Observe the individual's behavior for unspoken messages and preferences.
- Repeat the interview at another time in a different location.

---

the fact that an individual frequently displayed aggressive behaviors was not told to the employment specialist during assessment because the teacher and family member wanted the individual to go to work. Unfortunately, the individual was terminated shortly after placement following an incident where he pulled a knife on co-workers. If the information had been made available, this might have been avoided by matching the individual to another job or implementing a behavioral intervention program immediately upon placement. It is important for the employment specialist to explain the supported employment model during the interview and to provide assurance that the information given will not be used to screen the individual out of employment.

Observing in Multiple Environments

The best way to determine how an individual functions is to actually observe him or her performing an activity. For example, instead of asking if the individual can add or subtract, provide a simple problem for him or her to perform and increase the complexity depending upon his or her skill level. Similarly, asking the individual to lift up a trash can or to tell the present time will provide a more accurate assessment than asking how strong they are or if they know how to tell time.

It is important to observe the individual in a variety of settings since everyone tends to act differently depending upon the environment they are in. For example, someone may yell and scream at school, sit quietly and watch television at home, wander in the workshop, or interact appropriately in the community. Observing the individual in only one environment can give a very distorted and unfair perception of the individual's actual skills and behaviors. Perhaps the individual is bored in one setting, doesn't like the people in another, or enjoys the activities in yet another. This information regarding an individual's likes and dislikes can be extremely valuable during job matching and may not be revealed during an interview situation. If the individual does not participate in many different environments, the employment specialist should create them. For example, take him or her out to lunch, get together somewhere in the community, or meet at your office to gain an indication of how the individual functions in the community, with other people, and in new situations.

Interpreting Formal Records

For many individuals referred for supported employment, formal records will be the primary source of information available. After all, IQ scores, performance on standardized tests, and workshop production rates are probably the main reason why the majority of individuals referred for supported employment services were at one time considered unemployable. While these records can help provide an overall profile of the individual, it is important to consider the nature of the evaluation and the context in which it was conducted. The key is to extrapolate relevant information without being biased by outdated or inappropriate interpretations.

The number and types of records available for each individual will vary depending upon his or her history and services received. Educational reports can provide a description of the individual's school curriculum, level of performance, extracurricular experiences, and effective training strategies. Vocational records can inform the employment specialist of the individual's previous work experiences, training programs, work performance, and outcome data. An individual's personal history, family relations, life experiences, and social interests can be gleaned from social reports. Psychological records may provide information about the individual's adaptive behaviors, cognitive abilities, mental health status, and the behavioral manifestations of the condition. Medical conditions, physical limitations, medications, and sensory abilities can be described in medical records, including doctor's reports, hospital discharge summaries, and medical evaluations. Other types of records that may be useful for a particular individual include those from an occupational, physical, or speech therapist; rehabilitation engineer; case manager; dietician or nutritionist; and recreational therapist.

Completing Situational Assessments

Situational assessments can be useful if more information is needed about an individual or for clarification of conflicting information that has been obtained. A situational assessment provides a person with a severe disability with the opportunity to perform job tasks in real work environments (Moon, Inge, Wehman, Brooke, and Barcus 1990). Usually a situational assessment is conducted for a four-hour period in three different jobs in the community. For scheduling purposes, it is often easier to conduct situational assessments at an employment site that has more than one type of job typically found in a locality, such as a hospital, hotel, or university.

A situational assessment can provide valuable information that will assist the employment specialist with identifying potential job matches. Actual performance in a job with appropriate training and support is the best predictor of an individual's performance in a supported employment situation (Parker, Szymanski, and Hanley-Maxwell 1989). Observing an individual perform real work in multiple environments will provide an indication of the individual's work characteristics, interests, skills, abilities, and training needs. Additional information about the individual's independent living and social skills can be obtained by also scheduling a break in the employee break area, cafeteria, or local restaurant, before or after the work period.

Communicating with Parents/Family Members

During the assessment process, it is important to meet with family members to address their questions and concerns regarding supported employment. For many of the parents or family members, the visit with the employment specialist may be their first introduction to supported employment or, maybe, competitive employment at all. Often several visits may be necessary to adequately explain the process and to gain their support. Important issues that frequently cause concern include transportation, social security and medical benefits, safety, co-worker and public reactions, employment specialist's role, type of work, and long-term support availability. Actively listening, providing accurate and honest information, and encouraging ongoing involvement are the best ways to facilitate family support. For some issues, such as Social Security, this may mean arranging a meeting with another information source, while others, such as service availability, may mean honestly stating that funds are available for three years and beyond that is uncertain. A more detailed discussion of the family's role and how to work with members effectively is provided in Chapter 5.

Summarizing Assessment Information

The information gathered during consumer assessment is summarized into a useable format for making job placement decisions. It is recommended that a form similar to the Consumer Screening Form be used to synthesize assessment information (a copy of this form is located in Appendix A). On the Consumer Screening Form, the individual is rated on 27 characteristics, ranging from availability and transportation to physical strength to unusual behavior. Extra space on the form for comments provides the employment specialist with room to record specific information or related observations. Synthesizing information on the Consumer Screening Form can assist the employment specialist with focusing job development efforts on those types of jobs that may be appropriate for this individual.

Summarizing assessment information gathered from a number of sources into one behavioral characteristic can sometimes be difficult, particularly if each interview and observation paints a different picture of the individual. For example, the mother may say the individual works slowly, while the teacher says he or she works at a moderate rate with frequent prompts, and the situational assessment may reveal a fast work-rate in the laundry room and a slow work-rate with multiple maladaptive behaviors in the stock room. It is likely that the employment specialist will have a general feeling regarding the individual's skills based upon all of the information gathered during the entire assessment process.

When in doubt, it is recommended that more information be obtained or that the descriptor at the lower end of the continuum be chosen, with a specific explanation added in the comment section. For example, if the individual waits for directions on all tasks except for delivering the trays, it would be best to check "waits for directions" for initiation/motivation (question 14) and keep in mind that directions may not be required on certain tasks, perhaps those that the individual enjoys or has mastered. The opposite response "always seeks work", to account for the individual's independence with delivering trays, is likely to result in longer training time and possibly termination if placement is made in a job where independently seeking work is critical for work performance. The information recorded on the Consumer Screening Form will later be used to assess the compatibility between the characteristics of the individual and the requirements of specific jobs identified when conducting job development activities.

JOB DEVELOPMENT

As employment specialists collect and study consumer assessment information, they are involved, simultaneously, in job development. Job development is the process of identifying and assessing appropriate employment opportunities in the business community for individuals with severe disabilities. It consists of four primary activities (1) conducting a community job market screening, (2) developing a marketing strategy, (3) making specific employer contact, and (4) completing a job analysis.

Completing a Job Market Screening

While some individuals referred for supported employment services will have established educational and work histories prior to encountering disabling conditions, other individuals may have little or no exposure to the world of work, due to limitations imposed by developmental disabilities. Consequently, it is important to recognize the diversity in interests, experiences, and abilities of individuals referred for supported employment services. Conducting a community job market screening allows employment specialists to investigate and make contacts in a cross section of industries and positions within a business community, with the eventual goal of meeting the needs of both consumers and employers. In addition, taking a close look at current and anticipated hiring trends in the business community at large will help prevent employment specialists from developing a mind set in which only some industries, such as food service, are considered as having potential for persons with disabilities.

Information gathering and the identification of possible employment opportunities, *rather than securing a job placement*, are the goals of a community job market screening. This process is especially helpful for employment specialists who are unfamiliar with a geographic area, are involved in implementing a new program, or are expanding to serve a different disability group. Since hiring trends change over time, particularly in high-growth areas, supported employment staff may want to update their screening every six to twelve months to keep abreast of new developments. Suggestions for completing a job market screening are located in Table 6.3. The Community Job Market Screening Form (a sample form is located in Appendix B) can be used to record information on types of work available and companies to be contacted.

Since the community job market screening is a preliminary step to actually contacting employers for job placement opportunities, employment specialists should keep in mind the importance of being professional and making a good first impression. During this stage of job development, an employer's interests may be piqued as a result of positive interactions with an enthusiastic employment specialist. In addition, literature on supported employment that is provided to an employer in a non-threatening way (Remember, the purpose is to gather information, not specifically seek a job!) can be a positive reminder of the employment specialist's visit.

Table 6.3   Helpful Hints for Conducting a Community Job Market Screening

- Visit, and perhaps join, the local Chamber of Commerce and other civic organizations in order to learn about area businesses and to meet employers.
- Establish a job networking system with rehabilitation personnel from other agencies.
- Check the state employment commission or college placement offices for job listings.
- Keep an eye on the business section of the local newspaper for articles on new and existing businesses as well as on hiring trends.
- Network with family members and friends to obtain information and referral to employers.
- Identify companies in the yellow pages and newspaper classified ads that look interesting and schedule an appointment for a tour, stressing that you are seeking information. During the visit, find out what types of positions exist, what the job duties are, and which positions are difficult to fill.
- Always send a thank-you letter to employers you have visited or who have been helpful in providing assistance.

Developing a Marketing Strategy

Information collected during the community job market screening can be used by supported employment program staff to develop a marketing plan that fits the needs of the program as well as the needs of consumers, employers, and funding sources. For example, a program located in a small, tight-knit community, where coal mining is the predominant industry, will probably have a much different approach to marketing than a program that operates in a large, metropolitan area, where a wide range of government jobs is typically available. Table 6.4 outlines the general and optional components to be included in a marketing plan. Obviously, the components of a program's marketing strategy need to be updated and fine-tuned periodically to reflect changes in the business community, the funding sources, or the provision of services. For example, a service provider may begin serving persons with traumatic brain injury and will need to make this known in the community.

Making Specific Employer Contact

With a marketing strategy in place, employment specialists are ready to contact employers in order to identify job vacancies for specific clients. It should be emphasized that a traditional approach to job development, which advises that an available job be matched to consumers in a program's referral pool, is not necessarily the best approach to apply to all persons with disabilities. The staff from one program, for example, spent numerous hours developing a job at a publishing

Table 6.4   Components of a Supported Employment Marketing Program

- An attractive brochure, which explains supported employment services, to be given out to employers.
- Individual business cards that identify the name of the employment specialist and the program, the mailing address, and the telephone number.
- Good quality letterhead and envelopes with the program's name and logo.
- A program name and logo that conveys a clear and positive image of the supported employment service.
- Training and simulated exercises for employment specialists on how to deliver an effective presentation to employers.

Optional elements that may be included:

- Newspaper clippings, journal articles, or other relevant literature describing supported employment placements in businesses.
- Presentations by supported employment program staff to professional and civic organizations.
- Referrals to other potential employers by employers who have used supported employment services or hired workers with disabilities.

company only to determine later that none of the consumers in the program's referral pool had the interest or ability to perform such work. Job development efforts that focus on developing jobs to meet the needs of consumers are likely to improve job retention in the long-run.

Identifying Job Vacancies

Job leads are often identified in the classified section of the newspaper, the yellow pages of the telephone book, or through personal friends and past employment experiences. Additional sources that may be used to locate job opportunities are listed in Table 6.5. For some consumers, utilizing these sources may frequently not yield appropriate job vacancies, due to the very specific nature of an individual's interests, abilities, or needs. In such instances, it can be useful to identify and to work with employers who are willing to negotiate job responsibilities or even create a new job to meet a consumer's needs. For example, a building and grounds maintenance position at a large toy store was identified by program staff for an individual with interest and experience in plumbing and general repair. One of the job duties for this position, however, involved changing light bulbs in a 50-foot-high ceiling. Because the individual being considered for the position had an unsteady gait and balance deficits, the job coach successfully negotiated with the employer to eliminate that job duty.

Making Initial Contact

Prior to making contact with an employer regarding a job opening, job developers should determine, if possible, *who* within the company has the power to hire for the position being investigated and direct all communication to that person. Otherwise, job developers run the risk of being screened out by secretaries, personnel assistants or, at the least, may waste valuable time speaking to someone who cannot provide the desired information.

Table 6.5   Resources for Locating Job Development Leads

- Classified ads
- Job hotlines
- Government listings
- Career planning and placement offices
- State employment commissions
- Personal contacts
- Networking with other agencies
- Employer referrals
- "Help wanted" signs posted in businesses
- Job bulletins distributed by personnel offices
- Employers contacted during community job market screening

Table 6.6   Helpful Hints for Contacting Employers by Telephone

---

- Experiment with different approaches until you find one you are comfortable using–then practice, practice, practice (caution: you want it smooth, not canned!).
- Make calls in a quiet office away from distractions (music, talking, or laughing in the background during a phone call sounds unprofessional).
- Have a specific purpose for calling and be clear about communicating that purpose.
- Be honest, but don't tell the employer more than is necessary to get the appointment.

Telephone contact   When contacting the appropriate company representative by telephone, job developers should identify themselves, their program, and their interest in obtaining information about the company's job opening (i.e., job responsibilities, skill requirements, pay rate, hours, location, benefits, etc.). If the position sounds as if it may match a consumer in the referral pool, job developers should *briefly* describe their program and ask to arrange an appointment with the employer in order to explain the program in more detail and to view the job being performed. Guidelines on how to conduct a telephone contact with an employer are described in Table 6.6. Regardless of the appropriateness of the position or the employer's response, log all information on a form, such as the Employer Contact Sheet, for future reference (a sample form is located in Appendix C).

Cold-calls   This method, which typically involves a visit or telephone call without any knowledge that a job opening exists, can often be an informal way of gaining information about businesses. A drop-in visit has the obvious advantage of enabling the job developer to get his or her "foot in the door," however, job developers should be sensitive to the time constraints placed on an employer who has not previously set aside time for such a visit. More than a few job openings have been found by talking to a restaurant manager while having dinner and setting up an appointment for another time. In most cases, job developers utilizing a cold-call method will want to schedule an appointment to meet with the employer at a later date if the job site sounds or looks promising. However, if the employer is interested and has the time, the employment specialist's presentation should be made on the spot.

Letters of introduction   An alternate method of contacting employers is to send a letter, along with the program brochure, introducing the supported employment program. This is followed by a telephone call to set up an appointment. Employers with small companies may respond more to letters of introduction than employers with large companies, who are often inundated with mail.

Removing the fear   Employment specialists often consider contacting employers for job development as their least favorite activity associated with supported employment. Preparation and practice can help to ease any feelings of trepidation that an employment specialist may have. One strategy for reducing anxiety is to rehearse a presentation with another employment specialist or with other employers in the community. For example, if a business is identified that offers little potential for appropriate job leads, the employment specialist may choose to contact the employer and give his or her presentation a try. The employer's response or feedback from another employment specialist who accompanies the job developer are the best ways to evaluate and modify a presentation to make it more effective for the next contact. Additional hints to help make the job development process less intimidating are listed in Table 6.7. It is important to remember that employer contacts get easier and better with practice and experience.

Employer Presentation   When meeting with a representative of the business community, an obvious consideration is how to dress. While employment specialists are accustomed to adapting their dress and personal appearance to match the requirements of the work environment during job-site training, the issue of dress is often overlooked during the critical activity of job development. It cannot be overemphasized that employment specialists should consider what type of message they want to convey to the employer and choose their clothes accordingly. An employment specialist may dress differently when meeting the personnel director of a Fortune 500 company than when meeting with a fork-lift-operator supervisor in a large warehouse. However, a good rule of thumb is: *always dress professionally*. An employment specialist can dress up or down a bit, but it is important to remember that appearance tells the employer that the employment specialist is serious about what he or she does and that the services and people represented are worthwhile. Research has shown that people respond largely to nonverbal cues and appearance and less to what someone actually says.

In addition, preparing for an employer presentation involves collecting and organizing any props or materials that are necessary for communicating effectively with an employer. These may include business cards, program brochures, newspaper clippings on supported employment, Employer Contact Sheet, and Employer Interview Form (located in Appendix D). It goes without saying that it is important to be on time for an appointment. If something happens to prevent punctuality, it is a good idea to call the employer and give him or her the option of rescheduling.

Employment specialists will develop unique styles, expertise, and preferences for approaches that are most effective for them. The following guidelines provide a framework for conducting a presentation to an employer; this should be adapted to fit the needs of the agency, the individual employment specialist, and the employer being visited.

Table 6.7   Strategies to Help Take the Fear Out of Job Development

- Pair inexperienced job developers with more seasoned individuals during employer presentations in order to provide opportunities for modeling and feedback.
- Role play with a co-worker or write a script in preparation for making an employer contact. If possible, videotape yourself or other job developers making simulated employer contacts. Provide constructive criticism for each other.
- Find out as much as possible about the employer prior to making contact (information can be obtained from the Chamber of Commerce, employment commission, Who's Who listings, the company's public relation's department, etc.).
- Anticipate the worst possible responses that you might get from an employer, the likelihood that each will occur, and what your response would be. For example, the employer could insult you (unlikely to occur), the employer could say no (might occur), or the employer might hang up on you (probably won't occur).
- Set aside a block of time each day to make your calls when you typically feel most energetic and enthusiastic. If you have an off-day, take a break and do some paperwork.
- Remember that the first employer contact is the hardest; it gets easier with time, experience and success!
- The bottom line in job development is: If employer contacts are not made, both in terms of quantity and quality, then placements will not occur.

Establish rapport   In order to break the ice during the first few minutes of an employer interview, engage the employer in a few moments of "small talk", prior to delivering the actual presentation. Diplomas, plaques, photographs, or even the weather can serve as the topic of some light conversation and also lay the groundwork for getting to know the employer. However, if the employer appears ready to "get down to business", the employment specialist should take the cue and move on to the purpose of the visit.

Introduce the agency   Establish the credibility of your program by providing information about your agency's mission and role as a supported employment provider, the length of time your agency has been providing services, and past and present populations of individuals served. In addition, explain to the employer how your agency fits into the continuum of services for someone with a disability so that he or she can see the "big picture".

Identify the population   Possibly one of the most important aspects of delivering a presentation to employers is to describe persons with disabilities in realistic but nonstigmatizing terms. Unfortunately, some employers conceptualize someone with a severe disability as being "crazy" or "dumb", so it is critical to consider how to counter these steps with both accuracy and diplomacy. Several guidelines to assist with introducing the concept of disability during an employer presentation are provided in Table 6.8.

Explain the supported employment model   Some employers will have been contacted by other supported employment providers or rehabilitation agencies, so it is a good idea to find out what an employer may already know about supported employment. For employers who are not familiar with supported employment, employment specialists may want to use their program brochure as a visual aid while reviewing the components of the model. Some points to include in the explanation of each component of the supported employment model are described in Table 6.9.

Appeal to vested interests   Inform the employer of any financial incentives, such as tax deductions, that may be available to businesses hiring persons with disabilities. In addition, be sure to mention that research indicates that workers with disabilities are, as a group, motivated, dependable, and tend to stay in jobs longer than nondisabled workers (Parent and Everson 1986).

Wrap-up   Answer any questions the employer has prior to closing the presentation. An indication of the employer's interest in working with the program can be

---

Table 6.8   Guidelines for Talking to an Employer About Individuals with Disabilities

- Find out what the employer's perception is of persons with disabilities. In many cases, employers will know someone, personally or even professionally, who has a disabling condition. Connecting with the employer on a personal level based on his/her experience can help prime the employer for the idea of hiring someone with a disability.
- Give brief examples, in functional terms, of impairments that may pertain to the disability group served. Do emphasize, however, that each person is different and, like anyone else, brings a unique combination of experiences, strengths, interests, and support needs to an employment situation.
- Cite placements that the program has made and, if permission has been obtained, provide names of employers who are willing to serve as references to prospective employers. The fact that other employers have "bought into" the concept of supported employment not only makes it safe for prospective employers to do so, but also demonstrates that people with disabilities can work competitively.

Table 6.9   Guidelines for Talking to an Employer About Supported Employment

- *Job Placement*—Explain that a detailed analysis of the requirements of a job is performed during job development; this information is then paired with information gathered about a potential worker's interests, abilities, and support need to determine whether a successful job match can be made. Emphasize that a job placement will not be pursued unless an appropriate candidate for the job opening is identified. Your primary interest is to meet the employer's needs; if you don't, your consumer's job retention will be affected negatively.
- *Job-Site Training*—Establish the role of the employment specialist in accompanying the new employee to the job site, at no cost to the employer, to provide training and support. If applicable, inform the employer that the employment specialist will actually contribute to the completion of job duties while the individual develops the speed and endurance necessary for completing the job. (Be warned that some companies have policies restricting nonemployees from performing unpaid work or are concerned about nonemployees having access to "trade secrets". Also, for some higher-level skilled and professional positions, employment specialists do not have the skills or training necessary for performing the job duties.)
- *Ongoing Assessment and Follow-along*—Explain that the employment specialist begins to fade gradually and systematically from the job site when the individual is able to perform the job independently, to the employer's satisfaction. Stress that the employment specialist continues to monitor the individual's performance for as long as he/she is employed in order to be proactive in addressing any problems or training needs.

---

determined by probing with open-ended questions and diplomacy. At this point, employment specialists need to be prepared to muster all the finesse they can to overcome any concerns or reservations the employer may have.

If the employment specialist had requested the appointment in response to a job opening, he or she may want to complete the Employer Interview Form and the Sequence of Job Duties Form (located in Appendix E) and, if time permits, ask to observe an employee performing the job. It is important to establish guidelines for further communication with the employer before leaving the job site. The meeting should always close with a thank-you, followed by a written thank-you letter, regardless of whether or not the employer expresses interest in the program.

Completing a Job Analysis

If it appears that an appropriate job opening exists, the employment specialist should complete a detailed analysis to gather as much information about the job as possible, including the job requirements, work environment, and social atmosphere. This information can best be obtained by observing an employee performing the same or a similar job, as well as interviewing employees and co-workers. It is important to make sure that a visit to the job site is done at a time that reflects "typical" work routines so that the employment specialist can get an accurate picture of what the job entails. For example, conducting a job analysis at a busy restaurant at 2:00 PM in the afternoon is likely to portray an entirely different image of the work flow than a visit during the lunch or dinner period. In addition, all environments that an individual who works in this position would be required to participate in should be included in the job analysis, such as the employee breakroom; time clock area, or parking lot, if trash removal is one of the job duties. Many jobs are lost after placement due to "surprises" that appear following an imcomplete job analysis.

Employment specialists who are inexperienced or those who are confronted with new or unique job tasks may also want to work the job themselves for a period of time, ranging from several hours to a day or two. In some cases, an employer may be hesitant to allow a nonemployee onto the job site to work. An explanation of the reason, what information the employment specialist needs and reassurance that the employment specialist is covered by the employer's workers' compensation insurance often alleviates concerns.

Characteristics of the job identified during the job analysis can be summarized on a form similar to the Job Screening Form (located in Appendix F). This instrument contains 23 items that have been found to be important factors when considering a suitable candidate for employment, such as work pace, communication requirements, motivation, appearance requirements, and availability of reinforcement.

JOB MATCHING

Once a job opening is identified, the appropriate candidate to fill it must be determined. In some instances, a consumer-specific approach will be utilized, where employment specialists conduct job development activities with one individual in mind. However, more frequently, general job-development activities are conducted, and using consumer assessment and job analysis information, appropriate job openings are matched to an individual in the referral pool. A good job-consumer match is important for job success and worker satisfaction.

Initial Screening

While conducting job development and consumer assessment activities, it is likely that the employment specialist will begin to get an idea of who might be a good candidate for a particular job. Typically, several individuals will initially appear to "stand out" as being a good match, and the person who would be most suited to the position needs to be identified from this group. For example, Fred may like to work around other people, Sally may have transportation arrangements, or Justin may have extensive support needs that a particular job offers. The first step involves conducting a general screening to begin narrowing the number of potential employees for the job. Important factors to consider are outlined in Table 6.10. For example, is the schedule convenient for the individual (evening hours, weekend work)? Is the type of work something that the individual has expressed an interest in doing? It is important to remember that this general comparison is primarily a subjective process, and caution should be used to prevent "screening" someone out of a job due to personal biases or lack of information. If there is any doubt about an individual's appropriateness for a job, more information should be obtained, or he or she should be included in the more detailed matching process to follow.

Staffing Approach

A second strategy that can be used to identify potential job candidates from the pool of referrals is the "staffing" approach, in which all available supported employment staff gather to exchange information about a job and to discuss possible candidates. The job analysis information is distributed and explained by the employment specialist who completed the job analysis; everyone present then brainstorms a list of possible applicants. Next, some individuals may be contacted by phone or presented with information about a possible job lead in order to determine interests and reasons for any reservations that are expressed. Applicants are considered and eliminated based on critical issues until one or two potential candidates for the job are targeted. Characteristics to think about when comparing an individual's compatibility to a job are located in Table 6.11. This process can only be effective if all of the staff are familiar with the consumers. Often, this strategy will make staff aware of "how little" they may actually know regarding an individual, prompting further consumer assessment activities to be conducted.

Job-Worker Compatibility Analysis

Once the number of individuals has been narrowed down with the general screening or staffing approach, the person best-suited for the job can be identified using the Compatibility Analysis (located in Appendix G). This technique can also be useful to validate or confirm the match selected with the staffing approach. The Compatibility Analysis compares consumer information summarized on the Con-

Table 6.10 Considerations for Making a Good Job Match

Job Characteristics	Consumer Characteristics
Job Location/Schedule	Transportation/Availability
Job Requirements	Skills/Abilities/Interests
Type of Work	Work Preferences
Integration Opportunities	Social Preferences
Formal/Informal Supports	Support Needs
Employer Satisfaction	Consumer/Family Satisfaction

sumer Employment Screening Form with the job information recorded on the Job Screening Form. The Compatibility Analysis Form assists with identifying the strengths of an individual in relation to a specific job as well as areas in which the individual may not be a good match for that job. In addition, the Compatibility Analysis provides information on the critical skills needed to perform the job and an indication of the training needs that may be required by each individual. This process does not give a "printout" of which candidate to place into a specific job, however, it can be a useful way of comparing one or several candidates to an available job and an objective way of viewing that information.

Client-Job Compatibility Screening

A new approach to assist employment specialists with making job placement decisions is the Consumer Job Match Program developed by the Rehabilitation Research & Training Center on Supported Employment at Virginia Commonwealth University (Kregel and Banks 1990). This microcomputer-based tool is designed to compare information identified on the Consumer and Job Screening Forms and predict the success of individuals with mental retardation in *specific supported* employment settings. The program enables employment specialists to predict the likelihood that an individual placed into a supported employment position will retain his or her job for one year after placement and the amount of service (intervention hours) that an individual will require during the first three months and twelve months of employment.

The Client-Job Compatibility Screening Instrument was validated on a sample of 512 individuals with mental retardation, who had a mean IQ score of 54. All of the individuals were Supplemental Security Income (SSI) or Social Security Disability Income (SSDI) recipients and worked an average of 25 hours a week, with an average earning of $3.68 per hour. The initial validation results indicate that the program can potentially promote employment retention and reduce the costs of employment services, thereby providing significant benefits for individuals participating in supported employment, for the local agencies providing services, and for state and federal funding agencies. Further development and field-testing is presently being conducted to establish its use for individuals with disability labels other than mental retardation.

JOB PLACEMENT

Job Interview

Once a specific candidate has been identified for a job opening, the employment specialist must contact the individual and ask if he or she is interested in interviewing for the position. The employment specialist may feel a certain job is an appropriate match for a specific consumer, but the person being considered for the job may not be interested. If that happens, it is important to determine *why* the indi-

Table 6.11   Critical Issues to Consider During Job Placement

- **Medical Considerations**

  Is the individual on any medication, and are there side effects? What are they?

- **Interests/Motivation**

  Is there an individual who has specifically expressed an interest in this type of position or employment setting?

  If so, why is the individual interested in the position (e.g., type of work, money, prestige)?

- **Experience, Training, Education**

  Does the individual have previous work experience in the field?

  If an individual has limited work history/experience, does the position serve as a stepping stone to a future job/career direction?

  Does the individual meet the minimum job requirements (e.g., communication skills)?

  What were the reasons for job separation in the past, and will the position place the person at risk for separation?

- **Cognitive Abilities**

  Does the position require that the individual capitalize on his/her abilities?

  Can the job be structured, or is worker judgment necessary?

  Are there compensatory strategies, adaptations, or modifications that will enable the individual to eventually perform job duties independently?

  What are the safety issues?

  Is there a possibility for renegotiation of job duties?

- **Physical Abilities**

  Does the individual have the physical abilities to perform the job?

  If not, are there modifications or adaptations that could be used in order to enable the individual to perform the duties?

  Is there a funding source for modifications/adaptations? Except in the case of severe physical disability, changes most often can be made to the work environment for a nominal fee.

  Are the hours of work in synch with the individual's best hours? Many individuals with disabilities may have sleep disturbances or experience fatigue at certain times of the day.

Note: Lack of stamina or endurance should not rule someone out as a candidate because stamina/endurance will likely increase as the individual works the job. If the individual is lacking in stamina, it may be wise to start out with a part-time position that will allow an increase in work hours over time. Also, remember whenever feasible, it is the role of an employment specialist to assist with the performance of job duties until the individual is at 100% production.

Table 6.11   Critical Issues to Consider During Job Placement *(continued)*

- **Sensory Abilities**

  Does the individual have the visual acumen to perform the job?

  If not, how can it be compensated for?

- **Social Skills**

  Does the individual have the minimal communication skills needed to perform the job?

  What level of social interactions are required, and can the individual respond appropriately? If not, is the individual willing to be trained to respond appropriately?

  If maladaptive behavior is present, will the environment tolerate it or allow time for corrective intervention?

  Will the work environment accommodate unusual behaviors?

- **Financial Status**

  Are the wages and benefits acceptable to the individual?

  How will this particular job affect the individual's current financial status/ medical coverage, housing, etc.?

  Does the employment site offer the opportunity for lateral/upward mobility?

- **Transportation**

  How will the individual get to the place of employment?

  If the individual drives, is he or she willing to travel the distance? Is the car in condition to withstand the travel? Is there an alternate source of transportation if the private vehicle fails?

  If the individual is restricted from driving, is public transportation available?

  Is specialized transportation available?

  Can transportation be arranged with co-workers or neighbors?

  Can transportation be arranged with a person who works on the route to the employment site?

  Can the individual take a taxi to and from work?

  Can the individual walk or ride a bike to and from work?

  Can the individual get involved with a public car-pooling program (i.e., Ride Finders)?

Note: If no travel options are available, the employment specialist may encourage the individual to explore alternative residential options in an area where he or she can get to work. If this is not feasible and all other options have been exhausted, the individual cannot be considered for the job. It should be noted that not knowing how to access or use the transportation system should not prevent an individual from being considered for a job. Travel training can be provided.

Table **6.11**   Critical Issues to Consider During Job Placement *(continued)*

- Support System

   Do significant others support the placement? If not, sabotage due to reasons such as possible fear of losing their role could occur.

- Work Environment

   Does the position allow the individual to be integrated with nondisabled workers?

   How does the supervisor interact with employees? How does the supervisor give feedback?

   What are co-worker interactions like?

   What is the rate of supervisor and co-worker turnover? Does this fact work in favor of the potential placement?

   Why does the employer want to hire individuals with disabilities?

   What are the group dynamics?

   Does the position allow opportunities for the individual to increase his or her self-esteem?

Note: These issues are not presented as an all-inclusive listing or in a hierarchical fashion. What is critical is variable from situation to situation.

vidual is not interested. For example, is it a general fear of going to work, concerns about transportation, or a dislike of certain job duties? It may take patience and skillful probing by the employment specialist to discover the real reasons. If it is determined that an individual has made an informed choice and does not want to interview, the next suitable candidate should be asked if he or she is interested. If none of the individuals want to pursue the job lead, the employment specialist has the difficult task of turning down a potential job placement.

Continual resistance to employment may be a way of informing the employment specialist that the individual does not really want to work. When an individual is interested in interviewing for a position, the employment specialist should arrange and/or confirm the date, place, and time of the interview with the individual, the employer, and, possibly, the individual's family. Guidelines to assist employment specialists with coordinating and conducting a job interview are located in Table 6.12.

Preparation for Starting the Job

Following acceptance of the job, and prior to the first day of work, the employment specialist must complete several important activities. The financial analysis status should be reviewed, and a letter should also be written to the individual and significant others explaining, "to the best of the employment specialist's knowledge," the effect that work income will have on current benefits. If the individual receives Social Security benefits, a letter should be sent to the local Social Security Administration office, notifying them of the individual's employment. The employment specialist should establish contact with someone in the Social Security office who could serve as a liaison with the supported employment program. A liaison could assist the supported employment program to stay current with the guidelines from Social Security regarding the effect of employment on benefits. Furthermore, individuals and significant others should be strongly encouraged to arrange a time to meet with a Social Security representative. The employment specialist may need to assist the individual or family with making the arrangements and may want to accompany them on their visit.

In addition, the employment specialist is responsible for making transportation arrangements, such as determining bus routes or contacting specialized transportation, and making work arrangements, such as purchasing uniforms or tools. Targeted Job Tax Credit (TJTC) forms must also be completed and can be obtained through the Vocational Rehabilitation agency, State Employment Commission, or the employer's TJTC office. The TJTC offers employers a tax credit of 40% of the first $6,000.00 in wages earned by the employee for one year (maximum amount = $2,400.00). The forms must be signed by the employer and consumer and, ideally, should be completed on or before the first day of work, but forms must be postmarked by the fifth day of employment.

Finally, a meeting should be scheduled with the individual and his or her family to discuss the new employee's work situation. It is important to review the individual's hours, wages, and benefits; appropriate dress and appearance; transportation arrangements; effect of work on benefits; the supported employment process; and the plan for the first day of work (Freeman 1991). Often, families have their own busy work schedule or life routines and may find it difficult to keep track of the policies and rules that the employee is expected to follow. The Employment Policy Form has been found to provide consumer's and family members with a concise summary of pertinent information that can be posted in an area for easy reference. A copy of this form is located in Appendix H.

Employment Specialist's Role

The responsibilities of the employment specialist should be defined in as much detail as possible for the consumer as well as his or her family. It should be emphasized that the employment specialist is there to assist the individual in becoming independent and that it is the employment specialist's role to give feedback on his or her work performance as needed. Also at this time, the importance of open and honest communication should be stressed. The employee should be given the information on who to contact should he or she have questions or concerns regarding training techniques or the activities of the employment specialist. It is impor-

Table 6.12   Guidelines for Conducting a Successful Job Interview

Before the Interview

Make sure that transportation to and from the interview is arranged for the individual.

Schedule the job interview so that there will be an opportunity for the individual to observe the job.

Review appropriate attire.

Ensure the individual has the necessary information to complete the application at the job site.

Discuss fears/concerns the individual may have regarding the interview; for example, are you nervous?

Role play meeting the employer. Review No-No's; i.e., no cigarette smoking, biting nails, etc.

Role play possible interview questions and provide the individual with feedback on their responses as well as opportunities to rehearse responses. Have the consumer play the role of the interviewer as well as the individual being interviewed.

From insight gained during job development, try to predict the questions that the employer may ask, and try to determine what the employer is looking for in a potential employee. Such questions may include

- Why do you want this job?
- What are your qualifications and why do you feel you are a good candidate for this job?
- Why did you separate from past employment?

If the individual is competing among several applicants, make him or her aware of this fact.

Develop a list of questions that the individual may want to ask the employer.

Review pay/benefits and impact on current financial benefits; i.e., Social Security, Workman's Comp., Pending Law Suit.

Establish a potential start date.

If the individual has a tendency to ramble on or say too little, you may establish a cueing system to use during the actual interview to prompt the individual to stop talking or expand on what is being said.

Note: An individual may do well in a mock interview setting, but due to deficits in short-term memory and in the processing of information, this may not generalize over to the actual interview. Therefore, expect the unexpected, and do not spend a lot of time preparing for the interview. Instead it may be helpful to use a short list of helpful hints that the individual can study prior to the interview.

Table 6.12 Guidelines for Conducting a Successful Job Interview *(continued)*

During the Interview

Introduce the employer and potential employee.

Redirect the individual, if needed, during the interview to the topic at hand.

Contribute to the conversation if the individual has not discussed his/her attributes.

Remind the individual of earlier discussions to prompt him or her.

Rephrase questions, if needed, so that the individual can respond independently.

Ensure that the employer and individual interact, and be conscientious of not taking over and speaking for the consumer.

Explain past separations and obstacles to employment, with emphasis on the role of employment specialist.

Reiterate the positive attributes of the consumer.

After the Interview

Observe the job, if possible.

Establish a timeline for the next communication.

Compliment the individual and give him or her feedback. Also, if needed, remind client of other candidates who are applying for the job.

Write a thank-you letter to the employer from the individual and employment specialist.

Note: Each time an individual interviews is a learning experience. The employment specialist and the individual should discuss the strengths and weaknesses of the event.

tant to discuss the individual's preferences for receiving feedback and any other concerns that he or she may have. The major goal for the employment specialist is to open all lines of communication so that a positive and productive partnership can be established.

Summary

Due to the diversity in education, work histories, and experiences of persons with severe disabilities, job development efforts are most effective when they are driven by the individual needs, characteristics, interests, and abilities of each consumer. Utilizing the input of individuals with disabilities and their family members, throughout job development, not only yields valuable information regarding a direction for job development, but encourages them to become invested in the process, thus increasing the chances that a successful job placement will occur.

Employment specialists have a unique opportunity during job development to represent both their program and their consumers to potential employers. The ability of employment specialists to place persons with disabilities into competitive employment hinges on the image they project as well as the content of the message they deliver during *all* job development activities.

During placement, it is important to think optimistically and in terms of what the individual "can do" and "may be able to do" with support, emphasizing ability rather than disability. It is important to not be swayed by the negativism that is often a common theme throughout standardized testing results and outdated records. Supported employment is a consumer-driven model that emphasizes individualization at its CORE. If a person is motivated to try a job that does not present a safety risk to himself or herself or others and there is even a slight chance that the individual will experience success, the employment specialist should *go for it.* There is no magical way to ensure that a job match will always be successful. However, the employment specialist can increase the likelihood of a successful match by using good judgement and by making accurate information available to the individual and his or her family so that informed choices can be made.

Appendix A: Consumer Screening Form

Please overlay your letterhead in this space. The letterhead should designate the supported employment provider, not a state agency which represents more than one provider. Take care not to cover the page number designation or the title of the form. Also, do not change the layout of the form in any way.

CONSUMER EMPLOYMENT SCREENING FORM (Revised 6/90)

Consumer	Staff Member Completing Form
Name: _____	Name: _____
SSN: _____	ID Code: _____

Date of screening (month/day/year): __ __ / __ __ / __ __

Type of screening: Initial_____   Ongoing/Employed_____   Ongoing/Unemployed_____

Total number of hours per week presently working: _____   Months per year: _____

General Directions: PLEASE DO NOT LEAVE ANY ITEM UNANSWERED!

Indicate the most appropriate response for each item based on observations of the consumer and interviews with individuals who know the consumer (i.e. family members, adult service providers, school personnel, employers).

1. Availability: (Circle Yes or No for each item)	Will Work Weekends	Will Work Evenings	Will Work Part-Time	Will Work Full-Time
	Yes / No	Yes / No	Yes / No	Yes / No

Specifics/Comments:

2. Transportation: (Circle Yes or No for each item)	Transport. Available	Access to Specialized Travel Services	Lives on Bus Route	Family Will Transport	Provides Own Transport. (Bike, Car, Walks, Etc.)
	Yes / No	Yes / No	Yes / No	Yes / No	Yes / No

Specifics/Comments:

3. Strength; Lifting and Carrying:	Poor (<10 lbs)___	Fair (10-20 lbs)___	Average (30-40 lbs)___	Strong (>50 lbs)___

Specifics/Comments:

4. Endurance: (Without Break)	Works < 2 hours___	Works 2-3 hours___	Works 3-4 hours___	Works > 4 hours___

Specifics/Comments:

5. Orienting:	Small Area Only___	One Room___	Several Rooms___	Building Wide___	Building and Grounds___

Specifics/Comments:

Appendix A: Consumer Screening Form (cont.)

6. Physical Mobility:	Sits/Stands In One Area___	Fair Ambulation___	Stairs/Minor Obstacles___	Full Physical Abilities___

Specifics/Comments:

7. Independent Work Rate: (No Prompts)	Slow Pace___	Steady/Average Pace___	Above Average/ Sometimes Fast Pace___	Continual Fast Pace___

Specifics/Comments:

8. Appearance:	Unkempt/Poor Hygiene___	Unkempt/ Clean___	Neat/Clean but Clothing Unmatched___	Neat/Clean and Clothing Matched___

Specifics/Comments:

9. Communication:	Uses Sounds/ Gestures___	Uses Key Words/Signs ___	Speaks Unclearly___	Communicates Clearly, Intelligible to Strangers___

Specifics/Comments:

10. Appropriate Social Interactions:	Rarely Interacts Appropriately___	Polite, Responses Appropriate___	Initiates Social Interactions Infrequently___	Initiates Social Interactions Frequently___

Specifics/Comments:

11. Unusual Behavior:	Many Unusual Behaviors___	Few Unusual Behaviors___	No Unusual Behaviors___	

Specifics/Comments:

12. Attention to Task/ Perseverance:	Frequent Prompts Required___	Intermittent Prompts/High Supervision Required___	Intermittent Prompts/Low Supervision Required___	Infrequent Prompts/Low Supervision Required___

Specifics/Comments:

13. Independent Sequencing of Job Duties:	Cannot Perform Tasks in Sequence___	Performs 2-3 Tasks in Sequence___	Performs 4-6 Tasks in Sequence___	Performs 7 or more Tasks in Sequence___

Specifics/Comments:

14. Initiative/ Motivation:	Always Seeks Work___	Sometimes Volunteers___	Waits for Directions___	Avoids Next Task___

Specifics/Comments:

Appendix A: Consumer Screening Form (cont.)

15. Adapting to Change:	Adapts to Change___	Adapts to Change With Some Difficulty___	Adapts to Change With Great Difficulty___	Rigid Routine Required___

Specifics/Comments:

16. Reinforcement Needs:	Frequent Required___	Intermittent (daily) Sufficient___	Infrequent (weekly) Sufficient___	Pay Check Sufficient___

Specifics/Comments:

17. Family Support:	Very Supportive of Work___	Supportive with Reservations___	Indifferent about Work___	Negative About Work___

Specifics/Comments:

18. Consumer's Financial Situation:	Financial Ramifications No Obstacle___	Requires Job With Benefits___	Reduction of Financial Aid is a Concern___	Unwilling to Give Up Financial Aid___

Specifics/Comments:

19. Discrimination Skills:	Cannot Distinguish Between Work Supplies___	Distinguishes Between Work Supplies with an External Cue___	Distinguishes Between Work Supplies___

Specifics/Comments:

20. Time Awareness:	Unaware of Time and Clock Function___	Identifies Breaks and Lunch___	Can Tell Time to the Hour___	Must Tell Time in Hours and Minutes___

Specifics/Comments:

21. Functional Reading:	None___	Sight Words/ Symbols___	Simple Reading___	Fluent Reading___

Specifics/Comments:

22. Functional Math:	None___	Simple Counting___	Simple Addition/ Subtraction___	Computational Skills___

Specifics/Comments:

23. Independent Street Crossing:	None___	Crosses 2 Lane Street with Light___	Crosses 2 Lane Street W/O Light___	Crosses 4 Lane Street with Light___	Crosses 4 Lane Street W/O Light___

Specifics/Comments:

Appendix A: Consumer Screening Form (cont.)

- -

24. Handling
Criticism/
Stress: Resistive/   Withdraws Into   Accepts   Accepts
                 Argumentative__   Silence___   Criticism/Does   Criticism/
                                                     not Change   Changes
                                                     Behavior___   Behavior___

Specifics/Comments:

- -

25. Acts/Speaks
Aggressively: Hourly___   Daily___   Weekly___   Monthly___   Never___

Specifics/Comments:

- -

26. Travel Skills: Uses Bus   Uses Bus   Able to Make
(Circle Yes or   Requires Bus   Independently/   Independently/   Own Travel
No for each   Training   No Transfer   Makes Transfer   Arrangements
item)

                    Yes / No   Yes / No   Yes / No   Yes / No

Specifics/Comments:

- -

27. Benefits Consumer Needs (Circle Yes or No for each choice):

Yes / No	0	=	None
Yes / No	1	=	Sick Leave
Yes / No	2	=	Medical/Health Benefits
Yes / No	3	=	Paid Vacation/Annual Leave
Yes / No	4	=	Dental Benefits
Yes / No	5	=	Employee Discounts
Yes / No	6	=	Free or Reduced Meals
Yes / No	7	=	Other(Specify):_____

- -

27. CHECK ALL THAT CONSUMER HAS PERFORMED:

Bus Tables ___	Sweeping ___	Dish Machine Use ___	"Keeping Busy" ___
Food Prep. ___	Assembly ___	Mopping(Indust.) ___	Clerical ___
Buffing ___	Vacuuming ___	Food Line Supply ___	Pot Scrubbing ___
Dusting ___	Restroom Cleaning ___	Trash Disposal ___	Other ___
Stocking ___	Washing Equipment ___	Food Serving ___	_____

- -

Medications? _____

Medical Complications/Conditions? _____

_____

Additional Comments: _____

_____

_____

FORM DEVELOPED BY THE REHABILITATION RESEARCH AND TRAINING CENTER
VIRGINIA COMMONWEALTH UNIVERSITY

Appendix B: Community Job Market Screening Form

VIRGINIA COMMONWEALTH UNIVERSITY
REHABILITATION RESEARCH AND TRAINING CENTER
Community Job Market Screening Form

Date Completed: _____   Completed by: _____

1.   GENERAL SCREENING

List job openings that occur frequently (derive from classified ads, employment service listings, public services ads, etc.):

JOB TITLE/TYPE OF WORK   GENERAL REQUIREMENTS

_____
_____
_____
_____
_____
_____
_____

2.   SPECIFIC SCREENING

List potential appropriate companies or industries in this community to contact for job openings.

CURRENT

Company/Contact Person   Type of Work   Address/Phone

_____
_____
_____
_____

DEVELOPING

Company/Contact Person   Type of Work   Address/Phone

_____
_____
_____
_____

©Virginia Commonwealth University
Rehabilitation Research and Training Center, 1986.

Appendix C: Employer Contact Sheet

VIRGINIA COMMONWEALTH UNIVERSITY
REHABILITATION RESEARCH AND TRAINING CENTER
Employer Interview Form

Company: _____   Date: _____
_____   Phone: _____

Person Interviewed: _____
Title: _____
_____

Job Title: _____   Rate of Pay: _____
Company benefits:_____

Size of company (or number of employees):_____
Volume and/or pace of work:_____
Overall:_____ This position:_____
Number of employees in this position:_____
During the same hours:_____
Written job description available:_____
Description of job duties:_____
Availability of supervision (estimate percentage of time): _____

Availability of coworkers (direct or indirect):_____

Orientation skills needed (size and layout of work area): _____

What are important aspects of position:
Speed ___ vs. Thoroughness ___   Judgment ___ vs. Routine ___
Teamwork ___ vs. Independence ___   Repetition ___ vs. Variability ___
Other:_____
What are absolute "don'ts" for employee in this position (e.g., manager's
pet peeves, reasons for dismissal, etc.)? _____

Describe any reading or number work that is required: _____

What machinery or equipment will the employee need to
operate?_____

OBSERVATIONAL INFORMATION:
Appearance of employees:_____

Atmosphere:
_____ Friendly, cheerful   _____ Aloof, indifferent
_____ Busy, relaxed   _____ Busy, tense
_____ Slow, relaxed   _____ Slow, tense
_____ Structured, orderly   _____ Unstructured, disorderly
Other:_____
Environmental characteristics (physical barriers, extremes in temperature, etc.): _____

Comments:_____
_____
_____

SIGNATURE/TITLE:_____

© Virginia Commonwealth University, Rehabilitation Research and Training Center, 1990

Appendix D: Employer Interview Form

EMPLOYER CONTACT SHEET

Company name:_____

Address:_____ Follow up date:

City/St:_____ Zip:_____

Contact Person:_____ Telephone:_____

Type of company:_____ Consumer:

Type of position:_____

Directions to the site:

CONTACTS

Date:	Type:	Emp. Spec.	Comments:

Additional on file:

Thank-you sent: By:

Job analysis complete: By:

Placement information:

© Virginia Commonwealth University, Rehabilitation, Research & Training Center

Appendix E: Sequence of Job Duties Form

Sequence of Job Duties Form

_____ Daily
    (Job duties remain the
       same from day to day)

_____ Varies day to day
    (If checked here, complete a
       separate form for each
       different sequence)

If above box is checked, indicate day for which
this form is completed:

___ ___ ___ ___ ___ ___ ___
Mon Tue Wed Thu Fri Sat Sun

Approximate Time   **Job Duty**

_____   _____

_____   _____

_____   _____

_____   _____

_____   _____

_____   _____

_____   _____

_____   _____

_____   _____

_____   _____

_____   _____

Comments: _____

_____

_____

_____   _____
Signature/Title   Date

Appendix F: Job Screening Form

Please overlay your letterhead in this space. The letterhead should designate the supported employment provider, not a state agency which represents more than one provider. Take care not to cover the page number designation or the title of the form. Also, do not change the layout of the form in any way.

JOB SCREENING FORM (Revised 6/90)

Please complete one Job Screening Form for each job the consumer had during the period in question. All items refer to this particular position at this particular company for this particular location.

- -

    Consumer   **Staff Member Completing Form**

Name: _____ Name: _____
SSN: _____ ID Code: _____

- -

          Company

Name: _____ Screening Date: __ __ / __ __ / __ __
ID Code: _____   mo day yr

- -

Type of Service/Employment for this Report (Select one): _____

  1 = Work activity or Sheltered employment
  2 = Entrepreneurial
  3 = Mobile work crew
  4 = Enclave
  5 = Supported job
  6 = Supported competitive employment
  7 = Time-limited (No ongoing services anticipated)
  8 = Other (Specify: _____)

Type of Screening: Initial _____ Ongoing _____ Final _____

Job Title: _____

Current hourly wage (or wage at last date of employment in this position): _____
Did a wage change occur since the last Job Screening or Job Update? Yes____ No____

  If yes, complete this section:
    Hourly rate changed from $_____ to $_____ on ___/___/___
    Hourly rate changed from $_____ to $_____ on ___/___/___
Number of Hours per Week: _____ Months per Year: _____
If less than 12 months per year, what months is the job not available? _____

Number of employees in this company at this location: _____
Number of employees without disabilities in immediate area (50 ft. radius): _____
Number of other employees with disabilities: _____
  In immediate area (50 ft. radius): _____
Number of other employees in this position: _____
  During the same hours: _____

Appendix F: Job Screening Form (cont.)

General Directions: PLEASE DO NOT LEAVE ANY ITEM UNANSWERED!
Indicate the most appropriate response for each item based on observations of the job and interviews with employers, supervisors, and coworkers. Also circle CI (critically important), I (important), LI (less important), or NI (not important) for each item, to indicate its level of importance in this position.

1. Schedule:
(Circle Yes or No for each item)

Weekend Work Required	Evening Work Required	Part-Time Job	Full-Time Job
Yes / No	Yes / No	Yes / No	Yes / No

CI / I / LI / NI
Specifics/Comments:

2. Travel Location:
(Circle Yes or No for each item)

	On Public Transportation Route	On Handicapped Transportation Route
	Yes / No	Yes / No

CI / I / LI / NI
Specifics/Comments:

3. Strength; Lifting and Carrying:

Very Light Work (<10 lbs)___	Light Work (10-20 lbs)___	Average Work (30-40 lbs)___	Heavy Work (>50 lbs)___

CI / I / LI / NI
Specifics/Comments:

4. Endurance:
(No Breaks)

Work Required for <2 hours___	Work Required for 2-3 hours___	Work Required for 3-4 hours___	Work Required for >4 hours___

CI / I / LI / NI
Specifics/Comments:

5. Orienting:

Small Area Only___	One Room___	Several Rooms___	Building Wide___	Building and Grounds___

CI / I / LI / NI
Specifics/Comments:

6. Physical Mobility:

Sit/Stand In One Area___	Fair Ambulation Required___	Stairs/Minor Obstacles___	Full Physical Requirements___

CI / I / LI / NI
Specifics/Comments:

7. Work Pace:

Slow Pace___	Average Steady Pace___	Sometimes Fast Pace___	Continual Fast Pace___

CI / I / LI / NI
Specifics/Comments:

Appendix F: Job Screening Form (cont.)

- -

| **8. Appearance Requirements:** | Grooming of Little Importance___ | Cleanliness Only Required___ | Neat and Clean Required___ | Grooming Very Important___ |

CI / I / LI / NI
Specifics/Comments:

- -

| **9. Communication Required:** | None/ Minimal___ | Key Words/Signs Needed___ | Unclear Speech Accepted___ | Clear Speech in Sentences/Signs Needed___ |

CI / I / LI / NI
Specifics/Comments:

- -

| **10. Social Interactions:** | Social Interactions Not Required___ | Appropriate Responses Required___ | Social Interactions Required Infrequently___ | Social Interactions Required Frequently___ |

CI / I / LI / NI
Specifics/Comments:

- -

| **11. Behavior Acceptance Range:** | Many Unusual Behaviors Accepted___ | Few Unusual Behaviors Accepted___ | No Unusual Behaviors Accepted___ |

CI / I / LI / NI
Specifics/Comments:

- -

| **12. Attention to Task/ Perseverance:** | Frequent Prompts Available___ | Intermittent Prompts/High Supervision Available___ | Intermittent Prompts/Low Supervision Available___ | Infrequent Prompts/Low Supervision Available___ |

CI / I / LI / NI
Specifics/Comments:

- -

| **13. Sequencing of Job Duties:** | Only One Task Required at a Time___ | 2-3 Tasks Required in Sequence___ | 4-6 Tasks Required in Sequence___ | 7 or more Tasks Required in Sequence___ |

CI / I / LI / NI
Specifics/Comments:

- -

| **14. Initiation of Work/ Motivation:** | Initiation of Work Required___ | Volunteering Helpful___ | Staff will Prompt to Next Task___ |

CI / I / LI / NI
Specifics/Comments:

- -

Appendix F: Job Screening Form (cont.)

Indicate the most appropriate response for each item based on observations of the job and interviews with employers, supervisors, and coworkers. Also circle CI (critically important), I (important), LI (less important), or NI (not important) for each item, to indicate its level of importance in <u>this position</u>.

---

15. Daily Changes In Routine:

| 7 or More Changes___ | 4-6 Task Changes___ | 2-3 Task Changes___ | No Task Changes___ |

CI / I / LI / NI
Specifics/Comments:

---

16. Reinforcement Available:

| Frequent Reinforcement Available___ | Reinforcement Intermittent (daily)___ | Reinforcement Infrequent (weekly)___ | Minimal Reinforcement (pay check)___ |

CI / I / LI / NI
Specifics/Comments:

---

17. Employer Attitude:

| Very Supportive of Workers with Disabilities___ | Supportive with Reservations__ | Indifferent to Workers With Disabilities___ | Negative toward Workers with Disabilities___ |

CI / I / LI / NI
Specifics/Comments:

---

18. Employer's Financial Requirements:

| Financial Incentives Not Necessary___ | Tax Credit or Incentive (e.g., TJTC, OJT)___ | Subminimum Wage___ |

CI / I / LI / NI
Specifics/Comments:

---

19. Object Discrimination:

| Does Not Need to Distinguish Between Work Supplies___ | Must Distinguish Between Work Supplies with an External Cue___ | Must Distinguish Between Work Supplies___ |

CI / I / LI / NI
Specifics/Comments:

---

20. Time:

| Time Factors Not Important___ | Must Identify Breaks/Meals/ Etc.___ | Must Tell Time to the Hour___ | Must Tell Time to the Minute___ |

CI / I / LI / NI
Specifics/Comments:

---

21. Functional Reading:

| None___ | Sight Words/ Symbols___ | Simple Reading___ | Fluent Reading___ |

CI / I / LI / NI
Specifics/Comments:

Appendix F: Job Screening Form (cont.)

- -

22. Functional Math:

		Simple	Simple Addition/	Complex Computational
	None___	Counting___	Subtraction___	Skills___

CI / I / LI / NI
Specifics/Comments:

- -

23. Street Crossing:

		Must Cross 2 Lane Street with	Must Cross 2 Lane Street W/O	Must Cross 4 Lane Street with	Must Cross 4 Lane Street W/O
	None___	Light___	Light___	Light___	Light___

CI / I / LI / NI
Specifics/Comments:

- -

24. Visibility To Public:

	Consumer Not Visible____	Occasionally Visible___	Regularly Visible___	Visible Throughout the Day/Ongoing___

CI / I / LI / NI
Specifics/Comments:

- -

25. Benefits of Job:

Yes / No	0	=	None
Yes / No	1	=	Sick Leave
Yes / No	2	=	Medical/Health Benefits
Yes / No	3	=	Paid Vacation/Annual Leave
Yes / No	4	=	Dental Benefits
Yes / No	5	=	Employee Discounts
Yes / No	6	=	Free or Reduced Meals
Yes / No	7	=	Other(Specify):_____

- -

26. Level of Social Contact: (circle one)

(0) - Employment in a segregated setting in which the majority of interactions with persons without disabilities are with caregivers or service providers. Example: Adult Activity Center.

(1) - Employment in an integrated environment on a shift or position which is isolated. Contact with coworkers without disabilities or supervisors is minimal. Example: Night Janitor.

(2) - Employment in an integrated environment on a shift or position which is relatively isolated. Contact with coworkers without disabilities or supervisors is available at lunch or break. Example: Pot Scrubber.

(3) - Employment in an integrated environment in a position requiring a moderate level of task dependency and coworker interaction. Example: Dishwasher required to keep plate supply stacked for cooks.

(4) - Employment in an integrated environment in a position requiring a high degree of task dependency and coworker interaction and/or high level of contact with customers. Example: Busperson/Porter.

- -

Appendix F: Job Screening Form (cont.)

- -

27. CHECK ALL THAT APPLY TO POSITION:

Bus Tables ___	Sweeping ___	Dish Machine Use ___	"Keeping Busy" ___
Food Prep. ___	Assembly ___	Mopping(Indust.) ___	Clerical ___
Buffing ___	Vacuuming ___	Food Line Supply ___	Pot Scrubbing ___
Dusting ___	Restroom Cleaning ___	Trash Disposal ___	Other ___
Stocking ___	Washing Equipment ___	Food Serving ___	_____

- -

COMMENTS:

Rate of employee turnover (annual percentage):

      Overall: _____   This position: _____

Number of supervisors: _____   Rate of supervisor turnover: _____

Written job description available? _____

What are absolute "don'ts" for an employee in this position? (Manager's pet peeves, reasons for dismissal,etc.)_____

_____

_____

Environmental characteristics (physical barriers, temperature extremes, etc.):

_____

_____

_____

_____

Additional Comments: _____

_____

_____

_____

_____

**FORM DEVELOPED BY THE REHABILITATION RESEARCH AND TRAINING CENTER
VIRGINIA COMMONWEALTH UNIVERSITY**

Appendix G: Job/Worker Compatibility Analysis

<u>Job/Worker Compatibility Analysis</u>

Date: ___/___/___   Company: _____   Job Title: _____

Consumer A:	Consumer C:	Consumer E:
Name:_____	Name:_____	Name:_____
SSN:____/____/____	SSN:____/____/____	SSN:____/____/____
Consumer B:	Consumer D:	Consumer F:
Name:_____	Name:_____	Name:_____
SSN:____/____/____	SSN:____/____/____	SSN:____/____/____

INSTRUCTIONS: Indicate whether the factor is critically important for the position in question by placing an "X" in the first column. For each critical factor, rank from most (1) to least (23), the order of importance in the second column. For factors considered critical to the position, use the following symbols to indicate compatibility:

(=)   indicates current compatibility between job requirement and consumer ability.
(+)   indicates consumer is over qualified in this area.
(-+) indicates the discrepancy can be eliminated by intervention.
(-)   indicates a discrepancy without reasonable means of elimination.

Employment Factor:	Critical to Position	Order	Consumer A	B	C	D	E	F
(1) Availability								
(2) Transportation								
(3) Strength								
(4) Endurance								
(5) Orienting								
(6) Physical Mobility								
(7) Work Rate								
(8) Appearance								
(9) Communication								
(10) Social Interactions								
(11) Unusual Behavior								
(12) Attention to Task								
(13) Sequencing of Tasks								
(14) Initiation/Motivation								
(15) Adapting to Change								
(16) Reinforcement Needs								
(17) Attitude/Support								
(18) Financial Concerns								
(19) Object Discrimination								
(20) Time Awareness								
(21) Functional Reading								
(22) Functional Math								
(23) Street Crossing								
TOTAL:								

Compatibility: Consumers with negative (-) indication(s) of compatibility in areas critical to this position with no reasonable means of eliminating the discrepancy should not be considered for placement in this position.

Appendix H: Employment Policy Form

Employment Policy Form

(Employee Name)_____will begin

working as a (Position)_____at

(Employer)_____on

(Date of Hire)_____His/Her work schedule is:

Monday	_____	Friday	_____
Tuesday	_____	Saturday	_____
Wednesday	_____	Sunday	_____
Thursday	_____	Other	_____

_____ is his/her immediate supervisor.   The

benefits of the company include:_____

_____

The company offers the following holidays and vacation benefits:

_____

_____

The company policies regarding absences, tardiness, or inclement

weather are:_____

_____

The person to contact is:

Employer Name:_____

Address:_____

Phone Number:_____

(Employee Name)_____is an

employee of the company and is expected to follow the above
policies.

If you have any questions, please contact:

Employment Specialist_____

Address_____

Phone Number_____

developed by Rehabilitation Research & Training Center
Virginia Commonwealth University

7

Job-Site Interventions

The *creation* of effective interventions on the job site, or intervention related to the performance of job duties but off of the job site, can greatly enhance the initial and continued employment of consumers with severe disabilities. The converse is also true—ineffective, intrusive, and/or dependency-creating job-site interventions can lead to underemployment, termination of employment, and in many cases, the building of a "failure-set" among individuals who may have already experienced many employment setbacks. We have chosen to use *create* because of our belief that job-site interventions must be designed with specific consumers and job sites/ duties in mind. Thus, it is our belief that there cannot ever be a text that can provide pat solutions to given problems on a job site. Indeed, one of the most valuable attributes of a supervisor, co-worker, or employment specialist is the ability to design unobtrusive strategies to increase the quality and productivity of a worker on the job. The purpose of this chapter is to provide a basic foundation and a framework upon which the primary job-site intervention person can build creative strategies for efficient task and workplace social skill development and maintenance.

WHAT IS AN INTERVENTION?

For the purposes of this chapter an *intervention* is any act, strategy, or structure put into place for, with, or by a consumer that does not ordinarily exist for the consumer's co-workers who perform the same job. Indeed, effective interventions are generally an interwoven set of acts, strategies, and structures set into place by the primary intervention person(s). An act may be as simple as a co-worker reminding a supported employee that it is time to go for break, or as complex as a supervisor engaging in the application of differential reinforcement procedures. A strategy may involve a consumer simply counting to ten before responding to a hostile co-worker, or the systematic utilization of a series of checklists to perform a task. Structures may vary from uncomplicated physical aids, such as a marking on the floor or a line on the sink wall, to more complex aids, such as devices to assist standing, mobility, or communication.

*Types of Job Site Interventions

Type		Example
Act	-	Ad Hoc interruption of an argument between co-worker and supported employee
	-	Assisting with a job skill which has not yet been acquired by the supported employee
Strategy	-	Design of a reward system to increase production
	-	Creating a "transportation tree" that provides alternative methods of getting to work should the primary method fail
Structure	-	Building and using a light table to see stains on laundry
	-	Providing a keyboard guard to assist in programming by a consumer with significant upper extremity disabilities

The distinctions between acts, strategies, and structures are not discreet, i.e., for any given intervention may be labeled differently by different practitioners. The reader is advised not obsess on the categorization of intervention but rather to use a variety as needed!

Figure 7.1

Interventions that directly impact job performance may occur either on the job site or off of the job site. For example, an intervention for a given consumer with traumatic brain injury may be to refer him or her to a substance abuse professional. An individual with profound cognitive disabilities may need an intensive sequence of prompting to acquire a job duty. A person with physical disabilities may need to have a consult with a rehabilitation engineer. Thus, in this chapter, the term *interventions* covers a wide array of acts, strategies, or structures that may be accessed at various locations.

THE PURPOSE OF INTERVENTION

Generally, the purpose of all vocational intervention is to improve the overall quality of life of an individual. Depending on the setting, the purposes may be more narrowly defined. In supported employment, the purposes of intervention are very reflective of supported employment's underlying values of fair wages and integration. Most interventions are related to increasing the quality of work performed, the quantity of work performed, and building positive relationships with co-workers, supervisors, and others with whom the consumer comes into daily contact. Learning new job duties, increasing production, and adapting to the work culture are primary foci of interventions. Chronologically speaking, most interventions begin prior to the initial day of placement as the worker gets prepared for the new job. In supported employment, interventions continue for the life of the job.

WHO INTERVENES?

Traditionally, the chief individuals facilitating employment for consumers with disabilities have been rehabilitation professionals (e.g., employment specialists, placement specialists, vocational rehabilitation counselors, etc.). While supported employment was initially conceptualized as an intervention model relying heavily on service-provider-based employment specialists, there has recently been a rethinking and broadening of perspectives on who is suited to provide intervention on the job site.

While the employment specialist is still the most utilized intervention agent, supported employment has begun using co-workers (see Nisbet and Hagner 1988) and employer-based employment specialists (e.g., the Marriot Corporation). The utilization of co-workers and employer-based employment specialists offers seemingly more natural and less intrusive methodologies for facilitating employment because they limit, or sometimes totally remove, an outside agent from the training and retention processes. In addition, these new options may be attractive because the cost of intervention is shifted to the chief benefactor, the employer. While these methodologies hold great promise, because they are new and still evolving, their effectiveness has yet to be demonstrated to the degree of models utilizing provider-based employment specialists. Common sense dictates that there will be no "best" intervention person or model, but rather the best "chief" intervention individual will be one matched to specific consumer and employer needs.

For ease of communication within this chapter, the chief intervention person is identified as the employment specialist. However, the guidelines and strategies discussed below apply to all persons providing job-site intervention.

PREFERRED CHARACTERISTICS OF INTERVENTIONS

As stated earlier, the variety of intervention techniques used to facilitate integrated employment are actually limited only by the creativity of the employment specialist. However, there are critical attributes associated with the design of good job-site interventions. Regardless of whether the intervention is designed to change quality or quantity of work, or change interpersonal interchanges on the job site, the following characteristics of the interventions should be present: minimal intrusion; access to reinforcement; minimal aversion; involve maximum consumer input; maximum effectiveness and efficiency; appropriately systematic; allow appropriate levels of interdependence after the initial intervention has ceased; and involve data-based decision making. It is instructive to note that all of the characteristics should be considered in relative rather than absolute terms. Good interventions balance each of these characteristics to gain the ultimate desired result of stable and integrated employment. Figure 7.2 provides an overview of the preferred characteristics of intervention. Each characteristic is further explained below.

Preferred Characteristics of Interventions

Characteristic	Questions to Ask
Minimal Intrusiveness	Does the intervention -
	- Insure consumer dignity?
	- Fit into the worksite task flow or culture?
	- Match the instructional need?
Access to Reinforcement	- Utilize naturally occurring reinforcers?
	- Reflect consumer preferences?
	- Allow for systematic removal as necessary?
Minimal Aversion	- Minimize risk of psychological and physical pain?
	- Utilize naturally occurring events?

Figure 7.2

	-	Represent only a minute role when compared to reinforcement?
Consumer Input	-	Allow for ongoing input?
	-	Allow for input from consumer with verbal communication disorders?
	-	Allow for clinical judgments by the employment specialist?
Effectiveness & Efficiency	-	Aid in documentable skill acquisition, production, or maintenance?
	-	Represent the quickest route to success?
	-	Represent the least costly alternative?
Appropriately Systematic	-	Insure consumer dignity?
	-	Incorporate naturally occurring cues and consequences?
	-	Utilize cues according to consumer learning style and/or preference?
Allow Appropriate Interdependence	-	Facilitate natural job task collaboration?
	-	Enhance communication between consumers and others?
	-	Facilitate an equal balance of give and take in task and non task interventions?
Data Based Decision Making	-	Is information collected routinely?
	-	Maintain consumer dignity?
	-	Utilize the collected information in decision making?

Figure 7.2 *(continued)*

Minimal Intrusiveness

Intrusiveness in supported employment refers to the degree to which an act, strategy, or structure varies from the typically available interventions that occur naturally at the job site. Consideration of the intrusiveness of an intervention is important because interventions that vary drastically from the normal job processes (i.e., are very intrusive) have the potential to be demeaning to the consumer and may give co-workers, supervisors, and others a negative view of both the specific consumer and persons with disabilities in general.

Supported employment, by definition, is an intrusive process in that the consumers participating in supported employment need additional support not normally available to their nondisabled co-workers. For example, instituting a time-delay prompting procedure (a systematic, behavioral prompting procedure) to increase the production rate of a person who works slowly is usually a deviation from the normal procedures at a job site and is therefore intrusive. Likewise, utilization of paid co-workers to assist a person eat at a job site is also intrusive.

While both of the above examples illustrate intrusiveness, both examples also illustrate an acceptable amount of intrusion for a given job site. Generally speaking, the variance from normal job-site procedures should be kept as small as possible. It is important to remember that intrusiveness varies from one job site to another. For example, the use of a check list to mark off completed tasks would be less intrusive in an electronics production assembly position than it would be in some other positions because many electronic assembly persons routinely mark off completed circuits once they are assembled. The employment specialist must also weigh the degree of intrusion against the other characteristics discussed in this section. For example, while frequent consumption of snacks as a reinforcement could be considered very intrusive, it could be very justifiable if it is effective, and can be easily withdrawn, and meets the other characteristics of good interventions.

Efforts to reduce intrusiveness are greatly augmented by the use of naturally occurring events in the workplace. For example, teaching the supported employee to observe the break-time behaviors exhibited by co-workers may be easier than teaching the individual to tell time and less intrusive than a co-worker's reminder. Many times, naturally occurring events signal the beginning or end of a task sequence and should be maximally used to teach skill acquisition and maintenance.

Access to Reinforcement

Reinforcement is, by definition, any stimuli following a behavior that increases the occurrence of that behavior. Naturally occurring reinforcing events on the job site include praise from co-workers, supervisors, and the public; company perks, such as outings; access to friends; and the paycheck. Each of these reinforcers occur naturally after the performance of a job or task. Other reinforcers frequently used on supported employment sites include praise from the employment specialist, token reinforcement (e.g., checkmarks to be turned in at a later time for a preferred activity or object), incremental pay schedules, and in some cases, reinforcement from support groups and other treatment professionals. Frequently, because of consumer personalities, learning styles, and employment histories, reinforcers must initially be manipulated within the context of training programs in order to facilitate skill acquisition, an increase in production rates, and behavioral and cognitive modifications leading to better interpersonal relations within the work culture. One of the most important job-site intervention skills that can be learned and practiced is the systematic use of reinforcers to shape job performance.

Since no event is intrinsically reinforcing, except for very basic needs (e.g., food, water, shelter, etc.), the first step in utilizing reinforcement during job-site intervention is the identification of what is reinforcing to a given individual at a given time. Any consideration of reinforcement must include consumer input, along with other information sources, such as observation, record review, and input from previous personnel and significant others who have worked with the consumer. In addition to choosing effective reinforcers for a particular individual and situation, the method of delivering those reinforcements must be carefully considered. Timing is crucial, since ill-timed delivery can significantly reduce the effectiveness of a reinforcer.

While reinforcement is probably the most powerful tool available for use when intervening on the job site, its utilization does not come without risks. Improper selection of reinforcers and delivery strategies can be demeaning to the consumer (e.g., selection of age inappropriate reinforcers, such as smiley-face stickers, or the presentation of reinforcers in a manner that may cause embarrassment to a consumer). Additionally, reliance on non-naturally occurring reinforcers (e.g., tokens or incremental pay schedules) may be difficult to stop without careful planning. Again, reinforcement strategies must be considered in the context of the other components of effective intervention discussed in this section. For a more detailed discussion of reinforcement procedures see Meyer and Evans (1989), O'Brien and Repp (1990), and Walker and Shea (1988).

Minimal Aversion

Aversion refers to situations that cause the consumer real or anticipated physical or psychological pain. Historically, aversive procedures have included such things as electric shock, physical restraint, and the application of noxious chemicals (e.g., ammonia, hot sauce, etc.). While these more extreme procedures are not generally considered for use on the job site (thankfully), other more subtle aversive procedures have also been used on job sites in the past. For example, withholding or threatening to withhold a meal, contingent upon consumer performance, could easily cause psychological distress and perhaps physical distress if consumer performance never reached criteria levels for receiving lunch. Verbal statements, delivered abusively or too strongly could also certainly be considered aversive. Creating consumer embarrassment could also be aversive. Finally, it has also been argued that *not* receiving reinforcing events because of failure to meet job performance standards is aversive in that it causes psychological pain. Unfortunately, like the design of effective interventions, the forms that aversive procedures may take are ultimately limited by the creativity of misguided individuals. For an extended philosophical discussion regarding the use and non-use of aversive procedures and a more detailed description of aversive procedures see Horner, et al. (1990), Evans and Meyer (1990), Thompson (1990), Durand (1990), Turnbull and Turnbull (1990) and Morgan (1989).

In reality, all job sites have aversive components, and most employees encounter aversive events at one time or another. For example, verbal or written reprimands for absenteeism are designed to create psychological harm to deter future absences. Therefore, the removal of all aversive events for a person with disabilities would be very intrusive as previously defined. The employment specialist must balance naturally occurring aversive events along with potentially aversive interventions to ensure that the minimal amount of aversive procedures are utilized in the acquisition and maintenance of job skills. For example, given the above definition, withholding eye contact during target situations could be considered mildly aversive if it upset the consumer. However, this procedure is often used to decelerate behavior and is quite acceptable.

As simple as it sounds, the guiding rule of thumb regarding creating potentially aversive situations is "Do unto others as you would have them do unto you." Most of us enjoy reinforcement, endure typical aversive situations, and avoid situations that have the potential of causing either physical or psychological harm. Employment specialists should rely almost exclusively on interventions that provide the most potential access to reinforcement rather than creating interventions that could lead to physical or psychological pain.

Maximum Consumer Input

The concept of supported employment embodies the notion of deliberate consumer and, in some cases, family input in decision making. The best supported employment programs have developed processes to ensure that consumer input occurs. While consumer input begins during screening and referral and continues through job development, placement, and follow-along, the present discussion will focus on illustrations of how consumer input can be utilized during the job-site intervention phase.

Probable (nonexclusive) points of consumer input during job-site intervention include selection of prompting methodologies; selection of reinforcing stimuli and delivery mechanisms; decision making with regards to fading from the job site; and primary decision making on the utilization of augmentative therapies, such as psychological and substance abuse counseling, physical therapy, occupational therapy, cognitive retraining, etc. How consumers provide input varies considerably across the disability groupings and the functioning levels within disability groups. For example, for consumers with severe cognitive and communication deficits, input may be obtained from observation, presentation of alternatives, and knowledge of previous experiences. For individuals with more cognitive abilities and communication skills, verbal input may be easy to obtain in addition to the previous strategies.

Several points of consideration are noteworthy when soliciting consumer input. First, while expressive communication difficulties make consumer input more difficult to obtain, these difficulties should not preclude consumer input. Instead, alternative methods of obtaining input should be utilized. Second, a consumer's ability to speak articulately does not equate with effective communication. Sometimes, part of a consumer's disability might be the inability to identify and communicate true feelings about a given choice. It is instructive to listen to both the words (i.e., what is actually said) and the "music" (i.e., the affect and intonation that accompany the words). This type of listening involves good clinical skills.

The final consideration, which also requires good clinical skills, is the ability of the employment specialist to know when to choose not to follow consumer wishes *carte blanche*. For example, while a potentially alcoholic consumer may not wish to be evaluated for substance abuse treatment, an employment specialist sometimes must intervene to see that the consumer does receive evaluation. Similarly, while a consumer who has been prescribed psychotropic medication to stabilize affect may not wish to take the medication, it could be very crucial for the employment specialist to develop strategies to ensure that medication is taken. Depending on the intervention strategies chosen in these two illustrative scenarios, the consumer will most likely still have choices.

Maximum Effectiveness and Efficiency

Effectiveness refers to the ability of the selected intervention to reach the goal of that intervention. *Efficiency* refers to how the intervention interfaces with time with respect to the desired goal, effort, expense, and disruption of normal work flow. Given alternative intervention strategies, some interventions may be very effective, but require massive resources or call for intrusive or aversive procedures. Or, some potential interventions may be very easy to implement quickly and at low cost, but have little or no chance of reaching the goal of the intervention.

Consider the following example: A supported employee is working as a machinist designing metal cabinetry for air-conditioning units and must operate an extrusion machine to bend metal. She puts the metal in with her left hand and pushes a spring-operated switch with her right hand. The employee is frequently slow to release the sheet metal, causing her left hand to occasionally be bruised by the machine. Given her learning history, it is likely that between 150 and 200 trials with a simulated machine would allow her to acquire quick enough hand movements to prevent her hand being bruised. The probability of this intervention reaching the goal of "no hand bruising" is quite high, thus it would be considered an effective choice. It would require off-site training, acquiring or building a simulated machine, and until she learned to move quicker, her hand would probably continue to be periodically bruised. Another intervention strategy would be to have the plant electrician wire a second starting switch that would require the use of her left hand to operate. The starting sequence would require simultaneous pushing of both switches. With the addition of the switch, the possibility of her hand getting bruised is nonexistent, thus it, too, is a highly effective strategy. However, given the time for the intervention to work, the expense, and the trouble, compared to the 150-200 trial strategy, the switch intervention is clearly a more efficient intervention.

It is not possible to provide a sequence of most to least effective or efficient interventions. The ability to choose the most effective and efficient intervention from available alternatives is enhanced through employment specialist experience, knowledge of the consumer and job site, and sheer practice with interventions. It is important to note, too, that the employment specialist's facility with an intervention impacts the intervention's effectiveness and efficiency. Thus, given the exact same situation and consumer, two employment specialists may appropriately choose different interventions because of their familiarity with one or the other intervention. Variance in employment specialist style is an important consideration for program managers, who may inadvertently push one intervention over another. It is also an important consideration for the employment specialist. Frequently, considered interventions are not chosen because the employment specialist has little experience with the intervention. This may be indicative of the need for more training and practice on those types of interventions.

Appropriately Systematic

Learning theory teaches us that the presentation of consistent cues and consequences facilitates the quickest initial learning. While most tasks have many variations that could occur during their performance, when providing the initial training for a skill, it is best to structure the situation, if possible, to limit those variations. *Systematic* intervention refers to making *a priori* decisions about which cues should elicit certain behaviors and which consequences will follow desired and undesired responses to those cues. Inconsistent, spurious reinforcement or cues will impede the pace at which learning occurs for all people, regardless of disability. After learning correct responses to a very narrow range of potential cues, cue variations can be taught.

Consider the following example: When a bagger in a grocery check-out line in a certain store sees a frozen item (a cue), he should pick that item up and put it in a plastic "frozen food" bag (a response). While many people might learn this task with verbal instructions only, people with severe cognitive disabilities or extreme memory deficits may require many chances to perform this response (and receive reinforcement for correct decisions and corrective feedback for incorrect responses) before it is learned. If the individual is allowed to put the frozen food in a regular bag without consistent correction, he may, in fact, learn the wrong response pattern (Remember, bad habits are hard to break!). Indeed, if the bagger receives inadvertent praise for incorrect behavior, the wrong response pattern may become very ingrained. Consistent feedback will enhance both the training effectiveness and efficiency of task performance in this case.

When designing interventions, the employment specialist and others must decide what the supported employee should do in likely-to-occur situations. Systematic intervention begins as the job analysis is conducted and when the employment specialist can observe other workers in similar situations perform their duties at that job site. For example, during job analysis, the many ways in which work is presented to workers (cues), the procedures for completing that work (responses), how fast that work must be completed (response), and what happens when the work is completed (consequences) can all be observed and noted. In addition to task related information, the employment specialist can also observe the interaction patterns among co-workers, supervisors, and customers to identify which times and places might result in the most stress for an individual.

Again, with the job analysis information in hand, plans can be made with the consumer to facilitate successful job acquisition and retention. For example; task analyses can be developed; training and assessment times on the job site, during the work day, can be identified; strategies for dealing with stressors (e.g., rehearsing proper responses, resolving fears, etc.); or memory enhancement strategies can be implemented (e.g., check lists, maps, etc.) as needed. This thoughtful planning should occur throughout the period of active intervention by the employment specialist.

Systematic intervention also requires careful planning to allow for the exiting (fading) of the employment specialist from the job site. Planning for this exit should occur during the initial development of systematic interventions. It is important, for all involved, that the substantive reduction of employment specialist effort be carefully planned.

Several points regarding systematic instruction warrant discussion. First, the planning and implementation of any plan must take into account, and where possible involve, specific consumer attributes and input. Second, while systematic planning must be done for (and with) consumers for all items that are believed to require intervention processes, even the best plans will need to be modified during the first few days and weeks of the job ("The best laid plans of mice and men...") Factors that may cause these modifications include changes in work duties, identifying previously unnoted requirements, and consumer learning style and preferences. While it is important not to make voluminous changes all at once, it is also important to "fit" the plan to the consumer and job. This fit is usually refined as the job-site intervention phase continues.

Finally, while systematic instruction in human services had its beginnings with interventions designed for persons with severe cognitive disabilities, the need for systematic intervention is universal to any supported employment situation, during which previously vocationally unsuccessful consumers are striving to acquire and maintain a job. Persons with higher cognitive functioning (e.g., persons with long-term mental illness, traumatic brain injury, etc.) may, as a group, need more interventions planned for interpersonal skill development or memory enhancement than specific job-skill training. However, these interventions must be as equally and carefully thought out.

Allow Appropriate Interdependence

Interdependence in supported employment refers to the ways and degree to which the supported employee must rely on others within and outside of the workplace in order to be successfully employed. One goal of the supported employment specialist is to create balanced interdependence between the supported employee, co-workers, supervisor, employer, employment specialist, and others outside of the job site. Interdependence is natural for all employees on all job sites. Each of us rely on others within and outside of the job to provide guidance, new learning, assistance during difficult periods (both job and non-job related), and other supports in order to remain happily employed.

During the initial intervention period for supported employees, the balance of dependence is usually tipped toward others in the workplace, most notably, the employment specialist. For example, often the employment specialist will perform part of the job for the consumer, will intercede in interpersonal problems with co-workers, provide more than the usual feedback, etc. However, after job duties and related skills are learned by the new employee, the employment specialist must ensure that the interdependence scales tip back toward normalcy so that others on and off the job site will feel the continued employment of the consumer is mutually beneficial. For example, the employer and co-workers must not feel as if they are having to take more time than it's worth to show an employee how to perform job duties. As with any employment situation, if the employer does not feel the employee is "pulling their own weight" or is creating too many problems, the job is likely to be terminated.

The chapter that follows will describe in detail the strategies employment specialists can utilize to ensure the appropriate level of interdependence. At this point, however, it is important to understand that creating interdependence (as opposed to complete *independence*) is a necessary outcome of supported employment. It is also vital that any interventions planned take into account the need for eventually balanced interdependence.

Data-Based Decision Making

Decisions made regarding the design, implementation, and modification of interventions must be based upon the unique consumer attributes and the history of observable job and interpersonal performance of that consumer in past, similar situations. Information on past performance is called *data*. It is very important for the employment specialist to devise methods for each job site to ensure that these data are recorded so that decisions about how to intervene in future similar situations can be made effectively. Data collection is a requirement for effective supported employment implementation.

Again, the purpose of data collection is to provide analysis information that will increase the likelihood of employment success. For example, recording how fast a supported employee completes a task relative to co-workers may provide an opportunity to ask for a raise. Alternatively, the collected production data may indicate the need for an intervention to help the employee work faster. As another example, information regarding periodic and rhythmic affect and mood changes may help the employment specialist assist in medication modification decisions or indicate the need for referral for extensive evaluation for other services. Often, patterns that are revealed by the conscientious recording of information cannot be ascertained by the employment specialist's memory alone.

Common misconceptions about data collection are that it is too unnatural, that the act of data collection must be intrusive, and that data collection on a job site is too difficult to undertake. First, it should be noted that all workers' performance is measured in some way (i.e., it is natural). Number of case closures, number of clients served, and how many refereed articles are accepted for publication are examples of data that are collected on vocational rehabilitation counselors, case managers, and university professors, respectively. Written reprimands, letters of commendation, and other information regarding task and non task performance are potentially part of every personnel file. Indeed, many a job grievance has been initiated because of decisions made in the absence of data. Second, data collection can be as unobtrusive and simple as counting on one's fingers the number of prompts needed to complete a task (and recording them later) or counting the number of units completed. An experienced employment specialist will make the data collection techniques simple and unobtrusive. Like interventions, the variety and creativity of data collection techniques are limited only by the employment specialist's imagination.

Data collection is a means to an end. The result of data collection should be the constant reappraisal of intervention effectiveness. Based on the recorded information and paired with employment specialist experience, knowledge, and intuition, programs are frequently modified to increase their effectiveness and efficiency as well as to better meet the characteristics discussed above.

A GENERAL INTERVENTION MODEL

Like many applied sciences, the creation of job-site interventions is both a science and an art. While there are general processes and parameters to follow when developing job-site interventions, the development of interventions cannot be precisely outlined to suit every case and situation. Indeed, it is useful to consider job-site intervention as a *practice,* similar to the *practice* of medicine or other professions where practitioner knowledge is continually gained through assessment, attempts at effective intervention, and reassessment of individual cases and situations. The purpose of this section is to present a general process that is utilized by most employment specialists to intervene on the job site. As indicated in Figure 7.3, the process includes initial job and consumer assessment, preliminary intervention program development, in-depth assessment, intensive program development and modification, program implementation, and ongoing program assessment. Each of these components of the job-site intervention process will be discussed in more detail below.

Initial Assessment

The initial assessment phase involves two components: the analysis of the job and the assessment of the consumer. As the reader will recall from previous chapters, job analysis involves assessing the requirements (both job-duty and interpersonal) of a given job situation. Consumer assessment involves an array of activities, which could include record reviews and interviews, standardized and/or criterion referenced assessment of skills, and situational assessment on the job or similar site. Both of these components have been discussed extensively in previous chapters. It may be useful to reread those chapters prior to continuing this chapter.

Preliminary Program Development

During preliminary program development, the employment specialist hypothesizes about issues that have a high probability of needing intervention. Although a good job match will somewhat limit the high probability intervention areas, all supported employment placements will require some (often extensive) interventions. Intervention areas may include specific job-duty acquisition (e.g., learning how to operate a computer), nontask specific duties (learning how to clock in and out), or interpersonal skill building (e.g., how to mediate feelings regarding co-workers). Since supported employment is a *place-train* approach, specific skill development within these areas is expected to occur on the job site rather than as a prerequisite to placement.

Job Site Intervention Components

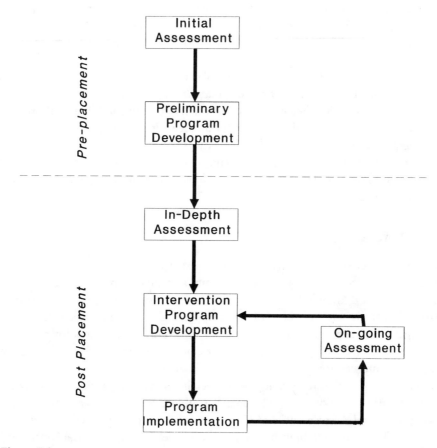

Figure 7.3

There are many examples of intervention needs on job sites. For a consumer with significant cognitive impairments who will soon be a maintenance worker and who has no experience performing the tasks associated with the job (not uncommon for entry-level positions), detailed task analyses (listings of component steps required to perform a task) are likely to be required prior to placement. A pharmacist returning to work after a head injury may also need task analyses to perform her duties, but they may be much less detailed. A retail clerk whose psychiatric disabilities have limited her steady employment may need few task analyses developed, but may need strategies for anger control with supervisors. Preliminary intervention strategies for a consumer with severe physical disabilities may involve very limited pre-employment trials with on-site job equipment to facilitate expeditious building of adaptations or development of job-sharing strategies.

The illustrative examples above all require initial planning that should occur prior to placement. These preliminary intervention programs should include a brief statement of criterion objectives, materials needed, procedures for assessment, task sequences, contingency planning, and measurement strategies and materials (these items are described fully below in the discussion of *Intervention Program Development*). It is wise for the employment specialist to use pencil or some other alterable media when developing preliminary plans, as they are likely to be modified after the completion of the next stage, *In-depth Assessment.*

It is important for the employment specialist to only conduct initial program development on high-probability intervention areas. It is fruitless to spend the time and energy developing a detailed task analysis on a skill that the consumer has repeatedly demonstrated during assessment. Again, the decision as to the likelihood of the need for an intervention program will become easier with employment specialist experience.

In-depth Assessment

On the first day of placement, the employment specialist will arrive on the job armed with job analysis materials (including a sequence of job duties and task analyses), a good knowledge of the consumer based on consumer assessment activities (hopefully with a notion of what things make the consumer really happy and potentially distressed), and preliminary intervention programs for skills that are likely to need development. The purposes of the *In-depth Assessment* phase of the job-site intervention process are to (1) validate that the consumer can, indeed, exhibit those skills that the employment specialist presumed (during Initial Assessment) the consumer possessed, (2) identify problem areas that were not identified during the Initial Assessment, and (3) obtain information on exactly which component skills within each high-probability skill development areas the consumer is able to perform (down to specific steps on task analyses, as appropriate).

Validation of Existing Skills

The validation of presumed skills is a relatively easy process. Using the sequence of job duties, the employment specialist need only observe the consumer perform the tasks as they are presented. If the task is completed correctly, within a normal time span, and with little or no assistance across several trials, the employment specialist can note this and periodically check on the skill throughout the life of the job. Sometimes the consumer will require minimal assistance during the first or second presentation of a task, but will then require no further assistance. In these cases, it is beneficial to observe several additional trials before beginning the development of an intervention program.

Identification of Skills Errantly Thought to Be Existing

Frequently, skills that the employment specialist thought the consumer would possess are, indeed, not present. There may be many reasons why a consumer is not able to perform previously acquired skills. For example, two common factors that inhibit demonstration of previously acquired skills are regression (i.e., if you don't use it, you lose it) and generalization across materials, situations, and trainers (i.e., slight differences in materials, situations, or trainers can cause major problems in task performance). It is important the employment specialist understand the many potential reasons previously learned skills are lost, and not think a consumer just does not want to perform the task. Obviously, during this phase, tasks that are deemed to require significant intervention from the employment specialist need to have preliminary intervention programs developed so that a more comprehensive assessment can be completed.

Comprehensive Assessment

Detailed, step-by-step listings of each skill needing intervention should have already been completed during either preplacement activities or after the first few days, for skill areas identified after placement. During the comprehensive assessment process, the consumer is presented with the job duty or task and given instructions to perform the task. The employment specialist must record which parts (steps) of the task the consumer can perform without assistance and which parts (steps) the consumer needs assistance to complete. The resulting data for each problem task or skill will be the beginning baseline for the intervention program. Figure 7.4 provides an example of this task analysis data. There are several methodologies that can be used to collect this task analysis assessment data. The reader is referred to Barcus, et al. (1987) for a detailed procedures for initial assessment on the job site.

As indicated throughout this chapter, some intervention programs will focus on areas that cannot be task analyzed, for example, controlling verbal utterances (e.g., talking too much, swearing, inappropriate verbal comments), excessive touching, disruptive displays of mood, and other types of interpersonal relationship issues. The assessment of these types of behaviors can be accomplished through careful recording of the behavior.

Consider "John", who is known to frequently be depressed and has lost several jobs because his affect has disgruntled co-workers. The assessment process begins by carefully defining the problem in behavioral terms (e.g., refusing to return greetings of co-workers). As the behavior is observed, the employment specialist records the context in which the behavior was exhibited, including time, place, parties involved, and other information that may be even remotely related (e.g., "Monday, 9:50 A.M., Paul F., John entered the job site sulking, he commented that he had just returned from a visit with his children"). An exact, but brief description of the specific behavior is also recorded (e.g., "Paul said good morning to John. John turned and walked away"). Finally, the employment spe-

*Task Analytic Assessment Data

Employee: Frank
Location: Moneysavers Bank
Employment Specialist: Ming Li
Instructional Cue: "Process the checks"
Natural Cue: Stacks of checks on his desk waiting to be processed

		11/30	12-4	12-7	12-11	12-14
	Steps	B	P	P	P	P
1.	Take the top check from the pile	+	+	+	+	+
2.	Find the vendor number (top left hand corner of check)	+	+	+	+	+
3.	Match vendor number on check with vendor number on work order (top left corner on green and white computer sheet.)	+	+	+	+	+
4.	Tear off all work orders with corresponding vendor numbers	+	+	+	+	+
5.	Put check on top of work orders	+	+	+	+	+
6.	Remove al staples and stack papers (match top left hand corner; papers must be facing forward as you read them)	–	–	+	+	+
7.	Pull out any cash register or credit card receipts	–	–	+	+	+
8.	Paper clip the check to the work order (top left corner)	–	–	–	–	+
9.	Place receipts in envelope	–	–	–	–	+
10.	Tape envelope closed	–	–	–	–	+
11.	Write "Check number" on envelope	–	–	–	–	+
12.	Paper clip envelope to back of check and back ups	–	–	–	–	–
13.	Place paper clipped stack on center of work table. (Checks MUST be in order, so when stacking work, place at bottom of pile facing up.)	–	–	–	–	–
14.	Stamp work completed	–	–	–	–	–
15.	Stack work upside down with the work facing same direction (paper clips should stack on top of each other	–	–	–	–	–
16.	When this pile becomes large enough that it begins to fall (not stack easily), place it in rear of box (with work facing toward front of box, paper clips should be on left side of papers laying sideways)	–	–	–	–	–

*This task analysis was developed by Wendy Parent and Jane Everson

Figure 7.4

cialist should record what happened after the behavior was exhibited ("Paul said 'OK, I won't talk to you'").

Recorded information can be very useful in the development of an intervention program. In the scenario above, repeated data collection could aid in the identification of patterns. For example, this behavior may be more likely to occur on Mondays, or it may occur only with selected co-workers. For example, if repeated occurrences from the above scenario indicate that "sulking" can cue the employment specialist that the behavior is likely to occur, perhaps a self-monitoring pro-

Behavior Recording Form

Consumer: _____   Location: _____

Date: _____

Time Beginning: _____

Time Ending: _____

Employment Specialist: _____

Antecedents

(Record here what happened immediately before the behavior or incident. Include people, tasks, environmental information etc.).

Behavior

(Record here an exact description of what happened, include frequency and intensity.

Consequence

(Record here how people in the environment responded to the behavior. Also indicate immediate and potentially deferred consequences of the behavior).

Figure 7.5

gram can be put into place. It is very unlikely that, without recording these data, effective intervention programs can be developed. The reader is referred to Chapter 9 entitled "Behavior Management at the Job Site" for a more detailed description of these analysis techniques.

In addition to the development of forms and assessment methodologies as described above, the employment specialist must develop a workable schedule for assessment. As a rule of thumb, assessment of tasks should occur at the times that the tasks normally occur. This will provide the most accurate picture of the demands of a task. However, this rule of thumb does not hold true for tasks that are performed only at peak production times. Tasks occurring during peak production hours should be assessed at slower times during the day so that the work flow will be minimally disrupted.

Intervention Program Development

Intervention programs, while varied, generally consist of a description of the exact focus of the program, an objective to be reached, materials needed to implement the program, a task analysis (previously developed for assessment purposes), intervention procedures, contingency plans, data collection methodologies and forms, and plans for generalization, fading, and maintenance. Figures 7.6a and 7.6b provide an illustrative example of an intervention program. Each component of an intervention program is described below.

Description of Program Focus

This section should describe, in observable terms, the target behavior. Good descriptions detail target behaviors that can be measured. For example, in the "John" scenario previously presented, the target behavior was "not returning greetings" rather than displaying depressed affect. Although this is a rather narrow view of the behavior, failure to return greetings was the primary behavior creating interpersonal problems on the job site. Descriptions that describe target behaviors with words such as "understand," "know," "process," etc. are not acceptable. One can only be sure that a consumer understands, has knowledge, and processes through their observable actions.

Target Objective

The objective quantifies the behavior that is expected at the end of the intervention. Objectives must be measurable and should be stated in a positive fashion. Each objective consists of three parts: a contextual statement, the behavior to be performed, and the criteria against which intervention success is to be measured. Again using the "John" scenario, an example objective may be: "Given a verbal or gestural greeting from co-workers, John will return 90% of the greetings in a cheerful manner for five consecutive work days." This objective allows for reasonably accurate measurement and provides specific criteria for completion. Purists may argue that "cheerful" should be more clearly defined, however too much specificity will make program development unwieldy. The objective also gives John some slack for bad days or for people who he specifically has an interpersonal problem with and justifiably does not want to greet.

Materials

It is helpful to list any non-job-task materials needed to implement the intervention program. Frequently, stop watches, timers, tokens, etc. are needed to implement the intervention. Listing them provides the employment specialist with a chance to consider material availability.

Illustrative Intervention Program

"Frank"

Program Focus: Frank's job is to process checks at a local bank. While he has each individual skill task component necessary, (see Figure 7.4) his head injury inhibits correct sequencing of the component steps. Although steps should be modeled at the typical speed as appropriate, acquisition of speed is not a specific focus of this intervention.

Target Objective: Given a stack of 10 checks, Frank will process each of the checks according to the task analysis on 5 consecutive work days.

Materials: Only task related materials (paperclips, staple remover, tape, pen, envelopes, and stamp) and this intervention program as required.

Task Analysis: See attached (Figure 7.4).

*Procedures: When Frank seats himself at the desk, wait 3-5 seconds to see if he starts the task. If he does start the task, move to either baseline (B, P) or training (T) procedures. If he does not initiate the task, say "Frank, process these checks." Mondays and Fridays are baseline/probe days. On these days, give the instructional cue if needed, a record a (+) for each step completed with assistance. When the first error is made, say "stop" and begin training. Use this procedure on checks 1 and 10. Checks 2-9 should be taught using the training procedures below.

All checks on Tuesday-Thursday and checks 2-9 on Mondays and Fridays should be taught using the following procedure. If Frank does not self initiate the task using the natural cue, give the instructional cue (Frank, process the checks). Wait 3-5 seconds, if step 1 is initiated and completed correctly, mark a (+) for that step and wait for initiation of the next step. If the step is not initiated, use a verbal cue (see underlined words on TA), wait 3-5 seconds. If task is initiated and completed correctly, mark a (v) by the step and wait for initiation of next step. If the step is again is not initiated or completed incorrectly within 3-5 seconds, restate the verbal cue and gesture to the appropriate items. If the step is then initiated and completed correctly, mark a (G) beside the step and wait for initiation of next step. If the step is not initiated or completed incorrectly, show Frank how to complete the step, reset the material for that step and reissue the verbal cue. If Frank completes the step correctly, mark a (M) by the step and wait for initiation of the next step. If Frank does not initiate the step correctly or at all reshow him how to do it. Mark a (-) beside the step and wait for initiation of next step. During training, proceed through all checks using this procedure. Record data only on the first and last check. Completion of steps 1-16 constitutes 1 trial. Give verbal reinforcement (Good Work" or "Nice Job") to Frank for each step of the task completed better than the corresponding step on the second most previous trial.

Contingency Plans - If materials or checks are not available to Frank, ask Mr. Shaklee, his supervisor, for help. If Frank seems to be getting frustrated, allow him to switch to a preferable task for 5 to 10 minutes, (i.e., microfilming or moving processed checks to storage areas). Always complete this task before the end of the day.

Data collection: Record data as indicated in the intervention procedures above. Graph baseline/probe data on Mondays and Fridays.

Plans for Fading: When any combination of Probe and Training data shows 10 consecutive trials completed without assistance. Reinforce successfully completed trial (checks 1-5, 7, 10). When Frank completes five consecutive days, move to assessment of production rate and intervention to increase rate if needed.

*This procedure was developed with Frank's needs in mind. Procedures often vary with different consumers

Figure 7.6a

*Task Analytic Training Data

Employee: **Frank**
Location: **Moneysavers Bank**
Employment Specialist: **Ming Li**
Instructional Cue: **"Process the checks"**
Natural Cue: **Stacks of checks on his desk waiting to be processed**

	12-1a	12-1b	12-2a	12-2b	12-3a
Steps	B	P	P	P	P
1. Take the top check from the pile	+	+	+	+	+
2. Find the vendor number (top left hand corner of check)	+	+	+	+	+
3. Match vendor number on check with vendor number on work order (top left corner on green and white computer sheet.)	+	+	+	+	+
4. Tear off all work orders with corresponding vendor numbers	+	+	+	+	+
5. Put check on top of work orders	+	+	+	+	+
6. Remove all staples and stack papers (match top left hand corner; papers must be facing forward as you read them)	M	G	+	+	+
7. Pull out any cash register or credit card receipts	V	V	+	+	+
8. Paper clip the check to the work order (top left corner)	M	G	G	V	+
9. Place receipts in envelope	M	M	G	V	+
10. Tape envelope closed	G	V	G	V	+
11. Write "Check number" on envelope	V	V	V	V	+
12. Paper clip envelope to back of check and back ups	M	M	G	G	V
13. Place paper clipped stack on center of work table. (Checks MUST be in order, so when stacking work, place at bottom of pile facing up.)	M	M	M	G	V
14. Stamp work completed	G	V	V	+	V
15. Stack work upside down with the work facing same direction (paper clips should stack on top of each other	M	M	M	M	M
16. When this pile becomes large enough that it begins to fall (not stack easily), place it in rear of box (with work facing toward front of box, paper clips should be on left side of papers laying sideways)	M	M	M	M	M

This task analysis was developed in part by Wendy Parent and Jane Everson

Figure 7.6b

Task Analysis

As indicated earlier, most job tasks can be broken down into component steps. Breaking the job down to small steps is often very helpful in determining where intervention is needed. Development of task analyses should occur for any job task needing intervention, regardless of the cognitive level of the consumer. Sometimes employment specialists believe higher functioning consumers do not need to have tasks analyzed. It is important to note that we all use task analyses in the performance of our jobs (e.g., computer operation manuals, procedures manuals, etc.). Therefore, while the delineation of component steps may not need to be as detailed for consumers with higher functioning levels, a listing of task components is required for effective and efficient interventions to occur.

When developing task analyses, several points should be remembered. First, only observable behaviors should be listed as steps. For example, instead of, "Identify the starter button," a more precise wording would be, "Push the starter button," since the act of pushing the correct button indicates proper identification. Second, steps should be of the same general size. For example, for a data-entry position task analysis, the step, "Enter demographic information into the computer," requires much more effort than "Press enter." Steps requiring disparate effort can cause confusion when trying to measure and interpret the effectiveness of an intervention program.

Intervention Procedures

This section is the heart of the program. Intervention procedures should describe step-by-step procedures to be followed by all who will be trying to facilitate the acquisition of the objective. Frequently, the step-by-step procedures will detail specific prompting strategies to be used during skill acquisition processes. Prompting procedures generally move from more intrusive to less intrusive (e.g., physical guidance to a verbal prompt). Reinforcement strategies (including the precise reinforcer to be used, under what conditions the reinforcer will be delivered, and a "schedule" that shows how the reinforcer will be gradually withdrawn) are also typically integrated during this process. Intervention procedures should be written with enough specificity so that a stranger, unfamiliar with typical training methodologies, could understand the intervention. This will not only help the employment specialist think about detail, but will also be useful, in the inevitable case, when a secondary employment specialist must cover for an absent primary specialist.

In its embryonic stage, supported employment used interventions developed primarily for persons with mental retardation. Interventions typically focused on task analysis procedures, "try another way" methodologies, and so-called systematic behavioral instructional techniques. Because it is now also used with persons with other disabilities, supported employment interventions have been expanded to include other categories of strategies, such as adaptations, compensation, and psychosupportive strategies. It is important to remember that these procedures are best utilized when interwoven with one another. For example, utilization of compensation strategies will likely involve the development of a behavioral training program. The development of these strategies within the context of supported employment has both diversified the range of intervention options for all people with severe disabilities and created the need for employment specialists with increased competencies.

Contingency Plans

Contingency planning helps the employment specialist think about potential places where things can go very wrong within an intervention. Contingency plans are not developed for incorrect responses (these are handled in the intervention procedures), but are designed to take care of major, generally nontask related responses that a consumer may exhibit during the performance of job duties. For example, given a specific consumer, it may be necessary for the employment specialist to think about what to do if the consumer simply refuses to work and sits down on the job. Preparing for psychomotor seizure activity for a consumer with epilepsy is also an example of contingency planning. For a consumer with a long history of depression and associated suicide attempts, contingency planning would involve detailing potential indicators of the person becoming suicidal and developing referral/management procedures.

It is not possible to anticipate all situations that may occur on the job site. However, with a good knowledge of the consumer, it should be possible to anticipate some of the potential problems that may arise. Planning for these "unexpected" events could potentially save a placement.

Data Collection Methodologies

As indicated in the *Characteristics of Interventions* section, good intervention programs have methods of collecting data that provide enough information relating to consumer learning to facilitate informed decision making while not inhibiting the intervention processes. This balance is critical if data collection methodologies are to be used and serve a real function in the intervention. Data collection methodologies often fall into three general categories: acquisition-data collection techniques, production-data collection techniques, and interpersonal/behavior-data collection techniques.

Most frequently acquisition-data collection procedures involve recording how the consumer performs on individual components (steps) of the task analyses. During assessment, performance is generally recorded using a system of pluses (+) and minuses (-) to indicate independent and incorrect responses, respectively. During intervention, other codes are used to record what level of assistance was needed to correctly perform each component (e.g., verbal, gestural, model, or physical). Programs that are facilitating acquisition would, of course, have more pluses (+) over time. Lack of pluses (+) (or unchanging levels of assistance) generally indicates a need for change in intervention strategies.

Production-data methodologies involve counting the number of units completed in a given period of time or measuring the length of time required to complete one unit of work. For example, on an assembly task, a worker may complete 6 assemblies per hour. In a janitorial position, a worker may complete cleaning one bathroom in 20 minutes. Production data is relatively easy to keep, since the employment specialist must merely note a beginning and ending time for the task or series of units and perform simple mathematical calculations.

Typically, the rate of work is converted to a standard unit of time, such as minutes or hours. This simple process involves dividing the time into the number completed. For example, the work rate of an individual who completed 75 units in 60 minutes is 1.25 units per minute (often expressed as 1.25/minute). Of course, the most important consideration for production is how the consumer's rate compares to the expected work rate (often called the standard work rate). At the end of training, the consumer's work rate should equal or be acceptably close to the standard work rate.

Most interpersonal data are gathered using event recording methodologies, as described above in the comprehensive assessment section. In these methodologies, contextual information (often called antecedents), a description of the behavior, and events following the behavior (often called consequences) are recorded. In addition to examining the data for patterns as in the assessment phase, the frequency and intensity of interpersonal data should move in the expected direction (either up or down) if the intervention program is effective.

Plans for Fading
Fading refers to the systematic withdrawal of external supports on the job site from a consumer. Most intervention programs use external supports, such as prompting strategies, reinforcement strategies, employment specialist presence, and production assistance, to initially facilitate reaching the intervention goal. It is important to consider strategies to reduce the levels of these supports within the intervention program as soon as possible so that the consumer does not become overly dependent upon them.

There are several strategies for fading that are used independently and/or together to remove external supports while maintaining the goal of the intervention. Reduction of reinforcement to "normal" levels is accomplished by gradually reducing the intensity of reinforcement (e.g., less enthusiastic praise) and the frequency of reinforcement (e.g., requiring more correct responses prior to giving praise). This reduction process, called thinning, should continue until the amount of reinforcement received by the consumer matches that of co-workers. In addition to the reduction of reinforcement, the delivery of all reinforcement should be transferred to the supervisor (and to co-workers, as appropriate) as soon as it is feasible. Like reinforcement, external prompts should also be removed, to the greatest extent possible, while still maintaining the intervention goals. Prompts administered by people should be reduced as much as possible and transferred to co-workers and supervisors prior to fading. Some prompts, such as memory devices (e.g., maps), need not be removed if they do not interfere with the performance of the job or are not demeaning (most of us use written prompts to remind us to do things).

Plans for fading begin prior to the first day of intervention. A well-planned intervention program will involve co-worker and supervisor prompting and reinforcement strategies early on. Sometimes, it is easy for employment specialists to become very involved in a case and resist fading because of employment specialist needs rather than consumer needs. While this "mother hen" syndrome is natural, it is also often counterproductive. Avoiding the "mother hen" syndrome is a very important skill for employment specialist to learn and practice.

Program Implementation

The next step in job-site intervention is the implementation of the program. The employment specialist must decide when program implementation is to begin and during which parts of the day the programs will be implemented. The employment specialist is usually running several intervention programs simultaneously. It is important to ensure, however, that too many intervention programs not start at once. This situation could occur if the consumer has many training needs. In this case, a good rule of thumb is to start intervention on the areas that are performed most frequently during the day, as long as intervention does not significantly interfere with production. This will usually facilitate quicker acquisition because of the number of trials available for intervention. If intervention will greatly interfere with production, it is best to choose less hectic times for program implementation. Less frequently performed task interventions are started later in the placement.

Following the In-depth Assessment phase, job task interventions, generally speaking, should start as soon as possible. Intervention programs designed specifically to increase production rates are usually implemented near the completion of skill acquisition interventions for the given task. The initiation of interventions to facilitate interpersonal relationships on the job are often started before placement or immediately on placement as supervisors and co-workers often remember first impressions.

Ongoing Assessment

Supported employment intervention decisions should be data-based and re-evaluated frequently. Evaluation of the effectiveness and efficiency of each intervention program must be ongoing. This evaluation involves careful inspection of the data on a daily basis. Adjustments should be made after prudent consideration of the data. Since some interventions will take longer to be effective, it is important not to change interventions too quickly or drastically, lest the consumer be confused, involving the employment specialist in a series of unneeded modifications. It is difficult to give a rule of thumb of how long to wait before changing a seemingly ineffective intervention. Consideration should be given to the complexity of the goal of the intervention program (e.g., is the goal really hard to achieve?), the level of consumer disability impacting the intervention (e.g., someone with very low cognitive functioning may take longer to acquire certain skills), and the performance of the consumer relative to reaching the goal (e.g., is there any positive movement toward achieving the goal, and if so, how much, and over what period of time).

Ongoing assessment not only refers to the re-evaluation of the intervention during implementation, but also is important after fading has occurred. A hallmark of supported employment is that ongoing support is provided for the life of the job. Part of this support is the monitoring of performance of tasks and behaviors that have previously required intervention. During the follow-along phase of supported employment, it is imperative that the skills developed during the initial training period are maintained. Periodic assessment, often utilizing the same techniques used during the *In-depth Assessment* phase, must be conducted. Other techniques for conducting ongoing assessment are discussed in the next chapter.

SUMMARY

Effective job-site intervention requires extraordinary inventiveness on the part of the employment specialist. He or she must be familiar with a variety of approaches for enhancing employment. Given the increasingly wide array of consumers with diverse abilities and disabilities, it is important that employment specialists are familiar with the range of intervention options currently available. This chapter has provided an overview of good intervention characteristics and a general model for intervention.

8

Job Retention: Toward Vocational Competence, Self-Management, and Natural Supports

Michael D. West, M.Ed.

The emergence and explosive growth of supported employment providers, services, and funding during the 1980s has created employment opportunities for individuals who, beyond the sheltered workshop or activity center, had previously been considered unemployable, including persons with significant mental retardation, physical disabilities, traumatic brain injury, deaf-blindness, and multiple disabilities. The supported employment initiative has also generated a number of policy and implementation problems, issues, and concerns, not the least of which involve how to most effectively and efficiently provide extended support services that enhance job retention of clients. How can agencies determine which clients will need ongoing support services in order to maintain employment? How does an agency plan and fund the types and amounts of extended services that clients will need? Why do so many supported employees lose their jobs despite intensive ongoing support services?

This chapter will examine some of the major issues, strategies, and techniques related to the provision of ongoing support services within a program of supported employment. Emphasis will be given to two programmatic trends that are receiving and will likely continue to receive increasing attention in the supported employment literature and direct services: (1) The development of strategies by which supported employees can monitor and alter their own task-related and social behaviors at the worksite; and (2) incorporating cues, consequences, and change agents found naturally in the work environment into a plan of follow-along services. First, extended services and the need for extended services will be operationally defined, and funding and cost issues explored.

DEFINING EXTENDED SERVICES AND NEED FOR ONGOING SUPPORT

The distinguishing characteristic between "supported employment" and "traditionally time-limited vocational services" is the provision of postemployment support services by a rehabilitation professional, often referred to as a "job coach" or "employment specialist." While time-limited vocational services may incorporate supportive and follow-along methods, a program of supported employment will, by necessity, include interventions at the job site due to the nature of its service consumers. The final regulations for the Rehabilitation Act Amendments of 1986 (*Federal Register*, August 14, 1987) state:

> The need for job skills reinforcement under this program distinguishes supported employment from other rehabilitation programs where job accommodations or independent living services, such as readers, transportation, or housing may be the only needed postemployment services...individuals with severe handicaps, with the exception of the chronically mentally ill, would be inappropriate candidates for supported employment if they do not need job skill training at least twice monthly (p. 30549).

The Amendments differentiate between supported employment service consumers who are severely disabled and those disabled by mental illness who may need continuing off-site interventions after employment without additional job-skill training. For those individuals, and those alone, supported employment monies may fund transitional employment services without a clear need for follow-along services provided at the job site (p. 30551).

Moreover, individuals targeted for supported employment programs would be expected to require ongoing support services for the duration of their employment (p. 30546). Traditionally time-limited postemployment services, by statutory definition, do not extend beyond 18 months from the date of employment (p. 30551). While many individuals with even severe disabilities are able to obtain and sustain employment through time-limited services alone, many cannot without regular provision of intervention and support.

This leads to a dilemma that provider agencies frequently face: how to determine *a priori* the need for extended services and, by extension, appropriate candidates for supported employment. In some cases, this has led to conflicts between the provider and funding agency, when individuals identified for supported employment prove able to function adequately with little or no follow-along services, or those identified for time-limited services only evidence a need for extended support. Client screening, for either supported employment services or transitional services only, should be done on an individual client basis that requires consideration of the types and severity of disabilities, the presence of unusual or dangerous behaviors, functional skills and limitations, prior work and employment service history, motivations and aspirations for work, and the personal social support networks that already exist. To some extent, the agency must also consider the generic services and supports that are available to the client and family members, the types of jobs or work settings that have been targeted for the individual, and the overall level of integration and acceptance of persons with severe disabilities within the community at large. The difficulty of prior selection also underscores the need for state policies that have some flexibility in terms of client placement, funding, and movement between transitional and supported employment services.

The types of activities authorized by the Rehabilitation Act Amendments of 1986 as extended services are *on-site interventions* and *off-site interventions*, with authorization for off-site interventions conditional on provision of on-site interventions. These interventions will be explained more fully later in this chapter.

FUNDING EXTENDED SERVICES

Coordination of Funding Sources

Time-limited vocational training services for supported employment consumers are generally funded by state vocational rehabilitation agencies, following the identification of an appropriate state or private nonprofit funding source for extended services (*Federal Register,* August 14, 1987, p. 30552). The coordination of funding from time-limited services to ongoing support has often been problematic for supported employment providers (Arkansas Research and Training Center 1985), resulting in either the absence of follow-along or the abandonment of the supported employment concept.

Extended services funding may be even more problematic for individuals with primary disabilities other than mental retardation or long-term mental illness, who may not fall under the traditional state mental health/mental retardation funding "umbrella." In a recent survey of the 27 states awarded Title III supported employment systems change grants in 1986 and 1987, conducted by the Rehabilitation Research and Training Center on Supported Employment (RRTC), Kregel, Shafer, Wehman, and West (1989) found that nine or fewer had mandated extended services and identified public funding sources for persons with cerebral palsy (33%), other physical disabilities (30%), traumatic brain injury (TBI) (19%), and hearing and visual impairments (19% each). In contrast, 100% of the 27 states had identified resources for persons with mental retardation (MR), and 77% for persons with chronic mental illness (CMI). In addition, many of those states, which had identified resources for supported employees with nontraditional disabilities, required that those individuals also meet the eligibility criteria of the state Mental Health/Mental Retardation/Developmental Disability agency.

As this book goes to press, the RRTC is surveying vocational rehabilitation services in all 50 states and the District of Columbia, and again asking if funding resources have been identified for extended services across disability categories. Only time will tell if the influx of individuals with disabilities other than MI or MR into supported employment programs has influenced states to amend their policies to provide extended service funds for these nontraditional consumer populations.

Problems with obtaining follow-along funds have inspired many supported employment providers to approach private agencies or groups to ensure ongoing funding. These sources have included private insurance carriers, the United Way, civic groups, corporate or private foundations, and individual donations. Another alternative has been to have the consumer set aside his or her own resources for later follow-along activities and utilizing the Plan for Achieving Self-Support (PASS) income exclusion offered for SSI recipients (Nielson 1986). Thus, consumers pay for their own follow-along services, but retain SSI cash benefits to offset the costs. Using the PASS exclusion has one serious drawback in that it can be extended only for a maximum of 48 months. However, this strategy may give the program time to locate permanent funding for ongoing support.

Time and Money for Follow-along Services

Funding formulas, units of service, and costs for transitional and follow-along services vary tremendously from state to state (Wehman, Shafer, Kregel, and Twardzik 1989). In Virginia, the unit of service is defined as client-specific intervention time, in clock hours. Time devoted to activities required for the general operation of the program are not tracked or billed. Types of client-specific activities that are billable to the Virginia Department of Rehabilitative Services (DRS) are presented in Table 8.1, and Figure 8.1 shows how intervention time was distributed across the billable categories. Hourly client-contact rates are calculated to recover personnel costs (direct service, administrative, and support), fringe benefits, occupancy, transportation, and other miscellaneous costs, and are adjusted for approximately 35% nonbillable time required for the operation of the program. In Virginia, a supported employment client is considered to be stabilized in his or her job when weekly staff intervention time required for job maintenance falls below 20% of the client's weekly work hours, at which point funding responsibility is shifted to the extended-services funding agency (Hill 1988). Although policies regarding cooperative funding agreements vary from state to state, this specific level of intervention provides an indication of the relative funding obligations for time-limited and extended-service funding agencies.

Figure 8.2 shows the average amount of staff intervention per week as a percentage of work hours aggregated for over 2600 supported employment clients tracked by Virginia's Supported Employment Information System (SEIS). This chart shows the ideal fading of intervention over time as the supported employee devel-

Table 8.1   Service Categories for Consumer-Specific Intervention Time

Time Active is time at the job site actually spent working with the consumer, including active observation. It includes any active training for the consumer.

Time Inactive is time spent on the job site between periods of active intervention. This is time during which the employment specialist has removed him/herself from active involvement and/or active observation of the consumer.

Travel/Transport Time is time used in traveling to a job site, to a meeting concerning a consumer, to the consumer's home, or in transporting a consumer anywhere.

Consumer Training Time is time spent training the consumer, in other than directly related job skills, while he/she is not at work. Examples are money handling, grooming, counseling, bus training, family matters, etc.

Consumer Program Development indicates time spent developing appropriate instructional plans, including task analyses and behavioral intervention programs.

Direct Employment Advocacy indicates time advocating for the consumer with job-site personnel for purposes directly related to employment, including job development.

Indirect Employment Advocacy indicates time advocating with persons not directly affiliated with the employment site.

Consumer Screening/Evaluation indicates time screening the consumers for eligibility or evaluating eligible consumers, including consumer assessment.

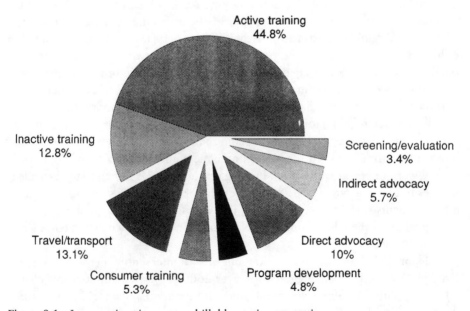

Figure 8.1   Intervention time across billable service categories.

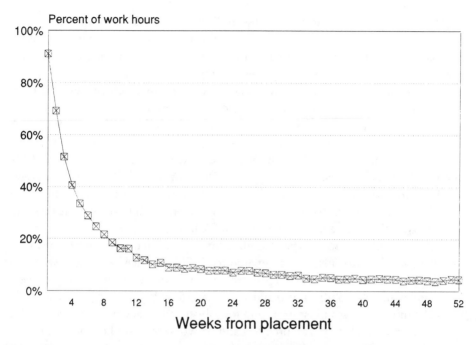

Figure 8.2   Intervention time as a percentage of work time.

ops competence in the job, leveling off at approximately 5% of work time. Of course, no individual client will (or should) show such an ideal pattern. Most individuals will have peaks and valleys of intervention as retraining need or other problems arise that require action by the rehabilitation agency. Additionally, there is tremendous variance in the level of intervention required by supported employment clients on a weekly basis for job maintenance activities, which should discourage funding agencies from setting limits on funds based upon average levels of intervention.

On average, clients stabilized in their jobs by week 12 (4 weeks after intervention time falls below 20% of work time). Post-stabilization intervention time thereafter averaged 5% of client work time (mean of 27 hours per week), or approximately 1.45 hours per week. The annualized cost of providing extended services based upon an average cost of services of $28 per contact hour was $2,111. Again, these are gross averages based on highly variable data.

The types and amounts of intervention time required for job maintenance appear to be heavily influenced by the primary disabilities of clients. McDonald-Wilson, Revell, Nguyen, and Peterson* (1991) compared interventions for persons with CMI with those of all other persons in the SEIS, a group comprised primarily of persons with MR. They found that supported employees with CMI, on av-

*On reference list - *Journal of Vocational Rehabilitation, 1* (3), 30-44.

erage, required less time to reach job stabilization and less time for job maintenance, but that interventions for persons with CMI showed dramatic "peaks", whereas interventions for other supported employees were provided in relatively consistent weekly amounts. This pattern undoubtedly reflects the episodic nature of impairments attributable to CMI. They also found that persons with CMI required proportionally less time with job-site training and retraining activities, and more time in training activities away from the job site and in advocacy efforts both within and apart from the job site. However, over half of all intervention time (57%) for persons with CMI was provided at the workplace, compared with 67% for all other supported employment clients. They note that this finding contradicts the basis for the regulatory exemption for at least two job-site interventions per month during the extended service phase for persons with CMI, in that these individuals continue to require significant job-skills reinforcement.

West, Callahan et al. (1991) studied intervention patterns for persons with severe physical impairments as compared to all SEIS participants and also found that proportionally less time was spent training and more in program development time (including job modifications) and advocacy efforts both at the job site and off-site. The difference was most profound for job-site advocacy time, evidencing the need to nurture and support employers and co-workers as well as the client.

West, Wehman et al. (1991) studied intervention patterns for supported employment clients with severe TBI and for clients with mental retardation. They found that clients with TBI required more time and expenditures to reach stabilization and to maintain their jobs. Ongoing services required 1.64 hours per week, at an annual cost of $2,476. They found tremendous variability in transitional service needs, but on a per client basis, average weekly extended service needs were relatively consistent at one to two hours per week. As with the CMI population, interventions for persons with TBI will typically show peaks and valleys, again indicative of the episodic nature of neurobehavioral impairments that frequently result from the injury (Kreutzer and Morton 1988).

Kregel, Hill, and Banks (1988) compared supported employment clients with mild or borderline MR with supported employment clients with moderate or severe MR represented in the SEIS. There was no significant difference between the two groups on total intervention time required for the first year of employment. The group with moderate or severe retardation required more initial training time, but required fewer hours of weekly ongoing services.

It should be noted that each of these intervention time studies used the SEIS data base for analyses, which has both positive and negative implications. On the positive side, the internal validity of the findings is high because the provider agencies serving the study groups used consistent operational definitions of intervention time, billable activities, and job stabilization and received uniform and consistent training in supported employment practices and documentation. On the negative side, the generalizability of these findings to other state systems is open to question.

ISSUES RELATED TO PROVIDING EXTENDED SERVICES

Why Do Supported Employees Lose Their Jobs?

Prior to describing strategies for helping supported employees keep their jobs, it will be helpful to explore the reasons they may lose their jobs. There is considerable evidence that a significant percentage of individuals who enter a supported employment position will be separated, most within six months of placement (Lagomarcino 1990; RRTC 1990). Within the SEIS data base of over 2600 supported employees, only about 62% will still be employed in their first placement after six months, and fewer than half will still be in their first position after one year (see Figure 8.3). The primary reason for job separation is employee-initiated resignation from the position (44.5%), followed by termination (37.5%), lay-off (16.7%), and extended leave of absence (1.1%). From the available literature, specific factors that contribute to separation can be related to (1) the worker's production, (2) the worker's social skills, (3) his or her physical or mental health status, (4) the worker's responsibility to the job, (5) economic factors, and (6) other external factors.

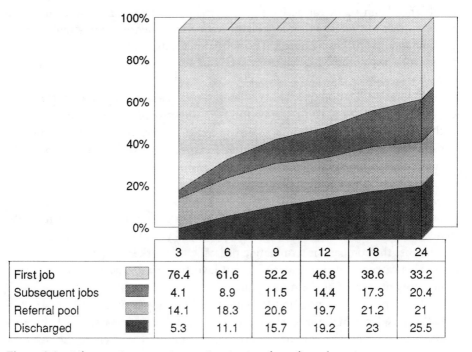

		3	6	9	12	18	24
First job		76.4	61.6	52.2	46.8	38.6	33.2
Subsequent jobs		4.1	8.9	11.5	14.4	17.3	20.4
Referral pool		14.1	18.3	20.6	19.7	21.2	21
Discharged		5.3	11.1	15.7	19.2	23	25.5

Figure 8.3   Job retention at various points in time from first placement.

Production Factors

Production problems typically relate to the worker's speed or quality of work, the inability to perform certain tasks, or the need for continual prompting to initiate or complete work. Within the SEIS (RRTC 1990), these are given as the primary reasons for 17.5% of all separations. In a study by Lagomarcino (1990), production factors accounted for 12% of separations.

Production factors may be mitigated early in the placement process through careful job analysis and client-job matching. Job demand should be assessed under the conditions in which the supported worker will be expected to perform them. Initially, supported workers need not be able to perform the job as expected, of course, but employment specialists should be realistic about dissonance between client capabilities and job expectations and the extent to which training, adaptation, and support can lessen these differences over the long term.

Changes in production speed, work quality, or self-initiation during the follow-along phase may signal several things, including boredom with the job, supervisor, or co-workers.

Physical and Mental Health Factors

Physical and mental health factors contribute substantially to job separations of persons with TBI (Sale et al. 1991) and CMI (Lagomarcino 1990; McDonald-Wilson et al. 1991). These disabilities frequently require intermittent hospitalization or absence from work for active psychiatric impairment, for medical or health problems, or for receiving other rehabilitative treatments. Interestingly, in the Lagomarcino (1990) study, medical reasons also accounted for 9% of terminations for persons with mild MR, which may be due to the presence of other disabling conditions, such as epilepsy.

If occasional hospitalization or other prolonged absence from work for physical or mental health reasons can be foreseen, the provider agency can negotiate with the employer to job-share a position. When the regular worker is absent, a substitute (with training by the employment specialist) will be provided by the agency to fill in.

Economic Factors

Economic factors account for 16.7% of all separations in the SEIS and for 17% of separations in the Lagomarcino (1990) study. Typically, these separations occur because the company is terminating or laying off workers because of slow business. This category also includes seasonal layoffs during slow times of the year, which are anticipated at the time of hire.

The types of jobs targeted for supported employment consumers are frequently entry-level, high turnover jobs in service related businesses, largely because they are usually the easiest points of access for supported workers to the competitive work world. Unfortunately, they are also the positions most susceptible to cuts when business is slow. If the skills and interests of the individual client warrant placement in such a position, the agency should be prepared for occasional job changes. Agencies should also examine their local labor market to identify industries and specific businesses in which economic layoffs are likely. In addition, Lagomarcino (1990) recommends caution in placing supported employees in new businesses, which tend to fail at higher rates than older, established businesses.

Job Responsibility

An absence of job responsibility is a significant contributor to job separation across disability groups, but particularly for persons with mild MR (Hill, Wehman, Hill, and Goodall 1986) and with CMI (Lagomarcino 1990). A substantial group of supported employees simply decide that they no longer desire to be employed. In addition, problems with attendance, punctuality, and general attitude toward their job are frequently given as reasons for separation. As with production problems, absence of job responsibility may be outward signs of dissatisfaction or boredom with the job.

Other External Factors

In this broad category, a number of factors contribute to job separation. These include problems with transportation to and from work, parental or spousal interference, potential loss of government benefits, or the client moving away. Also in this category are positive separations, such as the supported employee finding a better job or retiring.

From the above discussion, it should be apparent that supported employment providers need to be diligent about maintaining close contact with the supported employee, the family, the employer, and any other service providers or involved parties, and also need to be prepared to respond to any and all threats to the job security of their clients. It should also be apparent that agencies should attempt to proactively plan extended service needs by identifying a client's potential problems in each of the above areas, anticipating methods of intervention, and considering the individuals responsible for each anticipated intervention. Ideally, the follow-along plan should be written and developed jointly by all involved participants, describing in concrete terms how each problem will be addressed. While no follow-along plan will identify every future problem, nor ensure that a problem will be addressed as planned, a written plan is the agency's first and best assurance that problems affecting employment will come to their attention and that there is a commitment to solve them before a separation occurs.

While many of the studies related to job separation cited above attempted to isolate single causes, it is unlikely that a job separation truly has a single, discreet cause. Separation is more likely the culmination of any number of events, attitudes, and decisions on both the part of the employee and the employer—in the words of Sale et al. (1990), "More a process rather than an event"—with the end result being that either the employee or the employer decide the employment situation is not worth pursuing further. As an elementary example, an individual may have been terminated primarily because he was repeatedly absent from work. He may have been absent because he had no reliable transportation, which resulted because his parents, who originally agreed to provide transportation, failed to do so. Yet, if the job paid more, they might have been more likely to follow through with their commitment. Yet again, if the job were more interesting and reinforcing to the employee, he might very well have pushed his parents harder or made other arrangements for getting to work.

Viewing separation as a process has positive connotations for a supported employment program. First, the separation process can be reversed if the client and employer have mutual feelings that the placement can be saved and is worth saving. In addition, incidents, behaviors, or production deficits need not lead to separation if the employee is able to compensate by being a worthwhile employee in other ways.

Given the nature of supported employment consumers (the severity of their disabilities, their historical exclusion from vocational preparation and other adult services, their limited competitive work experience, etc.) and the entry-level jobs into which they are frequently placed, it should not be too surprising that many eventually lose their jobs. Perhaps the larger issue facing the field is not that many supported employees are separated, but what happens to them afterward. While many are placed again (and many again and again), an approximately equal number are either discharged from the program or returned to a "waiting-list" status without replacement (RRTC 1990). For many supported employees and their families, the promise of long-term support only lasts as long as the first job. The reasons for this phenomenon, including the influence that providers, funding agencies, consumers, and families have in the decision to terminate supported employment services after a separation, certainly require further scrutiny.

Family Involvement and Job Retention

Family roles in supported employment services are described more fully in Chapter 5, but the role of the family in job retention services deserves mention here as well. Without full support from the family, long-term job retention is unlikely (Kernan and Koegel 1980; Kochany and Keller 1981; Wehman 1981). This support is usually manifested in agreements to monitor medication, to report health or psychological status, to provide transportation, to ensure that the supported employee is adequately prepared to go to work, and to provide emotional support and encouragement. Depending on his or her age and level of dependency, a supported employment consumer may require these or other supports as part of a job retention plan. It is also helpful for family members to understand the difference between active involvement in job retention and overprotection. In some cases, this may involve agreements to not engage in certain activities, such as unnecessary contact with the employer or supervisor, "covering" for the supported employee, etc.

Service providers should also be attuned to the psychological health of family relationships, particularly for clients with emotional or behavioral disabilities associated with CMI or TBI. In some cases, family-based therapeutic intervention may be vital to achieving employment success. Support programs for these families will need to focus attention on three areas that directly influence job placement and retention: (1) helping the parents or spouse develop realistic vocational and independent living goals, (2) helping families develop mechanisms and skills for relieving family stress and dysfunction, and (3) helping family members understand and prepare for the financial implications of full-time or part-time employment, such as the loss or reduction of SSI, SSDI, Medicaid, or other entitlements. The role of the employment specialist would be to help families obtain family-based therapeutic resources, not to provide them.

The Importance of Choice in Job Retention

Issues related to consumer empowerment and choice in supported employment are discussed more fully in Chapter 2, but merit a brief mention here. Consumer participation and choice in identifying and selecting from vocational options during the placement phase is the first step towards long-term job retention. In some cases, this will likely mean balancing the desires and expectations of the client and his or her family with the constraints of the local labor market or realistic expectations for achieving specific occupational goals. It also may involve an attitude adjustment on the part of service providers, who frequently explore available jobs first and consumer skills and aspirations afterward. Consumers may be advised to take the available job now (even it it presents no challenge or gratification), until the job they want comes along. As with any member of the general population, a supported employee who feels that his or her job is trivial, dead-end, uninteresting, beneath or out of line with his or her level of skill or education will not likely be motivated to alter behaviors or increase productivity in order to keep that job.

Once a desirable position has been found and obtained, the decision to remain in the position is also a matter of choice for the supported employee. The myth of the worker with disabilities who toils away year after year in an entry-level or monotonous job, just happy to be working, is fast giving way to reality. While many individuals with disabilities do, indeed, stay with these types of jobs for many years, the relative size of this group is probably not much different from that found in the general work force. Persons with disabilities, as do most members of the work force, need to be given the opportunity to make voluntary career moves upward, downward, or laterally; to change scenery; or to begin anew. When such times arise, job terminations should not necessarily be viewed as a failure on the part of the consumer, the employment specialist, the employer, or the program, but as evolutionary stages in the development, growth, and self-determination of the consumer.

PLANNING SERVICES FOR ENHANCING JOB RETENTION POTENTIAL

Fading From the Job Site

Fading of the employment specialist from the job site is perhaps the most difficult adjustment period for both the supported employee and the employer. Fading too rapidly may result in a loss of skill and behavioral gains that had been previously made; fading too slowly may increase employee and employer dependence on the employment specialist. The determination of the rate of fading must be made on an individual basis, using all the available client data (i.e., supervisor's evaluations, production rates, etc.) as guides (Wehman 1981).

Fortunately, there are strategies that the employment specialist can employ to mediate the effects of fading. Two approaches that are particularly relevant to the discussion of follow-along services, *self-management strategies* and the *use of co-workers as providers of support*, will be reviewed here.

Developing Self-management Strategies

The most powerful antecedents and consequences to behavior are those that occur in natural vocational, social, or academic environments (Stokes and Baer 1977). When the learner seems unable or unwilling to respond to natural antecedents and consequences, alternative strategies, such as self-management procedures, are in order. Self-management, according to Baer (1984), involves training the learner to (a) recognize his or her own problem, (b) translate problems into behaviors to be altered, (c) locate or contrive natural contingencies, and (d) arrange contingencies to promote behavioral change. Self-management procedures have been successfully used in the instruction of children and adults with developmental disabilities in social, academic, daily-living, and vocational applications (Crouch, Rusch, and Karlan 1984; Wacker and Berg 1983; Karlan and Rusch 1982). Wacker and Berg (1986) describe the use of self-management within an employment situation. Although they specifically address strategies for workers with MR, as do the overwhelming majority of self-management studies, similar strategies may be useful for workers with other primary disabilities, who have deficits of memory, concentration, or disinhibition. By teaching self-control of behavior, the employment specialist is closer to ensuring that the worker can function in the workplace in the absence of external guidance and instruction.

Lagomarcino, Hughes, and Rusch (1989) describe the steps that employment specialists should follow in developing a self-management program to promote job independence for workers with disabilities:

1. Identify the problem through routine work performance evaluations. Self-management programs can be developed for problems with both productivity and social skills.
2. Verify the problem by direct observation of the worker and interviews with the supervisor and co-workers.
3. Establish a range of acceptable behavior based on observations of co-workers and negotiations with the employer.
4. Assess the work environment for naturally occurring cues and reinforcers to prompt and maintain behavior. Natural cues can be in the form of clocks or timers, employee check lists, whistles, and actions or statements of co-workers or supervisors, and natural reinforcers can be food items from a vending machine, supervisor praise, preferred tasks, etc. If no natural cues or reinforcers are present, or if natural cues and reinforcers are not sufficient for the individual worker, then socially acceptable, artificial cues and reinforcers must be developed.
5. Select a self-management procedure that will be compatible with specific job requirements and that will not draw negative attention to the worker. A few examples of these procedures will be described further in this chapter.
6. Teach self-management skills using techniques based on established learning principles (such as fading, shaping, modeling, etc.), which gradually withdraws external assistance from the trainer.
7. Evaluate the effects of self-management training by comparing his or her performance pre- and post-training, and comparing post-training performance with that of co-workers.

Some specific types of self-management strategies will now be described. These strategies are grouped as those that rely on self-administered cues and those that rely on self-administered consequences. These may be used in isolation or in any combination.

Self-administered Cues
Wacker and Berg (1986) describe three methods of self-cuing. The most frequently used form is *self-instruction*, in which the worker is first taught to perform the task, and then to produce self-generated verbal prompts to initiate and complete the task. For example, after instructing a motel housekeeper in the various tasks associated with room cleaning, the employment specialist might train the employee to initiate each task with an instruction (i.e., "First, clean the bathroom. Next, dust the furniture") immediately prior to the performance of each step. Self-instruction might also be utilized for initiating social contacts on the job, such as lunch or break behavior, greeting the supervisor or co-workers, or appropriate responses to stressful situations.

Moore, Agran, and Fodor-Davis (1989) used a similar procedure, which they termed verbal training, to teach workers with mental retardation to increase their productivity in sheltered work tasks. These workers were instructed to tell themselves that they needed to work faster with positive results, with no instruction specifically given in improving speed or efficiency. Although this particular strategy was used in a sheltered workshop, where workers verbally motivating themselves may be socially accepted, this type of behavior might go unnoticed or be acceptable in some competitive settings.

A strategy similar to self-instruction is *verbal labeling,* in which tools, workpieces, or aspects of a job are made more concrete and salient by the worker verbalizing their name or label. For example, in a data-entry position, which requires separate entry formats for various forms or lists, the employment specialist might instruct the worker to verbally name each form prior to entry. This verbal cue then triggers the appropriate response, in this case, the selection of the appropriate format.

The third method of self-cuing is the use of a *permanent prompt,* such as a written list of duties or task sequences, or picture prompts bound into a book or posted in an unobtrusive place. For example, a dining room attendant in a fast-food restaurant may have a picture sequence of duties taped on the inside of the door to a utility room or on the lid of a garbage bin. The worker can refer to this picture prompt regularly to ensure that tasks are not neglected.

Another form of permanent prompt might be a timer or clock, which can be used by workers to set production goals, either for producing a set number of units or for completing a duty or set of duties within a time limit. Moore et al. (1989) trained workers with MR to use timers to establish their own production goals for sorting washers.

Another permanent prompting system, one which might be less stigmatizing to the supported worker, is the use of taped instructions and a portable cassette player with earphones (Berg and Wacker 1983). The worker is instructed to start and stop the tape at appropriate times in order to receive task or sequencing instructions. In many work environments, personal cassette players are acceptable and common among workers, and this adaptation will not call attention to itself or to the worker. For example, personal cassette players might be acceptable in a motel setting for room cleaners or laundry workers, but not for desk clerks or accountants.

Self-administered Consequences

Training workers with disabilities to self-administer reinforcement and/or punishments has two potential benefits. First, by self-administering reinforcement, the worker has the opportunity to receive greater amounts of reinforcement when natural reinforcement is scarce. Second, an employee who self-reinforces or self-punishes is less likely to be affected by disruptions at the job site, such as changes in supervision (Wacker and Berg 1986).

Self-administered reinforcements and punishments at the job site are an individual determination, based on the likes and dislikes of the worker and the level of tolerance at the job site. For example, as reinforcement for completing assignments or responding appropriately to his co-workers, a supported employee may be trained to allow himself a special treat at break periods. This type of self-reinforcement would be easily tolerated at almost any job, whereas allowing extra break periods might not be. Moore et al. (1989) taught sheltered workshop employees to reinforce themselves by taking nickles from a cup and placing them in another cup to keep. In most competitive work situations, this form of self-reinforcement would probably call attention to the worker by making him or her appear juvenile.

Co-worker Involvement and Support

One of the primary goals of integrated employment is the natural development of friendships and social contacts between the worker with disabilities and his or her co-workers. Co-workers have also been recognized as active and passive resources in providing follow-along services. Passive functions include the use of co-workers as (1) normative references for assessing consumer work skills and behaviors and (2) subjective evaluators of consumer work performance (White 1986). The use of co-workers as active change agents has been suggested as a means of controlling program costs (Hill and Wehman 1982) as well as maintaining job performance through daily contact (Rusch, Martin, and White 1985; Wehman 1981).

Shafer (1986) describes three active functions that co-workers can perform as part of a job retention plan. The first is that of *advocates* for the supported employee, ensuring that the supported employee is treated fairly and with dignity while at work. Second, co-workers can be active *observers* and *reporters* of job performance and potential problems that may be developing. Finally, co-workers may function as *trainers*, providing either direct instruction in new work tasks or periodic reinforcement for correct performance or appropriate behaviors. It is important in planning co-worker involvement that individuals are selected who are willing and able to perform the duties as instructed by the employment specialist, and that their involvement with the supported employee will only minimally intrude upon their own job duties.

MODELS OF SUPPORTED EMPLOYMENT BASED ON NATURAL SUPPORTS

The nurturing and utilization of natural supports in the workplace, such as supervisors, co-workers, customers, and other employer resources, has received increased attention in supported employment literature in recent years. While social integration and co-worker involvement have been recognized as primary goals of supported employment since its inception, the movement toward systems of natural support appears to be gaining considerable momentum within the vocational rehabilitation field. Indeed, Nisbet and Hagner (1989) have proposed four new models of supported employment that utilize co-workers and other employer resources as the primary means of providing job-site interventions: the mentoring option, the training consultant option, the job sharing option, and the attendant option. One can deduce from the nomenclature that these models rely upon designated co-workers, supervisors, or other assistants who are already a part of the work culture or, in the case of the assistant option, who become part of the culture along with the supported employee.

The impetus for the movement toward natural supports comes from two interrelated theorems; first, as stated previously, naturally occurring cues, consequences, and change agents are more effective for training and generalizing new behaviors and skills than are cues, consequences, and agents that are externally imposed (Stokes and Baer 1977); and second, training and other interventions provided by a rehabilitation specialist are likely to be "rehabilitation-centered" and unnecessarily formal, rather than constructed around the existing work culture, and in the process may ignore or supplant informal resources and expertise that may already be available. While these theorems and the criticisms of current models of supported employment presented by Nisbet and Hagner (1989) are undeniable, service providers and funding agencies should have concerns about developing and implementing extended services that rely exclusively or predominantly on co-workers, employers, or assistants, both in terms of the research base of these proposed models and the practicality of implementation. Because of the potential impact of the natural supports movement on supported employment services for persons with severe disabilities, these two areas warrant a thorough examination.

A Second Look at Research on Workplace Support Systems

Nisbet and Hagner (1989) review research from the industrial sociology and management literature and arrive at three conclusions: (1) informal interactions flourish at work; (2) patterns of social interaction vary widely across and within work environments; and (3) some support is available naturally within work environments (p. 262). They use these conclusions to justify new models of supported employment based upon natural supports that exist in the workplace. This author's own review of this literature yields two further conclusions: first, social interaction and support are selectively shared; and second, social interaction with co-workers and supervisors has limited utility in problem-solving situations.

Social Interaction and Support Are Selectively Shared
Much of the organizational research of the past 20 years has focused upon the psychological sense of community, defined by McMillan and Chavis (1986) as "a feeling that members have of belonging, a feeling that members matter to each other and to the group, and a shared faith that members' needs will be met through their commitment to be together" (p. 9). McMillan and Chavis (1986) and Klein and D'Aunno (1986) have reviewed this research as it relates to organizations in gen-

eral and to places of employment, respectively. Both groups came to the conclusion that sense of community is, in Klein and D'Aunno's (1986) words, a "double-edged sword with potentially negative consequences for work organizations and individuals" (p. 373). Those individuals within the social and normative boundaries of the collective may enjoy increased self-respect, self-esteem, coping abilities, and sense of purpose Those perceived as different or deviant may be insulated, polarized, or ostracized from the larger group. Sathe (1983), using the term "corporate culture" to describe the shared understandings of a work community, states that cultures ensure self-perpetuation only by retaining employees who fit into the culture and by weeding out those who do not.

Studies of the nature and degree of interpersonal relations in work environments have yielded inconsistent findings (Henderson and Argyle 1985). Relationships may range from close friendship to active dislike, and interactions with co-workers may range from helpful to stressful. Much of this literature consists of single case studies of industries and jobs described by the researchers as demeaning, degrading, or monotonous and describes the coping mechanisms, both positive and negative, that employees develop (Thompson 1983; Lawler, Hackman, and Kaufman 1973).

Summarizing research related to physical proximity of workers and the development of friendships, Sundstrom (1986) concludes:

> A few field studies found friendships among people in adjacent
> workspaces, where conditions allowed them to talk with each other during
> work. However, friendships only formed among a fraction of the neigh-
> boring workers who conversed, and often involved people with similar
> backgrounds. (p. 396).

As examples, Brass (1985) and Burke, Weir, and Duncan (1976) found a network of helping relationships within work environments, but typically among individuals of similar age, sex, type of job, and status. Similar findings were reported by Lincoln and Miller (1979), who suggest that individuals prefer to socialize and seek friendships at work with those whom they perceive to be similar to themselves.

Thus, friendship and social support are not necessarily available to all employees within an organization and are likely to be unavailable to those perceived as different or deviant from other members of the organizational culture. Rehabilitation literature in the area of employer and co-worker acceptance (Albrecht, Walker, and Levy 1982; Bordieri and Drehmer 1987; Florian 1978) indicates that persons with disabilities are among those for whom acceptance and social support are not readily available.

Social Support Has Limited Significance in Problem-solving
Burke, Weir, and Duncan (1976) found that informal helping relationships develop among co-workers. However, they also found that "the majority of helping rela-

tionships appear to be restricted to formal working hours and within corporate walls, giving the impression that work relationships are perceived as having a limited and circumscribed value to the lives of individuals" (p. 374). They further suggest that "individuals in organizations are not likely to develop close, personal relationships with one another...[this] might inhibit individuals from turning to others with their problems or from reaching out when they sense an individual is under stress" (p. 375). They also found that members of organizations were reluctant to help co-workers deal with problems of an intimate, personal, or emotional nature, preferring instead to help co-workers with impersonal work-related matters. In one of the few similar studies of supported employment consumers, Shafer, Rice, Metzler, and Haring (1989) surveyed co-workers of individuals with mental retardation, also finding that interaction was primarily work-related.

Kaplan and Cowen's (1981) finding that industrial foremen self-reported spending 2.5 hours per week helping employees with personal problems is widely cited in the sociology of work literature. In describing the types of personal problems they encountered, these foremen included problems that are, indeed, work-related, but not task-centered, such as an employee's problems with co-workers, concern over opportunity for advancement and job security, and job dissatisfaction (p. 636). These accounted for 42.4% of all the "personal" problems with which the foremen were approached. These types of problems would appear to be within the work scope of a supervisor or foreman and thus falsely inflate the meantime reported for helping with personal problems.

Perhaps more instructive are the self-reported problem-solving strategies these foremen used with their employees. In less than half of the times (42.4%) that foremen were approached with problems did they help the employee find a solution. The remaining times, they responded by "offering support or sympathy, just listening, trying to be light-hearted, telling the person to count their blessings, trying not to get involved, or changing the subject" (p. 636). The effectiveness of the foremen's help was not assessed.

Practicality of Natural Support Models

The criticisms of current supported employment methods presented by Nisbet and Hagner (1989) focus primarily on extreme cases, where the culture and resources of the workplace are totally ignored or supplanted in favor of externally imposed interventions. There should be equal concern about service providers who would totally eschew external interventions and, instead, give their programs and their clients over to the dynamics of the workplace. Service providers should have legitimate concerns about how well co-workers and other job-site personnel can serve as effective interventionists for supported employees who have challenging behaviors, psychotic episodes, or intensive training or adaptation needs. Service providers should also have concerns about how long other personnel can perform these activities before the company decides that continued employment of the supported employee is not worth the time, personnel, and financial commitment. Service providers should be concerned about staff turnover, changes in assignments within companies that hire their clients, and the effect of frequent changes in assigned co-workers on the continuity of services (admittedly also a problem with supported employment provider agencies). They should also be concerned about exploitation of the supported worker when advocates cannot be objective. In short, it is not an illogical leap from dependence on the natural supports of the workplace to the "place and pray" approach of old.

From a policy perspective, two related concerns arise that must ultimately be addressed at either state or federal funding and policy levels. First, do models of supported employment that rely predominantly or totally on informal, nonrehabilitation supports conform to the letter and spirit of the 1986 Amendments to the Rehabilitation Act, which currently define the characteristics of supported employment? Second, given mounting evidence that target populations are already being underserved (Kregel and Wehman 1990; Wehman, Kregel, Shafer, and West 1989), are natural support models another means by which states and provider agencies can avoid providing services to people with truly severe disabilities? That is, can individuals who are capable of maintaining employment with enhanced natural supports or the presence of an attendant, with minimal intervention from a rehabilitation specialist, be considered appropriate candidates for a program that is expressly designed for those who could not be competitively employed otherwise?

Conclusions and Cautions on Natural Support Models

It is undeniable that the psychological sense of community exists in most, if not all, workplaces and that it provides a natural and unintrusive social support network for employees. This author's own many positive experiences placing persons with severe disabilities confirm the belief of Nisbet and Hagner (1989) that workers with disabilities can participate in this community with their co-workers and supervisors and develop nurturing support networks and friendships within the organization. Co-workers frequently agree, and even volunteer, to serve in valuable ways that enhance the employment experience and job retention for supported employees, such as assisting with personal tasks and problems, providing transportation, and training in new tasks or monitoring performance on previously learned tasks. When those individuals can be found, they should be used to their full advantage, for such contacts promote not only employment success, but valuable opportunities for social integration as well. And there is no doubt that the current research and service delivery emphasis on enhancing these natural supports and resources will serve to strengthen vocational and social outcomes for all supported employees, as well as address many of the problems and concerns of current supported employment practices expressed by Nisbet and Hagner (1989).

However, not all employees with disabilities will be so fortunate. There is no evidence from either the industrial sociology literature or the rehabilitation literature to suggest that natural supports will be consistently available to workers with severe learning, physical, or behavioral disabilities, and service providers should avoid programmatic assumptions that they will be available. Furthermore, there is no evidence to suggest that the acceptance, social support, and assistance found in work cultures are equivalent to the work skills, behavioral training, problem-solving assistance, and advocacy needs frequently required by individuals with severe disabilities for long-term job retention, and service providers should not make programmatic assumptions that they *will* be sufficient.

Natural support models as presented by Nisbet and Hagner (1989) are very seductive, with their emphasis on maximal integration, limited staff utilization, and relatively low-cost service designs. However, the underlying assumptions for supported employment models based on natural support mechanisms may be more wishful thinking than fact. Social support networks in the workplace are not just *there* to be exploited; they develop from months and even years of daily contact and positive experiences, and for many workers, disabled or not, a social support network never develops. Therefore, service providers should exercise caution in relinquishing their obligations of training, support, and advocacy for their clients.

PLANNING AND IMPLEMENTING EXTENDED SERVICES

As mentioned previously, the identification and provision of appropriate support services should, to the greatest extent possible, be a proactive rather than a reactive process. Potential problem areas, antecedents, and consequences should be identified during the job stabilization phase, and a prescriptive, written follow-along plan developed by the employment specialist, the employer, the co-workers, the family members, the consumer, and any other concerned parties. For the benefit of both the client and the employer, response to crisis or requests for assistance should be immediate and according to the agreed plan.

Effective follow-along utilizes both formal and informal strategies of problem analysis and data collection. Informal methods include discussions with the supervisor and/or co-workers at the job site, discussions with family members, accessing community support services, and other direct and indirect consumer-related activities. Formal methods are used to collect outcome data that are used for ongoing assessment of work performance or data that is aggregated for the purpose of evaluating program effectiveness.

Informal Follow-along Strategies

On-site Interventions

Following job stabilizatioon, contacts with employers will typically involve site visits or telephone contacts concerning the employee's job performance. In most cases, the site visit will elicit the most useful information about the employee's adjustment to the workplace, to the supervisor, and to the co-workers (Hill, Cleveland, Pendleton, and Wehman 1982). Retraining activities may be necessary in the event that the employee's work quality or speed diminishes over time or if job duties change (Moon, Goodall, Barcus, and Brooke 1986).

For employees with CMI or TBI, another vital concern may be monitoring the emotional stability of the employee. Disinhibition, temper outbursts, and other inappropriate behaviors are often latent responses to employment stress (Kreutzer and Morton 1988) and may not be predictable, especially if the client has little or no other employment experience. Employers will need to be informed of any known symptoms of an impending flair-up and appropriate means of supervisory response, including time-out procedures, suspensions, or calling the employment specialist for crisis intervention. In some instances, part of the initial negotiations between the employer and the employment specialist may be obtaining permission for "psychosocial first aid" (Isbister and Donaldson 1987) to be administered at the job site by the employment specialist or a qualified therapist if the employee's behaviors escalate beyond the supervisor's control.

It should be evident from the preceding discussion that many individuals with severe production deficits or emotional or behavioral anomalies will require sympathetic and understanding employers in order for placement to be successful. It is vitally important that employers know what to expect from the employee, both in terms of productivity and potential problems, and the degree to which the employment specialist and other crisis intervention staff or consultants may be used as resources in correcting problems in either area.

Off-site Interventions

As mentioned earlier in this chapter, family members are often vital to employment success by providing either direct assistance, emotional support, or both. The employment specialist's contacts with family members should focus on aspects of home life that are likely to impinge upon the work environment. These would include the ongoing assessments of the consumer's emotional stability; use or abuse of prescription and non-prescription drugs, including alcohol; and problems related to finances, health, and family functioning. The employment specialist should perform educational and referral functions, such as informing the consumer and family members of treatment programs (i.e., residential services, Alcoholics Anonymous, respite care) and other services and entitlements (i.e., SSI, SSDI) that are available in their community and helping them to access these services.

A comprehensive retention plan will also include advocacy efforts with related service personnel or other individuals on behalf of the consumer. This might include progress or status reports to the consumer's vocational rehabilitation counselor, neuropsychologist, or physician For individuals who reside in supervised apartments or group homes, changes in work schedule or problems with dress, medication, or finances will need to be communicated to the appropriate staff. Individuals who live independently or semi-independently may require an intermediary for dealing with a landlord or creditor. In short, any problem that may affect the individual's job placement becomes the concern of the employment specialist.

Scheduling Follow-along Contacts

Although a number of writers have addressed the *types* of activities that constitute follow-along services, little direction has been given as to the *frequency* and *intensity* of contacts. The determination of "sufficient" or "necessary" contacts to maintain employment has generally been left to the discretion of the employment specialist, provided that legal minimum levels are met.

Rusch (1986) describes two types of schedules, the *adjusted* schedule and the *fixed* schedule. The adjusted schedule varies with the consumer's success in meeting the employer's expectations and in ratings of progress. If an employer cannot tolerate this arrangement, then a predetermined, or fixed, schedule of follow-along contacts is negotiated.

One problem with using a fixed schedule of contact is that job duties, production demands, co-workers, and even supervisors may vary according to the day or time of day. An obvious example is restaurant work, where peak hours are during lunch and dinner "rushes". For restaurants located in business districts, weekday lunch periods will likely be more hectic than weekend lunches. Weekend dinner volume may be greater than weekdays. Or the employee's work schedule may bridge two shifts with different co-workers or supervisors. On a fixed schedule of visits based on employer request or convenience of the program staff, subtle and overt differences in work demands, the atmosphere of the workplace, and acceptance of the supported employee may go unnoticed.

As much as the setting allows, the employment specialist should obtain a variety of opinions regarding the performance and social adjustment of the supported worker. Of course, the observations and opinions of the supervisor are of paramount importance, as are those of any designated helper. But other co-workers (or possibly regular customers) may also have made observations or have valid opinions, which the supervisor cannot or will not share with the program staff.

The Support Group

The "job retention support group" for workers with disabilities (see Fabian and Wiedefeld 1989; Isbister and Donaldson 1987; West and Hughes 1990) can be a valuable medium for assisting and monitoring ongoing adjustment to employment, particularly for individuals with severe TBI or psychiatric impairment. Members of the support group meet voluntarily to discuss problems or stresses associated with work and to provide mutual emotional support. Through these exchanges, supported employment staff are also able to monitor the emotional stability of the group members and identify potential problem areas at the job site or at home.

Formal Follow-along Strategies

This section will describe formal data collection instruments from the SEIS that are completed as part of the follow-along process. In addition, schedules for completion of the forms are described.

Supervisor's Evaluation Form

Formal supervisor evaluations provide insight not only into the work performance of a supported employee, but also the expectations and priorities of the supervisor. For example, Shafer, Kregel, Banks, and Hill (1988) examined scores on the RRTC's Supervisor's Evaluation Form (see Figure 8.4) for initial and terminal evaluations for 125 workers with mental retardation. They found that employees who eventually were separated from their job tended to score lower than successful placements in the areas of attendance, punctuality, and timeliness of lunch and breaks. They concluded that employers may be willing to lower performance standards of speed and quality for a dependable, loyal worker. Although these findings have yet to be generalized to other disability groups, supervisor evaluation forms have utility for examining worker-supervisor relationships in both aggregated data and individual cases.

In the RRTC's data collection schedule, the Supervisor's Evaluation Form is completed by the employee's job-site supervisor, ideally with the employment specialist and the employee present, at a minimum of one month, three months, and six months postplacement, and every six months thereafter. The evaluation form is also completed immediately following job termination. If deemed necessary and feasible, employment specialists may request evaluations from the supervisor on a more frequent schedule. Because the work performance evaluations often used in businesses and industries are usually not sufficiently expansive or behavioral for supported employment purposes (Rusch 1986), employers are requested to use the RRTC's Supervisor's Evaluation Form in addition to any other employee evaluation forms or methods that they would normally use.

Job Update Form

The Job Update Form (Figure 8.5) is used to collect data related to changes in job elements, such as wages, work hours, and level of integration with customers or co-workers. This form is a shortened version of the RRTC's Job Screening Form,

Using the following scale, please check *one* number to the right of each question that *best* represents your opinion about this employee's present situation:

1   Extremely dissatisfied
2   Somewhat dissatisfied
3   Satisfied
4   Very satisfied
5   Extremely satisfied

                                                                    1 2 3 4 5

How satisfied are you with this employee's...

1.   timeliness of arrival and departure from work?   _____
2.   attendance?   _____
3.   timeliness of breaks and lunch?   _____
4.   appearance?   _____
5.   general performance *as compared to other workers?*   _____
6.   communication skills?   _____
7.   consistency in task performance?   _____
8.   work speed?   _____
9.   quality of work?   _____
10.   overall proficiency at this time?   _____

Additional Comments:

Figure 8.4   Items on the Supervisor's Evaluation Form.

which also provides an analysis of job parameters, requirements, and expected competencies.

The Job Update Form is completed by the employment specialist at three and six months postplacement, every six months thereafter, and at job termination.

Consumer Update Form

The Consumer Update Form (Figure 8.6) collects data related to the supported employee's level of independence. The areas of interest include (a) the employee's vocational rehabilitation case status, (b) residential situation, (c) mode of transportation to and from work, and (d) the types and amounts of government financial aid and entitlements. The form is completed on the same schedule as the Job Update Form. Because this information is also collected either prior to or at initial placement, changes in the employee's status, as a direct result of employment, can be tracked over time. Thus, this form provides significant information necessary for consumer-level benefit-cost analysis. This form is completed by the employment specialist on the same schedule as the Job Update Form.

1.   Type of service/employment for this report (select one):____
    1 = Work activity or sheltered employment
    2 = Entrepreneurial
    3 = Mobile work crew
    4 = Enclave
    5 = Supported job
    6 = Supported competitive employment
    7 = Time-limited (no ongoing services anticipated)
    8 = Other (specify:_____)
2.   Type of update: Ongoing_____ Final_____
3.   Job title:_____
4.   Current hourly wage (or last wage in this position):_____
5.   Did a wage change occur since the last Job Screening or Job Update?
    ____Yes ____No
6.   If yes, then complete this section:
    Hourly rate changed from $_____to $_____ on __/__/__
    Hourly rate changed from $_____to $_____ on __/__/__
7.   Number of hours worked per week:____ Months worked per year: ____
8.   If less than 12 months per year, what months is the job not available?
    _____

9.   Number of employees in this company at this location:_____
    Number without disabilities in immediate area (50' radius):_____
    Number of other employees with disabilities:_____
    In immediate area (50' radius):_____
    Number of other employees in this position:_____
    During the same hours:_____
10. Level of social contact (circle one):
    0 Employment in a segregated setting in which the majority of interactions
       with persons without disabilities are with caregivers or service providers.
       Example: Adult Activity Center.
    1 Employment in an integrated environment on a shift or position that is
       isolated. Contact with co-workers without disabilities or supervisors is
       minimal. Example: Night Janitor.
    2 Employment in an integrated environment on a shift or position that is
       relatively isolated. Contact with co-workers without disabilities is avail-
       able at lunch or break. Example: Pot Scrubber.
    3 Employment in an integrated environment in a position requiring a
       moderate level of task dependency and co-worker interaction. Example:
       Dishwasher required to keep plate supply stacked for cooks.
    4 Employment in an integrated environment in a position requiring a high
       degree of task dependency and co-worker or customer interaction.
       Example: Bus person/Porter.

Figure 8.5   Items on the Job Update Form.

1. Current DRS case status for this consumer (enter DRS code):_____
    If *never* served by DRS, enter *none* in the space provided.

2. Current residential situation (select one only):_____
    > 1 = Independent
    > 2 = Supported living arrangement
    > 3 = Sponsored placement (foster care)
    > 4 = Domiciliary care apartment (home for adults)
    > 5 = Supervised apartment
    > 6 = Parents
    > 7 = Other relatives
    > 8 = Group home/halfway house
    > 9 = Other (specify:_____)

3. Current primary mode of transportation to work (select one only):_____
    > 1 = Independent use of public transportation
    > 2 = Walks/rides bike or moped
    > 3 = Dependent use of public transportation (needed bus training)
    > 4 = Arranged car pool
    > 5 = Parent/friend drives
    > 6 = Handicapped transportation
    > 7 = Taxi
    > 8 = Drives own vehicle
    > 9 = Other (specify:_____)

4. Financial aid received by consumer at present or as of last day of work. Circle yes or no for each selection. If yes, write the amount received to the left of the selection.
    > _____Yes/No None
    > _____Yes/No SSI
    > _____Yes/No SSDI
    > _____Yes/No Medicaid
    > _____Yes/No Medicare
    > _____Yes/No Food Stamps
    > _____Yes/No Public Assistance (Welfare)
    > _____Yes/No Other (specify:_____)

5. Total income from all government financial aid during the past month:_____

Figure 8.6   Items on the Consumer Update Form.

Consumer Self-evaluation

This form was developed by the RRTC's TBI project and closely mirrors the Supervisor's Evaluation Form in its content (refer to Figure 8.4). At the time that the job-site supervisor completes an evaluation, the TBI consumer also completes an identical form, assessing his or her own work performance. This procedure has two related functions. First, it provides the employment specialist insight to the consumer's perceptions of strengths and weaknesses. Second, it may reveal areas of dissonance between the consumer's perceptions and the supervisor's, thus providing the employment specialist with general areas in which to concentrate intervention.

SUMMARY OF MAJOR POINTS

Extended services in supported employment should be prescriptive and proactive. The identification of employment barriers and interventions should occur during the initial phases of client screening, assessment, and placement, and a written plan developed for addressing anticipated training, support, and advocacy needs. Using natural cues, consequences, and supports can increase the supported worker's independence and social integration in the work area and improve the prognosis for long-term job retention. However, if these are inadequate for the particular worker, artificial cues, reinforcers, and supports can be effectively imposed.

Although the ultimate purpose of extended support services is to avoid unnecessary job separations, many individuals in supported employment are separated from their jobs. Job separations are not necessarily undesirable in and of themselves. In fact, job retention should be viewed less as an absolute, static state and more as gradual improvements in the supported employee's ability to function in the competitive work force. These improvements are frequently dependent upon refinement of the individual's career goals, productive abilities, and social skills and may involve movement from one employment setting to another, voluntarily or involuntarily. Such a dynamic view of job retention requires that provider and funding agencies be committed to continually provide supported employment services beyond the first separation.

9

Behavior Management
at the Job Site

John directs verbally abusive comments toward his employment specialist and his restaurant co-workers. Mary cries continuously for no apparent reason while learning to perform her job as a laundry attendant at a large hospital. Sam engages in socially inappropriate actions by making sexual advances toward his employer at a merchandise warehouse.

Do these situations sound familiar? Verbally abusive comments, crying on the job, and inappropriate social interactions are just a small sample of the behavior challenges that may prevent persons with severe disabilities from obtaining and maintaining integrated employment. Low production rates, infrequent on-task behavior, and poor quality performance are additional challenging behaviors that represent major obstacles to maintenance of employment.

Individuals who work for natural reinforcers available on the work site, such as paychecks, supervisor/co-worker praise, positive written evaluations, pay raises, bonuses, and social interactions are more likely to be successful in supported employment and to not present challenging behaviors. However, many individuals with severe disabilities have had little or no opportunity to experience these natural reinforcers within integrated employment settings and have difficulty managing their own behaviors. This presents a challenge to the employment specialist, who must assist the worker in learning to function within the work environment.

It is the employment specialist's responsibility to teach the worker to respond to naturally occurring reinforcers and, ultimately, to engage in socially appropriate behaviors. Initially, it may be necessary to identify items that are not naturally occurring reinforcers for use on the job site. In some instances, simply asking the new worker about likes and dislikes is sufficient; however, this method is frequently ineffective with employees who are severely disabled. The employment specialist should then observe the individual in a variety of settings and interview family members and other professionals familiar with the person's reinforcement needs. Regardless of the reinforcer identified, the employment specialist must consider several factors, including the timing, scheduling, and eventual fading of the reinforcer to those that occur naturally on the job site.

DEVELOPING AN INTERVENTION PROGRAM

Usually, there is no single "right" way to modify a particular behavior. There are, however, strategies that can be used to make an educated guess about the best place to begin intervention. While the steps described here may look like a lot of extra work, in the long run following them will save work—and headaches. More importantly, the client will benefit by careful planning and recording.

Perform Functional Analysis of Behavior

A functional analysis of behavior is merely an informal description of events that occur just before and after the behavior of concern. Events that occur prior to the behavior may include commands, instructions, or prompts. Events that follow the behavior may include food, praise, activities, or reprimands, or there may be no consequence.

Maintaining this "anecdotal" record can help set instructional objectives and zero in on when and where there should be intervention. For instance, a client might hit himself after he is given a command to begin work. Seeing this pattern unfold can help devise different ways to present cues and materials.

Define the Behavior

It is not enough to say that a child engages in stereotyped behaviors or that she has inappropriate hand movements. The target behavior should be specifically defined to allow anyone observing the child to measure the behavior accurately. This clearness of description permits the behavior to be monitored correctly. In addition, it ensures that all staff apply the same intervention procedure to the same behavior.

The importance of defining a behavior is evidenced in the example of inappropriate vocalizations. A client may engage in annoying throat-clearing sounds or other repetitive noises. Yet, scoring every vocalization (and intervening on them) would probably not be in the client's best interest. Thus, specifically pinpointing the behavior of concern leads to better programming.

Collect Baseline Data

Collecting data before beginning intervention helps to observe the gradual changes in behavior that are often undetectible day-to-day. Rather than spending the entire day trying to record every instance of a behavior, times and places for observation can be selected. Ask the following questions prior to collecting baseline data:

> When and where is the behavior most troublesome?
> When and where is the teacher or aide able to observe and record the behavior?
> When and where will it be possible to intervene?

Whenever possible, observe the behavior at various times during the day so that the data accurately reflect the extent of the problem. The functional analysis performed initially should help determine these times.

There are several methods of collecting baseline data. The choice depends largely upon the type and frequency of the behavior. The data collection techniques that follow are especially useful for stereotyped and self-injurious behaviors.

Frequency

To use this technique, simply count the number of times a particular behavior occurs. For instance, mark on a piece of paper each time the client puts an inedible object in her mouth. Many stereotyped behaviors, however, do not lend themselves to frequency recording, since they occur too often and have no clear beginning or end. Try counting the number of times a client body-rocks, for example, and one soon will become thoroughly exhausted (as well as inaccurate).

When conducting a frequency count, the observation periods should be for the same amount of time (e.g., always 15 minutes). If the observation time cannot always be the same, it is necessary to frequently convert into an average rate by dividing the number of occurrences by the unit of time. For instance, it is noted that a client pinches his arm four times during one 15-minute observation period and 12 times during a second 35-minute observation period later in the day. Divide the total number of pinches—16—by the total observational time—50 minutes—to get an average rate of 0.32 pinches per minute.

Duration

The duration of a behavior should be recorded by determining the number of seconds or minutes it occurs. This recording is especially useful for behaviors that occur at a high rate or that may vary in length from beginning to end.

As with frequency recording, a behavior can be timed across different sessions that vary in length. Rather than arriving at an average rate, however, learn the percentage of time the behavior occurs. For example, client can be timed gazing at her hand for 6 minutes in one 12-minute period. Later that day, this gazing is discovered for 18 minutes in a 20-minute period. Her percentage of handgazing is

$$\frac{(6 + 18) - 32}{100} = 75\%$$

Interval and Time Sample

In both types of recording, divide the observation unit (e.g., 2 minutes, 10 minutes) into equal periods (e.g., 5 seconds, 10 seconds) and note for each smaller period whether or not the behavior occurs. There are different types of interval recording, depending on the behavior being recorded. While it is not possible to detail the specific procedures of these techniques in this chapter, they are useful to learn. Time sampling, in particular, may be appealing because it does not require continuous observation.

Write Management Objective

The management objective is a precisely stated goal that contains three parts: (a) the desired behavior, (b) the conditions under which the behavior is to occur, and (c) the criteria for determining when the objective has been accomplished.

Behavior

In measuring the behavior, first describe it clearly so one can be sure of what to count or time. Rather than writing in the objective that "John will not self-stimulate," it is important to describe the specific behavior on which intervention is planned. An alternative approach is to choose one or more behaviors that Johnny should do in place of his stereotyped behavior. That way, the behavioral description is positive (e.g., "Johnny will interact appropriately with instructional materials...") rather than negative (e.g., "Johnny will not twirl object...").

Conditions

These refer to settings, times, materials, and instructional cues under which the client's behavior is to be altered. There should be full concentration initially, for example, on reducing Susie's inappropriate vocalizations during instructional settings. Self-injurious behaviors, on the other hand, are usually undesirable at any time.

Criteria

Criteria should be carefully developed, since they enable you to determine when the client has succeeded or failed. The criteria should match the type of recording used in collecting baseline data. If frequency data are converted to rate data, the criterion must reflect rate (e.g., "Tony will hit himself fewer than once per half hour."). Similarly, duration data should yield a criterion statement referring to time or percentage of time. A criterion level should be selected that is acceptable to all significant people who work with the client, including teacher, aide, parents, and therapist.

A complete objective, containing all three parts, might be written as follows: "When told to go to work session, Joel will comply within ten seconds for four out of five requests for each of three consecutive school days."

Select Intervention Technique

Selecting a method to reduce an inappropriate behavior should be done thoughtfully. Use previous observations of the client to help determine where to begin. Since stereotyped and self-injurious behaviors can be frustratingly difficult to modify, do not be afraid to seek outside help.

Before trying a complex behavioral intervention, rule out any obvious medical causes. While not typical, physical causes, such as middle-ear infection, can sometimes lead to inappropriate behaviors, such as ear-digging.

After eliminating medical reasons for the behavior, determine if it appears to be maintained by social reinforcement. Although many stereotyped behaviors seem to be intrinsically reinforcing, occasionally clients will behave inappropriately due to the positive or negative attention they get from teachers or peers. If this seems to be the case, extinction would be an appropriate strategy. It is not ethically justifiable, however, to use extinction, that is planned ignoring, for self-injurious behaviors.

If extinction fails to eliminate or significantly reduce the behavior, it will be helpful to determine if it is maintained by negative reinforcement. In that situation, the inappropriate behavior leads to the termination of an aversive stimulus. Thus, the client escapes a situation he doesn't "like." Strategies to break this cycle are to "put the client through" a task after presenting a command and to regulate the rate of delivery of commands. The task can be varied to ensure it is at the client's level and the materials altered to make them reinforcing.

Collect and Graph Data

As intervention on a behavior occurs, continue to collect data to determine the program's degree of success. Data collection techniques should be the same as those used in gathering baseline data. Do not attempt to record every instance of every behavior all day long—it is impossible to do so easily, and the data will be unreliable. How often data are collected will depend on the type, frequency, and severity of the behaviors as well as how many other clients and client behavior problems there are as well as the level of organization and support. Find a format that is accurate and workable.

Graphing data is essential in helping to make decisions about how the client is progressing. The graph does not have to be elaborate, but it should be monitored on a regular basis. Once a few graphs are developed, the entire process becomes easier.

A final note: Many job coaches will say that they "don't have time to take data." That may be because they're trying to gather too much unnecessary information. When set up properly, a data management system actually facilitates work toward clients' goals, thereby saving time previously spent worrying about lack of progress and trying numerous unsuccessful approaches.

WHAT SHOULD BE KNOWN ABOUT IMPLEMENTING BEHAVIOR PROGRAMS IN SUPPORTED EMPLOYMENT SITES?

Should individuals with behavior management problems be included in supported employment programs? Wouldn't it be better to get the behaviors under control in a sheltered workshop setting before community placement?

Attempting to eliminate problem behaviors prior to placement in the community may be an unsuccessful, as well as an unnecessary, program goal. For instance, many individuals with severe disabilities do not generalize well from one environment to another. Therefore, the staff of a sheltered workshop could work very hard to eliminate a behavior that would return as soon as the individual was exposed to a new environment. In addition, some behaviors may occur in one setting and not in another. The simple removal of an individual from the sheltered workshop and placement into a community work environment may eliminate the behavior problem. In summary, training should, whenever possible, take place within the natural environment in which the person is to ultimately function.

What reinforcers should be used on a job site for behavior management programs?

The best reinforcers to utilize during job-site training are those that occur naturally in the work environment. This might include the paycheck, co-worker praise, or supervisor praise. To identify naturally occurring reinforcers as well as naturally occurring times for delivery, the employment specialist must take time to make observations in the work site. For instance, the supervisor may walk by the consumer's work station on a regular schedule; this contact with the supervisor could be incorporated into a behavior management program.

However, sometimes it is necessary to consider using more tangible reinforcers, such as magazines, coffee, money, or food items. The employment specialist should try to use these items in a nonintrusive way in order to not draw attention to the consumer. In addition, tangible items should only be used on a job site if a procedure has been developed to fade use to a naturally occurring reinforcer.

When should reinforcement be delivered?

The timing of reinforcement is critical. All reinforcement should be given quickly and immediately following the occurrence of the appropriate worker behavior. Sometimes it may not be feasible to deliver a particular reinforcer immediately, particularly in the case of tangible reinforcers. In these situations, exchangeable reinforcers, such as points, tokens, or checks, should be immediately provided and exchanged at a later time, i.e., a soda during break time.

The employment specialist must also determine a schedule of reinforcement, which dictates how often the item will be delivered. During initial instruction, a continuous schedule is generally recommended. This means that the worker receives reinforcement for each behavior or step in a task that is performed correctly. As the worker's performance increases or improves, the reinforcement is gradually decreased to a predetermined period of time or number of correct responses. As the worker performs the behavior or task, the reinforcement schedule should be gradually changed until the individual is reinforced on a natural schedule for the work place. The timing and scheduling of reinforcement should always be based on the skill level of the worker and the demands of the environment.

How can one collect data on behavior management programs when one is already busy with skill acquisition programs?

Data collection can be problematic for the busy employment specialist who is try-ing to track several programs at one time. The solution is to develop innovative data collection techniques that fit into the daily routine. Frequency counts could be taken using golf counters or marking on a piece of tape attached to the employ-ment specialist's wrist. One job trainer used the change in his pockets to take a fre-quency count by transferring coins from one pocket to another when the targeted behavior occurred. This information can then be recorded on a formal data sheet during break time or at the end of the day.

How can a behavior management program be implemented when one is already busy with all the other demands of the work environment?

The employment specialist can determine the most appropriate time of day for pro-gram implementation by observing the events that occur on the job before and after a behavior occurs. For instance, the employment specialist may determine that the worker swears loudly whenever he has to perform a particular job duty. Therefore, the behavior strategy would be implemented during this time period.

However, if no particular time of day can be identified, several decisions must be made. For example, the employment specialist must determine if it is possible to use the behavior strategy throughout the day, whenever the identified problem occurs. This would be the strategy of choice, since it is important to be consistent, in order to see behavior changes. If the work environment is such that this is im-possible, the employment specialist should identify blocks of time, during the day, during which intensive programming can be provided. As the individual learns his or her job and begins to perform to job-site expectations, the program can be used during other portions of the day.

How does one know if one's program is working, and when should changes in behavior management strategies be made?

Prior to program implementation at the job site, a baseline period of performance should be established; this is used as a comparison measure with program imple-mentation data. As long as a steady decrease in negative behaviors or increase in appropriate behaviors and speed of performance is noted, the employment specialist should continue with programming. No changes over a series of days indicate that modifications are necessary, which might include the use of another reinforcer or program strategy that includes new compensatory measures. The employment specialist is cautioned to remember that maladaptive behaviors will often return on a short-term basis in the middle of a behavior management program. This is especially true as program criteria are changed, such as increasing the length of time for appropriate behavior to occur before delivery of the reinforcer. In this instance, consistency and patience is important. The employment specialist may need to revert to a previous program level and increase program requirements at a slower rate.

What should be done with a consumer who is creating such a disturbance on the job that the co-workers are beginning to notice? Just leave the job site?

Supported employment programs should develop a policy concerning sudden, inappropriate behaviors on a job site. For instance, the employment specialist should first attempt to bring the consumer's behavior under control with an immediate positive strategy. This could include trying several reinforcers as well as an impromptu behavior program. If this is unsuccessful, a call to the program supervisor for additional ideas on strategy should be the next step. A more formal program can be developed for implementation at the end of the work day. Removal from the site should be the last resort when the positive strategies have proven unsuccessful. A time limit may be provided as a guideline for the employment specialist in order to ensure that every effort for success has been made. (Obviously, if the consumer is causing damage to the property or to other individuals, he or she should be removed immediately.)

Should negative consequences/punishment be used as part of a behavior management program on a supported employment job site?

Only positive behavior management strategies should be used on a job site. However, it is possible to use naturally occurring contingencies to effectively deal with difficult problem situations. Natural contingencies might include corrections from persons in the environment, such as comments from the supervisor that a job has not been completed to satisfaction. In addition, the employment specialist should make certain that the supervisor is providing positive input when work has been completed efficiently and correctly.

Should parents and/or group-home staff be involved in behavior management programs on a supported employment job site?

Typically, the most appropriate person to implement an employment-related behavior management program is the employment specialist. However, the parents or group-home staff may be involved in providing feedback and encouragement to the consumer when he or she has had a particularly successful day at work. These individuals will also know what types of reinforcement may be useful to ensure program success. Keeping families involved and informed of job-site progress will go a long way in guaranteeing the success of the new employee.

So what if a behavior management program is developed that works? Won't the consumer's behavior return when the employment specialist is not around?

Yes, it certainly will if one does not ensure that the worker is performing to the expectations of the work place before leaving the job site! This would include the gradual elimination of any reinforcers or supervision that the employment specialist provided that do not occur naturally. For example, spending break time with a worker to reinforce the completion of a specific job duty. Gradually, one must decrease the amount of time spent with the worker until he/she is reinforced by social interactions with the co-workers.

It is also important to remember that a consumer's behavior might return to "test" the work environment, even after a long period of job stability. If the employment specialist returns and consistently implements a behavior management program, the consumer's behavior should quickly come under control.

SUMMARY

The purpose of this chapter has been to provide specific guidelines in how to develop and implement a behavior management program at a job site. Behavioral interventions in natural environments can be very challenging to provide in an effective yet humanistic way. This chapter has attempted to provide direction and practical information for resolving the types of problems which can cause a person with a severe disability to lose his or her job.

The reader who requires considerably more depth in implementation is referred to Smith (1989).

Part III

Special Issues in
Supported Employment

10

Program Evaluation: Toward Quality Assurance

As was noted in Chapter One there has been a significant move toward the establishment of supported employment programs, within the past five years especially (Bellamy, Rhodes, Mank, and Albin 1988; Garner, Chapman, Donaldson, and Jacobsen 1988). Local programs have increased from less than 300 to well over 2000 in only a few years (Wehman, Kregel, and Shafer 1989). Clearly, service providers and individuals with disabilities alike are interested in seeing more supported employment opportunities available.

With the dramatic increase toward this less restrictive vocational alternative, there is a need to evaluate the quality of these new programs. Rhodes and his colleagues (1990) have written eloquently in this regard warning that, without strict attention to standards of quality, supported employment will fail, become diluted in its integrity, and rapidly lose credibility among people with disabilities and their families. For example, they suggest:

> Supported employment is at a critical point in its development. Service
> providers and other state and community personnel need ways to promote
> and ensure quality as it expands...quality assurance mechanisms are neces-
> sary to protect the rights of persons with severe disabilities(p. 5)

Supported employment programs have been a source of controversy (e.g., Lam 1986) in the past, and failure to deliver on promises of integrated employment will give many second thoughts about the wisdom of this approach.

There have not been a lack of "one shot" demonstrations (Bates 1986; Vogelsburg 1986; Farel, Dineen and Hall 1984); also longitudinal studies of supported employment workers (Wehman et al. 1982; Wehman et al. 1985; Wehman and Kregel 1989) who are placed in competitive employment have also been completed. For example, in Wehman et al. (1985), it was reported that 167 workers, with a mean IQ of 49, were placed into 252 positions. After six years, the average length of employment was 19 months. An updated report of this study was published by Kregel and Wehman (1989) and indicated that 255 clients, with a mean IQ level of 53, were placed into competitive employment, with the average hour wage being $3.56, and mostly in service jobs for people who are predominantly labeled as mentally-retarded or mentally ill.

For the most part, studies like the one above as well as the excellent work of Vogelsburg (1986), Bates (1986), Rusch (1986), Moss (1988), and others indicate that previously unemployed persons with developmental disabilities were able to work only after a supported employment approach was utilized. However, there efforts were not evaluated in an experimental design similar to the study recently published by Goldberg, McLean, LaVigne, Fratolillo, and Sullivan (1990). In this study 49 persons with developmental disabilities were assigned randomly to either a supported employment work program or sheltered work program. The major finding of this important study was that these clients when assigned to supported work did significantly better in the competitive labor market than did those clients in extended sheltered work. Clients were considered to be successfully employed in competitive employment if they remained employed for 60 days.

Another effort at supported employment program evaluation, which was quite creative, was published by McDonnell, Nofs, Hardman, and Chambless (1989). These authors attempted to isolate the procedures and program features that contributed to the efficacy of supported employment programs in Utah. Specifically, the study, which included 120 individuals with disabilities in Utah, examined the relationship between the procedure included in the Utah program and employment *outcomes* achieved for these 120 persons. As Table 10.1 indicates these investigators were able to identify those variables that were instrumental in relating to hours worked, average weekly wages, job retention, and level of integration. A number of these model components were found significant; for example, a formal marketing plan was a key aspect in programs that yielded effective job retention.

Kregel, Wehman, and Banks (1989) also did an in-depth analysis of supported employment outcomes of 1550 persons with severe disabilities from 96 local programs. While this analysis was wide ranging and looked at many relationships between different outcome variables (e.g., wages, hours worked) and client characteristics, such as IQ, one of the more significant contributions of this paper was the before-supported-employment versus during-supported-employment analysis.

In Table 10.2 one can see the large percentage changes of 200%, 300%, and 400% that occurred in earnings for the 1550 clients once supported employment opportunities were made available.

The McDonnell et al. (1989) Goldberg et al. (1990), and Kregel, Wehman, and Banks (1989) studies are among the few that do significant analyses of supported employment data[1] and provide an important first step in evaluation research

---

[1] Kiernan and his colleagues (1989) have also done extensive national surveying, but these studies have tended to be more focus on all employment alternatives not just supported employment.

Table 10.1   Procedural Components

Pearson-Product Correlation Coefficients Between Supported Employment Outcomes and Utah (N = 120)

Model components	Average Hours worked	Weekly wages	Job retention	Level of integration
Individualized program planning procedures	.53*	.46*	.40*	.48*
Client assessment and job matching procedures	.72*	.78*	.39*	.50*
Job analysis procedures	.64*	.67*	.37*	.50*
Design of training programs	.68*	.68*	.35*	.53*
Progress in training programs	.59*	.70*	.32*	.35*
Supervisor observation of training programs	.42*	.30**	.07	.59*
Board of directors	.10	.06	.02	.10
Nonprofit status	.33*	.30**	.18	.28**
Workshop certification	.53*	.58*	.34*	.55*
Formal marketing plans	.41*	.36*	.23***	.44*
Accounting procedures	.49*	.48*	.10	.46*
Formal services contracts	.40*	.41*	.18	.53*
Standard job descriptions	.43*	.41*	.27**	.40*
Weekly staff meetings	.45*	.58*	.40*	.51*

*p≤ .001.

**p ≤ .01.

***p ≤ .05.

(Reprinted from McDonnell et al. 1989)

Table 10.2   Wage Outcomes for Individuals in Various Employment Models (N = 1,550)

Employment model	Hourly wage	Hours worked per week	Monthly earnings prior to supported employment	Monthly earnings during supported employment	Percentage change
Individual placement	$3.68	26.5	$80	$424**	430
Enclaves	3.25	28.7	67	301	349
Work crews	2.32	27.6	96	253	164
Small business	1.30	25.4	46	149	224

*$F_{(3, 2549)} = 243.27$, $p < .0001$.

**$F_{(3, 1549)} = 69.16$, $p < .0001$.

(From Kregel, Wehman and Banks 1989)

of supported employment programs. These studies tend to lend support to the hypothesis that supported employment is an excellent vocational approach for those individuals with severe disabilities who have been historically unemployed.

It will be the purpose of this chapter to provide information on program evaluation for supported work programs. Our approach will have a strong, local community bias. We will not review or critique the economics of supported employment or benefit-cost analyses, which falls outside the scope of this chapter.[2]

While the above reports provide one level of knowledge, they are more clearly of a research nature and not particularly useful for the program manager who wishes to assess the performance of a local program.

To address this need, DeStefano (1990) does an excellent job of identifying the following four considerations in evaluating a supported employment program. They are:

1. The focus of program evaluation may differ based on the interests, information needs, and capabilities of evaluators and their clients.
2. Supported employment involves the interaction of individual, employment, and program characteristics to produce a set of outcomes.
3. Evaluations can be used summarily and formatively.
4. Evaluation can be multi-level and multi-user. (p. 230)

Perhaps the seminal work in the program evaluation area for human services is found in the book by Schalock and Thornton (1988). This book is superb and is recommended to all serious students of program evaluation and benefit-cost analysis in community living and employment programs.

Returning to the DeStefano chapter, she presents standards, data to be collected, and key criteria for consideration in the evaluation of supported employment programs. For local program providers, this organization is a very good way of establishing an evaluation plan. It is simple and straightforward, yet *directly* measures the key outcome measures that are linked to the integrity of a *supported employment* program. One can review Table 10.3 to see how *population, competitive work, integration*, and the *ongoing* aspect of a program are to be evaluated.

Program Evaluation Instruments: What is Available?

The previous discussion provides encouraging evidence that supported employment does work as an effective intervention strategy for difficult-to-place people who have severe disabilities. However, none of the previously cited studies have been able to show standardization of program quality or report quality assurance standards about the programs in which client data were drawn. This is clearly a short-

---

[2]The reader is referred to Chapter 9 for a description of benefit cost analyses of supported employment.

Table 10.3   Standards, Data to be Collected, and Criteria to Consider When Evaluating Supported Employment

Standard	Data	Criteria
Population	Primary/secondary handicapping condition	Persons with severe handicaps for whom employment has not occurred
	Previous work history	or has been intermittent or interrupted
Competitive work	Hours worked for each individual per pay period	Averaging at least 20 hours per week for each pay period
Integrated work setting	Extent of contact with nonhandicapped co-workers	Workgroup of not more than eight individuals with handicaps; regular contact with nonhandicapped co-workers
Ongoing support services	Number of contacts and nature of support services provided to employee at the job site	Continuous or periodic job skill training services provided at least twice monthly at the job site (except for individuals with chronic mental illness)
		(Reprinted from DeStefano 1990)

coming if supported employment programs are to attain and sustain a high professional level of credibility. Therefore, it is the purpose of this section to review and critique several program evaluation instruments that are now available. One of the larger efforts at development in this regard has been the Vocational Integration Index, developed by the authors (Parent, Kregel, and Wehman, 1991). This index is presented in-depth in the chapter, which immediately follows., on vocational integration.

Below is a discussion of four program evaluation tools that have been developed over the past five years as a means of monitoring supported employment quality.

Standards of Excellence of Supported Employment Programs

At the Institute for Human Resource Development in Connecticut, Wood, Steere, Powell, Rammler, and Butterworth (1988) developed a seven category program evaluation checklist. These categories are:

1. Presence and Participation
2. Career Development
3. Job Development
4. On-Site Instruction
5. Ongoing Supports
6. Empowerment
7. Organizational Support

Within these categories are a total of 30 items (see Appendix A at back of this chapter) that reflect more specific detail about each of the respective areas. The items partially reflect the supported employment regulations (i.e. number of hours which must be worked weekly), but also go beyond these minimum standards and place a major emphasis on consumer choice, growth, and development. The completion of the checklist is simple and is essentially one of occurrence versus nonoccurrence marked on a respected series of dates over time (See Appendix A).

While a tool such as this instrument is excellent in terms of ease of administration, even more helpful is the focus on the client's individual career development. No data was available to determine the number of programs in which this has been used; reliability and validity measures were absent; and at this point, it appears essentially as a descriptive program checklist. The authors indicate that the tool is being further developed and validated.

Assessing the Quality of Supported Employment Services

Nisbet and Callahan (1988) present another, somewhat more sophisticated, approach to evaluation of supported employment programs. The instrument is divided into three sections: (1) Administrative Issues, (2) Job Matching and Development, and (3) Job Training and Support. Within these sections are subcategories, and within the subcategories are descriptive items for the service provider to consider. The items are timely and very credible, but the instrument does not appear to have been statistically validated, nor is information available on how many programs have collected data using this tool. Table 10.4 presents the three major sections and subcategories within.

Items are coded as outstanding, acceptable, needs refinement, or unacceptable. The authors indicate that the function of this tool is not to yield a numerical score, but instead, should provide qualitative information about the integrity of the program being evaluated.

For those service providers who wish to undertake a fairly in-depth self-analysis of their program, this manual will be excellent. This tool will be more useful for determining what areas to work on and improve as opposed to quantitatively evaluating progress made.

Table 10.4

Administrative Issues	Job Matching and Development Issues	Job Training and Support Issues
A. Agency Philosophy and Mission	A. Employee Selection Procedures	A. Use of Ecological and Job Analyses
B. Agency Administration	B. Individualization in Job Matching: Applicant and Family Involvement	B. Use of Systematic Instruction
C. Fiscal Management		C. Use of Modifications, Adaptations, and Technology
D. Image Enhancement and Public Relations	C. Use of Job Creation Strategies	
E. Interaction and Coordination with School Programs	D. Use of a Variety of Payment Mechanisms	D. Coordination with Non-work Life Space Areas
F. Effective Use of Community Resources	E. Development of Work Sites that Enhance the Image of Employees	E. Emphasis on Social and Communication Skills
G. Positive Relationships with Employers	F. Integrated Work in Typical Businesses and Industries That Encourage Interactions with Nondisabled Co-workers and Supervisors	F. Use of Ongoing Supports
H. Effective Utilization of Personnel for Job Development and Job Training	G. Development of Quality Jobs	

(From Nisbet and Callahan 1987)

Quality Indicators Profile of the National Association of Rehabilitation Facilities (NARF)

During 1989 NARF developed a Quality Indicators Profile to provide guidance to facilities providing supported employment services. These indicators were divided accordingly into:

- Program Philosophy and Mission
- Quality of Life
- Appropriators of Supports
- Organizational Structure
- Safeguards

Under each of these categories are numerous items, some of which are similar to the previous two assessment tools, and some of which are completely different. The major contribution of this tool is the emphasis on quality of life, which is always a very difficult concept to study and evaluate. The Quality Indicators Pro-file items are scored by a simple check if the provider feels this aspect of the pro-gram is in place. Appendix B in this chapter provides all items for the reader to re-view.

The Degree of Implementation Scale

Trach and Rusch (1989) report the development of a scale that from a research perspective, is easily the best developed of any of the efforts to date. (The entire scale is in Appendix C).

There are 28 items in the Degree of Implementation Scale (DOI), and these items were gleaned from an analysis and review of the supported employment lit-erature. Thirty-three Illinois supported employment programs were evaluated us-ing the DOI and were scored with a 2, 1, or 0. Presence of an item such as "con-ducts a community survey to identify jobs" would yield a score of 2; if this item is in development then a 1, for emergent, would be recorded. Outcome measures from each program, such as client severity level, wage, hours worked, etc. were col-lected and subsequently correlated with scores from the DOI. Trach and Rusch (1989) indicate:

> "Results of this study lend support to the validity of an instrument devel-oped to measure the degree to which model supported employment pro-grams implemented services identified by federal regulations..."(p. 138)

This is a tool that programs that need quantitative analysis may find useful. However, the DOI clearly focuses more on process or "input" variables than it does on client outcome features, such as degrees of vocational integration, career development, and quality of life. In all probability, this is an instrument that should be used in combination with one or more different tools.

PROGRAM EVALUATION TOOLS: WHAT WE STILL NEED TO KNOW

Development of effective local program evaluation tools for determining quality assurance in supported employment is an important area in which much work re-mains. Much, much more attention has been given to individual client evaluation of work outcomes or, at the other extreme, to descriptively reporting national ag-gregates (see Chapter 2) of supported employment progress. While both of these efforts are important, they fall far short of helping community personnel determine how successful their programs are. There are a number of points that appear to be very important in the creation and implementation of a viable program evaluation tool for local program use. These are:

1. The evaluation instrument must be clear in focus and be easy to administer. With the diversity and skill level of the many human service professionals in adult programs, it is absolutely essential that the tool be one that people can read, understand, score, and interpret easily.
2. The items on the survey need to be directly related to supported employment program values and guidelines, such as amount of pay clients earn, hours worked, type of job, integrations, etc.
3. The items on the survey need to be able to discriminate between effective programs and those which do not reflect excellence in supported employment
4. The items on the survey need to be sufficiently sensitive to detect program improvement over time for repeated assessments.

Program evaluation needs to be an ongoing, dynamic activity that is not bureaucratic, cumbersome or that requires excessive paper involvement. It should be client-oriented and directly reflect *program outcomes*, not process activity. All programs should have an ongoing evaluation component in order to determine the effectiveness and efficiency of activities.

Appendix A: Standards of Excellence Longitudinal Review Summary

Institute for
HUMAN RESOURCE DEVELOPMENT
STANDARDS OF EXCELLENCE
for Supported Employment Programs
Longitudinal Review Summary

Program: _____ Director: _____

Review Dates: _____ _____ _____ _____

Reviewers: _____

MAJOR AREA		DATES				
1.0 Presence & Participation	1.1	Individuals work in regular community job settings				
	1.2	Individuals regularly use a variety of community resources near the job site				
	1.3	Individuals have meaningful relationships through work with people who are not disabled and who are not paid adult service personnel or volunteers				
		Total Category Score:				
2.0 Career Development	2.1	Individuals control their personal futures, including choosing their career				
	2.2	Planning for careers occurs for each individual on an ongoing basis				
	2.3	Assessment includes information obtained from career planning, situational assessments and compatability analyses.				
	2.4	Individuals are satisfied with their careers and the supports they receive from the placing agency				
		Total Category Score:				

Appendix A: Standards of Excellence Longitudinal Review Summary (cont.)

3.0 Job Development & Job Placement	3.1 A variety of job opportunities are available				
	3.2 Individuals are matched to jobs that they like and want and for which they have expectations of success.				
	3.3 Individuals are employed directly by the host company and receive wages, benefits and work schedules commensurate with coworkers without disabilities				
	Total Category Score:				
4.0 On-Site Instruction	4.1 Individuals learn tasks required for their particular jobs				
	4.2 Individuals learn a range of inter-personal and other work-related skills that enhance their employment				
	4.3 Instruction is planned, implemented, evaluated and modified according to individual needs				
	4.4 Adult service personnel use current state-of-the-art instructional technologies				
	4.5 Individuals learn appropriate behavior through planned interventions which are positive and appropriate for use with coworkers without disabilities in integrated community work environments				
	4.6 Employment sites/tasks are modified based on individuals' needs in order to facilitate acquisition of skills				
	Total Category Score:				
5.0 Ongoing Support	5.1 Individuals maintain their skills through planned interventions that emphasize natural supports				
	5.2 Individuals receive ongoing supports which are identified, provided and limited only by individual need				
	5.3 Feedback is obtained on a regular basis from employers, coworkers and others about their satisfaction with the agency's support services				
	Total Category Score:				

Appendix A: Standards of Excellence Longitudinal Review Summary (cont.)

6.0 Empowerment	6.1	Individuals learn about and understand their options, and make daily choices			
	6.2	Individuals know and exercise a full range of rights and responsibilities			
	6.3	Staff know the rights afforded by law to persons with disabilities			
	6.4	Work environments are safe, comfortable and value enhancing			
	6.5	Individuals are treated respectfully in an age-appropriate manner			
		Total Category Score:			
7.0 Organizational Supports	7.1	The placing agency has a clearly articulated mission statement which emphasizes enhancement of individuals' lives through work through integrated community employment			
	7.2	The placing agency's organizational operations facilitate implementation of its mission			
	7.3	Employees of the placing agency receive regular and ongoing support, training and supervision			
	7.4	The placing agency complies with all federal, state and local laws and regulations			
	7.5	The placing agency is fiscally solvent and stable and has resources to provide the supports needed by its consumers			
	7.6	Service outcomes of the placing agency are monitored through agency-wide self-evaluation and ongoing planning occurs that involves adult service personnel and individual consumers			
		Total Category Score:			

Appendix B: NARF's Quality Indicators Profile

Appendix B: NARF's Quality Indicators Profile

DRAFT: JANUARY 19, 1989

NARF'S QUALITY INDICATORS PROFILE*

Directions: For the site review rate each item as "yes" or "no" according to evidence of meeting the standard. Items followed by (unrated) are merely information items and may not be indicative of meeting quality standards.

---

*This is the master blueprint - including items which are to be evaluated through multiple screening processes. Items which will be rated during a site review will be identified and a separate site review instrument devised.

I. PROGRAM PHILOSOPHY AND MISSION

_____ A) Values, mission or policy statements, and individual habilitation plans of the agency reflect a commitment to improving the overall lives of persons with disabilities.

_____ B) The agency has publicly stated its commitment to integrated community employment.

_____ C) The agency is actively enabling support for community integrated employment, including supported employment, from staff, families, and the community.

_____ D) The agency has a position statement ensuring the participation of applicants with severe disabilities. (RSA Statement)

II. QUALITY OF LIFE

A. Development of Work Sites that Enhance the Image of Employees.

_____ 1) Work settings reflect the range of jobs, including jobs that are highly valued by the community.

_____ 2) The jobs performed are highly valued by the community.

_____ 3) There is no apparent physical segregation of workers with disabilities from non-disabled coworkers.

_____ 4) The hours of employment approximate those of the surrounding community.

_____ 5) Volunteer positions are utilized only when: a) they are time-limited, b) result in a marketable skill, c) lead to paid employment and/or are used to supplement paid work experiences, and d) they are in valued and in integrated sites and/or e) requested by worker or parent/guardian.

Appendix B: NARF's Quality Indicators Profile (continued)

B. Integrated Work in Typical Businesses and Industries that Encourage Interactions with Non-Disabled Coworkers and Supervisors.

_____ 1) Nondisabled coworkers and supervisors are present at the work site during the shift.

_____ 2) Opportunities occur for non-work interactions with non-disabled co-workers.

_____ 3) Interactions with non-disabled co-workers are a part of regular job responsibilities.

_____ 4) For the individual placement model, no more than two workers with disabilities work in the immediate work area.

_____ 5) Group based employment situations are integrated with 8 or fewer persons with disabilities.

_____ 6) If group jobs are developed, individuals are assured the opportunity to move into individualized jobs and there is evidence of such advancement.

_____ 7) Individuals are offered choices in the selections and maintenance of jobs.

C. Development of Quality Jobs for the Individual Worker

_____ 1) The general working conditions of the settings are safe, friendly, accessible and comfortable.

_____ 2) The jobs targeted for development are for stable rather than temporary or seasonal positions.

_____ 3) The jobs targeted for development have a low rate of coworker and supervisor turnover.

_____ 4) The jobs targeted for development have opportunities for advancement, pay increases, benefits, and increases in responsibilities.

_____ 5) Jobs are matched to interests and abilities of the worker.

Appendix B: NARF's Quality Indicators Profile (continued)

D. Empowerment

_____ 1) There is evidence of choice decision making for supported employees both at work and in the community.

_____ 2) Supported employees have access to a normal range of community activities and participate in these activities regularly as they choose.

_____ 3) Wages earned and benefits received by supported employees are sufficient to assure community participation.

_____ 4) Some degree of personal discretion in use of compensation received for work evident.

_____ 5) There is evidence that the supported employee has control over his/her environment (consider meals, medications, pets, friends visiting within one's home, coming and going, recreational/leisure activities, and basic routines/time usage).

III. APPROPRIATENESS OF SUPPORTS

A. General considerations

_____ 1) The program offers a variety of vocational options.

_____ 2) There is a plan to secure long-term supports for employees.   (Family/friend network; coworker/employer supports; case management, etc.).

_____ 3) Supported work services are provided for a range of persons with disabilities. Persons are not excluded due to behavior, social skills, communications ability, motivational issues or intellectual impairment.

B. Family & Community Support

_____ 1) The agency demonstrates it's commitment to supported work by offering staff and parents/families inservice training and forums for discussion.

_____ 2) The family/residential providers work cooperatively with the rehabilitation providers to assure quality community employment.

_____ 3) Assistance is offered to help workers use their pay to purchase recreation activities, to select and buy personal needs items and to do banking.

_____ 4) Coordination with community residential providers and others is carried out to assure the best possible options for community life.

_____ 5) Residential commitment is secured or attempts have been made to secure prior to participation in supported work services.

Appendix B: NARF's Quality Indicators Profile (continued)

C. Assessment and Planning

_____ 1) Family, friends, and significant others are described in the vocational profile.

_____ 2) Skills and learning characteristics are included in the vocational profile.

_____ 3) Past vocational experiences are used in assessment.

_____ 4) Assessment used to identify potential jobs are based on ecological factors (e.g. where applicant lives, transportation factors, as well as transitional vocational evaluation procedures.

_____ 5) Individual preferences are evaluated.

_____ 6) Employment possibilities beyond the immediate job have been considered and goals identified (career planning).

D. Use of Ecological and Job Analyses

_____ 1) Employment sites are assessed and selected on an array of quality indicators (potential for interactions with non-disabled coworkers, wages, working conditions, etc.) prior to employment.

_____ 2) Comprehensive inventories of environments and work-related activities are conducted before employment begins.

_____ 3) Detailed job analysis of all critical work and work related routines are compiled.

_____ 4) On-going individual employee assessments are conducted which reference ecology inventories and job analyses.

_____ 5) Job trainer performance and job routines are agreed upon with the employer before employees begin work.

E. Emphasis on Social and Communication Skills

_____ 1) Social and communication skill requirements of the job are included in the ecological inventories.

_____ 2) Social and communication skills are not considered to be prerequisites for employment and training needs can only be determined within the context of the individual setting.

_____ 3) The social and communication skill requirements of the job are taught within the natural job routines.

_____ 4) Flexibility and accommodations are negotiated as necessary to insure acceptable social and communication requirements.

_____ 5) When necessary, augmentative communication systems are utilized for the purpose of exchanging information with employees.

Appendix B: NARF's Quality Indicators Profile (continued)

F. Initial Training

___ 1) Breaks, lunch, and other non-work functions of the job are an important focus of training.

___ 2) Workers are taught to get to and from work.

___ 3) Workers are taught useful, productive and valued job skills.

___ 4) Individualized adaptations necessary for successful performance are routinely developed.

G. Use of On-going supports

___ 1) There are no standard time limits on access to placement, training and follow-along services.

___ 2) Intensity of support varies according to individual needs.

___ 3) Employers, coworkers and others are involved in providing long-term supports.

___ 4) Assistance is provided in maintaining the already existing friendships and other relationships of the employees.

___ 5) Adult education opportunities are provided and are coordinated with supported work activities.

___ 6) The intensity of supports potentially required to secure and maintain employment is not used to reject persons for supported work services.

___ 7) Resources necessary to design, develop and finance modifications and adaptations have been fully explored and used.

___ 8) On-going supports are readily available and can be easily accessed when needed.

___ 9) Individual adaptations necessary for successful performance are routinely developed (including equipment/work responsibility/task/procedural modifications).

___ 10) Changes in jobs or settings are made when it is clear that the worker is becoming dissatisfied with the job.

___ 11) Re-employment assistance is provided to workers changing jobs to insure the continuation of integrated employment.

Appendix B: NARF's Quality Indicators Profile (continued)

IV. ORGANIZATIONAL STRUCTURE

A. Attitude and Planning

   1) The attitude of the rehabilitation provider towards supported employment as evidenced in planning documents and interviews demonstrates a spirit of:

_____ a) innovation/dynamic orientation

_____ b) customer focus - consumer focus - employer focus

_____ c) cost/benefit concerns

_____ d) trust and openness to considering ideas from supported employment direct line staff

_____ e) ability to create quality supported employment

_____ f) inspiration and excitement over supported employment and quality of lives for persons with disabilities

_____ g) open communication flow

_____ h) understanding of how demanding the supported employment workload can be and the programmatic implications.

_____ 2) Plan to serve family/residential commitment is secured prior to participation in supported work services.

_____ 3) There is an existing plan for continued supported employment, including changes in staffing patterns; resource reallocation; and specific timeliness for implementation of supported employment.

_____ 4) Plans focus on future innovations and improvements of services.

_____ 5) Plans for stabilizing resources have been developed.

Appendix B: NARF's Quality Indicators Profile (continued)

B. The Agency's ability to manage changes associated with Supported Employment

___ 1) In terms of change processes, the supported employment program and the agency are effectively managing necessary changes brought about by supported employment. (The company may be in stages of initial awareness, visionary beginnings, second stage challenges to authority and conflict, third stage resolution of conflict, fourth stage intergroup conflict, fifth stage quasi-stationary equilibrium, or sixth stage program refinement).

___ 2) Conflicts and discomfort associated with changes are openly recognized.

___ 3) Conflict resolution occurs in a manner which improves and supports the Supported Employment process.

___ 4) Conflict resolution includes the process of technical assistance and open communication.

___ 5) A systematic needs assessment of agency, community, and consumers needs has been conducted.

___ 6) Strategic planning is evident, including adequate timeliness and pacing of activities.

___ 7) A feedback, monitoring system is utilized for implementing and evaluating change.

C. Organizational stability/capacity

1) The organization has been involved with supported employment for ___ yrs. ___ mos. (unrated).

___ 2) Organization has access to adequate resources; operating capital, services, etc.

___ 3) Budget projections indicated capacity to continue providing a high quality supported employment program.

___ 4) Long-term funding issues have been addressed in the plan.

___ 5) There is family representation on the Board.

___ 6) There is consumer representation on the Board.

___ 7) There is business and industry representation on the Board.

___ 8) Financial support has been secured from several available sources (unrated).

    a) MR/DD, VR, JTPA, KH

    b) 1619 (a) and (b), and SGA

Appendix B: NARF's Quality Indicators Profile (continued)

D. Fiscal Management

_____ 1) Discrete costs associated with specific employment services, i.e., job development, placement, training, follow-along can be identified.

_____ 2) Discrete resources are allocated for client transportation.

_____ 3) There are allocations for staff development and training costs.

_____ 4) It is possible to track costs for supporting each individual in employment.

_____ 5) Plans for securing revenue include modifications in utilization of existing resources.

_____ 6) Additional forms for revenue for the agency and the support services have been explored, e.g., employer participation.

_____ 7) Administrative costs are proportionate to the number of clients being served.

_____ 8) A range of payment options is available for supported work which includes sub-minimum wage certificates (unrated).

_____ 9) The agency has developed a costing system for supported employment which reflects actual costs to ensure a system for the ongoing development of supported employment (this could include the use of payments from employers and others).

10) Does the agency allocate administrative costs to supported employment? (unrated) _____ How?:

_____

11) What is the indirect charge to supported employment? (unrated)

_____

Appendix B: NARF's Quality Indicators Profile (continued)

E. Marketing and Public Relations

_____ 1) There is a marketing plan that has specific objectives related to outcomes for supported employees.

_____ 2) The marketing plan has strategies, identified staff responsible for implementing the plan, materials that are enhancing, etc.

_____ 3) There are specific activities to interact with and present information to community businesses, community groups, families, schools, etc.

_____ 4) The agency staff is knowledgeable about current employment opportunities in the community.

_____ 5) The agency has developed "networks" and relationships with employers and employer groups, i.e., referral process, information, informal relations.

F. Effective Utilization of Personnel for Job Development and Job Training

_____ 1) The person responsible for job development has in-depth knowledge of both the targeted employee and the training and support procedures to be used on the job.

_____ 2) Thoughtful consideration has been given to the decision as to whether to combine or separate the roles of job development and job training.

_____ 3) Whenever feasible, jobs are developed in close proximity to already existing jobs so as to increase the number of workers a job trainer can supervise and support. (unrated)

_____ 4) Training for supported employment personnel reflects in understanding of the needs of the position and the community.

_____ 5) Supported employment staff indicate feelings of work satisfaction, challenging work, automony and creative possibilities to "stretch performance" and create quality programs.

_____ 6) Supported employment staff indicate satisfaction with the competence of the supervision they receive.

_____ 7) Supported employment staff take part in setting supported employment goals.

_____ 8) Staff indicates a sense of pride on their accomplishments and feelings of being valued with reasonable rewards for effective work, (The self values for supported employees permeate the supported employment program).

9) Turnover rate _____ (supported employment staff which have left in the past year) (unrated)

Supported employment staff salaries (range)_____

(unrated) _____ Average: _____

Appendix B: NARF's Quality Indicators Profile (continued)

G. Coordination with School/Community Programs

1) Supported work personnel are directly involved with students before graduation from high school (IEP's Transition Plans, direct training, consultation). _____ (unrated)

2) School and supported work personnel are involved in a task force that focuses on transitional and supported work.
_____ (unrated)

3) Strategies for transferring responsibility from school to supported work services are clearly documented and used.
_____ (unrated)

4) Supported work personnel provide feedback to school districts on outcomes and status of graduates.
_____ (unrated)

5) Local school districts are encouraged to prepare students for integrated supported work through non-school vocational experiences.
_____ (unrated)

_____ 6) Relationships with existing job providing agencies have been developed (e.g., Voc Rehab, Job Services, Community Developmental Services, JTPA).

_____ 7) Technical assistance support relationships have been established.

_____ 8) Family and home supports are used to facilitate employment (e.g., transportation, job development and training).

_____ 9) Coordination is provided so that each individual's financial benefits (e.g., pay, SSI, SSDI, employer insurance) are maximized.

Appendix B: NARF's Quality Indicators Profile (continued)

H) Relationships with Employers

_____ 1) A business/industry advisory board has been formed.

_____ 2) Employers provide referrals for developing new supported work opportunities.

_____ 3) Traditional vocational evaluations are not solely used to determine vocational options.

_____ 4) Employers are involved in the evaluation of worker's performance.

_____ 5) Employees provide feedback on supported work procedures and trainer's roles.

_____ 6) Presentations on supported work to local employer and civic groups are an on-going component of the service.

_____ 7) Employers indicate satisfaction with the services provided by the coordinating/supervising agency.

_____ 8) Employers indicate that supported employment staff are responsible, responsive and effective.

_____ 9) Employers contribute through their attitude and actions to an environment which enhances the quality of work and quality of life of the supported employee.

_____ 10) Employers are willing to allocate resources to assist with implementation of supported employment.

_____ 11) Job developers provide assistance to employers in securing TJTC.

_____ 12) Proper procedures for securing regular sub-minimum wages are documented and used.

_____ 13) Workers are paid directly by employer, both at regular and sub-minimum wage.

_____ 14) Commensurate and/or minimum wages are sought before considering sub-minimum wages.

_____ 15) Job developers communicate to employers the potential need for modifications and adaptations.

_____ 16) Job trainers clear all modifications and adaptations with the employer before implementation.

Appendix B: NARF's Quality Indicators Profile (continued)

V. SAFEGUARDS

____ A) Supported employment plans and procedures provide evidence of procedures to reduce risks to supported employees, including:

    1) consideration of effect on SSI, SSDI benefits
    2) plans for decisive and effective action when difficulties arise
    3) plans for "fallback" for ineffective or inappropriate placements

____ B) The agency engages in preventive action, including: environmental assessment, community-referenced skills assessment, and good employee-job matches.

____ C) Parents and prospective supported employees have been adequately prepared for and involved in supported employment placements (e.g., records of meetings held, evidence of preference).

____ D) Supported employment placements are made with effective planning of transportation and procedures for handling possible emergencies.

____ E) Backups for transportation and direct training supervision are documented.

____ F) On-site support is provided in a sensitive and non-intrusive way to minimize stigmatization or "specialness" of employee.

____ G) Fading of supervision is correctly timed and implemented and documented through performance records.

____ H) Staff are adequately trained and paid.

____ I) The work environment includes arrangement of supports from coworkers and supervisors.

____ J) The work environment includes arrangement of supports from coworkers and supervisors.

____ K) The physical layout of the worksite contributes to employee effectiveness.

____ L) Instructional and supplementary interventions (e.g. for transportation, health, and ancillary needs) are responsive, timely, and effective.

Appendix B: NARF's Quality Indicators Profile (continued)

____ M) Supported employee turnover is indicative of desire to advance or try other employment and does not reflect low quality job watches, staff deficiencies or agency incompetence. (Examine rate of turnover as well as stated reasons).

____ N) Placement into supported employment is made with consideration of trends in unemployment rates, work force needs, and prediction of the stability of the local economy.

____ O) There is evidence that program reviews itself critically in terms of quality control.

____ P) There is a Management Information System (MIS) used to manage the supported employment program.

Appendix C: Supported Employment Degree of Implementation

Supported Employment Degree of Implementation

The Degree of Implementation form may be completed for each program by the project director as part of job trainer supervision of university personnel on a site visit to deliver technical assistance. It will be necessary to examine job trainer logs and other program documentation in order to complete the form.

The instrument utilizes a 3-point scoring system to rate both the frequency and quality of the task performed. The point system works as follows:

2-Yes - The activity completed as regularly as mandated or as often as necessary at acceptable level of quality.

1-Emergent - The activity is being carried out but with less frequency or quality than is desirable. Technical assistance/staff development is indicated.

0-No-The activity is not carried out or is done so inappropriately. Those items considered "not applicable" to a program should be scored 0 then explained. Technical assistance/staff development is strongly indicated.

Job Survey and Analysis	No	Emergent	Yes
1. Conducts a community survey for potential jobs.	0	1	2
2. Develops a list of companies/agencies willing to employ clients.	0	1	2
3. Targets specific jobs within particular company/agency.	0	1	2
4. Socially validates targeted jobs.	0	1	2
5. Determines which company/agency is appropriate for placement.	0	1	2
6. Task analyzes targeted jobs within companies.	0	1	2
7. Socially validates task analysis for particular job.	0	1	2
8. Identifies requisite skills or modifications necessary for the job.	0	1	2
9. Socially validates necessary vocational skills.	0	1	2
10. Determines necessary social survival skills (e.g., appropriate communication skills, transportation skills).	0	1	2
11. Socially validates social survival skills.	0	1	2

Job Match

	No	Emergent	Yes
12. Assesses client's vocational skills with standardized assessment (e.g. Vocational Assessment and Curriculum Guide).	0	1	2
13. Assesses client's social skills with standardized assessment (e.g. Vineland Social Maturity Scale).	0	1	2
14. Assesses client's vocational and social skills through observation.	0	1	2
15. Determines match of client's characteristics to the job requisite skills.	0	1	2

Job Acquisition and Maintenance

	No	Emergent	Yes
16. Utilizes applied behavior analysis.	0	1	2
17. Modifies job to adapt to particular client's handicap.	0	1	2
18. Proposes plan to maintain the level of performance acquired through training (e.g. self-monitoring techniques).	0	1	2
19. Proposes plan for follow-up services.	0	1	2

Conjunctive Job Services/Interagency Coordination

	No	Emergent	Yes
20. Identifies potential agencies to provide vocational services.	0	1	2
21. Identifies potential agencies to provide social services.	0	1	2
22. Identifies services within each potential agency that promote continuation in present placement.	0	1	2
23. Proposes plan for agency coordination and job services from each agency to be provided in conjunction with job training.	0	1	2

Job Fit

	No	Emergent	Yes
24. Reassess client's vocational skills periodically with standardized assessment instruments.	0	1	2
25. Reassess client's social survival skills periodically with standardized assessment instruments.	0	1	2
26. Reassess client's social and vocational skills through monthly observation.	0	1	2
27. Socially validates the quality of performance on the job.	0	1	2
28. Modifies job training to meet client, employer, and parent/guardian expectations.	0	1	2

11

Vocational Integration

Joseph has mental retardation in the moderate range and a hearing impairment. He has been employed as a maintenance assistant in a large four-story office building for six years. Joseph works 40 hours a week and earns $6.50 per hour. Ten other maintenance assistants work on the crew and perform similar job tasks during the same hours as Joseph. All employees take lunch and break in the company cafeteria during the same hours. The employees on the maintenance crew typically purchase their lunches and sit at a large table together, except two workers who like to sit at a nearby table. Joseph takes a brown bag lunch and eats it alone at a table beside the other employees. Joseph never participates in the employees' parties or picnics and has never associated with them after work hours. He continues to receive follow-along supported employment services. Joseph tells his employment specialist he would like to have more friends at work.

Linda has sustained a traumatic brain injury, which has resulted in memory problems, poor concentration, and impaired speech. She has been employed as an office clerk in a large insurance company for one year. Linda works 25 hours a week and earns $4.00 per hour. The company employs eighty personnel who work in six major departments, with an office clerk assigned to each one. Several cliques have formed in the company and are primarily determined by an employee's job title and physical location in the building. Linda "hangs out" with a group of women from her department. They socialize throughout the work day and help each other out as needed. Members of the clique have birthday parties and showers for the other co-workers in their group. Linda rides to and from work each day with a co-worker from another department, an arrangement made through the company car-pooling program. She plays softball on the company team and often goes to the movies on weekends with a few of the other co-workers in her department. Follow-along supported employment services continue to be provided by the employment specialist. Linda tells her employment specialist that she loves her job.

David is 25 years old and has been diagnosed as having cerebral palsy and mental retardation. He attends a segregated day program for

150 individuals with disabilities. David spends most of his day in the sheltered workshop, performing either simulated or contracted assembly tasks. He is paid piece-rate wages and averages approximately $60.00 a month. He participates in a self-care instructional program and also spends time socializing with other individuals with a disability or with paid staff. The facility manager and workshop supervisor report that David does not perform the job tasks independently and needs assistance with personal care. They feel that David must receive additional training before he will be "ready for work" in the community. David attends the group activities sponsored by the facility, such as holiday parties and occasional bowling. The facility van transports David to and from the workshop each day, in addition to any other outing. David lives with his family and spends most of his evenings sitting home, watching television. David tells his workshop supervisor that he would like a job.

Joseph, Linda, and David are all receiving vocational rehabilitation services, however, each present very different employment outcomes. A major distinction between the above case studies is the degree of integration experienced by the individuals who are participating in each employment situation. Less than twenty years ago, the only vocational option available to individuals with severe disabilities was training in segregated employment settings similar to David's workshop placement. More recently, supported employment has extended the opportunities for vocational integration to those individuals previously excluded from working in community business environments. The growth in supported employment during the last half of the 1980s indicates that many individuals like Joseph, Linda, and David, who have a severe disability are performing real work in integrated settings.

The idea that individuals labeled severely disabled *can* and *should* work in regular business environments with nonhandicapped co-workers has been the guiding philosophy behind the supported employment movement. Work is a highly valued activity in American culture and offers numerous benefits to wage-earners both with and without a disability. First, society tends to judge the worth of an individual by his or her productivity. Performing real work and paying taxes can enhance an individual's status and self-worth. Second, wages and fringe benefits received through work offer employees increased financial security and greater control over personal life choices. Third, individuals who work are perceived in a productive and competent role, which decreases the stigma associated with being handicapped (Matson and Rusch 1986). Fourth, work offers the opportunity to interact with co-workers, develop interpersonal relationships, and arrange social activities after work hours (Mcloughlin, Garner, and Callahan 1987). The workplace is particularly conducive to the establishment of friendships, since employees have regular face-to-face contact and share common experiences (Pogrebin 1987). Fifth, participation in work and consequently earning a living contributes to increased independence, improved quality of life, and personal satisfaction (Mcloughlin, Garner, and Callahan 1987; Taylor 1987; Zautra and Goodhart 1979).

Quality of life is reported to be significantly effected by the quality of an individual's work life (Goode 1989; Near, Smith, Rice, and Hunt 1983; Inge, Banks, Wehman, Hill, and Shafer 1988). Jones (1989) investigated the quality of work life for thirty individuals who worked in a sheltered workshop or in an enclave setting. They reported that individuals in enclave positions had higher quality-of-work-life scores, wage levels, and integration levels as well as high positive correlations between the three measures. Seltzer (1984) investigated job satisfaction for 65 individuals with mental retardation. The study found that individuals who had held competitive jobs, but were currently unemployed or employed in a sheltered workshop, were less satisfied with their status than those individuals who were only competitively employed or only in sheltered workshops. Work satisfaction was reported to be associated with the individual's tasks, supervisors, and co-workers.

A review of the literature on job satisfaction suggests that, with many jobs, the work environment and relationships with co-workers may be the most important factors contributing to job success and satisfaction, particularly with positions requiring less skill and ability (Moseley 1988). Friendships play an integral role in the quality of one's working life, as evidenced by reports that work performance, job retention, and job satisfaction are related to an employee's participation in social relationships with co-workers (Kirmeyer 1988; Klein and D'Aunno 1986; Young 1986).

Given the importance of co-worker involvement to job satisfaction and quality of life, it is evident that integration, or the opportunity to interact and work with nonhandicapped employees, is a critical measure of the quality of supported employment (Rehabilitation Research & Training Center Newsletter 1990). Outcome data suggest that individuals with severe disabilities who receive supported employment services are working in integrated environments (Rehabilitation Research & Training Center 1990). However, as indicated with Joseph's vignette, physical integration alone does not necessarily ensure social integration. The study of integration in the workplace is receiving increased attention by supported employment researchers as questions related to quality of services are raised by individuals with a disability, parents/family members, and professionals.

Studies aimed at measuring integration have primarily focused upon comparing the social interactions of workers with a disability with those of their nonhandicapped co-workers (Chadsey-Rusch, Gonzalez, and Tines 1987; Lignugaris/Kraft, Rule, Salzberg, and Stowitschek 1986; Lignugaris/Kraft, Salzberg, Rule, and Stowitschek 1988; Parent, Kregel, Twardzik, and Metzler 1990; Test, Farebrother, and Spooner 1988; Yan, Rhodes, Sandow, Storey, Petheridge, and Loewinger 1990). Integration is frequently defined in terms of employee interactions, since this outcome is easily observed and measured. Although integration involves more than just interactions, it can be assumed that one's social participation in the workplace is a good indicator of an individual's social acceptance by co-workers and satisfaction with the job.

Overall, the findings from these studies indicate that employees with a disability are participating in the social interactions that occur during work with the same frequency as their co-workers. Unfortunately, differences are reported in the type, content, and settings of the interactions in which workers with and without a disability participate. The following findings have been reported: (1) employees with disabilities are less likely to be involved in nonwork related interactions (Chadsey-Rusch, Gonzalez, and Tines 1987), (2) nonhandicapped co-workers participate in interactions involving joking and laughing more often than workers with disabilities (Lignugaris/Kraft, Rule, Salzberg, and Stowitschek 1987; Lignugaris/Kraft, Salzberg, Rule, and Stowitschek 1988), (3) workers with disabilities receive more direction and participate in less informational exchanges than their co-workers without disabilities (Test, Farebrother, and Spooner 1988), and (4) nonhandicapped co-workers interact with others during break more frequently than workers with disabilities (Parent, Kregel, Metzler, and Twardzik 1990). These results are from a limited number of studies conducted with small groups of workers, however, the consistency in findings suggests that perhaps greater emphasis needs to be placed on the quality of integration experienced by individuals receiving supported employment services.

A valued goal of supported employment is quality integration, yet the operational parameters related to its implementation are not clearly defined (Mank and Buckley 1989; Mcloughlin, Garner, and Callahan 1987). Integration has been broadly defined as "...participation of a worker in the operation of the work culture at both the environment's required level and the worker's desired level" (Shafer and Nisbet 1988, 57). Hughes, Rusch, and Curl (1990) view employment integration as "participation of employees with and without disabilities as equal members within a workplace" (p.190). Decisions as to whether an individual is socially integrated are usually made based upon the number of people with a disability employed in the setting or the employee's level of co-worker involvement, as assessed by observation and informal interviews. Since quality of life and quality of the environment are very different across individuals, including workers with a disability and their employment specialists, it is important to identify those characteristics of a job that define integration so that an employee can be best matched to the social culture of the work setting (Taylor 1987). People are more apt to develop friendships with those individuals who share common interests, participate in similar activities, and follow the same job-site "cultural traditions" as themselves (Bell 1981; Fine 1986). In situations where people are a minority in one or two important characteristics, psychological and social problems may develop (Zautra and Goodhart 1979).

The purpose of this chapter is to assist supported employment professionals with identifying and promoting quality integration outcomes for individuals with severe disabilities. First, the indicators that are characteristic of vocational integration will be described. Second, systematic procedures for assessing integration opportunities in the workplace and an individual's social preferences will be discussed. Third, strategies for improving integration and quality-of-life outcomes will be presented.

CHARACTERISTICS OF VOCATIONAL INTEGRATION

Although employment in a nonsheltered setting *is* integrated employment, the degree to which a job is integrated will vary across job sites and across days or situations within the specific employment setting (Parent, Kregel, Wehman, and Metzler 1991). A definition of integration must be comprehensive enough to include all of the characteristics that constitute an integrated employment situation and be flexible enough to apply across a variety of job settings and individual differences. Four elements of the job site must be considered when defining vocational integration (Parent, Kregel, Wehman, and Metzler 1991). These include the entire company, the specific work area, other employees, and company benefits.

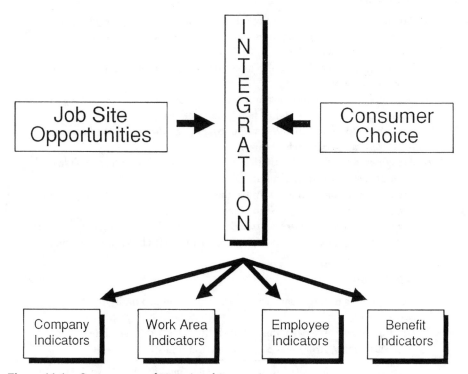

Figure 11.1   Components of Vocational Integration

It is important to note that each job site will vary in the number and type of opportunities for integration that it offers. These differences across jobs are what make one place of employment more attractive to a potential employee, thereby influencing an individual's choice to work in one setting over another.

The Rehabilitation Research and Training Center at Virginia Commonwealth University has developed an instrument that defines the specific indicators of quality integration. The Vocational Integration Index is a tool employment specialists can use when analyzing a job site to determine the opportunities available for vocational integration for all co-workers as well as to assess the degree to which an employee with a disability takes advantage of these opportunities (Parent, Kregel, Wehman, and Metzler 1991). The items on the Job Scale can assist employment specialists with determining if a job offers opportunities for true employment integration, while the Consumer Scale can help identify if an employee with a disability is socially integrated at the work site. Table 11.1 and 11.2 provide a listing of the items found on each of the scales.

These quality indicators of vocational integration are described below.

Table 11.1   Items on the Job Scale

Company Indicators

1. Are individuals with and without disabilities employed by the company?
2. Do employees have regular contact with other co-workers in the company throughout the work day?
3. Do employees have freedom to move around the different areas of the company during work hours?
4. Are employee assistance programs available for employees (e.g., drug or alcohol treatment, personal or family counseling?
5. Are other supports available for employees (e.g., direct deposit banking, organized car-pooling, child care)?
6. Are company sponsored activities available for employees (e.g., holiday celebrations, sports teams, picnics)?
7. Are employee common areas and gathering places available to employees (e.g., break room, lockers, Xerox machines, rest rooms)?
8. Are there formal or unwritten rules as to when talking among employees is acceptable (e.g., before work, at break, during shift changes, following task completion)?

Work Area Indicators

1. Do employees in the department work in physical proximity to other co-workers?
2. Do employees in the department follow the same work schedule (e.g., start times, stop times, task completion times)?

Adapted with permission from *Journal of Vocational Rehabilitation,* 1991, Vol. 1, No. 1, pp. 40-41.

Table 11.1   Items on the Job Scale *(continued)*

3. Do employees of the department work together with other co-workers to complete their tasks?
4. Does a company supervisor oversee the activities of the employees in the department?
5. Are staff meetings scheduled for employees of the department?
6. Are lunches and/or breaks scheduled at the same times for employees in the department?
7. Do employees provide assistance to each other when needed?
8. Do employees of the department have regular contact with the public throughout the work day?

Employee Indicators

1. Do employees follow similar work day routines (e.g., schedule, uniform, rules of conduct, job duty responsibilities)?
2. Do employees interact with other co-workers throughout the work day (e.g., socially, work-related)?
3. Do employees typically interact with one another in a certain manner during work hours (e.g., joking, conversing, greeting, slapping on the hand, discussing common topics)?
4. Do employees interact with each other during lunch and break times?
5. Do employees typically interact with one another in a certain manner during lunch and break times (e.g., joking, conversing, greeting, slapping on the hand, discussing common topics)?
6. Do employees of the department participate in social activities during work hours (e.g., pot-luck lunch, birthday celebrations, holiday parties)?
7. Do employees recognize special occasions and personal events in the lives of other co-workers (e.g., gifts or cards for birthdays, weddings, family deaths, or illnesses)?
8. Do employees participate in social activities with other co-workers outside of work hours (e.g., happy hour, party, dinner, movie, shopping, visiting)?

Benefit Indicators

1. Are employees paid for work performed?
2. Do employees who perform similar jobs earn comparable wages?
3. Are employees considered for raises on a regular basis?
4. Are medical benefits offered to employees (e.g., health insurance, dental insurance)?
5. Are other benefits offered to employees (e.g., employee discount, free meal, "Employee of the Month Award")?
6. Are vacation and holiday benefits offered to employees?
7. Are personal and sick leave benefits offered to employees?
8. Do employees have opportunities for advancement and mobility within the company?

Table 11.2   Items on the Consumer Scale

Company Indicators

1. Does the consumer work with other co-workers who are not handicapped?
2. Does the consumer have regular contact with other co-workers of the company throughout the day?
3. Does the consumer move around the different areas of the company during the work hours?
4. Does the consumer take full advantage of employee assistance programs (e.g., drug or alcohol treatment, personal or family counseling)?
5. Does the consumer take full advantage of other available supports offered by the company (e.g., direct-deposit banking, organized car-pooling, child care)?
6. Does the consumer regularly participate in company sponsored activities (e.g., holiday celebrations, sports teams, picnics)?
7. Does the consumer access employee common areas (e.g., break room, lockers, Xerox machines, rest rooms)?
8. Does the consumer follow the formal and unwritten social rules of the company?

Work Area Indicators

1. Does the consumer work in physical proximity to other co-workers in the department?
2. Does the consumer follow the same work schedules as the other co-workers in the department (e.g., start times, stop times, task completion times)?
3. Does the consumer work together with other co-workers to complete his or her job duties?
4. Does a company supervisor oversee the activities of the consumer?
5. Does the consumer attend staff meetings scheduled for employees of the department?
6. Does the consumer take lunch and/or breaks at the same time as the other co-workers in the department?
7. Does the consumer receive assistance from others when needed?
8. Does the consumer have regular contact with the public throughout the work day?

Employee Indicators

1. Does the consumer follow a similar work day routine as the other co-workers (e.g., schedule, uniform, rules of conduct, job duty responsibilities)?
2. Does the consumer interact with other co-workers throughout the work day (e.g., socially, work-related)?
3. Does the consumer interact throughout the work day in a manner similar to other co-workers (e.g., joking, conversing, greeting, slapping on the hand, discussing common topics)?
4. Does the consumer interact with other co-workers during lunch and break times?

Table 11.2   Items on the Consumer Scale *(continued)*

5. Does the consumer interact during lunch and break times in a manner similar to other co-workers (e.g., joking, conversing, greeting, slapping on the hand, discussing common topics)?
6. Does the consumer participate in social activities with other co-workers during work hours (e.g., pot-luck lunch, birthday celebrations, holiday parties)?
7. Does the consumer participate in recognizing special occasions and personal events in the lives of other co-workers (e.g., gifts or cards for birthdays, weddings, family deaths, or illnesses)?
8. Does the consumer participate in social activities with other co-workers outside of work hours (e.g., happy hour, party, dinner, movie, shopping, visiting)?

Benefit Indicators

1. Is the consumer paid for work performed?
2. Does the consumer earn comparable wages to other co-workers who perform similar job duties?
3. Is the consumer considered for raises on a regular basis?
4. Does the consumer receive medical benefits (e.g., health insurance, dental insurance)?
5. Does the consumer receive other benefits (e.g., employee discount, free meal, "Employee of the Month Award")?
6. Does the consumer receive vacation and holiday benefits?
7. Does the consumer receive personal and sick leave benefits?
8. Does the consumer have opportunities for advancement and mobility with the company?

Adapted with permission from *Journal of Vocational Rehabilitation*, 1991, Vol. 1, No. 1, pp. 40-41.

Company Indicators

Several features of the company dictate the overall opportunities for integration at a particular job setting. These can be as obvious as the number of people employed, the availability of formal supports, or the type of company sponsored activities or can be something less visible, such as the mechanism for evaluating employee work performance or the areas of the work site allowed access to by employees. For example, a company may or may not complete performance evaluations for its employees. If they do, it should be assumed that the employee with a disability will receive a performance evaluation that follows the same criteria and that is administered on the same schedule as the other co-workers who perform the same job. Similarly, co-workers may have access to the entire building and grounds at all times, while the employee with a disability may not be permitted to leave the immediate work area or may only be allowed to enter certain areas. A discrepancy between employee/co-worker practices may imply a very different set of expectations for the employee who is disabled.

Work Area Indicators

The features of the specific department or work area where employees perform their job duties are an important indicator of the usual opportunities for integration. This is where employees typically spend most of their work day with other employees who they see on a regular basis. Sharing the same work environment (proximity) and participating in common experiences (similarity) establishes the conditions that tend to promote the development of friendships among co-workers (Pogrebin 1987). Working during the same hours, performing similar job duties, wearing the same uniforms, taking breaks at the same time, sharing employee common areas, and attending the same staff meetings gives employees mutual topics for discussion and opportunities to engage in social interactions. For example, an employee with a disability who works in a separate area or during different hours than all of the other co-workers may never see an other employee to socialize with, despite the fact that he or she works at an integrated job.

Departmental practices frequently reflect and expand on the general policies and procedures specified by the company. Although these rules are often a subject of complaint by employees, the fact that they exist and that employees are expected to follow them creates a bond of similarity within the group. Differential treatment in the form of not being expected to follow the existing departmental rules, such as break schedules; or of having a different set of rules to follow, such as uniform requirements could alienate the employee with a disability or adversely affect employee/co-worker relationships. For example, consider the perceptions of an employee with a disability who is told not to attend a mandatory staff meeting that all of the other co-workers must go to. Although co-workers reactions may vary from envy to hostility to indifference, an image of being different would certainly be portrayed.

Employee Indicators

The interactions and activities of the employees of the company are critical indicators of the degree of social integration available at a particular job site. Employees may have the opportunity to interact with each other, the public, or their supervisor throughout the work day. For example, co-workers may socialize while performing their job duties together, such as a kitchen crew; or greet customers, such as a movie-ticket taker. In contrast, employees in another work environment may not participate in social exchanges with co-workers unless it is absolutely necessary. For example, employees may work side by side on an assembly line, but never talk to their work partner except to tell them to "hurry up" or to "pass a part." Similarly, co-workers of one company may participate in social activities during work hours, such as a going-away party or pot-luck lunch, while the majority of employees at another company may avoid company get-togethers. It is evident that the availability of opportunities for socialization does not necessarily mean that employees take advantage of a particular situation.

Equally important is how and when employees interact with one another. Employees may recognize special events of other co-workers, such as a birthday or birth of a child; or spend time together after work hours, such as a party or attending a play. Active involvement in any of the social functions that include the employees of the company would certainly contribute to feelings of membership or comradery among co-workers. It can be assumed that employees may be more apt to report co-workers to the supervisor for poor work performance if they do not like the individual or do not accept him or her as part of the work team. Or the alienation may be more subtle, as in situations where the employees do not help or "cover" for another co-worker when assistance is needed. Slight differences in an employee's uniform, expectations for performance, supervisor style, or availability to socialize can portray an image to co-workers that the supported employee is "special" and not "one of us."

Benefit Indicators

One of the primary values of work is the receipt of wages and fringe benefits in exchange for services performed. In addition to amount of wages, important indicators of integration include the method for distributing paychecks, the provisions for company raises, the scheduling of holiday or personal time, or the availability and use of fringe benefits, such as holiday time, medical insurance, or free employee meals. For example, consider the common bond shared between employees who receive their paychecks from their supervisor at the same time and then go out for lunch to celebrate. Certainly a message of being different would be portrayed for the worker with a disability who was required to go to the personnel department for his or her check or whose mother picked it up from the supervisor. Similarly, suppose all employees are entitled to receive a free meal from the company on the days they work, but the supported employee never received training to learn the skills needed to take advantage of this benefit. Instead, the individual carries a bag lunch and misses the opportunity to have lunch "like the rest of the gang."

The receipt of benefits establishes a shared topic for discussion among co-workers. Employees may rave about medical benefits, complain about vacation time, "second guess" the amount of raises, or discuss the next "Employee of the Month." Co-workers who are entitled to benefits share a vested interest and a common experience in receiving them. For example, co-workers may start joking and planning in November for the upcoming Christmas holiday. Similarly, employees may tease each other about being selected "Employee of the Month" or brag about the purchases made with an employee discount. Being excluded from receiving benefits or not using those that an employee is entitled to can reduce the number of opportunities for participation in peer interactions and activities.

PROCEDURES FOR ASSESSING VOCATIONAL INTEGRATION

Integration is a complex and dynamic phenomena that must be frequently assessed throughout the supported employment process. This is not surprising considering the high rates of supervisor and co-worker turnover that are often reported for entry-level jobs. Typically, changes in personnel will have a major impact on the work culture and social environment of the job site. For example, a new supervisor may decide to change company policies so that employees alternate lunch hours rather than everyone taking their break at the same time. Similarly, another job site with very little co-worker interaction may become a very social place as employees quit and are replaced with more friendly and outgoing staff.

In addition to the employment setting, a comprehensive assessment of integration must also include the individual with a disability who is a potential candidate for a particular job or who is already an employee of the company. It is important to know what type of working environment the individual would like, what his or her interests are, and the level of social contact that is desired. These characteristics can also change over time as work experience increases and the supported employee establishes a better foundation for judging the social desirability of a job setting.

Job-Site Integration Opportunities

The degree of integration available at a particular job site can be assessed by observing the work environment and interviewing supervisors and co-workers. It is likely that the employment specialist will obtain this information during the job analysis before placement, while providing job-site training after placement, and concurrently with data collection during ongoing follow-along services. Employment specialists can use this information to assist with making job placement decisions that enhance job-worker social compatibility and with monitoring individual employee satisfaction over time. Several questions can be addressed when conducting a systematic assessment of the work setting (Rehabilitation Research and Training Center Newsletter 1990). First, is this an integrated job? Second, what is the level of integration offered by this employment setting? Third, can modifications or interventions be made to enhance integration? Fourth, can (or are) the integration needs of a particular individual with a disability be (being) met by placement at this job site? In order to answer these questions, it is important to look at the multiple dimensions of the job site, including physical environment, social atmosphere, and co-worker activities.

Physical Environment

People need to have proximity to other people before integration on any level can occur (Pogrebin 1987; Stainback and Stainback 1987). At some jobs, employees may work side by side with constant opportunities to interact; while in another setting, employees may work in different areas of the building, but pass each other occasionally throughout the work day; and in other situations, employees may never have contact with another co-worker other than a supervisor. The frequency and consistency with which opportunities are available will depend upon the task requirements, production demands, layout of the work area, supervisor attitudes, and co-worker relationships.

Other features of the environment can affect the amount of social contact that is available to an employee with a disability. What is the level of task dependency? How much freedom do employees have to move around the building? Are there areas for employees to gather informally, such as a break room, locker room, employee rest room, Xerox machine, or time clock? Does the company organize activities for employees, such as softball teams, holiday celebrations, or family days? How much supervision is provided for employees? Do co-workers follow the same work schedule, such as start time, lunch and break times, and task completion times? For employees who have the same position, how similar are the work day routines, such as job duty responsibilities, type of uniform, and rules of conduct?

Perhaps the most obvious and controversial indicator of physical integration is the number of workers with a disability who are employed by the company. Federal regulations specify that no more than eight individuals with a disability may be employed in a single employment setting (*Federal Register*, August 14, 1987). Debates continue over whether this number is too restrictive or too liberal, with proponents at both extremes arguing for changes in regulations. More than likely, the re-authorization of the Rehabilitation Act Amendments in 1991 will continue to include a quantifiable definition of integration for program accountability. The key issues are presence and participation, with the assignment of a numerical figure to prevent segregated or congregated community placements.

Social Atmosphere

Interpersonal relationships tend to be facilitated when people have regular face-to-face contact and participate in social interactions with one another (Fine 1986; Pogrebin 1987). As mentioned previously, co-worker interactions and relationships occur more often when individuals have some interests, experiences, or characteristics in common. They type, style, and content of interactions that employees participate in can vary across job sites and across different times of day at the same employment setting. For example, at one job, employees may only discuss work topics; while another job may include a significant amount of joking and kidding; yet in another job, the co-workers may have developed a symbolic communication system, such as a thumbs-up, a slap on the back, or loud noise. In addition, employees may communicate one way during work hours and quite another at lunch, break times, or informal meetings.

A general assessment of the social environment at the job site can reveal the preferred or expected level of socialization for employees. Do co-workers engage in mutual social exchanges? Is there a usual way that employees respond to inter-actions initiated by other co-workers, such as joking, ignoring, smiling, or convers-ing? Does the supervisor exhibit a typical management style in response to em-ployee greetings and requests, such as yelling, assisting, criticizing, or answering? Is the job too fast-paced to permit talking? Are there unwritten rules as to when talking is acceptable, such as before work, at break, during shift changes, or fol-lowing task completion? Do co-worker and supervisor interactions occur regularly throughout the work day while the work is being completed?

Although individual co-workers may socialize differently or with more or less frequency, looking at the way the majority of employees relate to one another pro-vides an indication of just how social a potential job may be. For example, a job site with a friendly and relaxed atmosphere may encourage co-worker interactions. In contrast, the atmosphere of another work area may be pleasant and social in the absence of the supervisor; but cold, silent, and competitive when the management is present. Knowledge of the different social nuances of a particular job is impor-tant for making job placement decisions as well as helping the employee become an equal member of the work force.

Co-worker Activities

The number of opportunities for integration at a job site are meaningless if employ-ees do not participate in the interactions and activities that are available. Co-work-ers may make frequent use of a company lunch room, bowling team, departmen-tal picnic, or slow production times to socialize with other employees. At another job site, co-workers may not take advantage of similar opportunities, or some employees may do so at inconsistent times. For example, a job site that offered minimal co-worker contact during work hours, with a one hour lunch break sched-uled for all employees at the same time, may initially appear to be an appropriate match for a potential worker who expressed similar social interests. However, if after placement it is discovered that each employee goes out or eats at his or her work area alone, then a very different picture of socialization is presented.

Co-workers will certainly differ in the manner and frequency with which they interact with individual employees and at various times throughout each work day. It is important to assess the work environment on more than one occasion in or-der to gain an indication of the typical behavior of the majority of co-workers. Do employees go out of their way to talk to another worker, or do conversations usu-ally take place when the job demands co-worker contact?. Do employees talk about social topics or work related issues or both? How do employees interact with one another (i.e., teasing, joking, ignoring, or serious conversation)? Do employees "go out" together after work hours? Do employees appear to provide assistance or support to other co-workers when needed? Do the employees work together as a team? Observing how and when co-workers interact with one another will help the employment specialist identify the unwritten rules that dictate the expected behavior of the work area. Acceptance and comradery tends to increase when the supported employee is taught the social etiquette of the job site.

Individual Preferences

Judging the quality of integration opportunities available in the workplace is a highly subjective process. Regardless of disability label, individual employees are going to have very different desires, interests, and expectations regarding the degree of integration they would like. In addition, an individual's social needs and interests are likely to change with experience, which may redefine his or her preferred level of social involvement. A comprehensive assessment of an individual's interests and desires before placement and throughout his or her employment tenure is critical if quality integration is to be achieved. Important factors to consider in any decision related to integration include personal choice and level of participation.

Personal Choice

The quality of the employment situation and ultimately the individual's quality of life is enhanced when the individual is given opportunity to choose the determinants of a job (Mcloughlin, Garner, and Callahan 1988). These include such things as type of work, job duties, wages, hours, benefits, location, work conditions, schedule, advancement opportunities, co-worker characteristics, social environment, and degree of socialization. The job preferences of potential workers will vary considerably depending upon the value placed upon different job characteristics. For example, an individual may prefer to work at a job that pays minimum wage and offers few benefits if it is close to his or her home and offers a significant amount of socialization. Similarly, another individual may have a particular work interest, such as sports, computers, or gardening, and prefer a job related to his or her interest regardless of the opportunities for co-worker interactions that are offered. In many situations, opportunities for the development of friendships may be the only distinguishing feature between entry-level jobs, which typically offer similar wages, hours, and benefits (Rehabilitation Research & Training Center Newsletter 1990). To a great extent, employment success is related to the degree of autonomy and control that an individual with a disability can exert during the selection and placement decision process (Moseley 1988).

Information regarding an individual's social interests and preferences can be gathered by interviewing the potential worker and other significant persons, such as a friend, parent/guardian, or vocational trainer, as well as observing the individual in different environments. Although an individual with a severe disability may have had limited opportunities for interactions with nonhandicapped persons, a general indication of social preferences can be identified during the assessment process. For example, does the individual like to be around people? Does he or she like to interact frequently with others? Is the individual shy or outgoing? Does he or she prefer to spend time with individuals who have certain characteristics in common, such as age, gender, culture, or hobbies? Is the individual comfortable in a crowded, noisy room or is a quiet, isolated area preferred? Does he or she relate better to certain styles of interaction, such as kidding or serious conversation? What types of nonwork activities does the individual like to participate in? Answers to the above questions can help the employment specialist determine the compatibility between an individual's social preferences and the integration opportunities available at a particular work site so that a good job-employee match can be made.

Level of Participation

Job satisfaction and retention is often contingent upon the degree of social involvement that an employee has with supervisors and other co-workers (Greenspan and Shoultz 1981; Hanley-Maxwell, Rusch, Chadsey-Rusch, and Renzaglia 1986; Salzberg, Lignugaris /Kraft, and McCuller 1988). Co-worker relationships are a major source of natural support within a work environment (Nisbet and Hagner 1988). A co-worker can assist another employee with completing work responsibilities, handling personal problems, dealing with other co-workers, learning new job tasks, understanding the unwritten rules of the workplace, and responding to infrequent or emergency situations. In addition, co-workers fulfill multiple roles as friend, "confidant," and companion both at work and after hours. Although individuals will vary in their need for support and their desire to form relationships with co-workers, a lack of opportunity to do so would certainly make work an unenjoyable experience.

Changes in the opportunities available for developing relationships and the intensity of established relationships are not uncommon occurrences at the work site. Co-worker and supervisor turnover, absenteeism, departmental transfers, and schedule changes can be potentially serious threats to integration and job retention. For example, a supported employee who depends upon another co-worker for assistance with completing his or her work tasks may never get the job done the first time the co-worker does not show up for work. Similarly, an employee who has one good friend and advocate at work may find his or her job less satisfying if that co-worker is transferred to another company site. Proactive monitoring can assist the supported employee with maintaining and developing co-worker supports and meaningful relationships.

Assessing an individual's social participation is an important component of the follow-along process. Information regarding the degree of integration experienced by an individual with a disability can be obtained by interviewing the employee; talking with co-workers, the supervisor, and family members; and observing the work environment. Often, a decrease in an individual's level of involvement in co-worker activities or changes in the way in which co-workers interact with the supported employee is a signal of a potential or existing problem at the job site.

Systematic, ongoing assessment will assist the employment specialist with answering several key questions related to quality integration (Rehabilitation Research & Training Center Newsletter 1990). First, is the supported employee integrated in this job? Second, what is the degree of integration experienced by this employee? Third, does the level of integration reflect the individual's choice? Fourth, is intervention needed to increase the employee's level of integration? Fifth, can training strategies be identified to increase the individual's participation in available integration opportunities?

STRATEGIES FOR IMPROVING INTEGRATION OUTCOMES

Determining if an employee with a disability is truly integrated in his or her job is a challenging question to answer. There is no single indicator that can tell employment specialists whether an individual is experiencing maximum integration at the work site. Rather, a number of factors must be looked at when evaluating integration outcomes. In addition, each supported employee is going to have his or her own opinion as to what quality integration is and which characteristics of a work setting are rewarding. It is likely that an individual will be satisfied with some aspects of a job and desire change or improvement in other areas.

At what point, then, is intervention aimed at increasing integration appropriately implemented? This question can only be answered after looking at the job site's opportunities for integration, co-worker and supported employee participation in the opportunities that are available, and level of involvement desired by the individual with a disability (Parent, Kregel, Wehman, and Metzler 1991). Discrepancies between the activities of the supported employee and the other co-workers would suggest that intervention may be necessary *unless* the worker has made an informed choice not to participate in the same manner or with the same frequency as other co-workers. Similarly, differences between a worker's employment situation and his or her desired level of integration would signal a need for employment specialist intervention. Several strategies can be utilized to increase or enhance the degree of integration experienced by an individual with a severe disability. These include (1) making job-site modifications, (2) providing social skills instruction, (3) advocating on behalf of the employee, and (4) teaching the "social culture" of the job site. (Parent, Kregel, and Wehman, in press).

Making Job-Site Modifications

Often, a simple modification of the work environment, job duties, or work schedule can facilitate employee interactions (Judy 1989; Mallik 1979; Mallik 1990; Wehman, Wood, Everson, Goodwyn, and Conley 1988). For example, a laundry attendant who is responsible for folding towels alone at a work station that faces the opposite direction of co-workers would have a greater chance of being included in the verbal and nonverbal exchanges that take place if she moved behind the table and faced the other employees. In addition, a part-time file clerk who works four hours a day and does not receive a lunch hour would have more opportunities to socialize if she "hung around" and took break with the other employees after she punched out every day. It is important to assess the entire situation and brain-storm all possible solutions before making any changes at the job site. The least obtrusive modification should be implemented first, after receiving the employer's approval for any changes that can affect the work environment.

More complex modifications or the use of adaptive equipment may be necessary in other situations. For example, a maintenance assistant who performs all of his job tasks in areas where no other co-workers are present would have an increased chance to interact with other employees if his work schedule were changed to replace or add new job duties that another co-worker also performed or that required another person for completion. A second option might be to build in some informal meeting times throughout the work day, such as stopping by the employee break area, gathering at the time clock before and after work, or taking a different route between work areas that passes by co-workers. Adaptive aids, either commercially developed or handmade, can be used to assist an individual with being able to communicate with others, to participate in job-site activities, and to perform work tasks the same as nonhandicapped co-workers. Examples of adaptions include electronic calendars, computerized speech devices, ramps, Braille-output computers, elevated work stations, or environmental control units. Rehabilitation engineers and occupational therapists are a valuable resource for identifying and developing modifications and adaptations for the job site.

Providing Social Skills Instruction

Following the formal and informal social codes that dictate the expected behavior of employees at a job site is essential for co-worker and supervisor acceptance. For example, co-workers may be expected to say thank-you after a customer transaction, a supervisor may prefer a personal greeting at the beginning of every work shift, co-workers may slap hands when passing, or talking may not be allowed at certain times during the work day. One of the major responsibilities of an employment specialist is to identify and teach the valued work and nonwork-related social skills of a job site to the employee with a disability. For example, an employee may be taught to ask for assistance when the vacuum cleaner breaks down, to use appropriate social amenities with the public, to wave hello to the supervisor, or to maintain an acceptable social distance when conversing with co-workers.

Much of this learning occurs just from participating in an integrated employment setting, observing nonhandicapped peers, and modeling the appropriate interactions exhibited by others. Since the employment specialist is also an influential role model, it is important for him or her to engage in those behaviors that occur at the job site in the same manner as the employee is expected to participate. For example, an employment specialist who talks during work hours when it is not permitted is sending a message to the worker that talking is okay, which may jeopardize long-term employment success. Similarly, an employment specialist who allows a worker with a disability to greet her with a hug is perpetuating a behavior that is likely to interfere with co-worker relations.

Often, social skills training packages can be implemented that will increase an individual's social involvement at the work setting (Chadsey-Rusch 1990). The purpose of these interventions may be to teach an individual new skills or to reduce inappropriate behaviors. Effective training strategies that may be used alone or in combination include self-instruction, modeling, role-playing, social reinforcement, systematic instruction, supervisor prompting, co-worker assistance, and behavior management (Agran, Salzberg, and Stowitschek 1987; Breen, Haring, Pitts-Conway, and Gaylord-Ross 1985; Chadsey-Rusch 1990; Shafer, Tait, Keen, and Jesilowski 1989).

For example, an employment specialist could teach a parking lot attendant who is nonverbal to give directions by pointing in response to questions from customers; this could be done by modeling the behavior, providing verbal instruction, and praising a correct gesture. An individual employed as a microfiche clerk could be taught to initiate interactions during break or to ask for assistance when the equipment breaks down by role-playing situations, using co-worker prompting, or providing instructions and reinforcing appropriate interactions. Finally, a worker employed as a silver banisher, who cried every time she received positive or negative feedback from a co-worker, could be taught a more acceptable response by modeling, role-playing, reinforcement, or behavioral intervention. The type of intervention strategy that is implemented will depend upon the nature of the problem or skill deficit, the learning style of the individual, and the physical and social environment of the work area.

Advocating on Behalf of the Employee

Involvement in the job-site social network is enhanced when the vocational competence of a worker with a severe disability is conveyed. Employees may be reluctant to participate in interactions with a worker with a disability out of fear or uncertainty due to a lack of experience or preconceived stereotypes. Seeing the individual in a productive role and observing the day-to-day interactions of the employment specialist can have a powerful impact on changing incorrect perceptions. For example, having the worker complete a task while the employment specialist is "getting the job done" allows others to see the individual with a disability as an independent and contributing employee of the company. Similarly, social conversations between the employment specialist and the worker with a disability demonstrates to other co-workers that they can participate in meaningful and rewarding relationships with the supported employee.

Co-workers learn how to interact with the employee with a disability by observing the actions of the employment specialist. Acting in a respectful manner, being genuinely interested in the individual's well-being, and behaving in a nonjudgmental way portrays a positive and valued image of the individual with a severe disability. In contrast, laughing when the employee makes an inappropriate comment, ignoring an employee's social initiation, keeping silent when co-workers make fun of an employee, or answering a supervisor's question directed to the employee portrays the individual in a dependent and devalued role.

As advocate on behalf of the employee with a disability, it is the employment specialist's responsibility to identify and promote the individual's involvement in the social exchanges and activities that other co-workers participate in. For example, the employment specialist can assist the worker with signing up and playing on the company's softball team. Similarly, the employment specialist can encourage participation during informal social gatherings, such as at the time clock before work hours, by modeling appropriate interactions and providing instruction or by identifying a co-worker advocate to facilitate employee participation.

In addition, the function of an advocate is to "seek change by supporting, speaking out, or acting on behalf of" the supported employee (Moon, Inge, Wehman, Brooke, and Barcus 1990, 418). It is important for the employment specialist to eliminate discrepancies between the expectations or treatment of the co-workers and the supported employee that suggest the worker with a disability is not the same as the other employees or is a less valued member of the work force. For example, the employment specialist can talk to a supervisor who feels that the employee with a disability does not need to wear a uniform, even though all of the other co-workers are required to. In addition, the employment specialist can teach the employee to appropriately decline to complete the work responsibilities of another co-worker who is taking advantage of the supported employee. Examples of other guidelines for effective advocacy include talking informally with co-workers, sharing the employee's strengths with the co-workers, explaining the behavioral characteristics of the employee to the supervisor, and providing opportunities for the supervisor and employee to interact (Moon, Inge, Wehman, Brooke, and Barcus 1990).

Teaching the Employee the "Social Culture" of the Job Site

An employee's social adjustment depends upon the congruence or goodness-of-fit between the individual and the work environment (Schalock 1989; Schalock and Jensen 1986). In some situations, a worker will participate in social exchanges on the job site, but will not be included in interactions about social events or topics that co-workers who are friends engage in. For example, a co-worker may say "hello" to the worker with a disability while walking past him to go tell another employee about his exciting date the night before. Although the employee is not excluded from social interactions with co-workers, the opportunity to develop friendships can be limited by a lack of common or shared social interests with other employees.

It is important for the employment specialist to identify the valued social activities and conversations at a job site and to teach the worker a way that he or she can get involved. For example, consider a job site where the major topic of conversation is sporting events. An individual with a disability who knew little about sports could be a more active participant if he or she attended sporting games, watched televised events, or was prompted about upcoming competitions and significant outcomes, such as the Super Bowl. For an individual who is nonverbal, participation can be increased by bringing souvenirs, newspaper clippings, or pictures of current sporting events to the job site and showing them to the other co-workers.

Employees are more apt to include another co-worker in the interactions and activities that occur at a job site if he or she is perceived as being a contributing member of the social network. Talking about current events, mentioning a new music release, or speculating about possible work-site changes are examples of ways that the employee can increase his or her social involvement. Often, a worker with a disability will not have had previous opportunities to learn how to participate in interactions that promote positive relationships with others. For example, asking someone how they are doing or complimenting a worker on a new outfit is sure to elicit a favorable response. In addition, initiating a conversation, sharing information, asking questions, and responding appropriately are social exchanges that tend to encourage employee communication. Teaching a worker to participate in the valued social exchanges and activities that occur at a job site increases the likelihood that the individual with a disability will be included in the social interactions and relationships that develop among employees.

SUMMARY

Vocational integration is an important outcome measure of quality supported employment services. Multiple factors must be examined when determining if a particular job or employee are integrated. First, does the company offer opportunities for integration? Second, does the work area provide opportunities for physical and social integration? Third, do employees participate in the opportunities that are available? Fourth, does the company offer benefits for employees? Fifth, does the worker with a disability participate in the opportunities for integration that are offered? Finally, is the supported employee satisfied with the degree of physical and social integration that he or she is experiencing? A negative answer to any of the above questions could be an indication that intervention is necessary to improve the amount of integration available at a work site or to increase an individual's level of participation. Systematic and ongoing assessment of the job setting and the worker is critical if maximum integration is to be achieved and maintained.

The case studies presented at the beginning of this chapter illustrate the importance and difficulty associated with assessing integration. Most people would agree that Joseph and Linda are employed in integrated jobs, while David is working in a segregated setting. A more subtle, and perhaps controversial, distinction is evident in the quality of integration that Joseph and Linda are experiencing.

The following similarities with the two supported employment settings can be found: both companies offer opportunities for integration, opportunities are available in the work areas, employees are physically present and participate socially with one another, and employees earn greater than minimum wage. Linda "loves her job," is an active participant, and has developed meaningful relationships with her co-workers. In contrast, Joseph is often isolated, rarely participates in interactions and activities with co-workers, and expresses a desire for "more friends at work." It is evident that Joseph is not truly integrated at his job, despite the fact that he is working in an integrated, community business. The employment specialist may intervene to help Joseph achieve maximum integration at this work site or to assist him with finding another, more suitable job. The quality of vocational integration is enhanced when individuals with disabilities have choices and are empowered to make their own decisions regarding the employment settings that best meet their social needs and preferences.

12

Staffing and Recruiting for Supported Employment

Perhaps the most critical part of any organization is its personnel. This is especially true when the goods or services provided by an organization are primarily the result of human interactions. Such is the case with organizations providing supported employment services. The best mission statement, policies and procedures, and other organizational structures may be in place within supported employment programs, but will be ineffective without knowledgeable and dedicated staff who work well together and with the community.

Staffing is perhaps the most important task facing a program manager. This is true regardless of whether the manager is just starting a program or is replacing an employment or enclave specialist. Each staff hiring process is an opportunity to enhance a supported employment program. Quality staff will translate to better outcomes for persons with disabilities. Poorly qualified staff will either result in poor employment outcomes for consumers or, at best, disproportionate investments of time, energy, and fiscal resources dedicated to training and monitoring.

While a crucial task, effective staffing is a significant challenge. There has yet to be a consensus regarding the role of the employment specialist or enclave specialist. The field has not yet embraced the role of employment specialist as a professional role. Instead, many consider employment specialists to be paraprofessionals. Salary and benefits for employment specialists are very low when compared to others who perform similar duties. The purpose of this chapter is to provide information that will assist program managers in meeting these challenges by effectively recruiting, hiring, and maintaining a high-quality staff.

For the purposes of this chapter, the term "employment specialist" will be used to identify individuals who provide direct services to consumers across all supported employment approaches (i.e., individual, enclave, crew and entrepreneurial). As indicated in Chapters 3 and 4 and the Direct Services Technologies section, the actual provision of services to consumers is very similar across employment approaches. It is recognized that duties other than direct training and follow-along may vary across approaches. These variances will be discussed in the following appropriate sections.

STAFFING CONFIGURATIONS

Supported employment programs are organizationally configured in a variety of ways. The diversity of needs and the creativity of program managers meeting those needs makes it impossible to identify a finite set of staffing configurations for supported employment programs. Program size, number of supported employment approaches offered by a program, qualifications and experience of staff, and whether a supported employment program is administratively within a larger rehabilitation program are but a few of the factors contributing to staffing configuration decisions. The "right" configuration is the configuration that (1) leads most efficiently to the best outcomes for consumers and (2) satisfies both individual staff and organizational needs.

Three of the many different configurations are presented in Figure 12.1. Configuration 9A) represents what has been called the "holistic" configuration (Sale, Wood, Barcus, and Moon 1989). In this configuration, the employment specialist and the enclave specialist perform all direct-service duties, including assessment, job development, job-site placement, training and follow-along for each consumer on their caseload. One "partitioned" configuration (B) is also presented. In this configuration, the personnel specialize in certain duties associated with providing supported employment. In (B), each employment or enclave specialist handles his or her own job development. The employment specialists do their own job-site training and have as an additional responsibility, the initial training of new workers in the enclave (denoted by the dotted line). In this configuration there are employment specialists dedicated solely to the follow-along of all consumers except those in the enclave.

As illustrated in the Figure 12.1, the major difference in the configuration is whether or not certain individuals will specialize by doing one or two components of supported employment. To date, there is no empirical documentation that demonstrates that the holistic configuration is better in a given circumstance than the partitioned configuration. There are certainly pros and cons to both. For example, in some partitioned programs, there are different pay scales for job developers, employment specialists, enclave specialists, and follow-along persons. While this may have economic merit, the notion that one component requires more skills and is more valued than another is antithetical to the supported employment concept. Indeed, some programs use the follow-along position as an entry-level position. Experience demonstrates that follow-along often requires the most interpersonal savvy, the quickest assessment of problems, and the most timely resolution of issues, when compared to initial training. Figure 12.2 delineates additional pluses and minuses of the holistic and partitioned configurations.

For these and other reasons, it is recommended that the holistic configuration be the configuration of first choice, particularly in programs just starting. This

Staffing Considerations[1]

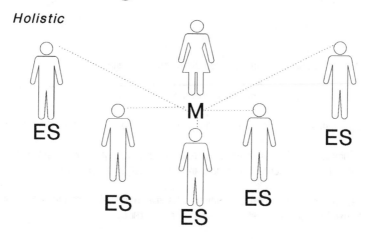

Holistic

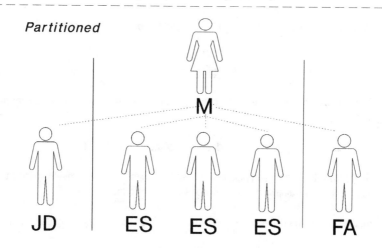

Partitioned

[1]
 *M=manager; ES=employment specialist; JD=job developer;
 FA=follow along*

Figure 12.1

Considerations of Holistic vs. Partitioned Staffing Configurations

Holistic

\+ Ownership and commitment to job and consumer enhanced

\+ Experience gained as trainer facilitates better job analysis

\+ Experience gained as trainer facilitates more accurate consumer assessment

\+ Eliminates need for information transfer to and from job developers or follow along personnel which sometimes results in communication breakdown

\+ Performing a variety of duties may be attractive to potential employment specialists and relieve long periods of stress, boredom, and burnout

\- The diversity of functions required may limit potential candidates

\- Most candidates hired initially will be proficient in only several aspects of the job

Partitioned

\+ The number of candidates who can perform the narrower scope of activity may be increased

\+ Specialization may increase the degree of competency of staff

\+ Staff "down-time" between placements can be minimized as job development can occur while intensive training or follow-along is being performed

\- Inadvertent status distinctions may occur, with job site training being devalued

\- Job and consumer match is more difficult if job developer is not the trainer

\- Follow-along, particularly crisis follow-along, will be degraded in the short term because of lack of knowledge of job site conditions during training

Figure 12.2

configuration allows the most continuity for employers and consumers. It provides the best "personal investment" in a job and a consumer. It provides a single point of contact for each consumer.

INITIAL RECRUITING AND HIRING CONSIDERATIONS

Prior to the initiation of job description development and actual recruiting, it is wise to complete a thoughtful assessment of the organization. As noted above, recruitment and ultimate staffing can be a powerful tool for making the organization better. A close look at the organization's mission and values, an analysis of past staffing concerns and successes, an examination of strengths of existing staff, and decisions regarding reconfiguration of staffing structures should all be completed prior to the development or redevelopment of a position description. Figure 12.3 delineates factors that a manager must examine prior to initiating position description development and subsequent recruiting processes. Each of these considerations will be discussed briefly below.

Considerations Prior to Recruiting

> What are the <u>current</u> organizational missions and values (both formal and informal)?

> If there were previous staff in this position, what personality, knowledge, and skill characteristics facilitated and inhibited effective job performance?

> What are the current strengths and weaknesses of remaining staff?

> What are the remaining staff's preferences related to personality, knowledge, and skills desired of the newly hired person?

> Would it be prudent to change staffing configurations at this time?

> Is it possible and desirable to move an existing employee into the vacated position?

Figure 12.3

Mission/Values

A mission statement of an organization should convey the purpose of the organization's work and the values that underlie that purpose. The mission of organizations providing supported employment services should therefore include the values of fair wages for valued and needed work, community integration of persons with severe disabilities, and a commitment to ongoing support. Additional values may also be embodied within the mission statement.

In addition to these formal mission statements, there are always informal missions and values that undergird every organization or unit. For example, organizations may choose to work only with individuals with certain types of disabilities and not with others. Or an organization might choose to work with the most challenging individuals available, regardless of disability labels. As another example, some organizations have extensive capital investments (e.g., large buildings, vans, etc.) and must generate money to continue these investments. These organizations may have different priorities than organizations with few capital investments.

As an employee leaves and a vacancy is created, it is a good time for the program manager to make a frank assessment to determine whether or not the organization or organizational unit is achieving its formal and informal missions. If discrepancies exist between the formal and informal missions, the program manager must evaluate whether or not personnel decisions can lessen the discrepancy.

For example, if the manager determines that the program is not adequately serving individuals with severe disabilities, and this is a formal or informal mission, it is possible that both the reward system for employment specialists and their training may need adjustment. Establishing a job description that emphasizes *severely* disabled persons and ultimately hiring someone who is experienced in working with persons with *severe* disabilities is likely to increase the number of persons with severe disabilities who are placed (obviously, if the reward system can also be changed, the mission may be even furthered).

Analysis of Previous Staff

Another piece of data that must be considered prior to developing a job description is the information obtained from the exit interview of a previous staff person. An exit interview is a discussion between the individual who is terminating their employment with the organization and either personnel officials or the supervisor. Information such as the actual work involved in carrying out the duties of the position, obstacles that impede effective job duty performance, and suggestions for improving the job are all things that should be gleaned from the exit interview. This information may prove helpful as the program manager decides how to improve his or her organization via the upcoming, new staffing.

Additionally, and especially for programs that are just beginning to provide supported employment services and are creating *new* positions, information should be gathered from other supported employment organizations in the community. Program managers should talk with other program managers and employment specialists to learn of their experiences. When possible, job duty descriptions should be shared across organizations. This will not only assist the program manager in writing a job description, but may also provide a basis for creating a job description that improves the likelihood of attracting high-quality individuals who may already be employed in similar positions.

Current Staff

An analysis of the strengths and weaknesses of current staff members should also be undertaken prior to developing a job description. Positive vocational outcomes for persons with disabilities are the result of teamwork on the part of employment specialists and program managers. It becomes important, then, to look at the aggregate strengths and weaknesses of a staff and to identify absent characteristics, which may help in meeting the mission of the organization.

For example, it may be that an existing staff is quite knowledgeable about job development techniques, yet knows little about systematic training. It would then behoove the manager to emphasize skills-training experience in the job description and during recruitment of the vacant position. Alternatively, the program manager may wish to change the staffing configuration to utilize personnel strengths more effectively.

Reconfiguration

When a staff member terminates, it may be a perfect time to reconfigure staffing arrangements. This reconfiguration may take the form of a total organizational or unit structural change or may involve simply moving an existing staff member into the vacant position. A total shift of organizational or unit structure should be undertaken only after very careful consideration, since the "cure" could end up worse than the original problem. However, in programs where a large discrepancy exists between mission and outcomes, this approach may be very useful.

A second reconfiguration option is to move an existing employee into the vacant position. This option is particularly attractive if (1) the existing employee has those special skills needed for the vacated position and (2) the existing employee views the move as a promotion (perhaps even an increased salary). Within organizations that offer an array of supported employment approaches, employees are often moved from enclave supervision positions to individual placement employment specialist positions. While these shifts still result in a vacant position, certain positions may be easier to fill than others.

JOB DESCRIPTION DEVELOPMENT

Subsequent to a thorough assessment of the organization, staff configurations and reconfiguration, and all internal staff reallocations, it is necessary to develop a job description. The job or position description is the single most important item needed for efficient recruitment of quality staff. A job description should provide both enough information for prospective applicants to make a decision about their qualifications related to the job and adequate criteria for the program manager to narrow the applicant pool to reflect only individuals truly qualified for the job. Existing job descriptions should not be reused *in toto* without careful consideration of the issues related to staffing configuration and initial considerations listed above.

Most job descriptions include a general description, a specific listing of duties and responsibilities, applicant qualifications, and salary and fringe benefits. Each of these components will be discussed below. The reader should note several points before reading further. First, the sections below are typical and may vary among organizations. Larger organizations who hire employment specialists may have a seemingly never-ending maze of rules and regulations relating to recruiting and hiring practices. Therefore, it is imperative that the program manager be intimately familiar with their own personnel policies prior to initiating the development of job descriptions and subsequent hiring procedures. Second, job descriptions must be individually tailored to the organizational needs at a given point in time. Therefore, no text, including this one, should provide "canned" job descriptions. Rather, general guidelines and prototypes should be given to provide a foundation upon which to build. Figure 12.4 provides such a prototype and will be used within the discussion below.

It should be noted that the sample description was developed for an employment specialist who will be using the individual approach and within a "holistic" staffing configuration. Obviously, programs using a partitioned model would only utilize the portions applicable to the specific position (e.g., job development, follow-along, etc.).

It should also be noted that Figure 12.4 portrays a position for a specialist who will be working with a generic disability. While many of the skills required for implementation of supported employment are consistent across disability groups, there are specific strategies that prospective employment specialists may need to possess in order to successfully work with a specific population. The discussion below will describe potential variations based on consumers with differing disabilities.

Sample Job Description

General Description

The employment specialist is involved in all aspects of community based vocational training, placement, and follow-along for persons with an array of severe disabilities as part of the Excel Rehabilitation Program. The successful candidate will meet with employers to secure placements, provide one-on-one training for job and other related skills, and maintain systematic and regular contact with employers after job training has been completed. The employment specialist will work as part of a team and will interact frequently with other professionals related to specific cases.

Specific Duties/Responsibilities

1. Job Development. The employment specialist will complete job market screening activities and regularly present the employment program to prospective employers until adequate numbers of appropriate open positions have been identified. The specialist will analyze job duties and requirements of potential jobs.

2. Consumer Assessment. The employment specialist will complete/and or secure assessment and evaluation information as necessary to assist the consumer with informed decision making. This may include referral to other professionals/agencies and subsequent interpretation of reports observations, and interviewing persons knowledgeable about the consumer.

3. Job Placement. The employment specialist will complete activities to secure placement of individuals with disabilities to include: vocational guidance, assistance with application procedures, support during interview processes, advice regarding job offers and negotiation, and initial planning for work.

4. Job Site Training. The employment specialist will work with the consumer on and off the job site until the consumer can maintain employment without regular or frequent assistance from the specialist. These duties may include development and implementation of instructional and/or behavioral programming strategies, conferences with the employer, coworkers, and/or consumer, and collection of performance information such as measures of quality and rate of work.

5. Follow-Along. The employment specialist will establish and maintain periodic contact with consumers, employers, and others as necessary to facilitate continued successful placement of the employee with disabilities. The employment specialist will be on-call to assist in the resolution of obstacles to continued employment.

6. Other. The employment specialist will perform other related duties including, but not limited to: participation in agency meetings, attend training and professional development meetings, development of materials, coordination of consumer services as necessary for continued placement, and maintaining accurate consumer case files.

Figure 12.4

Qualifications

In addition to excellent oral and written communication skills, effective interpersonal skills, and knowledge of vocational issues and strategies as they relate to persons with disabilities, the following specific qualifications apply:

1.   Education/experience.   Completion of a bachelor's degree in special education, vocational rehabilitation, psychology, or a closely related field and experience in direct training of persons with disabilities is preferred. Extensive and successful training experience will be considered in lieu of a degree.

2.   Transportation. The applicant must possess a valid driver's license and have own transportation.

3.   Other. The applicant must be able to work in a variety of service, manufacturing and professional settings and maintain flexible schedules.

Salary and Benefits

1.   Salary. $23,000 - $29,000

2.   Benefits. Two weeks paid vacation annually, one week sick leave. Group health insurance available.

Figure 12.4 *(continued)*

General Description

The purpose of the general description is to convey to prospective applicants the nature of the job and the overall parameters of the job duties. The general description will ideally entice truly interested individuals to read on and discourage others from pursuing the position. In this general description, the affiliation of the position is often stated up front. The major duties are usually stated, as are (is) the particular disability group(s) that the program serves. Variations within the general description will be based primarily on the staffing configuration of the program (i.e., holistic vs. partitioned) and the disability population being served. As can be noted in Figure 12.2, the general description is developed primarily from the headings of the specific duties. Often, this general description coupled with qualifications and application procedure information (see below) forms the basis of the advertising copy for the position.

Specific Duties/Responsibilities

After using the general description to entice the appropriate prospective applicants to read further, the specific duties/responsibilities delineate exactly what the incumbent will do on a daily basis. This section should be specific to further encourage applicants with appropriate knowledge, skills and abilities and discourage all others. Each *major* duty should be depicted in enough detail to allow for informed decision making by prospective applicants. Very often supported employment duties are listed in the order in which a placement is secured and maintained, as illustrated in Figure 12.4. An alternative, especially useful in partitioned staffing configurations, is listing job duties in the order of percentage of time that an employee performs those duties. For example, in a partitioned model trying to secure a job development specialist, the description would give initial position to those duties specifically related to acquiring jobs and perhaps list the occasional job-training duties much further down on the list.

While the general supported employment service delivery approach is generic across disability populations, the specific duties associated with various populations may vary drastically, and this variance must be conveyed in the job description. The description given in Figure 12.4 is written for a program serving people with a variety of disabilities and therefore does not emphasize a particular approach or job duty. If though, for example, the position was for an employment specialist working primarily with individuals who had traumatic brain injuries, the consumer assessment section may be modified to read as follows:

> *Consumer Assessment.* The employment specialist will complete and/or secure assessment and evaluation information as necessary to assist the consumer with informed decision making. This may include interpretation of and referral to other professionals/agencies, such as physicians, inpatient rehabilitation units, counseling and psychological services, and substance abuse programs.

Likewise, while the job-site training section of the job description in Figure 12.4 highlights behavioral training processes, programs serving individuals with persistent and long-term mental illness may emphasize other duties, such as behavioral rehearsal, vocational counseling, and development of cognitive compensation strategies. In short, the specific job duty listing must be tailored to specific supported employment programs and consider both the staffing configurations and the major disability population served.

The specific job duty listing is often used as a foundation for employee performance evaluation. For this reason, it is important to be as specific and as comprehensive as possible within this section. As mentioned earlier, when refilling a position, duties are often realigned to refine the position with respect to changing organizational needs. It is this job-duty section that will most frequently reflect the changing needs.

Qualifications

The qualifications section of the position description delineates educational, experiential, and other attributes that the organization either requires or prefers as prerequisites to employment. The qualifications section serves as a sieve, allowing only the applicants with certain qualities to be hired. Minimum qualifications must be judged in the context of the applicant pool of the community in which the organization operates and the minimum qualifications and salary required of similar positions in other agencies in the community. For example, in a community with few people who have any post-high school education, a high education level requirement may result in too few applicants.

The minimum criteria often required for employment specialists are good oral and written skills, good interpersonal skills, knowledge of business and/or disability population attributes, and some level of formal education. Also often required is the ability to work flexible schedules and to have reliable transportation. Preferred applicant qualifications generally include previous direct service and/or business experience, specific experience with the population to be served by the program, and preferred educational requirements.

The desired educational level of employment specialists should be, at minimum, completion of a two-year associate's degree in a related field, and probably should require a bachelor's degree. Although there continues to be debate over the educational level needed by employment specialists, (i.e., there are many examples of good employment specialists who do not meet this educational level, and there currently exists no empirical demonstration that the educational levels of employment specialists directly relate to consumer outcomes), currently existing educational and rehabilitation practices dictate these minimum levels of education for professionals (e.g., teachers, rehabilitation counselors, vocational evaluation specialists, etc.). The required educational level also relates to salary, as explained below.

The required and preferred types and amounts of experience also vary depending on the values of the organization. For example, some organizations prefer employment specialists with extensive business-related work histories as opposed to rehabilitation service delivery histories. Among other reasons, it is sometimes felt that real work experience benefits more effective job analysis and development of innovative compensations strategies.

Salary and Benefits

Like any position, salary and benefits are a critical factor in attracting good personnel who will remain with an organization over time. Sometimes the organization will have classification schema and experience "steps" that will make salary setting a relatively rigid process. In this case, accurate initial job classification is crucial. In many cases, the organization can set salaries each time a position is refilled. In either case, salaries must be set in the context of the community, other similar organizations within the community, and similar positions within the organization.

Most often a "salary survey" of other supported employment providers is completed when setting the initial salary range so that the selected salary is commensurate with (or preferably, slightly higher than) other supported employment providers in the area. Sometimes employment specialists will move among organizations toward the top-paying organization in the area. While this ensures experienced specialists at the top-paying organization, it may create very frequent turnover within the lower-paying organizations (all other organizational characteristics being equal).

Managers and administrators also like to ensure parity among workers who have similar duties within an organization. It should be pointed out at this juncture that the duties and demands associated with supported employment *vary drastically from those duties and demands of traditional rehabilitation direct-service staff, who provide training and other rehabilitation within workshops and other noncommunity-based settings.* Employment specialists most often operate much more independently and within much more diverse environments than workshop personnel (Rusch, Trach, Winking, Tines, and Johnson 1989). Therefore, it is imprudent to set salaries based upon those of workshop staff.

The salary range ultimately set for a position results from a mixture of data, values, and availability of resources. The data come from the community and an organization scan of similar positions. Organizational value is also important. For example, lower salaries could be indicative of the devaluing of the consumer service being provided and of the employment specialist position. If employment specialists are to be considered rehabilitation professionals (as they should be), salaries must be commensurate with other professionals. Lower salaries contribute to the view of employment specialists as paraprofessionals. Finally, fiscal resource limitations are a reality and must be considered. "You can't pay what you ain't got."

Most often, benefits are standard within an organization and evolve organizationally rather than position by position. The same logic that applies to salary setting also applies to initial benefits decisions. It is important to remember that sometimes benefits can offset lower salary, depending upon the applicant's situation. Common benefits include sick and vacation leave, health plans, and often compensation time.

RECRUITING

For managers, staff recruiting and hiring sometimes seems to be a painful and never-ending process. Specific recruiting and hiring activities are outlined in figure 12.5 and detailed below. Recruiting should be an ongoing process, punctuated by initiation of position description development, advertisement of a position, interviewing, and hiring flurries created by exiting staff. The program manager should always be on the lookout for potential quality staff, whether or not a current vacancy exists. This will facilitate acquisition of personnel who meet the job requirements and will fit in well with staff. A "constant recruiting" mindset will provide the ability to target recruits with already-known qualities.

Again, the recruiting process really starts with the development of the position description as described above. The next steps involve letting people know there is a vacancy within the organization, receiving and categorizing applications, interviewing selected candidates, and acquiring the desired applicant. What follows

Recruiting Strategies and Processes

Advertising

> Market your organization to potentially interested and qualified candidates on an on-going basis

> Use a word of mouth in a planful manner

> Communicate with professional colleagues in other organizations and businesses

> Balance length of ad, costs, and circulation when using of newspaper and other periodicals

Screening and Interviewing

> Use the position description to weed out unqualified individuals and to rank qualified candidates

> Develop standard questions and scenarios to ask each interviewed candidate

> Be sure to allow time for the candidate to ask questions about the organization and the vacant position

> Check references and be wary of ambiguous responses

> Do not ask personal questions that are not directly related to the position (e.g., marital status, political beliefs, etc.)

Final Selection

> BE CAREFUL! Resolve any uneasiness prior to hiring

> Allow time for the candidate to consider the offer and notify their former employer

> Notify unsuccessful applicants soon after the position has been accepted

Figure 12.5

is a brief description of each of those processes. It is recommended that the reader consult a current personnel management text for a more in-depth discussion of recruiting techniques.

Advertising

This phase of recruiting is designed to inform qualified candidates of the availability of a position, and usually consists of word-of-mouth, postings of position descriptions in strategic locations, and often newspaper and other paid advertisements. Word-of-mouth is an excellent way to obtain applicants. The program manager should call colleagues who have access to the types of individuals desired for the position. Likewise, colleagues and other organizations that are frequented by potentially good applicants should also be sent a position description and application instructions. Potential sources for these two forms of advertising include other organizations in the community that work with persons who have disabilities, Universities and other settings that train potential applicants, and business locations (this option is particularly good if the position is an established enclave or crew within industry).

The third advertising strategy most often utilized is the use of paid advertisements in local newspapers or other periodicals that specifically have readers who might meet the qualifications of the position. The content of these ads and the frequency with which they appear are both dictated by the money budgeted within an organization for the advertisement of positions. An ad that mirrors the position description is preferred, but is often cost prohibitive. Most frequently, only the general position description, abbreviated qualifications, salary, and application instructions are contained in the ad.

The rule of thumb for how many times to have an ad appear in the paper is to run the ad only enough to generate an adequate pool from which to select candidates for interviews and no more. Often one or two appearances in the local paper will be sufficient when coupled with word-of-mouth and position postings. While it is unlikely that too many *qualified* applicants will ever apply, sometimes, repeated placement of ads or placement in multiple sources can result in an inordinate number of *unqualified* applicants. Screening a large number of applications can be quite time-consuming. A properly selected advertising strategy will help to ensure a good balance.

Applicant Screening

The result of a good advertising strategy is a broad pool of applicants who at least meet the minimum qualifications of the position. The desired breadth of the pool will vary with the community size, demographics, and economic conditions and is hard to quantify. The program manager should feel good (and lucky) if she or he has five qualified applicants from which to choose.

The initial screening step is to cull all applicants who do not meet the minimum required qualifications (e.g., education, experience, etc.). These individuals are out unless they have some redeeming quality not thought of during the position description development stage.

The second step is to create a pool of "most viable" applicants by separating out applicants who exceed the minimum qualifications (probably meeting one or more of the preferred qualifications). It is not uncommon for one or more seemingly minimally-qualified applicants to be moved into the group of most viable candidates. Therefore, the manager should examine both the minimally-qualified and the more than minimally-qualified pools of applicants at this time to ensure that the qualification criteria used results in applicants with the most desired qualities falling into the smaller of the two groups. This is a check to make sure that what was conveyed within the advertisement and/or position description matches the manager's perception of a "good" candidate. Candidates that may be desirable but did not make the second application-screening cut should be moved into the pool of still viable candidates.

The final step in the screening process is to rank applicants based upon the written documentation that has been obtained. During this step, the manager will identify which group of applicants will be selected for first interviews.

Interviewing

The next step in the recruiting phase is selecting interview candidates. With a ranked listing of applicants, the manager must decide how many of the viable candidates he or she has time to interview. Note well that it is better to interview too many than too few of the most viable candidates, since a problem employee is much worse than a problem applicant.

The interview with each candidate is perhaps the most crucial element of the hiring process (other than the actual hiring decision). While the manager already has much data about the candidate on hand, personal impressions and in-depth probing will provide more information about concerns raised during the review of the applicant's material. It is a good idea to have a set of open-ended questions prior to the interview. It is important that the manager ascertain the candidate's philosophy and values regarding supported employment and persons with disabilities, knowledge of the locale's service system, prior experience related to the job duties, and expectations regarding the position. As the candidate responds to the questions, follow-up questions can be asked. Managers often present situations that have been encountered by employment specialists within their program and ask candidates what they would have done in a similar situation. This technique can provide invaluable insight to a candidate's knowledge and problem-solving abilities. If feasible, it is advisable to have more than one person interview the candidate so that multiple impressions can be obtained.

Remember that the interview is also a time for candidates to ask questions about the organization and the position. Ample time should be allowed to respond to these questions. The types of questions and the manner in which they are asked will often provide the manager with additional information regarding the candidate's ability and desire to meet the position requirements. The manager should use follow-up questions if concerns arise from the candidate's questions.

One final note about the interviewing process. The manager should be wary about asking questions that do not relate directly to the position. For example, marital status, religious and political affiliations, and other personal information not related to the position should not be asked lest the unsuccessful candidate perceive (and perhaps litigate!) some form of discrimination. Supported employment managers associated with larger agencies often have guidelines upon which to rely for more specific information on nondiscriminatory hiring practices. Smaller agencies should ensure that they develop such guidelines as a matter of practicality in today's suit-happy society.

Checking References

Checking references is an important part of the interview phase. When to check references is largely a matter of preference. Some managers may want to check references on all candidates prior to the interviews. Some managers check only the references on the selected candidate, just prior to the offer. While most references will give glowing reviews of the candidate, short, unclear, and ambivalent answers or letters should raise concern about a candidate. This concern should be checked out more fully by asking more probing questions of the candidate and/or requesting more references. The same caution relating to discriminatory questions as listed above should also be heeded when talking with references.

Final Decisions

The manager should, at this stage, step back and carefully consider all interviewed candidates. The best candidate may or may not be the candidate with the most education and/or experience. A close matching of personal and organizational philosophies, the ability to fit in with other workers, to learn new skills, and to identify one's own strengths and weaknesses are valuable employment specialist attributes. These and other factors should be considered in addition to the direct skills and education held by a candidate.

The old adage that it is easier to hire a problem than fire a problem should receive considerable attention by supported employment managers prior to making the final hiring decision and job offer. The person that is about to be hired can have considerable impact (both positive and negative) on a supported employment program and the consumers served by that program. A poor employee can easily destroy relationships with other agencies and employers. A careless employee can cause a consumer to lose benefits and suffer other personal losses.

Once a decision is made (and approved if necessary), the program manager offers the job to the selected candidate and negotiates the details as necessary. Although salary is often not negotiable, the manager should be prepared for a request for more money or other special consideration. The starting date is often a negotiated one. Usually the manager requires someone immediately, but can wait some period of time. It should be remembered that most organizations have a mandatory notice requirement, and it is unfair to the candidate to ask him or her to violate the policy ("Do unto others as you would have others do unto you"). After the candidate accepts the position, it is imperative that the terms of the employment be spelled out in writing through some type of employment agreement.

Accepting employment within a new organization is a major decision for the candidate. Therefore, the manager should be prepared to wait for an acceptance or rejection of the job offer. However, a time limit for a response should be mutually agreed upon, with the candidate realizing that the offer should be considered withdrawn after the agreed upon date.

The final step of the hiring process is to let unsuccessful applicants know they have not been selected. This is not only a mandatory courtesy, but timely written notification to these applicants will avoid sometimes uncomfortable telephone conversations. Obviously, since the top candidate may decline the job offer, notification of unsuccessful candidates should wait until the employment agreement with the selected candidate is executed.

EMPLOYEE TRAINING

At this time, and for several reasons, most employees hired will not be fully knowledgeable about how to work as an employment specialist. First, there is a current lack of availability of preservice training that provides employment specialists with the knowledge and skills on how to perform the required duties. Second, the relatively short period of time that supported employment has been a service delivery option means that large numbers of well-seasoned employment specialists are not readily available. Staffing of a supported employment program just begins when a candidate accepts a position and becomes the newest employee. Although the preceding hiring processes were arduous and time-consuming, employee training cannot be ignored nor delayed. The manager must now ensure that the employee becomes intimately familiar with the day-to-day, formal and informal organizational processes (orientation). Skill strengths and deficits must be identified, and training strategies must be put in place. Major deficits must be addressed *before* the employee is put into potentially compromising positions (training). Finally, the newest employee, along with "old-timers" need an opportunity to refine existing skills and gain new knowledge and skills (ongoing staff-development). The next sections will detail these processes. It should be noted that these processes are not linear, but rather are intertwined and ongoing.

Orientation

The purposes of employee orientation are to familiarize the new employee with organization policies and procedures, physical plant (if any), co-workers, and lines for gathering resources. Often, the program manager begins the orientation process by explaining the general policies and practices of the organization. After this initial meeting, the new job coach is often paired with a more senior employment specialist to visit sites, observe/participate in consumer assessment activities, do job development, follow-along, and/or training. In this way, the day-to-day culture of the organization and its common practices can be learned. This is also a time for the newly-hired employment specialist to identify areas in which he or she needs additional training or assistance.

Initial In-service Training

Many employment specialists come to their first supported employment job with little or no experience or training in supported employment (Everson 1989; Rusch, Trach, Winking, Tines, and Johnson 1989). At this point (and perhaps forever), there is no standard of previous training or experience mandated for employment specialists by any state. Supported employment providers who embrace quality should implement an effective in-service training program for their employment specialists. The training itself may not actually be provided by the supported employment provider organizations, but should be the organization's first line of quality assurance, as the training will reduce the likelihood of inappropriate placements, ineffective job-site training, and inadequate follow-along.

The focus and depth of the initial training will depend upon the roles associated with each position and any previous experience of each newly-hired employment specialist. Topics associated with supported employment training are provided in Figure 12.6. Training should include topics relating to values/philosophy, legal issues, and skills development in each major supported employment component (i.e., job development, consumer assessment and placement, job-site training, and follow-along strategies). Disability-specific knowledge and skills needed for facilitating employment should also be included during this initial training. In addition, case management and referral strategies should be included in the initial in-service training. Although important for employment specialists working with people who have any type of disability, these referral skills are especially critical for employment specialists who will be working with persons with traumatic brain injury, long-term mental illness, and other consumers who require a high degree of service integration from a variety of providers.

Training Clusters for Employment Specialist

Philosophical/Legal. Content in this cluster relates to values of supported employment (paid integrated real work, severe disabilities etc.), normalization theory and the nature of zero exclusion in supported employment, Federal and State statutes and regulations (e.g., The Rehabilitation Act, Carl Perkins Act, etc.), and consumer rights (e.g., eligibility, order of selection, confidentiality, etc.). The interrelationships of state systems and processes should also be focused upon within this cluster.

Population Specific Knowledge and Experience. The classification, etiologies, and general attributes associated with each disability population that the employment specialist works with is an important area of training. Training in these areas assist in interpretation of relevant diagnostic information that may be useful in job site training strategy development, referral indices, and retention strategies.

Supported Employment Processes. Topics within this cluster include familiarity with each supported employment approach (i.e., individual, enclave, crew, small business), job development and analysis techniques, consumer assessment strategies, job placement and orientation, systematic training procedures e.g., prompting, reinforcement, etc.), non-aversive management of job hindering behavior, counseling and referral indices and procedures. The training required in each area is highly dependent upon the disability population served.

Figure 12.6

Supported employment is often risky for consumers. The medical profession has a saying, "do no harm," which embodies the philosophy of making sure treatment effects do not leave the patient worse than if no treatment had been received. The effective training of employment specialists *prior to being placed in situations that could result in social, psychological, physical, or economic harm to consumers with disabilities* is of paramount importance if the potential for real harm is to be reduced. It is the responsibility of each manager to ensure, to the greatest degree possible, that training occurs prior to placing consumers at risk.

Ongoing Staff Development

Organizational theorists understand the importance of assisting employees in their professional growth. Professional growth opportunities can reduce burnout, which often results in employee turnover, and increase job productivity. Prudent supported employment managers will facilitate professional growth by providing opportunities for ongoing staff development activities, such as attendance at local, regional, state, and national meetings that bring together other employment specialists and related service personnel. Within the organization, training that provides information on state-of-the-art techniques associated with the provision of supported employment should also be regularly provided. In addition, some supported employment organizations provide financial stipends for employment specialists to upgrade their skills by completing coursework at local community colleges and universities. These and other proactive approaches will enhance the effectiveness of a program and help to keep the employment specialists happy.

SUMMARY

A major responsibility of the supported employment program manager is to ensure an effectively operating program structure and personnel. The decision on how to deploy staff and allocate roles and functions is crucial and must be done only after consideration of the variety of factors described in this chapter. Subsequent to deciding on a configuration, staffing and staff training become the first line of quality assurance and require significant effort to manage. While this chapter has detailed some very basic processes for recruiting and staffing, it is important to remember that experience is often the best teacher. The manager will generally get better at assessing organizational structure and personnel as he or she has a chance to perform some of the activities described above.

References

Agran, M., Salzberg, C.L., & Stowitschek, J.J. (1987). An analysis of the effects of a social skills training program using self-instruction on the acquisition and generalization of two social behaviors in a work setting. *The Journal of The Association for Persons with Severe Handicaps, 12,* (2), 131-139.

Anderson, E. (1977). *Rehabilitation facilities: A resource in the vocational rehabilitation of the severely handicapped.* Dallas, TX: Fourth Institute on Rehabilitation Issues.

Anthony, W. A., & Blanch, A. (1987). Supported employment for persons who are psychiatrically disabled: An historical and conceptual perspective. *Psychosocial Rehabilitation Journal, 11* (2), 5-23.

Anthony, W.A., & Blanch, A. (1987). Supported employment for persons who are psychiatrically disabled: An historical and conceptual perspective. *Psychosocial Rehabilitation Journal,* 11 (2), 45-54.

Arkansas Research & Training Center in Vocational Rehabilitation (1985). *Supported employment: Implications for rehabilitation services.* Little Rock, AR: University of Arkansas.

Bannerman, D. J., Sheldon, J. B., Sherman, J. A., and Harchik, A. E. (1990). Balancing the right to habitation with the right to personal liberties: The rights of people with developmental disabilities to eat too many doughnuts and take a nap. *Journal of Applied Behavior Analysis, 23,* 79-89.

Barcus, M., Brooke, V., Inge, K., Moon, S., & Goodall, P. (1987). *An instructional guide for training on a job site: A supported employment resource,* Richmond, VA: Virginia Commonwealth University Rehabilitation Research & Training Center.

Barke, L. T. (1986, July 31). *Development of performance measures for supported employment programs: Final report.* Berkeley, CA: Berkeley Planning Assoc.

Bateman, D. (1990, October). *The role of families in advocacy.* Presentation at the RRTC Sixth National Symposium on Supported Employment: Issues Facing the 1990's, Virginia Beach, VA.

Bater, P. (1986). Competitive employment in Southern Illinois: A transitional service delivery model for enhancing competitive employment outcomes for public school students. In F.R. Rusch (Ed.), *Competitive employment: Service delivery model, methods, and issues.* Baltimore, MD: Paul H. Brookes.

Bell, R. R. (1981). *Worlds of friendship.* Beverly Hills, CA: Sage Publications.

Bellamy, G. T., O'Connor, G., & Karan, O.C. (1979). *Vocational rehabilitation of the severely handicapped.* Baltimore: University Park Press.

Bellamy, G. T., Rhoes, L.E., Mank, D., & Albin, J. (1988). *Supported employment: A community implementation guide.* Baltimore, MD: Paul H. Brookes.

Bellamy, G. T., Sowers, J., & Bourbeau, P.E. (1983). Work and work related skills. In M. E. Snell (Ed.), *Systematic instruction of the moderately and severely handicapped* (2nd ed.) (p. 490-502). Columbus, OH: Charles E. Merrill.

Ben-Yishay, Y., Silver, S. M., Piasetsky, E., & Rattok, J. (1987). Relationship between employability and vocational outcome after intensive holistic cognitive rehabilitation. *Journal of Head Trauma Rehabilitation, 2,* 35-48.

Berg, W., & Wacker, D. (1983). *Effects of permanent prompts on the vocational performance of severely handicapped individuals.* Paper presented at the Association for Behavior Analysis, Milwaukee, WI.

Bitter, J. A. (1979). *Introduction to Rehabilitation.* St. Louis, MI: C.V. Mosby Company.

Boles, S. M., Bellamy, G. T., Horner, R. H., & Mank, D. M. (1984). Specialized Training Program: The structured employment model. In S. Paine, G. T. Bellamy, & B. Wilcox (Eds.), *Human services that work: From innovation to standard practice* (pp. 181-208) Baltimore: Paul H. Brookes.

Bourbeau, P. E. (1985). Mobile work crews: An approach to achieve long term supported employment. In P. McCarthy, J. Everson, S. Moon, & M. Barcus (Eds.), *School to work transition for youth with severe disabilities* (pp. 151-166). Richmond: Virginia Commonwealth University, Rehabilitation Research & Training Center.

Bourbeau, P. E. (1989). Mobile work crews. An approach to achieve long-term supported employment. In P. Wehman, & J. Kregel (Eds.), *Supported employment for persons with disabilities. Focus on excellence* (pp. 83-94). NY: Human Sciences Press.

Breen, C., Haring, T., Pitts-Conway, V., & Gaylord-Ross, R. (1984). The training and generalization of social interactions during breaktime at two job sites in the natural environment. In R. Gaylord-Ross, T. Haring, C. Breen, M. Lee, V. Pitts-Conway, & D. Roger(Eds.), *The social development of handicapped students.* San Francisco: San Francisco State University.

Brolin, D. (1982). *Vocational preparation of persons with handicaps.* Columbus, OH: Charles E. Merrill.

Brooks, D. N., Campsie, L, Symington, C., & Beattie, Al. (1986). The five year outcomes of severe blunt head injury: A relative's view. *Journal of Neurology, Neurosurgery and Psychiatry, 49*(7), 764-770.

Brooks, D. N., McKinlay, W., Symington, C., Beattie, A., & Campsie, L. (1987). Return to work within the first seven years of severe head injury. *Brain Injury, 1,* 5-19.

Bronicki, G. J., & Turnbull, A. P. (1987). Family-professional interactions. In M. E. Snell (Ed.), *Systematic instruction of persons with severe handicaps* (pp. 9-36). Columbus, OH: Charles E. Merrill.

Brown, F. (1987). Meaningful assessment of people with severe and profound handicaps. In M. E. Snell (Eds.), *Systematic instruction of persons with severe handicaps* (3rd ed.) (pp. 40-63). Columbus, OH: Charles E. Merrill.

Bruininks, R. H., & Lakin, K. C. (eds.). (1985). *Living and learning in the least restrictive environment.* Baltimore: Paul H. Brookes.

Butterfield, E. C. (1990). The compassion of distinguishing punishing behavioral treatment from aversive treatment. *American Journal on Mental Retardation, 95* (2), 137-141.

California State Department of Rehabilitation. (April-May, 1990). *Supported employment news, Vol. 3*(6).

Carney, I. H. (1987). Working with families. In F. P. Orelove & D. Sosbey (Eds.), *Educating children with multiple disabilities.* (pp. 315-338). Baltimore: Paul Brookes Publishing Co.

Certo, N., Haring, N., & York, R. (1983). *Public school integration of severely handicapped students.* Baltimore: Paul H. Brookes.

Chadsey-Rusch, J. (1990). Teaching social skills on the job. In F. R. Rusch (Ed.), *Supported employment models, methods and issues.* Sycamore, IL: Sycamore Publishing Co.

Chadsey-Rusch, J., Gonzalez, P., & Tines, J. (1988). Social ecology of the workplace: A study of interactions among employees with and without mental retardation. In J. Chadsey-Rusch (Ed.), *Social ecology of the workplace* (pp. 27-54). Champaign, IL: University of Illinois at Urbana-Champaign, The Secondary Transition Intervention Effectiveness Institute.

Colorado Rehabilitation Services. (1990). *Supported employment services outcome report, Oct. 1986-November, 1989.*

Conley, R. W., Noble, J. H., & Elder, J. K. (1986). Problems with the service system. In W. E. Kiernan & J. A. Start (Eds.), *Pathways to employment for adults with developmental disabilities* (pp. 67-83). Baltimore: Paul H. Brookes.

Cowdery, G. E., Iwata, B. A., & Pace, G. M. (1990). Effects and side effects of DRO as treatment for self-injurious behavior. *Journal of Applied Behavior Analysis, 23* (4) 497-506.

Crouch, K. P., Rusch, F. R., & Karlan, G. R. (1984). Competitive employment: Utilizing the correspondence training paradigm to enhance productivity. *Education and Training of the Mentally Retarded, 19,* 268-275.

Deaton, A. V. (1986). Denial in the aftermath of traumatic head injury: Its manifestations, measurement, and treatment. *Rehabilitation Psychology, 32,* 231-240.

Donovan, M. (1990). Help wanted: People with disabilities wanted. Rockville, Md.: Mariott Foundation.

Dougherty, B. (1987). A major link to employment training for special needs youth and adults. *The Journal for Vocational Special Needs Education, 9,* 3.

Durand, V. M. (1990). Reader response: The "aversives" debate is over: And now the work begins. *The Journal of the Association for Persons with Severe Handicaps, 15*(3), 140-141.

Elder, J. (1984). Job opportunities for developmentally disabled people. *American Rehabilitation, 10*(2), 26-30.

Elder, J., Conley, R., & Noble, J. (1986). The service system. In W. E. Kiernan & J. A. Start (Eds.), *Pathways to employment for adults with developmental disabilities* (pp. 53-66). Baltimore: Paul H. Brookes.

Evans, I. & Meyer, L. (1990). Reader Response: Toward a science in support of meaningful outcomes: A response to Horner, et al. *The Journal of the Association for Persons with Severe Handicaps, 15*(3), 133-135.

Everson, J. M., Barcus, J. M., Moon, M. S., & Morton, M. V. (Eds.). (1987). *Achieving outcomes: A guide to interagency training in transition and supported employment.* Richmond: Virginia Commonwealth University, Rehabilitation Research & Training Center.

Fabian, E. S. (1989). Work and the quality of life. *Psychosocial Rehabilitation Journal, 12*(4), 39-49.

Falvey, M. A. (1986). *Community-based curriculum: Instructional strategies for students with severe handicaps.* Baltimore: Paul H. Brookes.

Favell, J. E., Azrin, N. H., Baumeister, A. A., Carr, E. G., Dorsey, M. F., Forehand, R., Foxx, R. M., Lovaas, O. I., Rincover, A., Risley, T. R. Romanczyk, R. G., Russo, D. C., Schroeder, S. R., & Solnick, J. V. (1982). The treatment of self-injurious behavior. *Behavior Therapy, 13,* 529-554.

Federal Register. Supported employment regulations for Vocational Rehabilitation Act Amendments. (1987 August 14).

Fine, G. A. (1986). Friendships in the workplace. In V. J. Derlega & B. A. Winstead (Eds.), *Friendships and social interaction* (pp. 185-206). New York: Springer-Verlag.

Freeman, T. (1991 January). Placement Process. In M. Oppenheim (moderator), *Consumer assessment, matching, and placement issues.* Supported Employment Telecourse Network, Richmond, VA: Virginia Commonwealth University.

Gartner, A., Lipsky, D. K., & Turnbull, A. P. (1991). *Supporting families with a child with a disability.* Baltimore: Paul Brookes Publishing Co.

Geist, C., & Calzaretta, W. (1982). *Placement handbook for counseling disabled persons.* Springfield, IL: Charles E. Thomas.

Gettings, R. M., & Katz, R. E. (1987). *Supported employment: Federal policies and state activities related to integrated work opportunities for persons with developmental disabilities.* Alexandria, VA: National Association of State Mental Retardation Program Directors.

Getzel, E. E. (1987). Highlights of research activities on JTPA and special needs populations. *The Journal of Vocational Special Needs Education, 9*(3), 23-25.

Gold, M. W. (1980). *Try another way training manual.* Champaign, IL: Research Press.

Goode, D. A. (1989). Quality of life and quality of work life. In W. W. Kiernan & R. L. Schalock (Eds.), *Economic, industry and disability a look ahead.* Baltimore: Paul Brookes Publishing Co.

Greenspan, S., & Shoultz, B. (1981). Why mentally retarded adults lose their jobs: Social competence as a factor in work adjustment. *Applied Research in Mental Retardation, 2,* 23-28.

Grossman, H. J. (1983). *Classification in mental retardation.* Washington, DC: American Association on Mental Deficiency.

Guess, D., Benson, H. A., & Siegel-Causey, E. (1985). Concepts and issues related to choice-making and autonomy among persons with severe disabilities. *Journal of the Association for Persons with Severe Disabilities, 10,* 79-86.

Guess, D., Helmstetter, E. Turnbull, H. R. III, & Knowlton, S. (1986). *Use of aversive procedures with persons who are disabled: An historical review and critical analysis.* The Association for Persons with severe handicaps: Seattle, WA.

Goode, D. A. (1990). Thinking about and discussing quality of life. In R. L. Schalock (Ed.), *Quality of life* (pp. 41-57), Washington, DC: American Association on Mental Retardation.

Grant, P. C. (1989). *Multiple use job descriptions: A guide to analysis, preparation and application for human resource managers.* New York, NY: Quarum Books.

Hanley-Maxwell, C., Rusch, F. R., Chadsey-Rusch, J., & Renzaglia, A. (1986). Reported factors contributing to job terminations of individuals with severe disabilities. *The Journal of the Association for Persons with Severe Handicaps, 11*(1), 45-52.

Hasazi, S. B., Gordon, L. R.,& Roe, C. A. (1985). Factors associated with employment status of handicapped youth exiting from high school from 1979-1983. *Exceptional Children, 51*(6), 455-469.

Henne, D. & Locke, E. A. (1985). Job dissatisfaction: What are the consequences? *International Journal of Psychology, 20*(2), 221-240.

Hill, J., Cleveland, P., Pendleton, P., & Wehman, P. (1982). Strategies in the follow-up of moderately and severely handicapped competitively employed workers. In P. Wehman & M. Hill (Eds.) *Vocational Training and Placement of Severely Disabled Persons: Project Employability: Volume III* (pp. 160-171). Richmond, VA: Virginia Commonwealth University.

Hill, J. W., Seyfarth, J., Banks, P. D., Wehman, P., & Orelove, F. (1987). Parent attitudes about working conditions of their adult mentally retarded sons and daughters. *Exceptional Children, 54*(1), 9-23.

Hill, M. (1987). *Interagency vendorization services: Expanding supported employment* (Vol. 3). Richmond: Virginia Commonwealth University, Rehabilitation Research & Training Center.

Hill, M. (1988). An interagency perspective. In P. Wehman & M. S. Moon, *Vocational rehabilitation and supported employment* (p. 40). Baltimore, MD: Paul H. Brookes.

Hill, M., Banks, P. D., Handrich, R., Wehman, P., Hill, J., & Shafer, M. (1987). Benefit-cost analysis of supported competitive employment for persons with mental retardation. *Research in Developmental Disabilities, 8*(1), 71-89.

Hill, M., Hill, J. W., Wehman, P., Revell, G., Dickerson, A., & Noble, J. (1985). Time limited training and supported employment: A model for redistributing existing resources for persons with severe disabilities. In P. Wehman & J. W. Hill (Eds.) *Competitive employment for persons with mental retardation: From research to practice: Volume I* (pp. 132-168). Richmond, VA: Virginia Commonwealth University.

Hill, M. L., Wehman, P., Kregel, J., Banks, P. D., & Metzler, H. M. D. (1987). Employment outcomes for people with moderate and severe disabilities: An eight-year longitudinal analysis of supported competitive employment. *Journal of the Association for Persons with Severe Handicaps, 12*(3), 182-189.

Hill, M., Revell, G., Chernish, W., Morell, J. E., White, J., & McCarthy, P. (1985). Social service agency options for modifying existing systems to include transitional and supported work services for persons with severe disabilities. In P. McCarthy, J. Everson, M. S. Moon, & J. M. Barcus (Eds.), *School to work transition for youth with severe disabilities* (pp. 195-218). Richmond: Virginia Commonwealth University, Rehabilitation Research & Training Center.

Horner, R. H., Dunlap, G., Koegel, R. L., Carr, E. G., Sailor, W., Anderson, J., Albin, R., & O'Neil, R. E. (1990A). Toward a technology of "nonaversive" behavioral support. *The Journal of the Association for Persons with Severe Handicaps, 15*(3), 125-132.

Horner, R. H., Dunlap, G., Koegel, R. L., Carr, E. G., Sailor, W., Anderson, J., Albin, R., & O'Neil, R. E. (1990B). Author's response: In support of integration for people with severe problem behaviors: A response to four commentaries. *The Journal of the Association for Persons with Severe Handicaps, 15*(3), 145-147.

Hughes, C., Rusch, F. R., & Curl, R. (1990). Extending individual competencies, developing natural support, and promoting social acceptance. In F. R. Rusch (Ed.), *Supported employment models, methods, and issues*, Sycamore, IL: Sycamore Publishing Co.

Illinois Supported Employment Project. (1990). *Supported employment report.* University of Illinois, Urbana-Champaign, College of Education.

Inge, K. J., Banks, P. D., Wehman, P., Hill, J. W. & Shafer, M. J. (1988). Quality of life for individuals who are labeled mentally retarded: Evaluating competitive employment versus sheltered workshop employment. *Education and Training in Mental Retardation, 23*(2), 92-104.

Isbister, F., & Donaldson, G. (1987). Supported employment for individuals who are mentally ill: Program development. *Psychosocial Rehabilitation Journal, 11*(2), 45-54.

Johnson, J. R., & Rusch, F. R. (1990). Analysis of hours of direct training provided by employment specialists to supported employees. *American Journal of Mental Retardation, 94*, 674-682.

Jones, C. M. (1989). *Quality of work life experiences, segregated and integrated as you tell it.* Unpublished masters thesis, San Francisco State University, California.

Karlan, G., & Rusch, F. (1982). Correspondence between saying and doing: Some thoughts on defining correspondence and future directions for application. *Journal of Applied Behavior Analysis, 15*, 151-162.

Judy, B. J. (1989). Job accommodation in the workplace. In W. E. Kiernan & R. L. Schalock (Eds.), *Economics industry and disability a look ahead*. Baltimore: Paul Brookes Publishing Co.

Kazdin, A. E. (1980). *Behavior modification in applied settings* (2nd ed.) Dorsey Press: IL.

Kernan, K. & Koegel, R. (1980). *Employment experiences of community-based mildly retarded adults*. Working paper No. 14, Sociobehavioral Group, Mental Retardation Research Center, School of Medicine, University of California, Los Angeles.

Kiernan, W. E., & Brinkman, K. (1988). Disincentives and barriers to employment. In P. Wehman & M. S. Moon (Eds.), *Vocational rehabilitation and supported employment* (pp. 221-233). Baltimore: Paul H. Brookes.

Kiernan, W. E. & Knutson, K. (1990). Quality of work life. In R. L. Schalock (Ed.,), *Quality of life* (pp. 101-114), Washington, DC: American Association on Mental Retardation.

Kiernan, W. E., McGaughey, M., & Schalock, R. L. (1986). *National employment survey for adults with development disabilities*. Children's Hospital, Development Evaluation Clinic: Boston.

Kiernan, W. E., McGaughey, J. J., & Schalock, R. L. (1986). *Employment survey for adults with developmental disabilities*. Boston: Developmental Evaluation Clinic, Children's Hospital.

Kiernan, W. E., Schalock, R. L. (Eds.) (1989). *Economics, industry, and disability* (p. 12). Baltimore, MD: Paul H. Brookes.

Kiernan, W. E., Schalock, R. L., Knuston, K. (1989). Economic and demographic trends influencing employment opportunities for adults with disabilities. In W. E. Kiernan & R. L. Schalock, *Economics, industry, and disability*. Paul H. Brookes.

Kiernan, W E. Smith, B. C. & Ostrowsky, M. B. (1986). Developmental disabilities: Definitional issues. In W. E. Kiernan & J. A. Stark (Eds.,), *Pathways to employment for adults with developmental disabilities* (pp. 11-20). Baltimore: Paul H. Brookes.

Kiernan, W. E., & Stark, J. A. (1986). *Pathways to employment for adults with developmental disabilities*. Baltimore: Paul H. Brookes.

Kirmeyer, S. C. (1988). Observed communication in the workplace: Content, source and direction. *Journal of Community Psychology, 16*, 175-187.

Klein, K. J. & D'Aunno, T. A. (1986). Psychological sense of community in the workplace. *Journal of Community Psychology, 14*(4), 365-376.

Klonoff, P. S., Costa. L. D., & Snow, W.G. (1986). Predictors and indicators of quality of life in patients with closed-head injury. *Journal of Clinical and Experimental Neuropsychology, 8*, 469-485.

Kochany, L., & Keller, J. (1981). An analysis and evaluation of the failures of severely disabled individuals in competitive employment. In P. Wehman, *Competitive employment: New horizons for severely disabled individuals* (pp. 181-198). Baltimore: Paul H. Brookes.

Kregel, J. & Banks, P. D. (1990). *The Client-Job Compatibility Screening Instrument*, Richmond, VA: Virginia Commonwealth University, Rehabilitation Research & Training Center.

Kregel, J., Hill, M., & Banks, P. D. (1987). An analysis of employment specialist intervention time in supported competitive employment: 1979-1987. In P. Wehman, J. Kregel, M. Shafer, & M. Hill (Eds.), *Competitive employment for persons with mental retardation: From research to practice.* (pp. 84-111). Richmond: Virginia Commonwealth University, Rehabilitation Research & Training Center.

Kregel, J., & Sale, P. (1988). Personnel preparation of supported employment professionals. In P. Wehman, & S. Moon, *Vocational Rehabilitation and supported employment*. Baltimore, MD: Paul H. Brookes.

Kregel, J., Shafer, M., Wehman, P., & West, M. (1989). Policy and program development in supported employment: Current strategies to promote statewide systems change. In P. Wehman, J. Kregel, & M. Shafer (Eds.) *Emerging trends in the national supported employment initiative: A preliminary analysis of 27 states* (pp. 15-45). Richmond, VA: Virginia Commonwealth University.

Kregel, J., & Wehman, P. (1989). Supported employment: Promises deferred for people with severe disabilities. *Journal of the Association for the Severely Handicapped*, 14(4), 293-303.

Kregel, J., & Wehman, P. (1990). Supported employment: Promises deferred for persons with severe handicaps. In J. Kregel, P. Wehman, & M. S. Shafer (Eds.), *Supported employment for persons with severe disabilities: From research to practice*, Vol. II, (pp. 31-62). Richmond, VA: Virginia Commonwealth University, Rehabilitation Research & Training Center.

Kregel, J., Wehman, P., & Banks, D. (1990). The effect of consumer characteristics and type of employment model on individual outcomes in supported employment. In J. Kregel, P. Wehman, & M. S. Shafer (Eds.). *Supported employment for persons with severe disabilities: From research to practice*, Vol. III, (p. 63-80). Richmond, VA: Virginia Commonwealth University, Rehabilitation Research & Training Center.

Kreutzer, J. S., & Morton, M .V. (1988). Traumatic brain injury: Supported employment and compensatory strategies for enhancing vocational outcomes. In P. Wehman & M. S. Moon (Eds.) *Vocational rehabilitation and supported employment* (pp. 291-311). Baltimore: Paul H. Brookes.

Lagomarcino, T. R. (1990). Job separation issues in supported employment. In F. R. Rusch (Ed.), *Supported employment: Models, methods, and issues* (pp. 301-316). Sycamore, IL: Sycamore Publishing Co.

Levy, J. M., & Levy, P. H. (1986). Issues and models in the delivery of respite services. In C. L. Salisbury & J. Intaglita (Eds.), *Respite care: Support for persons with developmental disabilities and their families* (pp. 99-166). Baltimore: Paul H. Brookes.

Lignugaris/Kraft, B., Rule, S., Salzberg, C. L., & Stowitschek, J. J. (1986). Social interpersonal skills of handicapped and nonhandicapped adults at work. *Journal of Employment Counseling*, 23(1), 20-31.

Lignugaris/Kraft, B., Salzberg, C. L., Rule, S., & Stowitschek, J. J. (1988). Social vocational skills of workers with and without mental retardation in two community employment sites. *Mental Retardation*, 26(5), 297-305. Lovett, H. (1991). Empowerment and choices. In L. H. Meyer, C. A. Peck, & L. Brown (Eds.), *Critical issues in the lives of people with severe disabilities* (pp. 625-626).

Livingston, M. G., Brooks, D. N., & Bond, M. R. (1985). Patient outcome in the year following severe head injury and relative's psychiatric and social functioning. *Journal of Neurology, Neurosurgery and Psychiatry*, 48(9), 876-881.

Lovett, H. (1991). Empowerment and choices. In L. H. Meyer, C. A. Peck & L. Brown (Eds.), *Critical issues in the lives of people with severe disabilities* (pp. 625-626).

MacDonald-Wilson, K. L., Revell, W. G., Nguyen, N., & Peterson, M. E. (1991). Supported employment outcomes for people with psychiatric disability: A comparative analysis. *Journal of Vocational Rehabilitation, 1* (3), 30-44.

Mallik, K. (1979). Job accommodation through job restructuring and environment modification. In D. Vandergoot, & J. D. Worrall (Eds.), *Placement in rehabilitation a career development prospective*. Baltimore: University Park Press.

Mallik, K. (1990). Rehabilitation engineering and environmental modifications. In P. Wehman & J. S. Kreutzer (Eds.), *Vocational rehabilitation for persons with traumatic brain injury*. Rockville, MD: Aspen Publishers Inc.

Mandeville, K., & Brabham, R. (1987). The federal-state vocational rehabilitation program. In R. M. Parker (Ed.), *Rehabilitation counseling: Basic and beyond* (pp. 31-64). Austin, TX: Pro-Ed.

Mank, D. M., & Buckley, J. (1989). Strategies for integrated employment. In W. E. Kiernan & R. L. Schalock (Eds.), *Economics, Industry, and disability, a look ahead*. Baltimore: Paul Brookes Publishing Co.

Mank, D. M., & Buckley, J. (1988). Supported employment for persons with severe and profound mental retardation. In P. Wehman & M. S. Moon, *Vocational rehabilitation and supported employment*. Baltimore, MD: Paul H. Brookes.

Mank, D. M., Rhodes, L. E. & Bellamy, G. T. (1986). Four supported employment alternatives. In W. E. Kiernan, & J. A. Start (Eds.), *Pathways to employment for adults with developmental disabilities* (pp. 139-153). Baltimore: Paul H. Brookes.

Martin, J., & Husch, J. V. (1987). School-based vocational programs and labor laws. *Journal of The Association for Persons with Severe Handicaps, 12* (2), 140-144.

Martin, J. E., & Mithaug, D. E. (1990). Consumer-directed placement. In F. R. Rusch (Ed.), *Supported employment: Models, methods, and issues* (pp. 87-110). Sycamore, IL: Sycamore Publishing Co.

Matich-Folds, L. (1991, January). Supported employment for persons with physical disabilities. *The Advance, 2* (3), p. 10, 12.

Matson, J. L. & McCartney, J. R. (Eds.). (1981). *Handbook of behavior modification with the mentally retarded*. New York, NY: Plenum Press.

Matson, J. L., Rusch, F. R. (1986). Quality of life: Does competitive employment make a difference? In F. R. Rusch (Ed.), *Competitive employment issues and strategies*. Baltimore: Paul Brookes Publishing Co.

McDonnell, J. J., Wilcox, B., Boles, S. M., & Bellamy, G. T. (1985). Transition issues facing youth with severe disabilities: Parent's perspective. *Journal of the Association for Persons with Severe Handicaps. 10*(1), 61-65.

Mcloughlin, C. Garner, J. B., & Callahan, M. (1987). *Getting employment, staying employed*. Baltimore: Paul H. Brookes.

Menchetti, B. M. & Udvari-Solner, A. (1990). Supported employment: New challenges for vocational evaluators. *Rehabilitation Education, 4*, 301-317.

Moon, M. S., Goodall, P., Barcus, M., & Brooke, V. (1987). *The supported work model for competitive employment for citizens with severe handicaps: A guide for job trainers*. Richmond, VA: Virginia Commonwealth University, Rehabilitation Research & Training Center.

Moon, M. S., Goodall, P., & Wehman, P. (1985). *Critical issues related to supported competitive employment*. Richmond: Virginia Commonwealth University, Rehabilitation Research & Training Center.

Moon, M. S., & Griffin, S. L. (1988). Supported employment service delivery models. In P. Wehman & M. S. Moon, *Vocational rehabilitation and supported employment* (pp. 17-30). Baltimore, MD: Paul H. Brooke.

Moon, M. S., Inge, K. J., Wehman, P., Brookes, V., & Barcus, J. M. (1990). *Helping persons with severe mental retardation get and keep employment*. Baltimore: Paul Brookes Publishing Co.

Moore, C. (1988). Parents and transition: "Make it or Break it." *The Pointer, 32*(2), 12-14.

Mosley, C. R. (1988). Job satisfaction research: Implications for supported employment. *The Journal of the Association for Persons with Severe Handicaps, 13*(3), 211-219.

Mulick, J. A. (1990.) The compassion of distinguishing punishing behavioral treatment for aversive treatment. *American Journal on Mental Retardation, 95* (2), 137-141.

Mulick, J. A., & Linscheid, T.R. (1988). A review of LaVigna and Donnellan's "Alternatives to punishment: solving behavior problems with non-aversive strategies." *Research in Developmental Disabilities, 9*, 317-327.

Near, J. P., Smith, C. A., Rice, R. W., & Hunt, R. G. (1983.) Job satisfaction. *Journal of Applied Social Psychology, 13* (2), 126-144.

Newman, S. (1984). The social and emotional consequences of head injury and stroke. *International Review of Applied Psychology, 33,* 427-455.

Nielson, G. B. (1986). *Using the Plan to Achieve Self-support, a SSI work incentive program to fund supported employment: From rationale to case examples.* Manuscript submitted for publication.

Nirje, B. (1969). The normalization principle and its human management implications. In R. Kugel & W. Wolfensberger (Eds.), *Changing patterns in residential services for the mentally retarded* (pp. 179-195). Washington, DC: President's Commission on Mental Retardation.

Nirje, B. (1980). The normalization principle. In R. J. Flynn & K. E. Nitsh (Eds.), *Normalization, social integration, and community services* (pp. 32-49). Baltimore: University Park Press.

Nisbet, J., & Hagner, D. (1988). Natural supports in the workplace: A reexamination of supported employment. *Journal of the Association for Persons with Severe Handicaps, 13*(4), 260-267.

Noble, J. H., & Collignon, F. C. (1987). Systems barriers to supported employment for persons with chronic mental illness. *Psychosocial Rehabilitation Journal, 11*(2), 25-44.

Noble, J. H., & Collignon, F. C. (1988). Systems barriers to supported employment for persons with chronic mental illness. In P. Wehman & M. S. Moon, *Vocational rehabilitation and supported employment* (pp. 325-340). Baltimore, MD: Paul H. Brookes.

Noble, J. H., & Conley, R. W. (1987). Accumulating evidence on the benefits and costs of supported and transitional employment for persons with severe disabilities. *Journal of The Association for Persons with Severe Handicaps, 12* (3), 163-174.

Nockleby, D. M., & Deaton, A. V. (1987). Denial versus distress: Coping patterns in post head trauma patients. *International Journal of Clinical Neuropsychology, 9*(4), 145-148.

O'Brien, S. & Repp, A. (1990). Reinforcement-based Reductive procedures: A review of 20 years of their use with persons with severe or profound mental retardation. *The Journal of the Association for Persons with Severe Handicaps, 13* (3), 148-159.

O'Bryan, A. (1985). The STP benchwork model. In P. McCarthy, J. M. Everson, M. S. Moon, & J. M. Barcus (Eds.), *School-to-work transition for youth with severe disabilities* (Monograph, pp. 183-194). Richmond: Virginia Commonwealth University, Project Transition into Employment, Rehabilitation Research & Training Center.

O'Bryan, A. (1989). The small-business supported employment option for persons with severe handicaps. In P. Wehman, & J. Kregel (Eds.), *Supported employment for persons with disabilities. Focus on excellence* (pp. 69-82). NY: Human Sciences Press.

Oddy, M., Coughlan, T., Tyerman, A., & Jenkins, D. (1985). Social adjustment after closed head injury: A further follow-up seven years after injury. *Journal of Neurology, Neurosurgery and Psychiatry, 48,* 564-568.

Oddy, M., Humphrey, M., & Uttley, D. (1978). Stresses upon the relatives of head-injured patients. *British Journal of Psychiatry, 133,* 507-513.

Parent, W. S., & Everson, J. M. (1986). Competencies of disabled workers in industry: A review of business literature. *Journal of Rehabilitation, 52*(4), 16-23.

Parent, W. S., Kregel, J., Twardzik, G., Metzler, H. (1990). Social integration in the work-places: An analysis of the interaction activities of workers and mental retardation and their coworkers. In J. Kregel, P. Wehman & M. Shafer (Eds.), *Supported employment for persons with severe disabilities: From research to practice, Vol. III,* (p. 171-195). Richmond, VA; Virginia Commonwealth University Rehabilitation Research & Training Center.

Parent, W., Kregel, J., & Wehman, P. (in press). *Vocational Integration Index: Measuring Integration of Workers with Disabilities.* Stoneham, MA: Andover Medical Publishers, Inc.

Parent, W., Kregel, J., Wehman, P., & Metzler, H. (1991). Measuring the social integration of supported employment workers. *Journal of Vocational Rehabilitation, 1*(1),35-49.

Parker, R. M. (1987). *Rehabilitation counseling: Basics and beyond.* Austin, TX: Pro-Ed.

Parker, R. M., Szymanski, E. M. & Hanley-Maxwell, C. (1989). Ecological assessment in supported employment. *Journal of Applied Rehabilitation Counseling, 20*(3), 26-33.

Peck, G., Fulton, C., Cohen, C., Warren, J. R., & Antonello, J. (1984). *Neuropsychological, physical and psychological factors affecting long-term vocational outcomes following severe head injury.* Paper presented at the annual meeting of the International Neuropsychological Society, Houston, TX.

Pogrebin, L. C. (1987). *Among Friends.* New York: McGraw Hill Book Company.

Poling, A., & Ryan, C. (1982). Differential reinforcement of other behavior schedules. *Behavior Modification, 6,* 3-21.

Rehabilitation Research & Training Center Newsletter. (1987). *From research to practice: The supported work model of competitive employment, 3*(2).

Rehabilitation Research & Training Center (1988). *Interagency vendorization: Expanded supported employment services.* Richmond, VA: Virginia Commonwealth University.

Rehabilitation Research & Training Center (October, 1988). *Quarterly report: Successful outcomes in supported employment.*

Rehabilitation Research & Training Center (1990). *A national analysis of supported employment growth and implementation.* Richmond, VA: Rehabilitation Research & Training Center, Virginia Commonwealth University.

Rehabilitation Research & Training Center Newsletter (1990, Summer). *The many "faces" of vocational integration.* Richmond, VA: Rehabilitation Research & Training Center, Virginia Commonwealth University.

Rehabilitation Research & Training Center Newsletter (1990). *Parents and families: Advocating vocational outcomes for young adults with disabilities, 5*(3).

Revell, G., Wehman, P., & Arnold, S. (1984). Supported work model for competitive employment for persons with mental retardation: Implications for rehabilitative services. *Journal of Rehabilitation, 50*(4), 33-38.

Rhodes, L. E., & Valenta, L. (1985a). Industry-based supported employment. An enclave approach. *Journal of The Association for Persons with Severe Handicaps 10*(1),12-20.

Rhodes, L. E., & Valenta, L. (1985b). Enclaves in industry. In P. McCarthy, J. M. Everson, M. S. Moon, & J. M. Barcus (Eds.), *School-to-work transition for youth with severe disabilities* (Monograph, pp. 129-149). Richmond: Virginia Commonwealth University, Project Transition into Employment, Rehabilitation Research & Training Center.

Rhodes, S. R. (1986). *Interagency cooperative/collaboration agreements.* Washington, DC: National Association of Developmental Disabilities Council.

Rice, R. W., McFarlin, B., Hunt, R. G., & Near, J. P. (1985). Job importance as a moderator of the relationship between job satisfaction and life satisfaction. *Basic and Applied Psychology, 6*(4), 297-316.

Rosenthal, N. H. (1989). More than wages at issue in job quality debate. *Monthly Labor Review, 112*(2), 4-8.

Rothwell, W. J., & Kazanas, H. C. (1989). *Strategic human resource development,* (p. 236-258). New Jersey: Prentice Hall.

RRTC Research Division. (1987). *Data management system operations manual (2nd ed.). Richmond: Virginia Commonwealth University, Rehabilitation Research & Training Center.*

Ruegg, P. (1981). The meaning and use of work as modality to habilitation and rehabilitation of disabled persons in facilities providing vocational programs. In J. Lapadakis, J. Ansley, & J. Lowitt (Eds.), *Work, services and change: Proceedings from the National Institute on Rehabilitation Facilities* (pp. 5-22) Menomie, WI: University of Wisconsin-Stout.

Rusch, F. R. (1986). *Competitive employment issues and strategies.* Baltimore, MD: Paul H. Brookes.

Rusch, F. R. (1986). Developing a long-term follow-up program. In F. R. Rusch (Ed.) *Competitive employment: Issues and strategies* (pp. 225-232). Baltimore: Paul H. Brookes.

Rusch, F. R., Hughes, C., McNair, J., & Wilson, P. G. (1989). *Co-worker involvement scoring manual and index.* Champaign: University of Illinois.

Rusch, F. R., Johnson, J. R., & Hughes, C. (1990). Analysis of co-worker involvement in relation to level of disability versus placement approach among supported employees. *Journal of The Association for Persons with Severe Handicaps, 15*(1), 32-39.

Rusch, F. R., Martin, J. E., & White, D. M. (1985). Competitive employment: Teaching mentally retarded employees to maintain their work behavior. *Education and Training of the Mentally Retarded, 20,* 182-189.

Rusch, F. R. (1990). *Supported employment: Models, methods, and issues.* Sycamore, IL: Sycamore Publishing Co.

Sale, P., Barcus, M. Wood, W., & Moon, S. (1988). The role of the employment specialist. In B. Kiernan & B. Schalock (Eds.), *Economics, industry, and disability: A look ahead.* Baltimore, MD: Paul H. Brookes.

Salzberg, C. L., Agran, M., & Lignugaris/Kraft, B. (1986). Behaviors that contribute to entry-level employment: A profile of five jobs. *Applied Research in Mental Retardation, 7,* 299-314.

Salzberg, C. L., Lignugaris/Kraft, B., & McCuller, G. L. (1988). Reasons for job loss: A review of employment termination studies of mentally retarded workers. *Research in Developmental Disabilities, 9,* 153-170.

Schalock, R. L. (1989). Person-environment analysis: Short- and long-term perspectives. In W. E. Kiernan & R. L. Schalock (Eds.), *Economics, industry, and disability: A look ahead.* Baltimore: Paul Brookes Publishing Co.

Schalock, R. L. (1988). Critical performance evaluation indicators in supported employment. In P. Wehman & M. S. Moon, (Eds.). *Vocational rehabilitation and supported employment* (pp. 163-174). Baltimore: Paul H. Brookes.

Schultz, R. P. (1986). Establishing a parent-professional partnership to facilitate competitive employment. In F. R. Rusch (Ed.) *Competitive employment issues and strategies* (pp. 289-302). Baltimore: Paul Brookes Publishing Co.

Seltzer, M. M. (1984). Patterns of job satisfaction among mentally retarded adults. *Applied Research in Mental Retardation, 5,* 147-159.

Seyfarth, J., Hill, J., Orelove, F., McMillan, J., & Wehman, P. (1985). Factors influencing parents' vocational aspirations for their mentally retarded children. *Mental Retardation, 25*(6), 357-362.

Shafer, M., & Nisbet, J. (1988). Integration and empowerment in the workplace. In M. Barcus, S. Griffin, D. Mank, L. Rhodes, & S. Moon (Eds.), *Supported employment implementation issues,* (pp. 45-72). Richmond, VA: Virginia Commonwealth University, Rehabilitation Research & Training Center.

Shafer, M. S., Tait, K., Keen, R., & Jesiolowski, C. (1989). Supported competitive employment: Using co-workers to assist follow-along efforts. *Journal of Rehabilitation,* 55(2), 68-75.

Shafer, M. S. (1986). Utilizing co-workers as change agents. In F. R. Rusch (Ed.) *Competitive employment: Issues and strategies* (pp. 215-224). Baltimore: Paul H. Brookes.

Shafer, M. (1988). Supported employment in perspective: Traditions in vocational rehabilitation. In P. Wehman & M. S. Moon, (Eds.), *Vocational rehabilitation and supported employment.* Baltimore: Paul H. Brookes.

Shafer, M. S. (1990). The national supported employment initiative and its impact upon state agency rehabilitation counselors. In *Supported employment for persons with severe disabilities: From research to practice.* Richmond, VA: Virginia Commonwealth University, Rehabilitation Research & Training Center.

Shafer, M. S., Kregel, J., Banks, P. D., & Hill, M. L. (1988). An analysis of employer evaluations of workers with mental Retardation. *Research in Developmental Disabilities,* 9, 377-391.

Shafer, M., Parent, W., & Everson, J. M. (1988). Employers and supported employment: The need for responsive marketing by supported employment developers. In P. Wehman & M. S. Moon (Eds.), *Vocational rehabilitation and supported employment.* Baltimore: Paul H. Brookes.

Sharpton, W. R., & West, M. (1992). Severe and profound mental retardation. In P. J. McLaughlin & P. Wehman (Eds.), *Handbook of developmental disabilities: A guide to best practices.* (pp. 16-29) Stoneham, MA: Andover Medical Publishers.

Shevin, M., & Klein, N. K. (1984). The importance of choice-making skills for students with severe disabilities. *Journal of the Association for Persons with Severe Handicaps,* 9, 159-166.

Singer, G. H. S., & Irvin, L. K. (1991). Supporting families of persons with severe disabilities: Emerging findings, practices, and questions. In L. H. Meyer, L. A. Peck, & L. Brown (Eds.), *Critical issues in the lives of people with severe disabilities* (pp. 271-312). Baltimore: Paul Brookes Publishing Co.

Smith, M. (1989): Autism: life in the community. Baltimore: Paul Brookes, Publishing Co.

Smull, M. W. & Bellamy, G. T. (1991). Community services for adults with disabilities: Policy challenges in the emerging support paradigm. In L. H. Meyer, C. A. Peck, & L. Brown (Eds.), *Critical issues in the lives of people with severe disabilities.* Baltimore: Paul Brookes Publishing Company.

Snell, M. (Ed.) (1987). *Systematic instruction of persons with severe handicaps* (3rd edition). Columbus, OH: Charles E. Merrill.

Stainback, W., & Stainback, S. (1987). Facilitating friendships. *Education and Training in Mental Retardation,* 22(1), 18-25.

Stainback, W., Stainback, S., Nietupski, J., & Hamre-Nietupski, S. (1986). Establishing effective community-based training stations. In F. R. Rusch (Ed.), *Competitive employment issues and strategies* (pp. 103-114). Baltimore: Paul H. Brookes.

Stipek, D. J. (1988). Motivation to learn: From theory to practice (pp. 19-28.) Englewood Cliffs, NJ. Prentice-Hall, Inc.

Stokes, T., & Baer, D. (1977). An implicit technology of generalization. *Journal of Applied Behavior Analysis,* 10, 349-367.

Summers, J. A. (1986). *The right to grow up: An introduction to adults with developmental disabilities.* Baltimore: Paul H. Brookes.

Summers, J. A. (1986). Putting it all together: Administration and policy in developmental disabilities. In J. A. Summers (Ed.), *The right to grow up: An introduction to adults with developmental disabilities* (pp. 287-303). Baltimore: Paul H. Brookes.

Taylor, H. (1987). Evaluating our quality of life. *Industrial Development, 156*(2), 1-4.

Test, D. W., Farebrother, C., & Spooner, F. (1988). A comparison of the social interactions of workers with and without disabilities. *Journal of Employment Counseling, 25* (3), 122-131.

Thompson, T. (1990). Reader response: The Humpty Dumpty world of "aversive" interventions. *The Journal of the Association for Persons with Severe Handicaps,* 15(3), 136-139.

Thomsen, I.V. (1984). Late outcome of very severe blunt head trauma: A 10-15 year second follow-up. *Journal of Neurology, Neurosurgery and Psychiatry, 43* 260-268.

Tindall, L. W., Gugerty, J. J., & Dougherty, B. (1984). *JTPA youth competencies and handicapped youth.* (ERIC Document Reproduction Service No. ED 252 699).

Turnbull, A. P., Summers, J. A., Backus, L. Brenicki, G. J., Goodfriend, S. J., & Roeder-Gordon, C. (nd). *Stress and coping with families having a member with a developmental disability.* Washington, DC: DATA Institute.

Turnbull, A. P., Summers, J. A., & Brotherson, M. J. (1986). Family life cycle theoretical and empirical implications and future directions for families with mentally retarded members. In J. J. Gallagher & P. M. Vietze (Eds.), *Families of handicapped persons: Research, programs, and policy issues* (pp. 45-65). Baltimore: Paul Brookes Publishing Co.

Turnbull, A. P. & Turnbull, H. R. (1986). Toward great expectations for vocational opportunities: Family-professional partnerships. *Mental Retardation* 26(6), 337-342.

Turnbull, A. P., & Turnbull, H. R. (1990a). *Families, professionals and exceptionality: A special partnership* (2nd ed). Columbus, OH: Merrill Publishing Company.

Turnbull, A., & Turnbull, H.R. (1990b). Reader Response: A tale about lifestyle changes: Comments on "Toward a technology of "nonaversive" behavioral support." *The Journal of the Association for Persons with Severe Handicaps,* 15(3), 142-144.

Turnbull, A. P., & Turnbull, H. R. (1991). Family assessment and family empowerment: An ethical analysis. In L. H. Meyer, C. A. Peck, E. L. Brown (Eds.), *Critical issues in the lives of people with severe disabilities* (pp. 485-488). Baltimore: Paul Brookes Publishing Co.

Turnbull, H. R., Guess, D., et al. (1986). A model for analyzing the moral aspects of special education and behavioral interventions. In P. Dokecki and R. Zaner (Eds.), *Ethics of dealing with persons with severe handicaps: Toward a research agenda* (p. 168). Baltimore, MD: Paul H. Brookes.

Tyerman, A., & Humphrey, M. (1984). Changes in self-concept following severe head injury. *International Journal of Rehabilitation Research, 7*(1), 11-23.

Utah Supported Employment Program (1990). *Supported employment programs.* Utah Division of Rehabilitation Services and Division of Services to the Visually Handicapped.

Virginia Commonwealth University, Research Rehabilitation and Training Center. (1990). *Quarterly report. Successful outcomes in supported employment. Data analysis for North Dakota supported employment providers, Quarter 1, Jan 1, and March 31.*

Wacker, D., & Berg, W. (1983). Effects of picture prompts on the acquisition of complex vocational tasks by mentally retarded adolescents. *Journal of Applied Behavior Analysis, 16,* 417-433.

Wacker, D. P., & Berg, W. K. (1986). Generalizing and maintaining work behavior. In F. R. Rusch (Ed.) *Competitive employment: Issues and strategies* (pp. 129-140). Baltimore: Paul H. Brookes.

Walker, J. & Shea, T. (1988). *Behavior management: A practical approach for educators.* Columbus: Merrill.

Weddell, R., Oddy, M., & Jenkins, D. (1980). Social adjustment after rehabilitation: A two-year follow-up of patients with severe head injury. *Psychological Medicine, 10,* 257-263.

Wehman, P. (1988). Supported employment: Toward zero exclusion of persons with severe disabilities. In P. Wehman & M. S. Moon (Eds.), *Vocational rehabilitation and supported employment.* Baltimore: Paul H. Brookes.

Wehman, P. (1981). *Competitive employment: New horizons for severely disabled individuals.* Baltimore: Paul H. Brookes.

Wehman, P. (1990). *A national analysis of supported employment growth and implementation.* Rehabilitation Research & Training Center on Supported Employment, Virginia Commonwealth University, Richmond, VA.

Wehman, P. (1990). School-to-work transition: Elements of successful programs. *Teaching Exceptional Children, 23*(1) 40-43.

Wehman, P., Hill, M., Goodall, P., Cleveland, P., Brooke, V., Pentecost, J. (1982). Job placement and follow-up of moderately and severely handicapped individuals after three years. *Journal of the Association for the Severely Handicapped, 7*(2), 5-16.

Wehman, P., Hill, M., Hill, J., Brooke, V., Pendleton, P., & Britt, C. (1985). Competitive employment for persons with mental retardation: A follow-up six years later. *Mental Retardation, 23*(6), 274-281.

Wehman, P., & Kregel, J. (1985). A supported work approach to competitive employment of individuals with moderate and severe handicaps. *The Association for Persons with Severe Handicaps, 10*(1), 3-11.

Wehman, P., Kregel, J., Barcus, J. M., & Schalock, R. L. (1986). Vocational transition for students with developmental disabilities. In W. E. Kiernan & J. A. Stark (Eds.), *Pathways to employment for adults with developmental disabilities* (pp. 113-128). Baltimore: Paul H. Brookes.

Wehman, P., Kregel, J., & Seyfarth, J. (1985). Employment outlook for young adults with mental retardation. *Rehabilitation Counseling Bulletin, 29*(2), 91-99.

Wehman, P., Kregel, J., & Shafer, M. S. (1989). Emerging trends in the national supported employment initiative: A preliminary analysis of twenty-seven states. Richmond, VA: Virginia Commonwealth University Rehabilitation Research & Training Center.

Wehman, P., Kregel, J., Shafer, M. S., & West, M. (1989). Supported employment implementation I: Characteristics and outcomes of persons being served. *Emerging trends in the National supported employment initiative: A preliminary analysis of twenty-seven states* (Monograph, pp. 46-74). Rehabilitation Research & Training Center on Supported Employment. Virginia Commonwealth University.

Wehman, P., & Kreutzer, J. S. (1990). *Vocational rehabilitation for persons with traumatic brain injury.* Rockville, MD: Aspen Publishers, Inc.

Wehman, P., Kreutzer, J. S., West, M. 1989). Employment outcomes of persons following traumatic brain injury: Preinjury, post-injury and supported employment. *Brain Injury, 3,* 397-412.

Wehman, P., Kreutzer, J. S., West, M., Sherron, P., Zasler, N., Groah, C., Stonnington, H., Burns, C., & Sale, P. (1990). Return to work for persons with traumatic brain injury: A supported employment approach. *Archives of Physical Medicine and Rehabilitation, 71,* 1047-1052.

Wehman, P., & Kregel J. (1990). *A national analysis of supported employment growth and implementation.* Richmond, VA: Virginia Commonwealth University, Rehabilitation Research & Training Center.

Wehman, P., & Moon, M. S. (1987). Critical values in employment programs for persons with developmental disabilities: A position paper. *Journal of Applied Rehabilitation Counseling, 18*(1), 12-16.

Wehman, P., & Moon, M. S. (Eds.) (1988). *Vocational rehabilitation and supported employment.* Baltimore: Brookes Publishing Co.

Wehman, P., Moon, M. S., Everson, J. M., Wood, W., & Barcus, J. M. (1988). *Transition from school to work. New challenges for youth with severe disabilities.* Baltimore: Paul H. Brookes..

Wehman, P., Shafer, M. S., Kregel, J., & Twardzik, G. (1989). Supported employment implementation II: Service delivery characteristics associated with program development and costs. *Emerging trends in the National supported employment initiative: A preliminary analysis of twenty-seven states* (Monograph, pp. 75-69). Rehabilitation Research & Training Center on Supported Employment. Virginia Commonwealth University.

Wehman, P., Wood, W., Everson, J. M., Goodwyn, R., & Conley, S. (1988). *Vocational education for multihandicapped youth with Cerebral Palsy.* Baltimore: Paul Brookes Publishing Co.

West, M., Kregel, J., & Banks, D. (1990). Fringe benefits earned by supported employment participants. In J. Kregel, P. Wehman, & M. S. Shafer (Eds.), *Competitive employment for persons with severe disabilities: From research to practice, Vol. III* Monograph, pp. 116-133). Richmond: Rehabilitation Research & Training Center, VCU.

Western Michigan University Supported Employment Evaluation Project. (May, 1990). *Supported employment in Michigan. Fourteen quarterly statistical report: Summary version.* College of Arts and Sciences, Kalamazoo, Michigan.

White, D. M. (1986). Social validation. In F. R. Rusch (Ed.) *Competitive employment: Issues and strategies* (pp. 199-213). Baltimore: Paul H. Brookes.

Will, M. (1984). *Supported employment: An OSERS position paper.* Washington, DC: U.S. Department of Education.

Williams, R. (1991). Choices, communication, and control: A call for expanding them in the lives of people with severe disabilities. In L. H. Meyer, C. A. Peck & L. Brown (Eds.), *Critical issues in the lives of people with severe disabilities.* Baltimore: Paul Brookes Publishing Company.

Wolfensberger, W. (1972). *The principle of normalization in human services.* Toronto, Canada: National Institute on Mental Retardation.

Wood, W. (1988). Supported employment for persons with physical disabilities. In P. Wehman & M. S. Moon, *Vocational rehabilitation and supported employment* (p. 341-363). Baltimore, MD: Paul H. Brookes.

Yan, X., Rhodes, L., Sandow, D., Storey, K., Petheridge, R., & Loewinger, H. (1990). *Social Structure in a supported employment work setting: Clique analysis of interpersonal interactions.* Unpublished manuscript.

Young, J. L. (1986). What competencies do employees really need? A review of three studies. *Journal of Career Development, 12*(3), 240-249.

Zarsky, J. J., Hall, D. E., DePompei, R. (1987). Closed head injury patients: A family therapy approach to the rehabilitation process. *American Journal of Family Therapy, 15*(1), 62-68.

Zautra, A., & Goodhart, D. (1979). Quality of life indicators: A review of the literature. *Community Mental Health Review, 4*(1), 1-10.

Glossary of Supported Employment Terms and Concepts

Edited by Jane M. Everson

Compiled by:

Victoria Blackburn	Laura Gunther
Trudie Hughes	Susan Killam
Perry Matthews	Brenda McClelland
Debra Rabuk	Virginia Rios
Sharon Sikes	Lisa Tatum
Jeanette Thorpe	Karen Westmoreland
Michael Yeatts	

INTRODUCTION

The terms and concepts included in this glossary are frequently associated with the supported employment movement and with supported employment programs. Although many of the terms and concepts have definitions and usage apart from supported employment, they have been defined here with particular attention being paid to their relationship to the supported employment movement. Each listing includes resources indicating where more information on the term or concept can be found. This manual is designed for professionals who manage and/or provide supported employment services and for parents and individuals with disabilities, who continue to advocate for the provision of supported employment services. Many thanks to Patti Goodall, Sherril Moon, and Paul Wehman for their review and feedback and to Rachel Conrad for her typing.

Reference Listing of Defined Terms and Concepts

Administration on Developmental Disabilities (ADD)—ADD is a division of the U.S. Department of Health and Human Services. ADD funds a number of discretionary grants and contract activities designed to improve service systems to individuals with developmental disabilities (Summers 1986). These funds are usually short-term (not more than three years) and are provided as demonstration or start-up funds. ADD also funds 36 University Affiliated Programs (UAPs) and seven satellite centers that provide interdisciplinary personnel training, technical assistance, and product dissemination to professionals who work with persons with developmental disabilities (Elder, Conley, and Noble 1986). ADD has also enacted a major initiative to focus employment efforts on those persons who have not been served by traditional vocational rehabilitation services, and thus has played a leadership role in the national implementation of supported employment (Elder 1984).

Benchwork Model—See "Entrepreneurial Model"

Carl D. Perkins Act—The Carl D. Perkins Vocational Education Act of 1984 (P.L. 98-524) created new opportunities for youths with disabilities and disadvantages. P.L. 98-524 was the first change in federal vocational education policy since 1976. The language of the act places a strong emphasis on equal access to quality vocational education programs, including the provision of special support services to enhance students' participation in programs (Phelps and Frasier 1988). Title II, Part A specifies:

Each local education agency shall...provide information to handicapped and disadvantaged students and parents of such students concerning the opportunities available in vocational education at least one year before the students enter the grade level in which vocational education programs are first generally available in the State but in no event later than the beginning of the ninth grade, together with the requirements for eligibility for enrollment in such programs (Sect. 204).

Each student who enrolls in vocational education programs shall receive: (1) assessment of the interests, abilities, and special needs; (2) special services, including adaptation of curriculum, instruction, equipment, and facilities; (3) guidance, counseling, and career development activities; and (4) counseling services designed to facilitate the transition from school to postschool employment and career opportunities (Sect. 204).

The mandates of and philosophy behind the Carl D. Perkins Act promise to expand vocational education services to previously unserved populations, including students with disabilities, and thus should enhance the vocational skills foundation they bring to employment and supported employment programs. For more information, contact the division of vocational and adult education in your state department of education.

Case Closure—State vocational rehabilitation systems use status codes to indicate client statuses in the vocational rehabilitation process. Status codes for case closure include: closed from referral as ineligible for services (08); closed in extended evaluation (06); or either successful (26) or unsuccessful (28) placement of clients into employment (Mandeville and Brabham 1987). A case may be closed successfully when a client has been employed for a minimum of 60 continuous days. Because state vocational rehabilitation systems are time-limited services, individuals with severe disabilities who are eligible for supported employment programs will continue to have their cases closed by their state vocational rehabilitation agency, but their cases will be opened by the agency designated in their state to provide ongoing support and follow-along services.

Case Management—Case management involves the coordination of services and resources between many agencies and organizations whose goal is successful community living for individuals with disabilities. Effective case management services for supported employment ensure that the individual client is the focus of joint planning by agencies, such as education, vocational rehabilitation, and mental health/mental retardation (Wehman, Moon, Everson, Wood, and Barcus 1988). Lack of systematic and cooperative case management services have traditionally been an obstacle in the implementation of supported employment programs because of multiple legislative mandates and funding sources. Effective case management coordination efforts in vocational transition and supported employment programs have been described by Kiernan and Stark (1986); Rusch (1986); and Wehman et al. (1988).

Case Services Dollars (also known as 110 dollars and Title I funds)—Case services dollars are monies authorized under Title I of the Rehabilitation Act. Case services dollars are allotted to rehabilitation counselors to either directly provide or purchase services for clients assigned to their caseloads. If clients are deemed eligible for vocational rehabilitation services, rehabilitation counselors may provide any or all of the following services: guidance and counseling, vocational evaluation, medical services, vocational training, transportation, equipment and supplies, job placement services, and follow-up services (Parker 1987). Under the most recent amendments to the Rehabilitation Act (P.L. 99-506, 1986), case services dollars may be used to provide or purchase supported employment services.

Client Pool—A client pool is a group of individuals with severe disabilities who have been referred to a supported employment provider and assessed as appropriate clients. This pool is used for selection of individuals for specific job development, job placement, and job-site training (Moon, Goodall, Barcus, and Brooke 1986). A client pool approach ensures that eligible clients can be matched to a job that has been locally identified and that best meets their individual employment and support needs (Moon et al 1986).

Commensurate Wages—Commensurate wages are an underlying principle in all regulations covering subminimum wages under special certificates for workers with disabilities. Commensurate means proportionate. Wages paid to a disabled worker must be based on his or her productivity in proportion to the wages and productivity of nondisabled workers performing essentially the same work in the same geographic area. Commensurate wages must be based on the prevailing wage paid to nondisabled experienced workers in the same industry. For more information, contact the U.S. Department of Labor and review the provisions of the Fair Standards Labor Act.

Competitive Employment—Competitive employment is work that produces valued goods or services. Pay may be minimum wage or higher or lower. It must take place in a setting that includes nonhandicapped workers and provides opportunities for employment advancement (Rusch 1986). Competitive employment enhances feelings of self-worth and normalization for persons with disabilities, both in self-perception and the perception of society (Seyfarth, Hill, Orelove, McMillan and Wehman 1985). Competitive employment has been most recently and clearly defined for supported employment programs as "work that is performed on a full-time basis or on a part-time basis, averaging at least 20 hours per week for each pay period, and for which an individual is compensated in accordance with the Fair Standards Labor Act (FSLA)" (*Federal Register*, November 18, 1987, p. 44368).

Contract Procurement—Contract procurement describes a comprehensive process of public relations, marketing, and sales used to obtain work from private and public organizations. Contract procurement has become increasingly important as vocational services expand into different supported employment options. Supported employment managers must possess the skills to procure work for the entrepreneurial business and the mobile work crew models (Bellamy, Rhodes, Mank, and Albin 1988). Without adequate contract procurement, supported employment programs will be unable to provide consistent and stable employment opportunities in community settings for individuals with severe disabilities.

Council of State Administrators of Vocational Rehabilitation (CSAVR)—CSAVR was established in 1940 to provide state-level vocational rehabilitation input to the federal level Rehabilitation Services Administration (RSA). CSAVR membership is composed of the state administrators of all public vocational rehabilitation agencies in the United States and its territories.

Day Activity Centers (also known as developmental centers and adult day programs)—Day activity centers provide various nonvocational programming for adults with moderate to severe mental retardation (Bellamy, Sowers, and Bourbeau 1983). The programming is designed to provide self-help, work adjustment, and social skill instruction in order to help clients progress toward competitive employment and independent living. These centers are typically administered by social services or disabilities agencies in individual states. The clients typically served by these centers are on of the primary target populations for supported employment (Wehman, in press).

Developmental Disabilities—A developmental disability is attributable to a mental or physical impairment (or a combination of the two) that is manifested before 22 years of age; that is likely to continue indefinitely; and that results in substantial functional limitations in three or more of the following life areas: self care, receptive and expressive language, learning, mobility, self-direction, capacity for independent living, and economic self-sufficiency; and reflects the person's need for a combination and sequence of special, interdisciplinary, or generic care, treatment, or other services that are of lifelong or extended duration and individually planned and coordinated (Kiernan, Smith, and Ostrowsky 1986). A developmental disability is a disability that is viewed as substantial and chronic, with multiple impairments and that will require ongoing interdisciplinary services (Kiernan et al. 1986). Individuals with developmental disabilities have been identified as a target population for supported employment because a disproportionately large number of them remain jobless and economically dependent (Kiernan and Stark 1986, Summers 1986).

Dictionary of Occupational Titles (DOT)—The DOT is published by the U.S. Department of Labor. It lists over 20,000 occupations including job characteristics and general employment characteristics. The DOT may be useful for job development, vocational counseling, and career guidance (Shafer, Parent, and Everson, in press; Stainback, Stainback, Nietupski, and Hamre-Nietupski 1986). The scores on many standardized vocational assessments and work samples can be related to the DOT. Examples of these formal evaluations include the Philadelphia Jewish Employment and Vocational Service Work Sample battery (JEVS), the Ohio Vocational Interest Survey (OVIS), and the Valpar Component Work Sample Series (Bitter 1979). In many instances, rehabilitation counselors, job developers, and supported employment specialists may find the DOT useful for general community job market screening and as one mechanism of the vocational assessment process (Brolin 1976). For individuals with severe disabilities who have been referred to supported employment programs, however, it is important to recognize the limitations of formal vocational evaluations and general job development procedures.

Discretionary Funds—Discretionary funds are time-limited funds released as contracts or grants to meet the goals of specific initiatives. Discretionary funds may be public or private, federal, state, or local, and are distributed at the discretion of agencies or organizations. They are typically awarded in response to submitted proposals (See "Request for Proposal"). Discretionary funds provide a good start-up or conversion source for supported employment programs, but because they do not guarantee a permanent or long-term funding source, they should be combined with other funding sources.

Eligibility Services—Eligibility services are those services that require individuals to meet certain criteria or to display certain characteristics in order to be considered for service provision (Kiernan and Stark 1986). Individuals who are referred for eligibility services are assessed and/or diagnosed by the service agency. Eligible individuals are not necessarily guaranteed services and may be denied services because of funding or legislative barriers. Vocational rehabilitation is one example of an eligibility service; to be eligible for state vocational rehabilitation services, individuals must meet three criteria: (1) they must show the presence of a physical or mental disability; (2) that disability must be one that interferes with their ability to gain and maintain employment; and (3) they must be considered employable as a result of service provision. For more information on eligibility criteria for vocational rehabilitation services, contact your local vocational rehabilitation agency.

Employment Specialist (also known as job coach, job trainer, or employment training specialist)—An employment specialist is a direct service worker who provides supported employment services to an agency's or program's clients. An employment specialist or job coach is most frequently associated with individual placement models (Moon, et al. 1986) and may be responsible for all or part of the activities associated with the model. Job coaches or job trainers, as described by Moon et al. (1986), are responsible for job development, consumer assessment, job placement, job-site training and ongoing assessment, and follow-along for an individual client.

Enclaves (also known as sheltered enclaves or enclaves in industry)—The enclave is one of the commonly accepted supported employment models. It is characterized by a group of eight or fewer workers with severe disabilities who are trained and supervised by a human services worker. The individuals are employed in an integrated host-business or industry and access employment opportunities provided to all employees of the host-business or industry. Enclaves pay wages commensurate with the individual's productivity and may be paid directly by the host-business or industry, or the human services support organization (Rhodes and Valenta 1985). The human services worker does not fade from the job site. The ability to provide continuous supervision and flexible and shared decision making between the host-business or industry and the human services support organization is one of the advantages of the enclave model (Bellamy, Rhodes, Mank and Albin 1988).

Entitlement Services—Entitlements are cash income, noncash benefits, or services that all eligible clients have a legal right to receive. Any individual who meets the established criteria and/or who displays specified individual characteristics (e.g., income, age, level of disability) must be provided services. Special education is one example of a federal entitlement service. According to the mandates of the Education for All Handicapped Children Act (P.L. 94-142), all children who meet the eligibility requirements are entitled to a free appropriate public education. Other entitlements include Medicaid, Medicare, Food Stamps, Social Security Disability Income (SSDI), and Supplemental Security Income (SSI). For more information on these federal and state entitlement services, contact the appropriate state agency in your state.

Entrepreneurial Model (also known as the benchwork model)—The benchwork model was developed in the early 1970s by the Specialized Training Program (STP) at the University of Oregon. Early replications of this model were based on ideas and research conducted at the University of Oregon (Mank, Rhodes, and Bellamy 1986). The model was developed as an alternative to traditional day activity center programs for persons with severe disabilities. The model typically employs 15 or fewer workers with disabilities, who are trained and supervised by two to three human services workers. The human services workers do not fade from the job site. Recent attempts have been made to downsize the benchwork models and to employ nondisabled workers to meet federal integration and size guidelines for supported employment programs. The model relies on contractual work, which is typically electronics assembly (O'Bryan 1985); therefore, the success of the program depends upon the ability of the support agency to secure ongoing contract work from industry. More recent entrepreneurial models have met local labor market needs by establishing bakeries, restaurants, and small shops. Due to the restrictiveness of the model, it is intended for workers with the most severe disabilities and challenging behaviors, who need ongoing and intensive training and supervision. Workers are typically paid subminimum wages commensurate with their productivity (Boles, Bellamy, Horner and Mank 1984).

Fading—Fading is the term for a supported employment procedure implemented by an employment specialist after the placement and training of an individual in a job, involving the gradual reduction of intervention time on a competitive job site. Fading includes the general decrease of artificial prompts and reinforcement to more natural types and schedules (Snell 1987). When to start fading and the amount of time an employment specialist should spend on and off the job site depend upon the individual worker's work quality, work rate, amount of work performed independently, and the amount of time a worker is on task. Fading is a critical process in placing workers in individual placement supported employment models. Once fading has been completed, follow-along procedures are implemented (Barcus, Brooke, Inge, Moon, and Goodall 1987; Moon et al. 1986).

Fair Labor Standards Act (FSLA)—The Fair Labor Standards Act of 1938 allowed the U.S. Department of Labor to govern child labor, minimum wages, and overtime pay (Martin and Husch 1987). More recent amendments allow employers to pay workers with disabilities lower than minimum wage as long as the subminimum wage is based on the actual wage made by his or her nondisabled peers and the subminimum wage is based on the disabled person's productivity. The Act, therefore, allows a person to be employed in an integrated supported employment program, even though he or she may not be able to perform 100% of the job. The supported jobs and enclave models often use productivity rates to pay employees with disabilities (Bellamy et al. 1988). In order to pay less than minimum wage, a company or nonprofit organization must obtain a special certificate issued by the U.S. Department of Labor (DOL). In the past, DOL gave out two certificates, one for sheltered workshops that paid its clients 50% of the minimum wage and one for work activity centers that could pay below 50% of the minimum wage. DOL now issues only one certificate that enables workers with disabilities to be paid based on productivity (Gettings and Katz 1987).

Fee for Services Agreements—This is a compensation paid for professional services, usually by state departments of vocational rehabilitation to rehabilitation facilities (Anderson 1977). Similar agreements may be made with local vocational rehabilitation agencies for purchasing supported employment services, which can help programs offering those services to offset the time-limited costs (Revell, Wehman, and Arnold 1984). Fee-for-services agreements utilize a vendor approach by approving a program or agency to provide a defined service for individual clients at a predetermined rate. For more information on developing vendorship agreements with vocational rehabilitation, see Hill (1987).

Follow-along Services (also known as follow-up services and ongoing support services)—Follow-along services are the characteristic of supported employment that provides individuals with severe disabilities assistance in retaining their jobs and making job changes and advancements. Follow-along services include regularly and frequently visiting the job site to observe employees, interviewing supervisors, collecting data and providing re-training; making job modifications and adaptations; making telephone calls to assess employees' progress; mailing supervisor evaluation forms to measure supervisor satisfaction; conducting employee evaluations to assess the employee's satisfaction with employment; and mailing progress reports to the employee's family or residential service provider (Moon et al. 1986). Follow-along services must be individualized to the needs of the employee with severe disabilities. Maintaining regular and frequent contact with employees and employers long after the employee is stabilized in a job has been found to enhance job retention, maintain employee productivity and satisfaction, and maintain supervisor satisfaction (Wehman and Kregel 1985). Follow-along services are paid for by mental health, mental retardation, developmental disabilities funds, and/or general state revenues that have been allocated for services.

Follow-up Services—See Follow-along Services

Individualized Education Program (IEP)—The IEP is the primary mechanism mandated by P.L. 94-142 to ensure that students who receive special education services are in appropriate educational programs. During the mandatory annual planning meeting, a team of professionals and parents set educational and behavioral goals and objectives for individual students. IEPs for adolescents should include community-based vocational skill training that will enhance a student's success in employment and supported employment programs (Wehman et al. 1988).

Individualized Transition Plan (ITP)—The ITP is a formal written plan that specifies transition skills and services to be received by a student prior to and after graduation. This plan should encompass annual as well as short-term objectives that reflect the skills required to function on the job, at home, and in the community. Services needed should be specified to include referrals to appropriate agencies, as well as job placement, on-the-job training, and follow-up. Also, the agency/ person deliver these services should be listed. As the title states, it should be individualized and comprehensive in scope, including training in social skills, money management, and transportation to and from work. This plan should be instituted into a student's IEP or, if out of school, the person's IWRP (Wehman et al. 1988; Wehman, Kregel, Barcus and Schalock 1986).

Individualized Written Rehabilitation Plan (IWRP)—The IWRP is a plan that is jointly developed by a rehabilitation counselor and a client for all clients determined to be eligible for services. It was mandated by the Rehabilitation Act of 1973. It must include the ultimate employment goal and short-term objectives related to the rehabilitation services provided, the date of initiation and expected duration, and the procedures and schedule for progress reviews (Mandeville and Brabham 1987). The 1986 amendments to the Act reflect attention to individual support needs and to implications of supported employment services. These amendments require the IWRP to be developed on the basis of employability, specify the provision of rehabilitation engineering, and to assess and reassess the need for postemployment follow-along services after case closure (P.L. 99-506, Title I, Section 102, b). The whole of the IWRP provides a degree of accountability, actively involves the client in rehabilitation planning, and represents a shift in philosophy from medical to educational service programming in the vocational rehabilitation system (Shafer, in press).

Intermediate Care Facility for the Mentally Retarded (ICF-MR)—An ICF-MR is a residential facility for individuals with severe and/or multiple disabilities who need 24-hour-a-day services. ICF-MR facilities are subsidized by Medicaid funds, which provide all reasonable costs of providing care. Due to the strict eligibility requirements of Medicaid funding, ICF-MR residents often experience strong financial and medical disincentives to employment and supported employment (Conley, Noble and Elder, 1986; Levy and Levy, 1986).

Integrated Work—Integrated work is employment in a typical work setting in which the person with a disability works in close proximity to, and interacts with, nondisabled workers other than human services support personnel. The individual with a disability would perform tasks similar to other tasks performed in the particular industry (Mcloughlin, Garner and Callahan 1987). Integration at the work setting has been shown to enhance the disabled employee's work and social skills and, therefore, is a very important factor to consider in supported employment (Rusch 1986).

Interagency Agreements—Interagency agreements are written documents between federal, state, and/or local agencies that reflect the requirements, constraints, and discretionary authority of the participating agencies. They are used to coordinate resources and services between agencies with similar objectives in order to maximize existing services. This coordination clarifies each agency's responsibilities and helps identify areas where a cooperative effort would be advantageous (Wehman et al. 1988). The local vocational rehabilitation, local mental retardation, and local education authority (LEA), for example, may choose to develop a local interagency agreement to procure necessary transition and supported employment services for young adults with disabilities (Wehman et al.,1988).

Intervention Time—In supported employment, intervention time is time spent by an employment specialist with a specific client during the provision of supported employment services. This time may be recorded for all activities related to employment, including direct client training, employment advocacy, and client screening and evaluation. The recording of intervention time is very important in tracking a client's and a program's progress (Hill, Banks, Handrich, Wehman, Hill, and Shafer 1987). It is also an integral part of the benefit/cost analysis on all levels (client, program, and system). According to Kregel, Hill, and Banks (1987), an average of 161 hours of intervention time is spent per client by an employment specialist during the provision of supported competitive employment services to individuals with moderate mental retardation.

Job Coach—See "Employment Specialist"

Job Training Partnership Act (JTPA)—The JTPA was signed in 1982 to replace the Comprehensive Employment and Training Act (CETA) program and to establish a national program to prepare disadvantaged and disabled youths for productive employment. Currently, JTPA provides employment training through the State Grant Program (Title IIA) and through seven national demonstration projects (Title IV). To meet eligibility requirements, a person must have demonstrated difficulty in finding and/or sustaining employment. Individuals with disabilities comprise less than 10% of clients (Getzel 1987). In 1986, over 9,000 individuals were placed into employment. The JTPA funds are used primarily to support costs for time-limited training, employment staff, and for client-related expenses, such as wage subsidies for OJT (on-the-job training) and transportation. An advantage of the JTPA program is that it allows a great deal of flexibility in addressing local expenses and in encouraging private and public sectors to work together. Also, it may be effectively used to pay for job development and job-site training in supported employment (Dougherty 1987; Revell 1985). See "Private Industry Council."

Least Restrictive Environment (LRE)—"The primary social principle underlying the concept of least restrictive environment is the commitment to finding a place for handicapped individuals in settings that enhance their participation in society" (Bruininks and Lakin 1985, 16). A least restrictive educational environment is mandated by P.L. 94-142 as a placement that is closest to the educational environment of students without handicaps, including a curriculum that is appropriate to the special needs of the student with a disability (Bronicki and Turnbull 1987). These special needs should be met through an appropriate instructional program that can be delivered with the least abrogation of the student's right to be educated with nonhandicapped peers.

In supported employment, the concept of least restrictive environment has been defined as a community-based employment setting with "real work for real pay" and frequent integration with nondisabled co-workers (Wehman and Moon 1987). Support services are provided for individual workers in order to maintain them in the least restrictive employment setting for their individual needs.

Medicaid—Medicaid is a public health care program provided to individuals with low incomes and/or disabilities. Medicaid is federally administered and federally and state funded. In fiscal year 1989, an estimated 2.8 million people who are blind or disabled will receive SSI benefits. Most SSI (Supplemental Security Income) recipients are eligible for Medicaid benefits (i.e., individuals who are poor, aged, blind, disabled, or a member of a family with dependent children), although some states have separate eligibility criteria. Medicaid usually provides full reimbursement for costs of specific health services to eligible persons (Elder, Conley, and Noble 1986) and is the primary funding source for ICF-MR (Intermediate Care Facility for People with Mental Retardation) programs and many adult day programs.

With the permanent authorization of Section 1619 (a) and (b), Medicaid recipients may remain eligible even after obtaining substantial gainful activity levels (SGA) in which their income is too high to qualify for SSI payments. These benefits are continued with the stipulations that the recipient must continue to have a disability; have difficulty maintaining employment without medical coverage; and lack earnings sufficient to pay for benefits equivalent to the combined value of SSI payments and Medicaid coverage (Conley, Noble, and Elder 1986). Nevertheless, many SSI recipients and their family members continue to have legitimate questions and concerns about SSI benefits when they are considering supported employment opportunities. These questions must be addressed by knowledgeable supported employment providers and local social security counselors.

Medicare—Medicare is a public health care program providing health-related services to Americans who are 65 years of age or older and persons with disabilities who have a previous work history. In fiscal year 1989, the program will serve approximately 33 million Americans, including three million Americans with disabilities. It is federally funded and federally administered to those who qualify for SSDI/CDB (Social Security Disability Insurance/Childhood Disability Program). SSDI/CDB beneficiaries must wait for two years after SSDI/CDB eligibility before becoming eligible for Medicare (both Part A and Part B coverage). Although, unlike Medicaid, it has no asset requirements, it does contain co-insurance and deductible provisions that determine reimbursement levels for specific health services (Elder, Conley and Noble 1986). Part A covers inpatient hospital care, skilled nursing facility care, and home health care. Part B covers outpatient hospital services, physician services, therapeutic services, rehabilitation facility services, and other facility services. After an SSDI beneficiary is employed, Medicare coverage will continue for 36 months after he or she has been determined capable of working at a substantial gainful activity (SGA) level. Currently, this loss of Medicare eligibility serves as a substantial disincentive to supported employment opportunities for many SSDI recipients.

Mental Retardation—The most commonly used definition of mental retardation comes from Grossman (1983), who defines mental retardation as:

> "...significantly subaverage general intellectual functioning existing concurrently with deficits in adaptive behavior and manifested during the developmental period."

The subaverage general intellectual functioning is redefined as an IQ (intelligence quotient) of 70 points or lower on a standardized intelligence test. Adaptive behavior deficits indicate the inability to adapt to culturally determined social norms as measured by standardized adaptive behavior tests. Finally, both of these characteristics must be manifested before the age of 18.

Individuals with mental retardation have historically been excluded form community-based competitive work. A common misconception is that individuals with mental retardation are capable of work only in sheltered environments and that productivity and earnings correlate to developmental levels. Another misconception is that an individual's intellectual limitations are the primary reason why competitive work is not found (Elder, Conley and Noble 1986). Individuals with mental retardation have recently been employed in increasing numbers in supported and nonsupported employment programs nationally and have been identified as a primary target population for the supported employment movement. Brown (1987) has suggested that the level of an individual's functioning is determined by the availability of technology and the amount of resources society is willing to allocate. Gold (1980) has defined mental retardation as the level of power necessary when training the individual to learn, instead of limitations in what an individual can learn.

Mobile Work Crews—The mobile work crew model of supported employment is characterized by a group of four to eight severely disabled individuals and one supervisor, who operate a small business out of a van (Mank et al. 1986). The crew typically moves from one business to another during the day performing custodial work, grounds maintenance, or other needed services in the community. Work contracts are drawn up between different businesses and the human service agency. A human service worker supervises and trains the crew and does not fade from the job sites. Integration takes place during the day as crew members interact with the public. This model is flexible to the local job market and is able to meet the needs of urban, suburban, or rural areas (Bellamy et al. 1988; Bourbeau 1985; Mank et al. 1986).

National Industries for the Severely Handicapped (NISH)—NISH is a national not-for-profit agency that provides technical assistance to workshops in securing government contracts. NISH was established through congressional mandate in the Javits-Wagner-O'Day Act of 1971. Many sheltered workshops have sought the help of NISH in obtaining custodial contracts for government buildings, thus employing disabled individuals in the community. The mobile crew and enclave model have used NISH to gain contracts for adults with severe disabilities that will pay highly subsidized wages (Gettings and Katz 1987).

Normalization—According to Wolfensberg (1972), normalization is "utilization of means which are as culturally normative as possible, in order to establish and/or maintain behaviors and characteristics which are as culturally normative as possible" (p. 245). Also stated as the "normalization principle" is a doctrine that calls for "making available," as far as possible, "normal conditions of life" to persons who happen to have mental retardation (Nirje 1969, 1980, 7). Normalization for persons with disabilities would mean making available patterns of life and everyday living conditions that are as close as possible to the regular circumstances and cultures of society. These patterns of life and living conditions would mean a "real" job, a "regular" home to live in, privacy, and respect (Nirje 1980).

Office of Special Education and Rehabilitative Services (OSERS)—OSERS is part of the U.S. Department of Education and oversees the Rehabilitation Services Administration (RSA), Special Education Programs (SEP), and the National Institute on Disability and Rehabilitation Research (NIDRR). In 1985 and in 1986, OSERS released discretionary funds to initiate pilot programs for supported employment in 27 states. The purpose of the initiative as introduced by Will (1984) was to provide supported employment services to individuals with severe disabilities, who at the time were usually not served through traditional vocational rehabilitation services. Since 1984, OSERS has placed a funding and policy priority on vocational transition and supported employment for individuals with severe disabilities (Will 1984).

Ongoing Support Services—See "Follow-along Services"

On-the-Job Training Funds (OJT)—OJT is a federal program that provides time-limited wage assistance to eliminate risk to an employer who hires a worker with a disability (Anderson 1977). These funds provide a subsidy to the worker's wages while he or she is being trained on the job. OJT funds may be authorized by a rehabilitation counselor. This is an incentive that may make supported employment more attractive to potential employer (Moon et al. 1986). The Association for Retarded Citizens of the United States (ARC-US) also provides time-limited OJT funds for individuals with mental retardation. For more information on OJT funds, contact your local vocational rehabilitation agency and local or state ARC.

Prevocational Skills—Adequate vocational preparation is the key to successful employment outcomes for people with severe disabilities (Wehman et al. 1988) Prevocational skills are a function of the public school system—not the adult service system. Prevocational skills that are provided by adult service programs perpetuate the readiness and developmental model philosophies by preparing students and adults for experiences for which they may never demonstrate skills. Supported employment philosophy encourages school-sponsored vocational programs to build career awareness and specific vocational skills, but denies the need to continue prevocational training throughout a person's adult years. Prevocational skills should be built into an educational curriculum as early as possible to teach relevant work and work-related skills. Educational curricula would place students with disabilities into environments to provide them with community-based acquisition and production experiences that would prepare them for future work environments (Bellamy, O'Connor, and Karan 1979; Falvey 1986).

Private Industry Council (PIC)—PIC is a local organization that guides the JTPA program through Service Delivery Areas (SDAs). It provides the U.S. Department of Labor with information on how JTPA funds are used in the community. PICs identify employment needs through a formal assessment process and may be a useful resource when an employment specialist is doing job development. These councils have the authority to decide who will be served, what services will be provided, and who will deliver the training services and activities. Their responsibilities include (1) local planning and review of the JTPA programs; (2) coordination with other employment and training programs; and (3) the establishment of support services (Dougherty 1987; Tindall, Gugerty, and Doughery 1984). If a service organization is interested in acquiring JTPA funds to fund its supported employment program, the agency would need to contact the local PIC (Gettings and Katz 1987; Hill et al. 1985).

Projects With Industry (PWI)—Projects with Industry (PWIs) began under the Vocational Rehabilitation Act of 1973 and are funded through the vocational rehabilitation system. PWIs set up partnerships with private businesses and the vocational rehabilitation system and utilize business advisory groups in conducting placement programs for individuals with disabilities. Agencies developing supported employment programs may be able to use PWI funding for job placement, job-site training, and stabilization of workers in community job sites (Revell et al. 1984).

Public Law 94-142—P.L. 94-142, the Education for All Handicapped Children Act, was passed in 1975 to provide free, appropriate public education for youth with disabilities between the ages of three and 21 years. In 1986, P.L. 98-457 most recently amended P.L. 94-142 services and extended special education services to youth 0-3 years of age. P.L. 94-142 was a landmark piece of legislation that provides (a) due process procedures for parents and students with disabilities and (b) individualized education programs (IEPs) for students' instructional programs and delivery. Part C, Section 626 of the Act provides funding to encourage the development of transition, vocational training, employment, and supported employment services for youths with disabilities.

Public Law 99-506—P.L. 99-506 is the Rehabilitation Act Amendments of 1986. The major changes to the Rehabilitation Act relevant to supported employment include the authorization of Title I funds (case services dollars from the vocational rehabilitation system) to purchase supported employment services and the provision of demonstration money through Title VI-C to all states on a formula basis in order for them to develop supported employment programs. The definition of supported employment is competitive work in integrated settings for persons with severe disabilities who are traditionally excluded from job placement or for those who, because of their disability, need ongoing support to maintain a job. The definition of successful employment in the Act has changed from only full-time employment to include part-time employment, and the IWRP must have more specific information on vocational goals for persons with severe disabilities. Other major changes include fair hearing officers for case appeals and funding for rehabilitation engineering. Because supported employment services require long-term follow-up, Congress has mandated that the vocational rehabilitation system and the service provider come up with an interagency agreement to determine who will fund specific components of the programs (Gettings and Katz 1987; Shafer, in press). P.L. 99-506 is important because it not only reemphasizes that persons with the most severe disabilities benefit from vocational rehabilitation services, but it also provides funds to assist these individuals become successfully employed through supported employment.

Readiness Model (also known as "Developmental Model")—The readiness model is an approach that has been used throughout the educational and vocational rehabilitation systems. The concept emphasizes that before a person is placed into a community job-site, he or she must be trained and possess certain skills, such as correct work habits, social skills, and functional academic skills (Revell et al. 1984). Readiness equates with an evaluate/train/place procedure (Mandeville and Brabham 1987). In supported employment, possessing job readiness skills is not considered a prerequisite for job placement for individuals with severe disabilities; thus, the procedures for placing a person with severe disabilities are place/train/ follow-along (Wehman, in press).

Rehabilitation Engineering—Rehabilitation engineering is a service specified by P.L. 99-506, the Rehabilitation Act Amendments of 1986 to assist with job placement and job retention for individuals with physical disabilities. As defined by the Rehabilitation Act Amendments of 1986, rehabilitation engineering means the "systematic applications of technologies, engineering methodologies, or scientific principles to meet the needs of and address the barriers confronted by individuals with handicaps in areas that include education, rehabilitation, employment, transportation, independent living, and recreation." Rehabilitation engineering services may be provided by an engineer, an occupational or physical therapist, or any technician skilled in job restructuring, job modification, use of adaptive equipment, or environmental accommodations.

Rehabilitation Services Administration (RSA)—RSA is the federal level branch of the U.S. Department of Education that is responsible for overseeing the implementation of rehabilitation legislation. The office was created by the Rehabilitation Act of 1973 and is comprised of 10 regional offices. The 10 regional offices supervise activities within each state in their respective region. Recently, RSA has played a leadership role in the administration of grants in supported employment and personnel training.

Request for Proposal (RFP)—The RFP process is a method of dispersing discretionary grant monies to agencies and organizations. The agency or organization responds to the RFP through a formal proposal (Bellamy et al. 1988) indicating the method in which they would spend the grant monies. The funding organization reviews the proposals and awards funds to the agencies that submit the most appropriate proposals. The funds are typically from one to five years in duration. This mechanism has helped to finance new and innovative supported employment programs (Wehman et al. 1988).

Section 1619 (a) and (b)—Section 1619 (a) and (b) was established in 1981 to provide work incentives to recipients of Supplemental Security Income. Part (a) authorizes cash benefits to be paid to working beneficiaries as long as their earnings are below $713 per month. Part (b) authorizes the continuation of Medicaid coverage even if recipients earn more than $713 per month. SSI recipients who are employed through supported employment are now able to retain their Medicaid coverage as long as they remain within specified income guidelines. For more information, contact your local Social Security office.

Sheltered Workshop—A sheltered workshop is a nonprofit or charitable organization that provides vocational training and employment services within a facility. The organization's purpose is to provide rehabilitative programming for workers with disabilities, and/or to provide remunerative employment (Mcloughlin, Garner, and Callahan 1987). Sheltered workshops often subcontract with businesses to provide work for the sheltered employees and typically pay their employees subminimum wages commensurate with their production. Workshops generally employ from 25 to 200 disabled workers and have historically been the primary employment option for adults with severe disabilities.

Social Security Disability Insurance (SSDI)—SSDI is a federally funded program that provides monthly benefits to persons unable to engage in substantial work as a result of a disabling condition. Recipients are not required to meet an asset test, but to be eligible, they must be fully and currently insured at the onset of the disability (Elder, Conley, and Noble 1986). SSDI is seen as a work disincentive due to the fact that SSDI payments will stop if an individual reaches a level of substantial gainful activity (SGA). SGA is defined as earnings of $300 or more per month (Conley, Noble, and Elder 1986).

Stabilization—Stabilization is one of the necessary processes of the supported work model of competitive employment for persons with disabilities. It is initiated when the employee has performed every step of the individualized job-duty task analysis for that specific duty on three consecutive probe data trials. Stabilization is reached after (1) completion of training, adjustment, and fading activities; (2) the employment specialist intervention time levels off and does not significantly change for a 30-60 day period (Hill et al. 1987); and (3) the employer is satisfied with the employee's work performance.

Supplementary Security Income (SSI)—Supplementary Security Income (SSI) was established to provide a basic level of income for needy persons. These "needy" persons are aging or disabled, are not adequately covered by one of the Social Security retirement or disability programs, and must be unable to work due to a disability. Recipients must also have very limited assets (Elder, Conley, and Noble 1986). Due to asset limitations, SSI becomes a work disincentive to beneficiaries as they are limited in the amount of money they may earn and save (Conley, Noble, and Elder 1986).

Supported Competitive Employment—A supported employment approach for individuals with moderate and severe disabilities (Wehman and Kregel 1985). This approach employs individuals in community work settings with initially intensive job placement and job-site training support from a "job coach." This support is faded gradually and maintained by follow-along services (Moon et al. 1986). The supported competitive employment model, to date, has proven to be very successful for individuals with moderate mental retardation in terms of job retention and costs. Also known as the "supported work model of competitive employment" (Moon et al. 1986), this model places individuals only in positions that pay minimum wage or higher.

Supported Employment—Supported employment is defined in the Rehabilitation Act Amendments of 1986 as "competitive work in integrated work settings for individuals with severe handicaps for whom competitive employment has not traditionally occurred, or for individuals for whom competitive employment has been interrupted or intermittent as a result of a severe disability, and who because of their handicap, need ongoing support services to perform such work." Supported employment is an umbrella concept that includes typical models, such as enclaves, mobile work crews, supported jobs, supported competitive employment, and entrepreneurial models. Supported employment is characterized by the inclusion of individuals with the most severe disabilities in a place-and-train model where both integration and wages are highly valued (Kiernan and Stark 1986; Rusch 1986; Wehman and Moon, in press).

Supported Jobs—Supported jobs are typically found in conventional, private sector companies (Bellamy, Rhodes, Mank, and Albin 1988) and are staffed by individuals with disabilities needing ongoing support. If the Department of Labor has certified that the employer can pay subminimal commensurate wages, the employer may hire workers that produce substantially below production standards.

Targeted Jobs Tax Credit (TJTC)—TJTC is a federal tax credit program designed to provide financial incentives to potential employers when hiring from one of seven target groups. The program is administered on the state level (Elder, Conley, and Noble 1986). Some studies have indicated, however, that TJTC may actually play a minor role in the hiring decision process of employers (Shafer, Parent, and Everson in press), although many utilize the TJTC when it is offered.

Time-limited Services—Time-limited services have a beginning point and an ending point, but are not provided during the entire term of the worker's employment (Wehman, in press). These services are usually provided only to individuals thought to be capable of functioning on the job independently once services have been terminated (Moon, Goodall, and Wehman 1985). Time-limited services are one reason that persons with severe handicaps do not receive job placements from the Department of Rehabilitative Services. Supported employment provides ongoing services, which often make the difference in success or failure for the individual with severe disabilities.

Transitional Employment—Transitional employment is a time-limited service that provides intensive job-based training, support, and placement services to persons with severe disabilities. This process is provided to help persons with disabilities develop acceptable production and work behaviors in the community job market.

Trial Work Period (TWP)—Trial work period, as defined by the Social Security Administration, is a period of time during which an individual's ability to perform substantial gainful activity is determined (i.e., the individual's sustained work ability). The work period begins with the month of entitlement to SSDI benefits and ends after nine months of earning $75 or more per month (15 hours per month if self-employed). The determination of the individual's ability to perform substantial gainful activity is made upon completion of the trial work period. The trial work period allows individuals on SSDI to "try out" working while still receiving cash payments for a period of time. This may be an incentive to attempt a return to competitive or supported employment.

Vendorship—Agencies can provide services for a vocational rehabilitation (VR) department only if the VR system approves the agency as a vendor of services. Once a vendorship agreement has been reached for a defined service, the nonprofit agency receives an authorization from a rehabilitation counselor for funding to provide the service for a predetermined amount of units for an individual consumer. Vendorship agreements work on a fee-for-service basis with the fee for each unit of service determined before authorization. Nonprofit agencies are now becoming vendors of supported employment services and are asking the VR system to provide funds for the placing and training phases (Hill, Revell, et al. 1985; Wehman and Kregel 1985).

Vocational Evaluation—Vocational evaluation is a service provided by the Department of Rehabilitation Services, and is usually an assessment of the client's readiness to work (Wehman, in press). It has been defined as a process using real or simulated work to assess individuals and determine appropriate services (Geist and Calzaretta 1982). Supported employment placements are usually made from an assessment of support needs rather than an assessment of readiness for employment.

Vocational Rehabilitation—Vocational rehabilitation is the philosophy, services, and service delivery of the federal-state program that has been in existence in the United States since 1918 (Mandeville and Brabham 1987). The system is driven by the philosophy that we live in a work-oriented society, and that Americans, regardless of the type or degree of disability they may experience, are capable of and have an inherent right to work. A vocational rehabilitation (VR) agency is located in each state and is funded by 80% federal and 20% state funds based on state population and per capita income. The state VR agency may be an independent agency or a component of education, vocational education, health, welfare, or labor (Mandeville and Brabham 1987). The service delivery system is assured through the Rehabilitation Act of 1973 and subsequent amendments. The VR delivery system is coordinated through a numerical coding system (i.e., a case status code) and is managed by a professional rehabilitation counselor.

Work Activity Center—Work activity centers are a physically separated part of a sheltered workshop designed to serve and provide therapeutic activities to individuals with more severe handicaps. Work activity centers are intended for those adults whose evaluations indicate a lack of occupational readiness and who need personal and social adjustment training. Training generally includes basic living skills and any purposeful activity (so long as work is not the main purpose) that would eventually enable them to move to a regular program workshop (Bellamy, Sowers, and Bourbeau 1983).

Work Adjustment—Work adjustment traditionally refers to pre-employment training that helps develop appropriate work habits and social skills. Work adjustment training is funded by vocational rehabilitation and provided by sheltered workshop (Rusch 1986). Traditional work adjustment relies on fundamentally different thinking than supported employment, which believes that on-site, post employment training can adjust vocational and social deficiencies (Wehman, in press).

Index